THE LAW OF LIFE AND DEATH

THE LAW OF LIFE AND DEATH

ELIZABETH PRICE FOLEY

HARVARD UNIVERSITY PRESS
Cambridge, Massachusetts, and London, England 2011

Library of Congress Cataloging-in-Publication Data

Foley, Elizabeth Price.
The law of life and death / Elizabeth Price Foley.
p. cm.
Includes bibliographical references and index.
ISBN 978-0-674-05104-1 (alk. paper)
1. Death—Proof and certification—United States. 2. Life and death, Power
over—Moral and ethical aspects. 3. Life and death, Power over—Decision making.
4. Right to life—United States. 5. Right to die—Law and legislation—United States.
6. Euthanasia—Law and legislation—United States. I. Title.
KF3827.D4F65 2011
344.7304'19—dc22   2010047701

Lines from the Emily Dickinson poem *That it will never come again* reprinted by permission of the publishers and the Trustees of Amherst College from THE POEMS OF EMILY DICKINSON: VARIORUM EDITION, edited by Ralph W. Franklin, Cambridge, Mass.: The Belknap Press of Harvard University Press, Copyright © 1998 by the President and Fellows of Harvard College. Copyright © 1951, 1955, 1979, 1983 by the President and Fellows of Harvard College.

To Patrick and Katy,

with love and eternal thanks.

Contents

THE LAW OF LIFE AND DEATH

Introduction

> The boundaries which divide Life from Death are at best shadowy and vague. Who shall say where the one ends, and where the other begins?
>
> —Edgar Allan Poe, The Premature Burial (1844)

Are you alive? What makes you so sure? Admittedly, it would be hard to read this book if you were not alive. But an ability to read is not a reliable proxy for life; many living creatures are illiterate or otherwise unable to read. So what is it that defines one's status among the living? Is life biological—something akin to "I am breathing" or "My heart is beating"? Is it spiritual, as in "I have a soul that animates my body"? Or perhaps the definition of life should be more intellectual, such as "I think, therefore I am"?

If asked, most people would probably define life by these physical, spiritual, or intellectual references. Moreover, most people would assume that, whatever definition of life one employed, death would be its antithesis. So for example, if one used an intellectual definition of life, death would occur when the relevant intellectual characteristic disappeared, perhaps consciousness or the ability to reason.

But the seemingly incontrovertible notion of life and death as antonyms presents an array of potential pitfalls and ambiguities. Say that society decides to define life by reference to the physical characteristic of cardiopulmonary (heart and lung) function. If death is the absence of cardiopulmonary function, how long must we wait, after the heart and lungs stop, before death can be declared? If a person's heart stops, is the person automatically dead after the passage of a certain number of seconds or minutes, or do medical providers have a duty to attempt resuscitation? If resuscitation must be attempted, how long must or should these measures be taken before death can be declared? Do individuals, their families, or perhaps even medical providers have a right to refuse resuscitative attempts? If so, under what circumstances? Moreover, if society accepts cardiopulmonary function as the defining characteristic of life, is a person with irreversible brain damage whose cardiopulmonary function is being artificially maintained alive? Put another way, is it cardiopulmonary function that matters (even if artificially maintained), or must the function be spontaneous (unaided)? If the mere existence of function matters, does this mean that we must maintain individuals on life support indefinitely, no matter the cost, or can we turn off the machines? If spontaneity is what matters, is a person who receives technological support, such as a pacemaker, technically dead? Similarly, if cardiopulmonary function is the hallmark of life, does this mean that a fetus is a living person so long as its heart is beating? If so, would this imply that aborting such a fetus is the legal equivalent of murder?

It seems so basic, so simple, to assume that life and death are antithetical legal concepts—to say that someone who is alive cannot be dead, and vice versa. But as the preceding questions show, strict adherence to conceptualizing life and death as mutually exclusive may create results that society is not willing to accept. Yet it is hard to declare, with a straight face, that life and death are not the opposite of each other. It would also highlight the possibility that an individual may be considered alive for one legal purpose but not for another. Individuals could get caught in a strange kind of legal limbo, not fully alive, but not fully dead either. And it implies legal cognizance of multiple tiers of personhood, with higher-tier persons receiving greater legal protection than lower ones. A fetus, for example, might be considered living for some limited legal purposes, yet not be entitled to the same legal status and protections as a nine-year-old boy or a forty-three-year-old lawyer. A baby born without an upper brain may be considered alive, but may not be entitled to the same treatment or rights as a seventy-year-old woman with severe dementia. Is such a result legally acceptable, or must each living person enjoy the same rights and privileges as all other living persons? More specifically, are all living persons "legal" persons? Is there a difference, in other words, between being "alive" and being a "person" under the law?

Perhaps more importantly, if we insist on defining life and death as mutually exclusive concepts, we necessarily have to resolve a preliminary question: Which should come first, the proverbial chicken or the egg? Should the law anchor its analysis to a definition of life (thereby defining death as life's absence), or rather to a definition of death (thereby defining life as death's absence)? Which one is easier to define: life or death?

Perhaps tellingly, *Black's Law Dictionary* does not contain a definition for life. It does, however, define death as the "ending of life."[1] If this is our analytical structure—a definition of death as the antithesis of life—then a failure to agree on a definition of life will lead to massive intellectual confusion and evasion. If death is the antithesis of something that is left undefined, there is trouble brewing ahead.

But before you condemn the law for this glaring analytical deficiency, I ask you to consider whether it would be wise to demand a unitary, mutually exclusive definitional relationship between life and death. Governmentally imposed, one-size-fits-all definitions of life and death may deeply offend individual autonomy. Each of us, after all, has contemplated the meaning of life and death and arrived at our own basic understandings. Some of us formed them while sitting in a college philosophy or biology class, some while sitting in a house of worship, and some in moments of deep personal reflection, perhaps following the birth or death of a loved one. The definitions of life and death we internalize reveal a lot about who we are as individuals. They tell a story of the social, cultural, religious, political, and economic environments in which we live.

Given this wide variation in personal experiences and preferences, is it normatively desirable to have a univocal legal approach to life and death? Perhaps not, yet I suspect that most people believe there is a unitary law out there somewhere that defines one's status as living or dead for all purposes— the kind of black-and-white law that can be looked up and understood quickly by a skillful lawyer. But they would be (pardon the pun) dead wrong. Although the concepts of life and death are omnipresent in law, they have been devised in a wide variety of contexts, ranging from constitutional to contract law and from crimes to torts. Each context contains its own set of concepts and definitions of life and death that are often remarkably amorphous, often inconsistent, and sometimes bordering on the incoherent.

The range of legal questions is staggering. And in a surprising array of contexts, the law of life and death is still far from settled. Despite this lack of clarity, the law marches on, functioning as it must, grappling with a range of important legal questions that hinge on a definitive determination of whether someone was alive or dead at a specific moment in time. The law does not enjoy the luxury of debating difficult questions without the need to assign definitive answers, as do other disciplines such as philosophy or ethics. The law must provide an answer when properly asked a question. There is no "maybe" X is dead, or "maybe" X is alive. For purposes of interpreting contracts, determining inheritance, assigning monetary liability, declaring constitutional rights, or potentially sending someone to prison, the law cannot equivocate.

But just because the law must provide answers when questions are properly posed does not mean that the answers will always be consistent with legal decisions from other contexts. It also does not mean that all salient questions about life and death will be answered by the law. Many life-and-death questions—ones with significant legal implications—are never brought before the courts or become the subject of legislation. Many decisions are made privately by individuals, their family or loved ones, their medical providers, or some combination thereof. Indeed, the law often explicitly punts many of the difficult questions to these other non–legal decision makers, with little or no recourse to those who disagree with the decisions that are made.

Even when the law has tried to articulate answers to disputed questions, these answers have been ignored or lost in translation due to pragmatic, religious, or ethical considerations. In short, the law must sometimes provide answers to these perplexing life-and-death questions, but the answers are not simple, not always consistent across legal contexts, and often spawn even greater ambiguity.

This book will examine the law of life and death, offering a broad overview of the law's ambiguities and inconsistencies and the profound implications that flow therefrom. But lest you throw your hands up in the air and assume that you will not derive any useful answers from reading this book, I ask you to consider embracing these ambiguities and inconsistencies for the intellectual richness they offer. As it turns out, there are fascinating reasons for the frustrating fluidity of this area of the law, and these reasons tell a story all their own. The law's inability to provide simple answers to the seemingly simple questions, "Is X alive?" and "Is X dead?" is perhaps its greatest virtue. Fluidity may be frustrating, but it is often the only rational approach, in a pluralistic society, to questions about which there is passionate disagreement.

Surprisingly, there are few books that explore life and death from the perspective of the law. It is not that lawyers have stayed on the sidelines while life-and-death topics have been debated. There have been numerous well-researched legal books and journal articles focusing on discrete issues such as abortion, organ transplantation, and euthanasia. And of course there have been many more books and articles exploring these topics from other important disciplinary perspectives such as medicine, ethics, theology, and philosophy. Yet there have been only a handful of books that have attempted to tackle these issues within the larger context of the law, examining overarching connections, justifications, and themes.

The lack of attention to the law of life and death is remarkable given law's ubiquity and centrality to our lives. Because of the incredible variation in personal conceptions of the meaning of life and death, ultimately it is the law—not philosophy, morality, ethics, or any other discipline—that arguably matters most in pragmatic terms. There generally is no ability, after all, to choose your own, customized legal definitions of life and death (though some have argued forcefully that there should be). The definitions that are used have been chosen on a societal, not a personal, level. So while we may each have our own ideas of the meaning of life and death, the law must pick a definition and impose it upon us all. It is the law of life and death—in the richness and vastness of its multitude of contexts—that determines our entry and exit from the human community.

The good news is that, in the vast majority of situations, the law and most individuals' personal preferences are in agreement. A person walking down the street whistling a tune, a tiny baby crying for milk, and a ninety-nine-year-old blind and deaf man with an artificial heart valve are all alive in the eyes of the law. A stillborn baby, a body burned beyond recognition, decapitated in a car accident, or discovered putrefied in the woods, are all dead. But of course not all cases are so easy.

It is this vast gray area—the realm of discovery about society's values—that is the focus of this book. By examining the law's approach to life and death, *in toto,* we may come to understand these challenging issues in a more meaningful and productive way. We may also begin to see and appreciate them in a broader cultural and political context. Indeed, there is perhaps no better way to fully appreciate the cultural divide that our society faces than to study how our laws define life and death. On issues such as abortion, medical research, and punishment of injury to fetuses, U.S. law has assigned a high value to life (or at least its potentiality), influenced by a belief that life itself, without regard to the quality of that life, is the most important consideration. On issues such as informed consent, advance directives, and organ transplantation, by contrast, the law has assigned a high value to dying (or at least to controlling its circumstances), influenced by a belief that the quality of life, rather than life simpliciter, is the most important consideration. The clash between these values has created an odd mix of law, sometimes pro-life, sometimes pro-death. If we can spot these influences at work, perhaps we can improve, or at least better understand, the laws relating to life and death and, ultimately, society itself.

I

Statutory and Common Law Life

That it will never come again
Is what makes life so sweet.

—Emily Dickinson

It is a miracle that happens hundreds of thousands of times each day. Sperm meets egg. Their chromosomes begin intertwining, forming a unique genetic combination. The mysterious, awe-inspiring process of rapid cell division begins. Within a short time, if all conditions are right, the growing embryo will find a cozy spot on the uterine wall and attach, securing a life-giving bond with its mother. Somewhere between sixteen and twenty-one weeks after conception, the mother will begin to feel kicking or moving inside the womb. After about twenty-one weeks, the fetus may be able to live independently of its mother, though it may require extraordinary medical care. After thirty-five weeks, the fetus is considered full term.

We have all passed through these stages, each critical in our development. Out of all of them, when did your life begin? When did you become you? Conception, implantation, quickening, viability, live birth, consciousness, or when you became capable of rational decision making—all are plausible answers; none is dominant. Despite all the time, money, and energy spent, shockingly little consensus has been reached on the fundamental question of when life begins. Much of the division is due to deep religious, ethical, and philosophical differences that likely will never be resolved.

This book is not going to rehash these religious, ethical, or philosophical views on life. Instead, this book is about law. What does the law say about when life begins? The law is its own unique discipline, and more often than not, particularly in a republican form of government, the law represents a compromise among competing views. Unlike other disciplines such as philosophy or religion, the law does not have the luxury of equivocation. The law must answer when asked: Is X alive? Being alive (or not) has significant legal consequences that necessitate an answer; maybe is not an option.

But defining whether X is alive is harder than it seems. *Black's Law Dictionary's* refusal to define life is revealing. It signals that there may be more controversy surrounding life than death. Adopting a single definition for life would have heavy implications for divisive issues such as abortion, birth control, in vitro fertilization, and stem cell research. If the law defined life to begin at conception, for example, the legality of all of these activities would be brought into serious question.

The legal definition of death, by contrast, is arguably less political, due to the genesis and nature of the definitions of death that have been devised thus far. Historically, death was determined by the cessation of heart and/or lung function (cardiopulmonary death). Later, the law expanded the definition of death to also include cessation of the functioning of the entire brain (brain death). These definitions are the products of much debate and discussion within the scientific community and represent scientific consensus on when death occurs.

Once the criteria for death are satisfied, an individual is declared dead. What happens to a body after the declaration of death—for example, removal of organs, use in medical research, burial, cremation, et cetera—is relatively uncontroversial because society generally accepts the death criteria as trustworthy, morally justified, and not politically motivated. There is heated debate about quality of life—who would be "better off" dead, or who is "as good as" dead. But despite using the word "dead" in these descriptions, such debate is really about life, not death. The enormous controversy swirling around Terri Schiavo, for example, centered on her quality of life and the belief by many that she would be better off dead, not that she *was* actually dead. Like all patients in a permanent vegetative state (PVS), Terry Schiavo clearly was not legally dead. In terms of existing legal doctrine, her case highlighted the nature and extent of the right of the living to refuse medical treatment when it no longer comports with their wishes. Schiavo, in other words, illustrated the rights of the living, not controversy over the definition of death.

As Chapter 4, "Brain Death," will reveal, there is some opposition to the current definition of brain death—some think brain death should be eliminated entirely; others think it should be broadened to include PVS patients like Terry Schiavo. But at present these are mostly academic debates; ordinary people are not clamoring for brain death reform. Even those who oppose the concept of brain death are probably not losing much sleep worrying about it, for the simple reason that the vast majority of deaths do not involve brain death. Moreover, brain death opponents can lessen their concerns by refusing to consent to organ donation. If one is not an organ donor, this will significantly reduce any pressure health care providers may feel to declare brain death in the first place. Similarly, those who support brain death but think it should be defined more broadly (for example, higher brain death) can effectuate their preference by executing an advance directive (for example, a living will or health care power of attorney) that refuses medical treatment such as ventilation or nutrition when they lose higher brain function.

There is, in short, no real moral outrage associated with the application of the legal definition of death. Individuals have a certain amount of control over how their death will be declared, and this lessens any urgency of altering the status quo. In addition, because society generally perceives the legal definition of death as derived from dispassionate medical consensus, there is no overt connection between it and political ideology.

A legal definition of life—if one existed—would be a different situation. Picking a moment in time when life begins would have clear political consequences on a wide array of legal issues such as homicide, abortion, and stem cell research. Pro-life groups have proposed statutes and constitutional amendments that would define life as existing from the moment of conception.[1] If these laws were enacted, they would anger a significant portion of the population that supports contraception, abortion, or stem cell research, or believes life begins at some later point in time.

But what if the law picked a definition of life that was not based on religious or political viewpoints? In other words, what if life was defined—like death—by reference to generally accepted biological criteria? If a biological definition of death can be incorporated into law, could it likewise form the basis of a definition of life that would be accepted as morally just and not politically motivated?

The first step in dealing with this inquiry is to determine whether there is, in fact, a scientific consensus on the criteria for life. The short answer is yes, there does appear to be a set of biological criteria that identify the existence of life. Some scientists think certain criteria are more important than others, yet most agree that life (at least as known here on Earth) has identifiable characteristics. These characteristics include a genetic structure, metabolism, regeneration, homeostasis, and adaptation.[2]

A genetic structure—usually, a double helix DNA—is now accepted as the basic blueprint possessed by living organisms. Metabolism indicates that an entity is taking in substances from the environment, such as oxygen or sunlight, and using them to keep the entity functioning. Regeneration roughly refers to reproduction, whereby members of the life form have at least the potential (even if unexercised) to continue the life form's existence, given the right set of circumstances. A life form should also be able to maintain homeostasis, meaning an ability to protect against external toxins and regulate internal processes, such as blood, water or salt levels, or temperature. Adaptation describes the life form's ability to alter itself in response to a changing environment. Unlike homeostasis, which addresses a life form's basic ability to maintain, adaptability refers to its ability to change, such as through mutation or selection, or even to undergo simple physiological alterations, such as forming calluses on the hands or feet.

Application of the life criteria is not always easy. Scientists are not in agreement, for example, regarding whether viruses possess enough of these criteria to be classified as living organisms. Fortunately, some things are clear. Human beings exhibit all of these criteria and are clearly alive. Rocks, on the other hand, exhibit none of the criteria and consequently are not alive, not even the pet rock variety.

If there is a general consensus about the criteria for ascertaining life, why are they not used as the basis for law? Once again, politics lurks large. If biological criteria were the basis for the legal definition of life, there would be obvious and immediate implications for issues such as abortion, contraception, and stem cell research. An embryo has a genetic structure, metabolism, regenerative and adaptive potential, and at least some degree of homeostatic ability. Depending on which of these biological criteria were considered more important, a law that used them to determine when human life existed could consider most abortions, some contraceptives, and all embryonic stem cell research tantamount to murder.

If many in society do not philosophically or morally believe contraception, abortion, or stem cell research is murder, then the biological criteria for life will prove politically infeasible. Consequently, there is a political need to compartmentalize the biological criteria as, well, merely biological criteria. The question is thus rephrased, from "When does life begin?" to "When does human life, or personhood, begin?"[3] The former asks a raw biological question; the latter asks a philosophical or political one. Accordingly, even if one concedes that biological life begins at conception, the embryo is not entitled to full legal protection as a person until some later point in time. The law would choose some later moment—perhaps quickening, viability, or live birth—that reflects a political compromise among a plurality of competing religious, moral, and philosophical views.

Another problem posed by the biological criteria for life is that they seem to imply something interesting, but perhaps troubling, about death. More specifically, notice that the biological criteria for life do not include self-awareness, or consciousness. An oak tree, for example, is clearly alive under the biological criteria, even though there is no evidence that trees have moods, emotions, dreams, or any other form of self-awareness. But if consciousness is not required for life, this suggests that consciousness is also irrelevant for death. After all, if life does not require consciousness, would it make sense to define death in a way that requires its absence? Consider, for example, that some believe premature newborns or even full-term newborns lack robust consciousness,[4] and most agree that babies born without higher brains—called anencephalic infants—have no consciousness whatsoever. Should such newborns be classified as dead because consciousness is lacking or not fully developed?

If one were striving for intellectual consistency, one would think the answer to the previous question is yes. If consciousness is critical to life, then presumably a lack of consciousness would indicate death. Consciousness, in other words, would be the defining characteristic of both life and death. A tiny preemie or anencephalic infant could be "not alive" and hence, dead.

Yet this sort of intellectual consistency is rare. But before one writes off such inconsistency as hypocritical, consider that there may be a more subtle, less nefarious explanation. Is it possible that there is some message here about the relationship between life and death? More specifically, is it conceivable that life and death are not antithetical, mutually exclusive concepts? If so, it could be intellectually consistent to say that life is not defined by reference to consciousness, while death, on the other hand, is. If death is not just a simple antithesis of life, then death can be unmoored from the criteria for life, and vice versa. The truth is that the law of life is unrelated to the law of death; the two areas of law have no necessary linkage. Why this is true is worthy of some exploration.

There are also some interesting philosophical considerations—in addition to the political ones—that may justify the law's separation of life and death. First, and perhaps most prominently, some in science, philosophy, and ethics believe that both life and death are not so much distinct events as they are processes. It is common, for example, to hear talk about the "process of dying" rather than death itself,[5] though eventually, at some point, death must be declared.

In a very broad sense, we begin the process of dying from the moment we begin living. If life is also a process, then it seems logical to conclude that it is a process that begins prior to our birth. The process of life, in other words, takes us from point A to point B—that is, from some moment like conception to some moment when we achieve full legal status as a living person. Life itself is thus a culmination of the antecedent process of life. Once alive, the ineluctable slide toward the process of dying begins. The process of dying then takes us from point C to point D—for example, from a diagnosis of terminal disease to the cessation of our heartbeat (or some other death indicator). Death is thus the culmination of the process of dying.

The process of life takes us from A to B; the process of death takes us from C to D. There is, under this view, no necessary overlap or definitional connection between the process of life and the process of death. If the processes of life and death are distinct, then the culmination of these processes (that is, life and death) can be defined distinctly, without a necessary relationship to each other. It also means that in our journey between A (beginning of the life process) and D (death), there are large gray areas in which one may be in the process of life but not yet fully alive, or in the process of death but not yet fully dead. The question the law must then answer is: What should be the legal status of individuals who have begun the process of life but are not yet fully alive, or who have begun the process of death but are not yet fully dead? Should they be considered alive, dead, or something in between?

A second argument that may support delinking life and death is, as discussed briefly before, that life and death are philosophical, moral, or religious ideas, not scientific or medical ones. If this is the case, we should not be surprised to find that the laws relating to life or death reflect moments of capture—when a particular view wins out over the alternatives—or compromise, when courts or legislatures pick a position between the ideological extremes. Since the law of life and death is generally a matter decided on a state-by-state basis, each state can generally be expected to enact laws reflective of the dominant religion or culture of that particular state. Likewise, if there is no clearly dominant religion or culture, a state's law may reflect a political compromise between proffered extremes. Alternatively, in accord with special interest group theory, life or death laws may instead reflect the passionately held beliefs of a vocal minority. If the law of life and death is the end product of a political debate about philosophy, religion, or morality, we can (and should) expect that it will be richly varied and often seemingly inconsistent.

I will now exmaine the various nonconstitutional ways in which the law defines life. Tort, criminal, contract, and property law, for example, all experience moments when a definition of life must be used to help decide whether compensation or punishment is appropriate. I will attempt to identify common themes across these disparate areas of law and then proceed in Chapter 2 to compare these themes to those developed in constitutional law.

Criminal Law

HOMICIDE: THE "BORN ALIVE" RULE

Mr. and Mrs. Keeler divorced after sixteen years of marriage and two daughters. After the divorce, Mrs. Keeler began dating Ernest Vogt and became pregnant with his child. Mrs. Keeler moved in with Mr. Vogt, and Mr. Keeler then learned that his ex-wife was pregnant. After dropping her daughters off at their father's house, Mrs. Keeler began driving back to her home. After a couple of miles, she found the road blocked by Mr. Keeler's car. Mr. Keeler forced Mrs. Keeler out of her car, screaming, "I'm going to stomp it out of you!" He shoved his knee into her abdomen. Mrs. Keeler was rushed to the hospital, where an emergency C-section was performed. The fetus was stillborn, with a severely fractured skull. Physicians concluded that the fetus was approximately thirty-four to thirty-six weeks old.[6]

Should Mr. Keeler be charged with murder? Should he be charged with some lesser offense? Or perhaps he should not be charged at all? Does it matter that Mrs. Keeler's fetus had survived well past the point of viability?

Historically, under the common law inherited from England, aggressive acts committed against a child in utero would result in criminal liability only when the child died immediately following a live birth. This approach—known as the "born alive rule"—refused to recognize any fetus as a distinct person under homicide law until the fetus had survived the birthing process and exhibited biological independence from its mother. Indeed, in the *Keeler* case referenced above, the California Supreme Court in 1970 abided by the common law born alive rule, holding that an unborn but viable fetus was not a "human being" within the meaning of the state murder statute.

The born alive rule in criminal law serves an important evidentiary function, ensuring that only the clearest cases of fault are punished. Without it, it could be difficult to determine causation—namely, whether the death was caused by the defendant's act or was simply a natural miscarriage.[7] Because the stakes are particularly high in criminal cases—resulting in a potential loss of liberty to the defendant—criminal laws are construed strictly, resolving any ambiguity in favor of the defendant. The born alive rule is consonant with the criminal law's rule of strict construction, reflecting a belief that the defendant's liberty should be taken away only if the "person" killed under the homicide statute was unambiguously a person. Requiring a live birth thus reduces evidentiary ambiguities and furthers the general policy of erring on the side of the criminal defendant whenever possible.

But how do you know if a fetus has been "born alive"? It might seem commonsensical to answer this question by reference to the legal definition of death. If a fetus meets the legal definition of death, in other words, it seems logical to say that the fetus was not born alive. Yet only one state—Michigan—seems to have taken this approach. And on closer examination, this apparently logical connection—a fetus is not born alive if it meets the legal definition of death—presents challenges that are complex and perhaps insurmountable.

The Michigan decision that formally embraced the legal definition of death to ascertain whether a fetus is born alive was People v. Selwa, decided by the Court of Appeals in 1995.[8] In *Selwa*, the defendant was charged with negligent vehicular homicide after his car hit Heide Mielke's car head-on. Mielke was six and a half months pregnant. She was rushed to the hospital, where it was determined that her unborn child had a low heart rate. An emergency C-section was performed. The baby was born floppy and blue, and resuscitative efforts were begun.

A hole was made in the baby's trachea and a manual respiration bag was inserted. Pure oxygen was delivered, as were antibiotics, nutrients, and a blood transfusion. After about fifteen minutes, a faint heartbeat was detected. After twenty-five minutes, the heartbeat had increased to over one hundred beats per minute, and the baby took two or three gasping breaths on its own. It was taken immediately to the neonatal intensive care unit, where it was placed on a ventilator. The heartbeat began to slow down, however, and some two and a half hours after delivery, the ventilator was turned off, and death was called.

Two of the three judges in *Selwa* concluded that the baby had been born alive and was thus a person within the meaning of the Michigan vehicular homicide statute. In reaching this decision, the majority explicitly relied on the Michigan statute that defined death. Like most states, Michigan law defined death as either irreversible cessation of heart and lung function, or irreversible cessation of brain function.[9] The majority asserted,

> Because it is axiomatic that one who is not dead is alive and vice versa, we find that the definition of "death" becomes as equally helpful as the definition of "live birth" [in the vital records statute] in determining whether a child was "born alive" and hence is a "person." If one is not born dead, one is born alive and vice versa. . . . Accordingly, a child is "born alive" and thus a "person" under the negligent homicide statute if, following expulsion or extraction from the mother, there is *lacking* an irreversible cessation of respiratory and circulatory functions or brain functions.[10]

The *Selwa* majority then applied the definition of death to the facts of the case, concluding that the infant's heartbeat and gasping breaths indicated that it was not dead (and hence was born alive). The majority believed that the facts indicated cardiopulmonary function but also noted that "although . . .

an electroencephalograph (EEG) was not performed, it may be inferred from
the evidence that there was some brain activity."[11] The inference of brain activity was reasonable, reasoned the court, because breathing is a function
regulated by the brain stem.[12]

Judge Holbrook dissented, objecting to the majority's assumption that
life and death are mutually exclusive concepts—an assumption the majority
thought so obvious as to be axiomatic. Specifically, Judge Holbrook found the
Michigan statute defining death to be "wholly unhelpful" in determining
whether the baby was born alive because "the relevant axiom is: A 'person'
must be alive before the person can die. The majority's use of the [death stat-
ute] places the proverbial cart before the horse."[13] The Michigan death statute
was thus irrelevant to Holbrook because it answered the wrong question—
namely, "Is X dead?" when the salient question was instead, "Was X alive?"
Holbrook's point is that one cannot define life by reference to a statute defining death. Life and death, to Judge Holbrook, clearly are not antithetical concepts that can be defined by reference to each other: life is not the opposite of
death, and vice versa.

Judge Holbrook's dissent raises many interesting issues. It directly challenges the assumption that life and death are opposites—an assumption not
only made by the *Selwa* majority but also, I suspect, by most Americans. It
incorporates a view of legally cognizable life as something more than mere
biological life—something abstractly referred to as "personhood." The salient
question therefore becomes: how should the law define personhood, if it is
not by reference to the biological signs of life (cardiopulmonary or brain
function) that are used in the legal definition of death?

In attempting to answer this question, Judge Holbrook asserted that the
relevant standard for personhood was established in a prior decision, which
concluded that a "person" is one who is not only "born alive" but who also
"exist[s] independently of its mother's body."[14] Holbrook offered very little
guidance as to what these phrases mean, other than to cite the prior decision's statement that the fetus must be "fully brought forth" and an "independent circulation" established.[15] Holbrook's application of this standard of
personhood yielded the following conclusion: "The fetus' weak heartbeat at
the fifteen-minute mark and two or three spontaneous respirations at the
twenty-five minute mark were artificially induced and mechanically sustained. . . . An independently sustained life is not exhibited by forcing air into

a fetus' lungs either manually or mechanically, or by a heartbeat that is detectable but so weak that it fails to circulate the blood."[16] While breathing and heartbeat may be relevant, their existence is not enough to establish personhood per se. A few spontaneous respirations won after almost half an hour of intense resuscitative efforts, combined with a weak heartbeat that does not circulate blood through the body is insufficient, in Judge Holbrook's view, to establish an independent existence and hence, personhood.

Implicit in Judge Holbrook's analysis is the idea that cardiopulmonary function that is artificially or mechanically induced should not count as indicia of legally cognizable life, or personhood. He seems to say yes, there were a few breaths and yes, there was a faint heartbeat, but no, there was no life because these vital signs were the byproducts of extraordinary technological intervention. Vital signs that are artificially caused should not count in the legal determination of life.

Judge Holbrook's decision to discount technologically induced vital signs has some innate appeal. After all, why should the law consider relevant a few breaths or a faint heartbeat that are achieved only after many minutes of near-Herculean resuscitative efforts? Would it be more logical to conclude that such a baby was stillborn and that these extraordinary efforts ultimately proved futile? If a baby is delivered from its mother's womb and does not have a detectable heartbeat or spontaneous respiration within a certain period of time, should it be considered stillborn—that is, born dead instead of alive?

One of the difficulties posed by this position is that technologically induced bodily functions are universally considered legally relevant for both life and death. The law does not discount, for example, a heartbeat that is maintained by a pacemaker. Likewise, it does not disregard breathing maintained by a ventilator or kidney function maintained by dialysis. Without these technological interventions, those receiving them would inevitably die. If the law disregarded these technologically induced functions—such as the ventilator that sustained the life of actor Christopher Reeve for several years after an accident left him quadriplegic—the absurd result would be that such individuals would be considered legally dead. Obviously, technological supplementation or substitution for ordinary vital functions cannot be disregarded in the legal assessment of life or death.

To give Judge Holbrook proper credit, there does appear to be something different about a newborn who breathes only a few breaths and whose heart beats weakly for a couple of hours, but only because of extraordinary resuscitation efforts. But then again, all medical technology that restores life is extraordinary. And while there may be a temporal difference in most cases—the heartbeat of the newborn in *Selwa* stopped only two and a half hours after delivery, versus days or years of artificially maintained life in the case of pacemaker recipients or dialysis patients—should the amount of time really matter? The law thus far has taken a consistent position that artificially maintained life is life, no matter how short or long the technology works. Judge Holbrook's attempt to draw a meaningful legal line between artificial and natural life runs afoul of this basic understanding.

It may be that Judge Holbrook was trying to say something about artificially *induced* life versus artificially *maintained* life. In other words, it may be reasonable for the law to count biological functions that are technologically maintained after a person has been born and established an independent existence, but unreasonable to count them in a newborn who has never established an independent existence without such technological aid. Although Judge Holbrook never explicitly makes this point, it would make some sense, given his assertion that personhood (legally cognizable life) is a separate and distinct inquiry from legal death.

If life and death are not mutually exclusive legal concepts, it could be logical to take into account medical technology when determining whether death has occurred, yet disregard it when assessing whether life ever existed in the first place. In this way, a fetus would not be considered born alive (and hence would never achieve legal personhood) if heartbeat or respiration was obtained for a short time and then lost. The child could be considered stillborn, despite temporary, artificially induced indicia of life.

The difficulty with this position is that it potentially leads to arbitrary results. If a child is born without detectable heartbeat or respiration and resuscitative measures are begun, how long must these resuscitative measures be pursued before the child can be considered stillborn? And if the resuscitative measures are successful within the relevant time period, how long must the vital signs continue for the law to recognize the existence of a living person? Must the vital signs be sustained for five minutes, five hours, five days, or five years?

The infant in *Selwa,* for example, was subjected to aggressive resuscitative measures for fifteen minutes before a very faint heartbeat was detected. And it took twenty-five minutes before a few gasping breaths were achieved. Presumably, if the doctors in *Selwa* had decided to give up after ten minutes (before any heartbeat or breathing was detected), the majority would have agreed with Judge Holbrook that the infant was stillborn, and the defendant could not have been convicted of negligent homicide. As we will explore in the Chapter 3 on cardiopulmonary death, there are no legal standards regarding when or how long resuscitative measures must be attempted before giving up. The decision to initiate and continue resuscitative measures is left solely to the discretion of the attending physician.

But if resuscitative measures are begun and—regardless of how long they are attempted—succeed in generating heartbeat or respiration, how long must these vital signs continue before it is reasonable to conclude that life exists? To the majority in *Selwa,* the amount of time was not relevant; what was important was that there was uncontested evidence that the infant had a heartbeat and had taken a few spontaneous breaths. The presence of a heartbeat and breathing, no matter how short in duration, indicated to the majority that the infant was not legally dead and was therefore necessarily alive.

The *Selwa* majority's focus on the existence of the vital signs, rather than the amount of time they continue, reflects the approach used by most American courts today. To be "born alive" generally requires evidence that the infant exhibits independent circulation and/or respiration.[17] How long the circulation and/or respiration lasts, or whether it is the byproduct of resuscitative efforts, is not considered relevant. Courts carefully avoid drawing any definitive timelines by simply stating that whether sufficient evidence of independent circulation and/or respiration exists is a question of fact to be resolved by the fact finder (usually a jury).[18]

The *Selwa* court departs from legal norms, however, in its use of the legal definition of death to aid in its determination of whether life exists. The vast majority of courts do not use the legal definition of death as an interpretive aid in deciding what it means to be born alive. Indeed, in the few courts that have specifically considered the question, there has been a reluctance to do so, particularly with regard to brain death.

For example, in People v. Bolar, decided by the Illinois Court of Appeals, the defendant, Bolar, was charged with reckless homicide when he ran a stop sign and struck another car carrying Kelly Oswald, who was eight months pregnant. The force of the crash caused the placenta to separate from the uterine wall, and an emergency C-section was performed. A faint heartbeat was detected within fifteen seconds and resuscitation efforts began. After two minutes of attempted resuscitation, the heartbeat was checked again, at which time two slow beats and three rapid flutter beats were detected, followed by silence. Further resuscitative measures were stopped, and death was pronounced.

The majority in *Bolar* concluded that the infant had been born alive because, although no respiration occurred, the infant had a detectable heartbeat for two minutes.[19] The defendant in *Bolar* argued that he could not be charged with the homicide of the Oswald's child because the medical testimony suggested that the child was born without brain activity and was thus legally brain dead. Specifically, the defendant asserted that under Illinois law governing organ donation, an individual is considered dead—and thus eligible to donate life-sustaining organs—when the individual is diagnosed as having an irreversible loss of all brain function.[20] The Illinois Court of Appeals rejected this contention, stating, "Defendant's contention that brain activity be required for a finding of live birth is a luxury that is impossible to afford. Testimony at trial indicated that this could only be conclusively established through use of an electroencephalogram. Though no testimony was adduced we believe that constraints of time, availability of equipment, and incompatibility with life-saving measures renders this requirement totally impractical."[21]

The court does not want to open Pandora's box. If defendant's argument was correct, it could allow defendants to escape responsibility (either civil or criminal) whenever the plaintiff or prosecution (as the case may be) failed to prove that the fetus had discernible brain activity. Because newborns are rarely, if ever, hooked up to electroencephalographs (EEGs) that can detect higher brain function or given clinical tests to detect the existence of lower brain (brain stem) function, the Illinois Court of Appeals concluded that the defendant's insistence on evidence of brain "life" was a "luxury that [was] impossible to afford."

The *Bolar* court's conclusion—that testing for brain function and hence brain death is impossible—is correct. There are insufficient time and resources to test newborns for evidence of brain function. These newborns are quickly removed from the mother's body, often by C-section, and immediately tested for easily detected signs of vitality, such as heartbeat and breathing. There is no time to hook up EEGs or engage in the laborious and subtle detection of reflexes mediated by the brain stem. Indeed, the Michigan Court of Appeals' observation in *Selwa* was true: to the extent that any indicia of brain function at all is likely in the newborn scenario, it will be found inferentially through the fact that the newborn attempts to breathe on its own, as respiration is a function regulated by the brain stem.[22]

If one thinks about it logically, any attempt to use the legal definition of death to inform what it means to be "born alive," under civil and criminal laws that require it, inevitably leads to the sole use of cardiopulmonary function. This is so because while the legal definition of death is expressed in the alternative—that is, one is dead if one either has irreversible loss of cardiopulmonary function or brain function—it is only the former (cardiopulmonary function) that can realistically be invoked in newborn scenarios. It would be unrealistic to ask that newborns be routinely tested for brain function.

While arguably EEGs could be hooked up rather quickly, EEGs detect only higher brain (cerebral) function and are useless for detecting lower brain (brain stem) function. Testing for the existence of brain stem functions is complex and time consuming. To be accomplished with a degree of confidence, a diagnosis of brain stem death takes days or even weeks. It cannot be done within a matter of minutes while a team of providers struggles to resuscitate a newborn in crisis.

Inevitably, in the legal situations that employ the born alive rule, the only practical means of ascertaining whether the newborn is indeed alive is to monitor its heartbeat and breathing. Brain function—though it may well be useful for determining death—is an impractical standard for determining whether life exists in a newborn. One would think that the practical result of a case like *Selwa* would be that only cardiopulmonary death—or more precisely, the presence of cardiopulmonary function—could be used effectively. But this may be too rash a judgment. An unpublished 2003 per curiam opinion of the Michigan Court of Appeals, People v. French, illustrates how a defendant may well defeat the born alive rule by invoking the legal definition of brain death.[23]

In *French,* the defendant was charged with criminal counts of negligent homicide and causing the death of another while operating a vehicle on a suspended license. After crashing his car into the side of a train, the defendant's nine-months pregnant girlfriend was thrown from the car and the placenta separated. A C-section was performed, and baby Xavyor was immediately placed on a ventilator. Four days later, after bedside testing revealed brain death, Xavyor was disconnected from the ventilator.

The defendant asserted that the prosecution had insufficient evidence to establish that Xavyor was born alive and hence a person under the applicable statutes. The procedural posture of the case is interesting: The defendant was trying to get criminal charges dismissed, arguing that there wasn't enough evidence ("probable cause") to establish that he caused the death of Xavyor because the evidence suggested that Xavyor was brain dead when removed from the womb.

The trial court held a preliminary hearing to determine whether there was probable cause to bind the defendant over for trial. The hearing involved several witnesses, but only one medical witness, Dr. Cohle, the medical examiner who wrote the case report for Xavyor's death.[24] Dr. Cohle was not the treating physician and did not perform an autopsy, instead basing his opinions on discussions with the treating physicians and a review of the medical records.[25]

Dr. Cohle's testimony was ambiguous. On several occasions, he testified that Xavyor had "lived" for four days.[26] Yet he also testified that Xavyor "never had brain activity."[27] Just prior to disconnection of the ventilator—which had been connected for four days—Xavyor was tested (by another physician) and found to have no discernible brain activity.[28] In a fascinating exchange with counsel, Dr. Cohle concludes that Xavyor was brain dead:

> Q. Now is that the date [January 7] that this infant had no viable brain waves that you were referring to as being clinically dead, I believe?
>
> A. Well, yes, certainly. . . . Obviously the brain testing would have been conducted prior to that whether there was some degree of brain wave testing done on January 6 I don't know for sure. I just know that the child was found to have no brain activity, and apparently never did have any brain activity from the time of the—
>
> Q. Do your records reflect what date that brain activity was tested?
>
> A. Well, I don't have that kind of specificity. All I know is that the obviously the brain activity would have to be determined to be absent prior to the withdrawal of life support. Generally there is

a period of hours, sometimes longer depending on the case. But there are multiple tests at different times of brain activity. All of these have to be consistently negative before the child is pronounced dead.[29]

Shockingly, this is the only evidence that the lawyers in the case presented regarding the critical issue of whether Xavyor was born alive or dead. Dr. Cohle's testimony, unsurprisingly, shows what we would expect in a situation such as this—namely, that sometime after being hooked up to the ventilator, both higher and lower brain function testing was performed, and on day four, a diagnosis of brain death was made. The giant unanswered question is this: was Xavyor "alive" when he was removed from his mother's womb? According to the court's prior binding precedent in *Selwa,* an infant is born alive if it is not born dead. Because death is defined by law as either irreversible cessation of cardiopulmonary or brain function, evidence of either cardiopulmonary or brain function will establish that the infant was alive for purposes of the born alive rule.

So what should a court make of a situation such as this? Xavyor was born and immediately placed on a respirator. If being born "alive" is legally the equivalent of being born "not dead" (as it was pronounced to be in *Selwa*), then evidence of cardiopulmonary function—even artificially induced by a ventilator—will suffice to establish that the infant was born alive. Yet strangely, in *French,* this was not the court's conclusion.

Instead, the majority in *French* did not even discuss the fact that Dr. Cohle's uncontested testimony established that Xavyor had cardiopulmonary function (albeit ventilator-induced) for four days. It was only after clinical testing confirmed brain death several days later that the ventilator was disconnected. Why the *French* majority discounted this cardiopulmonary function is simply never discussed, so it is an enigma that will have to go unresolved. What is clear is that the *French* majority thought that the prosecutor had produced insufficient evidence to establish that Xavyor was not brain dead when removed from the womb, stating, "Our review of the rather minimal evidentiary record in this case causes us to come to the same inescapable conclusion as the circuit court: the prosecution did not present *any* evidence establishing that the child had *any* brain activity, respiration, etc., once removed from the mother, and therefore, there are no facts to rely upon in concluding that

Xavyor was born alive as defined in the controlling case of *Selwa*."[30] The majority believed that Dr. Cohle's testimony established that Xavyor had been
born brain dead, despite the fact that Dr. Cohle's testimony could only confirm that a diagnosis of brain death had been made four days after Xavyor
was ex utero. And the only mention of cardiopulmonary function comes
from the above-quoted statement that the prosecution did not present "any"
evidence that the child had "any" respiration once removed from the mother.

Presumably then, the *French* court did not believe that breathing and
heartbeat sustained by a ventilator "counted," though, as discussed earlier,
such artificially induced cardiopulmonary function in fact is always "counted"
for purposes of determining whether someone is legally dead. Thus, although
the *French* court professed its allegiance to *Selwa*, its application of *Selwa's* key
holding indicates otherwise. After all, the unusual legal nugget contained in
Selwa is the court's decision to determine whether an infant is "born alive" by
using the legal definition of death—that is, an infant is not born alive if it is
born dead. If this is indeed the case, then if the law of death declared Xavyor to
be "not dead," this would necessarily mean, under the rationale of *Selwa*, that
Xavyor was alive for purposes of the born alive rule. Applying this rule to Xavyor's situation, Xavyor was clearly "not dead" when placed on the ventilator,
for the simple reason that artificially induced cardiopulmonary function "counts"
to negate death under the law of death. Xavyor was declared legally dead due
to brain death four days ex utero, but during the four days prior to this determination, the law of death unequivocally considered Xavyor to be alive.

So how could the *French* court have so misconstrued and misapplied
Selwa? Perhaps the reason lies with the doubts expressed by Judge Holbrook's
dissent in *Selwa* about the legitimacy of "counting" artificially induced respiration for purposes of determining whether an infant is born alive. And while
the majority in *Selwa* rejected the idea that artificially induced respiration
should be disregarded, they did note that the Mielkes' child had taken several
spontaneous breaths after twenty-five minutes of resuscitative efforts and
prior to being placed on the ventilator.[31] It may well be that there is an unconscious judicial preference for some evidence—however slim—of independent
breathing, even though the law of death does not consider this relevant. In
this sense, it may be that *Selwa* and its progeny—most notably *French*—do not
really offer a significant change from the common law interpretation of the
born alive rule. Even courts that claim to define life by reference to death do

not actually do so, because the common law requirement that there be evidence of independent existence—evidenced by spontaneous breathing—is too well entrenched, even if unconsciously so. So while *Selwa* may seem to present a radical break—and a rare attempt at unifying the legal concept of life and death—its practical result appears far less than radical. As *French* reveals, the Michigan courts seem, albeit through some contorted reasoning, to require evidence of independent circulation and/or respiration; without this, the courts of all jurisdictions are unwilling to declare that a fetus has been born alive.

Another intriguing issue raised by the born alive rule is that it seems implicitly to acknowledge that embryos[32] and fetuses[33] have a right to be free from bodily harm. If this is the case, it poses a conceptual conflict with other areas of the law, such as abortion, which imply that the unborn—at least up to the point of viability—have no such right. This forces the question: how can the unborn have a right to bodily integrity yet no corresponding right to life?

The most likely answer is that the first assumption—that the unborn have a right to bodily integrity—is incorrect. The born alive rule suggests that the right to bodily integrity attaches only to those who are unambiguously alive—that is, those who have survived the birthing process. In this sense, the bodily integrity being protected is the body of the born, not the body of the unborn. Because the born child's body is not as healthy as it otherwise would have been (absent the injurious prenatal action), the born person's body has been harmed—and it is the born person's body that the law cares about.

One difficulty with this reasoning is that it seems to assume that personal harm can be inflicted before there is a person. How can it be against the law to harm something that is not even alive? Does the ability to recover damages inflicted prior to birth suggest that there is some judicial recognition of personal rights possessed by the unborn? Unlikely. Of the few courts that have bothered to provide a rationale for allowing recovery for prenatal injuries, some have reasoned that, where it is beneficial to do so, the law should assume that the person was in being from the moment of conception.[34] But this rationale is carefully circumscribed, intimating that this assumption—that personhood exists from the moment of conception—should be entertained only when there is an unequivocal, born person who has been harmed. There has been no judicial enthusiasm, in other words, for extending the life-begins-at-conception assumption beyond this rather limited scenario, although (as we will see) there has been *legislative* enthusiasm, as evidenced by the passage of specific feticide statutes.

There is also lurking in the recognition of a right to recover for prenatal injuries an idea analogous to what is known in property law as a future interest. For example, suppose a will gives Blackacre to Alex if and when Alex marries. Alex's interest in Blackacre is contingent, springing to life only if and when Alex gets married. Similarly, if Alex's mother is assaulted by Dan when Alex is ten weeks postconception, any prenatal injuries sustained by Alex do not accrue unless and until Alex is born alive. Alex's right to recover for prenatal injuries is a type of future legal interest that accrues (that is, becomes legally cognizable) only upon Alex's birth.[35]

Viewed this way, Alex's right to recover for injuries inflicted on him *in utero* is not endorsing the notion that a fetus has personal rights, but merely the notion that a person whose bodily injuries are attributable to a prebirth incident may recover under ordinary ideas of causation. The aggressor committed an act that subsequently caused harm to a (born) person, so that person has a right to recover.

The bottom line is that criminal law punishment for prenatal injuries within the context of the born alive rule does not signal that courts and legislators believe an unborn child has any status equivalent to personhood. If we want to know what courts and legislators really think about the legal rights of the unborn, we will need to look elsewhere. Specifically, for present purposes, we should determine what the law says when there is unequivocally no live birth—that is, when the act causes the death of an embryo or fetus.

FETICIDE

Despite the evidentiary benefits associated with the born alive rule, the vast majority of states now statutorily recognize the killing of an unborn as a criminal act. The new approach generally classifies the willful killing of a fetus as a separate and distinct crime, although there is considerable variation on the label and penalties attached to such an act. A small minority of states has simply jettisoned the born alive rule for homicide itself, accepting that the intentional destruction of a fetus can be punished as homicide, although generally only if the fetus has passed the point of viability (the point when the fetus can survive outside the mother's womb).[36] The majority of states, however, considers the intentional killing of a fetus to be a special kind of crime, generically referred to as "feticide."

Feticide is generally considered a lesser crime than murder, carrying a lighter penalty, though it is still uniformly classified as a felony. Feticide statutes often require the fetus to be past the point of viability in order for sanctions to be imposed. There is a growing trend, however, to expand feticide to include pre-viable fetuses. Indeed, at present about half the states impose criminal liability for the killing of a fetus at any stage of its development.[37]

A recent and interesting example of the breadth of current criminal liability for killing early-stage unborn is Lawrence v. State, a Texas prosecution for capital murder. In *Lawrence,* the defendant shot and killed his girlfriend, whom he recently learned was pregnant. An autopsy revealed that the embryo was approximately four to six weeks old at the time of the shooting. Lawrence was charged with capital murder for the death of both his girlfriend and her unborn child. Under the Texas Penal Code, a "person" murdered within the meaning of the capital murder statute is defined as "a human being who is alive, including an unborn child at every stage of gestation from fertilization until birth."[38] The Texas statute thus takes a very broad view of murder, encompassing the intentional killing of any unborn from the moment of conception onwards.

The defendant in *Lawrence* argued that Texas's broad murder statute violated the viability principles established in the Supreme Court's abortion jurisprudence. Specifically, Lawrence asserted that because the Texas law punished the killing of pre-viable unborn, the state lacked a sufficiently compelling state interest to justify its interest in punishing those who destroyed such early-stage life. It is only after the point of viability, Lawrence argued, that the state could constitutionally punish killing the unborn.

The Texas Court of Criminal Appeals—the state's highest court for criminal cases—rejected Lawrence's interpretation of the Supreme Court's abortion jurisprudence. While acknowledging that abortion cases draw an important distinction between pre-viable and post-viable unborn, the court correctly recognized that the viability distinction was apposite only in cases involving a woman's claim to liberty. When a woman asserts that state action infringes her right to terminate her pregnancy, the Supreme Court's abortion law requires courts to ask whether the woman's pregnancy had passed the point of viability. If a fetus has passed the point of viability, the state's interest in protecting its life is sufficiently compelling to trump the woman's liberty interest in terminating her pregnancy. Prior to viability, however, the state's interests are not sufficiently compelling to override the woman's liberty.

When a third party such as Lawrence is charged with causing the death of a pre-viable unborn, the viability framework is not implicated. There is no need, in such a case, to balance the woman's liberty interest against the state's interest in protecting the unborn. There was no evidence that the girlfriend in the *Lawrence* case wanted to terminate her pregnancy. The only interest at stake was the state's interest in protecting the unborn, an interest that the Supreme Court has acknowledged exists throughout pregnancy. In the absence of any counterbalancing liberty interest of the pregnant woman, the Texas Court of Appeals concluded that a state is "free to protect the lives of those whom it considers to be human beings."[39] Perhaps tellingly, the Supreme Court declined to review the *Lawrence* decision.[40]

Most states have not been as aggressive as Texas and have declined to apply homicide statutes to the unborn. The common law born alive rule, in other words, is still in place for the majority of state homicide laws. But this does not mean that criminal law declines to punish those who cause the death of the unborn. As stated earlier, feticide statutes exist in a majority of states, though the penalties generally are less harsh than under homicide statutes.

In a strange sort of way, feticide statutes represent a legislative attempt to split the baby (pun intended) by creating an intermediate class somewhere between inanimate matter and living persons. Feticide statutes send the message that fetuses are worthy of the protection of criminal law, but not quite as worthy as you or I. Perhaps a rough legal analogue would be animals, which are often protected by special statutes prohibiting either cruelty towards them or intentionally killing them.[41] In the eyes of the law, killing a fetus is more like killing your neighbor's dog than your neighbor, since the fetus, like the dog, is granted some meaningful legal protection, but not quite as much as persons who have been born. In the end, neither of the polar extremes in the culture wars gets its way, and perhaps this is the way it should be: the life-begins-at-conception crowd does not get its way (a declaration of the fetus as a full legal person), but neither does the life-begins-at-birth-or-later crowd get its way (no recognition of fetal worth).

Tort Law

Unlike criminal law, tort law is not concerned with punishing acts that are harmful to society at large, but in providing compensation for acts that are harmful to private individuals. There is, of course, tremendous overlap between criminal and tort law. If someone punches you in the face, the violent act indicates that the aggressor poses a threat to society, and a criminal prosecution for battery will likely ensue. But even if the prosecution is successful, you, as the victim, may wish to seek your own compensation for the medical bills and emotional harm you suffered. You can file a tort lawsuit alleging battery which, if successful, allows you to recover for this private harm.

There are several torts that have implications for the legal definition of life. The first one we will examine, wrongful death, is essentially the tort analogue to homicide or feticide. It involves an act—often negligent or reckless—that caused the death of an unborn fetus or embryo. The only difference is that, in the tort context, legal acknowledgment of the unborn's death will result only in monetary compensation, not a loss of the defendant's liberty.

WRONGFUL DEATH

Early one morning, twenty-one-year-old Megan Nelson was driving eastbound on State Road Ten in Newton County, Indiana. She was nine months pregnant, expecting the birth of her daughter Savannah any day. James Wilson was driving a semitruck, westbound, on the same road when he became impatient and decided to pass the truck in front of him. Wilson's semi collided head-on with Megan's car. Megan and Savannah died on the scene.[42]

Should Savannah's father be able to recover civil damages from Wilson for the "wrongful death" of his unborn daughter? The Indiana appellate court that considered this question in 2009 said no, ruling that only a child who is "born alive" can be considered a "person" under the state's wrongful death tort statute.[43] The born alive rule, as explored in the previous section, is still the norm for homicide statutes, though it has been effectively discarded through the adoption of special feticide statutes now in effect in most states.

Since the criminal law has decided to sanction the possible loss of liberty for acts that destroy the unborn, should courts still cling to the born alive rule in the context of tort law, as did the Indiana Court of Appeals? Unlike the Indiana Court of Appeals, most courts in the United States have answered this question no, concluding that the born alive rule does not make sense in wrongful death actions. The vast majority of American courts will now allow wrongful death recovery so long as the unborn has passed the point of viability at the time of the wrongful act.[44] If an injury is inflicted on a pregnant woman *prior* to the point of viability, the subsequent death of the unborn will not be compensable by tort law in most states.[45]

The importance of viability to wrongful death actions mirrors its importance in criminal law. And, as we will soon see, it also mirrors the Supreme Court's abortion jurisprudence, which recognizes a woman's right to terminate her pregnancy until the point of fetal viability. The general theme, in other words, is that viability is the defining moment for legal recognition of the value of unborn life. Once the fetus has passed the point of viability, the law generally seems comfortable with explicitly recognizing its worth, though it is still not as significant as those who have been born.

Other than wrongful death, tort law recognizes other causes of actions that provide a glimpse into the legal definition of life. Specifically, we will examine two general categories of torts: (1) wrongful birth and wrongful life; and (2) wrongful conception/pregnancy. The first of these two categories (wrongful birth and wrongful life) is conceptually moored to the Supreme Court's recognition of a constitutional right to abortion, in the sense that these torts presumably would not exist in the absence of such a right. They reaffirm the idea that the pre-viable unborn are not considered to be living persons, but are more akin to a type of property that, when still present in the womb, is under the exclusive control of the mother.

Wrongful Birth and Wrongful Life

Yvonne Smith became pregnant and started seeing an obstetrician, Dr. Saraf, for her prenatal care. An ultrasound performed at thirty-eight weeks revealed that the fetus had a significant spinal cord defect and water on the brain. Her son Elijah was born shortly thereafter, suffering from incontinence and permanent paralysis in both legs. Mrs. Smith and her husband believe that if Dr. Saraf had ordered a simple blood test, Elijah's severe disability would have been revealed. The failure to order this test deprived Mrs. Smith of her right to choose whether to terminate her pregnancy. Should the Smiths be able to sue Dr. Saraf for the "wrongful birth" of Elijah? Should Elijah be able to sue Dr. Saraf for his "wrongful life"?

With regard to the parents' suit for wrongful birth, almost half of the states will permit recovery.[46] With regard to the child's independent suit for its wrongful life, only a handful of states permit recovery.[47] The trend in the last few decades has been toward increasing judicial recognition of both wrongful birth and wrongful life. At present, however, wrongful birth is much more commonly allowed, following a steady trajectory of recognition for the past several decades. Wrongful life remains extremely controversial. Why the difference in acceptance between wrongful birth and wrongful life?

Wrongful birth is a claim by parents who allege that their disabled child's birth is wrongful. Specifically, they allege that because their provider negligently failed to discover the abnormality, this negligence caused them to lose the opportunity to either avoid conception or abort the pregnancy.[48] The growth in acceptance of wrongful birth has been fueled in large part by the Supreme Court's contraceptive and abortion jurisprudence. Since the 1965 decision in Griswold v. Connecticut, the Supreme Court has held that there is a constitutional right to use contraceptives. And since the 1973 decision in Roe v. Wade, the Supreme Court has held that pregnant women generally have a constitutional right to abortion. Once these constitutional decisions were made, the analytical door was opened for parents' recovery of costs associated with raising a disabled child. The essence of wrongful birth, after all, is that the provider's failure to disclose a threat of disability has deprived the woman of her right to either avoid conception or choose an abortion. The harm suffered is the deprivation of the right to either use contraception or abort, a deprivation that presumably would not be cognizable if such constitutional rights did not exist.[49]

A series of decisions from the New Jersey Supreme Court illustrates the analytical connection between the constitutional rights to contraception and abortion and the tort of wrongful birth. In 1967—six years before the Supreme Court's decision in Roe—the New Jersey Supreme Court was asked to consider the propriety of recovery for wrongful birth. Specifically, in Gleitman v. Cosgrove, the parents sought recovery of damages against physicians who allegedly failed to warn them that their son might be severely disabled as a result of exposure to German measles while in the womb. The Gleitmans contended that if they had been told of the risk of birth defects, they would have aborted the pregnancy. The lost opportunity to terminate the pregnancy was the harm for which they sought compensation.[50]

The *Gleitman* court refused to recognize wrongful birth, stating that even assuming the Gleitmans could have obtained a legal abortion "somehow or somewhere,"[51] New Jersey's criminal prohibition of abortions created "substantial policy reasons prevent[ing] this Court from allowing tort damages for the denial of the opportunity to take an embryonic life."[52]

Six years after Roe v. Wade, in 1979, the New Jersey Supreme Court was again asked to recognize wrongful birth. In Berman v. Allan, the Bermans sought to recover damages flowing from the failure of their physicians to perform amniocentesis. The Bermans alleged that if amniocentesis had been performed, it would have revealed that their daughter suffered from Down's Syndrome, and they would have aborted the pregnancy.[53]

The *Berman* court recognized that, given the U.S. Supreme Court's recognition of a constitutional right to abortion in 1973, the continuing validity of its earlier decision in *Gleitman* was brought into question.[54] It concluded:

> In light of changes in the law which have occurred in the 12 years since *Gleitman* was decided . . . [*Gleitman*] can no longer stand in the way of judicial recognition of a cause of action founded upon wrongful birth. The Supreme Court's ruling in *Roe v. Wade* clearly establishes that a woman possesses a constitutional right to decide whether her fetus should be aborted, at least during the first trimester of pregnancy. Public policy now supports, rather than militates against, the proposition that she should not be impermissibly denied a meaningful opportunity to make that decision. . . . Any other ruling would in effect immunize from liability those in the medical field providing inadequate guidance to persons who would choose to exercise their constitutional right to abort fetuses which, if born, would suffer from genetic defects.[55]

Berman made it clear that there was a necessary connection between the constitutional right to abortion and the tort of wrongful birth. But is this connection appropriate? Deprivation of constitutional rights is generally actionable through civil litigation.[56] Yet there is one significant difference between the usual claims for violations of constitutional rights and wrongful birth claims. In tort claims for violations of constitutional rights under federal civil rights statutes or so-called *Bivens* actions, the defendant is a state actor—that is, an agent of the state or federal government. Constitutional rights are not private rights; they are rights individuals possess against government. If an agent of the Federal Bureau of Investigation conducts an unreasonable search of your home in violation of the Fourth Amendment, you may sue the agent under the *Bivens* doctrine because the agent's actions constitute a governmental deprivation of your constitutional rights.

If your neighbor Bob conducts an unreasonable search of your home, by contrast, there is no constitutional violation for the simple reason that Bob is a private citizen, not a government agent. This does not mean that Bob can ransack your home whenever he likes and escape liability. Bob's act probably constitutes a tort, such as trespass, or a violation of criminal law, such as breaking and entering. But the right to recover under these tort or criminal law theories is conceptually unmoored from your Fourth Amendment rights. These bases for punishing Bob, in other words, are analytically independent from any constitutional rights. If there were no Fourth Amendment, Bob's act of ransacking your house would presumably still constitute a tort and/or violation of the criminal law.

In the case of wrongful birth actions, however, such analytical independence seems to be missing. Wrongful birth involves an allegation that due to a provider's failure to inform a pregnant woman of her child's potential disability, she has been deprived of her constitutional rights to either avoid or terminate her pregnancy. The deprivation of the woman's constitutional rights is a necessary prerequisite—in essence an element of—the wrongful death tort. Wrongful birth conceptually could not exist without the constitutional rights to contraception or abortion.

The conceptual difficulty is that wrongful birth claims are disputes between private citizens. A private citizen (a pregnant woman) is suing another private citizen (the health care provider). It is a purely private lawsuit, but it is being used to effectuate constitutional rights—something that is unusual, to say the least. Consider the following hypothetical to illustrate this point: you are engaged to be married to an individual of the opposite sex. On your wedding day, when the preacher asks the audience whether there are any objections to the union, an ex-lover of your fiancé stands up and shouts, "Yes! He/she is the love of my life!" Your fiancé is confused and calls off the wedding.

The Supreme Court has recognized the existence of a constitutional right to marry.[57] As such, any laws or other governmental actions that infringe upon one's right to marry are unconstitutional. But as with other constitutional rights, actions by private persons who interfere with your right to marry are not, per se, constitutional deprivations.

The ex-lover's acts have clearly prevented you from exercising your right to marry, much in the same way that a health care provider in the wrongful birth scenario prevents the pregnant woman from exercising her right to use contraception or obtain an abortion. In both cases, there is a private individual (ex-lover/health care provider) who has taken some action that has prevented another private individual from making a constitutionally protected choice. Of course, you do not have to get married, nor do you have to use contraceptives or choose abortion—they are choices that you are constitutionally permitted to make without undue interference by the government. But in both the marriage hypothetical and the wrongful birth scenario, there is a private individual preventing another private individual from exercising a constitutionally permitted choice.

In the wedding day hypothetical, would it be appropriate for the state to allow you to sue the ex-lover for infringing your constitutional right to marry? Of course not.[58] By definition, constitutional deprivations require that such deprivations occur through the acts of governmental agents, not private individuals. Private individuals, in other words, cannot deprive you of constitutional rights—only state actors can. The laws or judicial precedents of a given state may recognize the existence of a private tort action to compensate harms suffered at the hands of private actors, but these tort actions inherently are not vehicles by which the state provides recompense for constitutional violations. They are—as in the hypothetical where your neighbor Bob ransacks your house—conceptually unmoored from constitutional rights. Tort law provides compensation for actions by private individuals that harm the life, liberty, or property of other private individuals, not actions by private individuals that harm the constitutional rights of other private individuals.

The tort of wrongful birth thus rests on an odd analytical foundation. It provides compensation for the acts of private individuals (health care providers) that infringe on the constitutional rights (contraception or abortion) of other private individuals. Wrongful birth, as a private tort between individuals, is not designed to compensate for injury to the pregnant woman's life, liberty, or property, but instead to compensate for the deprivation of a constitutional right by a private actor. An argument could be made that wrongful birth compensates the pregnant woman for deprivation of her "property"—the embryo/fetus. Thus, a health care provider who fails to provide information regarding the unborn's disability could be seen as depriving the pregnant woman of her right to choose how to dispose of her property in the embryo/fetus. And indeed, cases involving frozen embryos (which we will discuss soon) seem to embrace this notion that the unborn—at least in the very early stage of development—is a type of "property." But wrongful birth cases have not seen fit to articulate this view, so this is merely a matter of speculation. As articulated by the courts, wrongful birth is a tort that compensates individuals for acts performed by private actors (health care providers) that result in a deprivation of their constitutional rights to abortion or contraception. As such, wrongful birth effectively does an end-run around the state action doctrine, allowing tort law to expand the constitutional right to abortion to encompass infringements by private, not state, actors.

Wrongful life suffers from the same conceptual challenge. A wrongful life claim is brought on behalf of a disabled child—not his parents. In it, the child asserts that the defendant's negligence prevented his parents from exercising their constitutional right to use contraceptives or abort the pregnancy. But for the defendant's negligence, the plaintiff (child) would not have been born. A wrongful life claim thus seeks compensation for being born with disabilities.[59]

As with wrongful birth, the child seeking recovery for his wrongful life must allege that the defendant's negligence prevented his parents from exercising their constitutional rights to prevent his conception (by using contraceptives) or terminate the pregnancy. The defendant's acts, in other words, deprived the child's parents of their constitutional rights, which in turn caused the child to be born disabled. The deprivation of constitutional rights is thus an element of the wrongful life cause of action, as it is with wrongful birth.

In much the same way as it did in the wrongful birth case of Berman v. Allan, the New Jersey Supreme Court has acknowledged the linkage between the constitutional right to abortion and the tort of wrongful life. In Hummel v. Reiss, Kelly Hummel sued her mother's doctor and hospital for wrongful life, alleging that their negligence prevented her mother from aborting her. Kelly was born blind, slightly deaf, and with severe brain damage.[60]

Kelly was born fifteen months before the Supreme Court's decision in Roe v. Wade. At the time she was born, her mother did not have a legal right to obtain an abortion in New Jersey.[61] As was the case in the wrongful birth case of *Berman*, the New Jersey Supreme Court ruled that Kelly could not maintain her wrongful life action because wrongful life (as well as wrongful birth) is "dependent on a woman's right to terminate a pregnancy for reasons other than the mother's health. . . . [P]ersons born before the decision in *Roe* are foreclosed from receiving the benefits of such a [wrongful life] claim."[62]

Further proof of the linkage between the constitutional right to abortion and the tort of wrongful life can be found in case law that denies recovery when the discovery of the fetal defect occurs after the point of fetal viability. In a recent case from California, Barrigan v. Lopez, premature twins born with cerebral palsy brought a wrongful life suit against their mother's obstetrician, claiming that he should have advised their mother of her right to abort them. The court found that the threat of disability became apparent only after the twins had passed the point of viability, a point beyond which California law—in keeping with the Supreme Court's abortion jurisprudence—did not permit abortions other than to save the life or health of the mother.[63] Because the mother had no right to abort her twins, the twins had no right to recover for wrongful life.[64] Admittedly, in the *Barrigan* case, the prohibition on post-viability abortions was statutorily, not constitutionally, based. But the California statute was undoubtedly designed to comport with the Supreme Court's abortion jurisprudence, which gives states the ability to ban completely most post-viability abortions. California's entire statutory framework regarding abortion—as well as other states—is driven by the Supreme Court's constitutional abortion case law. Because the Constitution is the supreme law of the land, the various states' ordinary laws regarding abortion must conform to the constitutional framework. In this sense, states' recognition (or nonrecognition, as was the case in *Barrigan*) of wrongful life claims is inherently defined by reference to constitutional principles.

Because wrongful life, like wrongful birth, permits recovery for a private actor's deprivation of constitutional rights, it seems to do the same end-run around the state action doctrine. This is not to say that states are not free to define torts as they wish or that torts are not appropriately aimed at remedying private harms (they are). Rather, it is merely to point out that the articulated justification for these torts is odd, allowing private actors (parents or children) to sue for violations of constitutional rights committed by purely private actors.

Wrongful life is also controversial because of the message it sends about the value of disabled life. The gravamen of a wrongful life claim is the child's assertion that he would be better off dead—that his very life, because riddled with disability or deformity, is inherently wrongful.[65] It implies that a life burdened by disability or deformity should never have been allowed to occur. The unmistakable message is that no life at all would have been preferable to disabled life. For this reason, wrongful life is more controversial than wrongful death, and the majority of courts that have considered wrongful life have refused to recognize it.[66] Indeed, resistance to wrongful life has been so strong that legislatures in at least ten states have enacted special laws prohibiting their state courts from recognizing it.[67]

We will now turn to our final category of tort law with significant implications for the legal definition of life—so-called wrongful conception/pregnancy claims. While this category of tort is not dependent on the recognition of a constitutional right to abortion (the way wrongful life and wrongful birth are), it is dependent on a related constitutional right—namely, the right to avoid procreation through the use of contraception.

Wrongful Conception/Pregnancy

Ann and her husband had two beautiful and healthy children. Following the birth of her second child, Ann asked her doctor to perform a surgical sterilization to prevent any future pregnancies. Despite undergoing this procedure, Ann bore a third healthy child. Following the birth of her third child, Ann asked the same physician to perform another sterilization procedure. But once again, Ann became pregnant, bearing a fourth healthy child. Should Ann and her husband be able to receive compensation from their doctor for having to bear or raise these two healthy children?[68]

Most jurisdictions would answer this question in the affirmative and permit recovery under a tort theory known as "wrongful conception" or "wrongful pregnancy." Wrongful conception/pregnancy is brought by the parents of a child who allege that the child's birth was unplanned and unwanted. This tort generally involves the birth of normal, healthy children.[69] This fact differentiates it from wrongful birth, as the latter seeks compensation for the unwanted birth of a disabled child, whereas with wrongful conception/pregnancy, the health of the child is irrelevant. More specifically, wrongful conception/pregnancy provides compensation for acts that cause an unwanted conception or pregnancy, whereas wrongful birth provides compensation for

an act that causes the birth of a disabled child, such as the failure to perform a
test that would have revealed a disability early enough to permit a lawful
abortion.

By their nature, wrongful conception/pregnancy lawsuits are filed against
those who have some causal responsibility for the parents' conception or
pregnancy, such as physicians, pharmacists, or pharmaceutical manufacturers. The essence of the claim is that the parents took reasonable precautions
to prevent conception or pregnancy from occurring—precautions that they
are constitutionally entitled to take—but notwithstanding those precautions,
the defendants' actions resulted in pregnancy or conception. Under this theory, parents have sued physicians who have improperly performed sterilization procedures.[70] They have also sued pharmacists who have improperly
dispensed contraceptives as well as the manufacturers of contraceptives that
have failed.[71]

One of the more difficult aspects of wrongful conception/pregnancy is
the determination of damages. Specifically, how much should parents be
compensated for the birth of a healthy, albeit unwanted, child? Answering
this question requires courts to place a dollar value on the burden of unwanted parenthood, a task that has caused much judicial consternation. In
the majority of jurisdictions, the approach settled upon has been the so-called
limited recovery rule, which limits the parents' recovery to any actual medical costs associated with the pregnancy and childbirth. It thus denies recovery
for expenses associated with raising and educating the child, thereby severely
reducing the financial attractiveness of such lawsuits. Courts that have settled
upon the limited recovery rule have employed various rationales for doing so,
including a belief that allowing compensation for raising the child would in-
centivize fraudulent claims and be disproportionate compared to the defendant's culpability, that the benefits derived from the birth of a healthy child
outweigh any expenses associated with raising it, and that permitting recovery for child-rearing expenses could cause psychological harm to the child if
she found out.[72]

Unlike wrongful birth and wrongful life, wrongful conception/preg-
nancy is not analytically moored to the constitutional right to abortion. But
there is a close relationship between wrongful conception/pregnancy and the
constitutional right to avoid procreation through the use of contraceptives. Unlike wrongful birth and wrongful life actions, however, parents in wrongful

pregnancy/conception actions are *not* alleging that the defendant has deprived them of their constitutional right to use contraceptives, so there is no odd sense of doing an end-run around the state action doctrine as there is with wrongful birth or wrongful life. Instead, in wrongful conception pregnancy claims, the parents assert that despite their having exercised their right to avoid pregnancy, pregnancy nonetheless occurred. The defendant, in other words, has acted negligently in his attempt to assist their exercise of their constitutional right. Viewed this way, wrongful conception/pregnancy is little different from run-of-the-mill negligence actions.[73] Nonetheless, if there were no constitutional right to avoid pregnancy (and hence use contraceptives), the tort of wrongful pregnancy/conception would not be so ubiquitous. If individuals did not enjoy a right to avoid procreation by using contraceptives or undergoing sterilization, there could still be state laws on the books prohibiting the use of contraception. And if such anticontraception laws still existed, there presumably would be no tort compensation allowed for negligent acts associated with illegal contraceptive activity. Nonetheless, even in the absence of a constitutional right to avoid procreation, some states would probably permit the use of contraceptives statutorily or by common law, at least by some portion of the population. In that instance, there would be logic to recognizing a tort cause of action in such jurisdictions for negligent performance of contraceptive-related acts.

Contract and Property Law

Though there are occasional exceptions, the general rule that has emerged in tort and criminal law is that after the point of viability, any act that causes harm to a fetus is punishable. Prior to viability, because the unborn can be aborted (or prevented altogether by contraception), there is substantially less legal protection—and indeed, several torts that compensate parents for deprivation of the right to abort or avoid pregnancy. We now turn to the other major areas of common law—namely, contract and property law—to compare relevant doctrines relating to the law of life.

EN VENTRE SA MERE

The first broad recognition of fetal rights emerged from English inheritance law. Since at least the eighteenth century, the common law has recognized that a child *en ventre sa mere* (in the mother's womb) has the same inheritance rights as a person who has been born.[74] Any reference in a will to children or heirs as a class is presumed to include children conceived before the testator's death but born afterwards.[75] The same holds true for inheritance when there is no will. The Uniform Probate Code, for example, follows the common law *en ventre sa mere* rule, providing that for purposes of intestate succession, an "individual in gestation at a decedent's death is deemed to be living at the decedent's death if the individual lives 120 hours after birth."[76]

The reason for such broad recognition of fetal rights under property law is that the focus of property law, at least in inheritance cases, is to effectuate the decedent's intent. It was presumed, therefore, that the testator whose will left his estate to his children as a class (without naming specific names) would intend to include unborn offspring still within the womb. Consider, for example, the case of Ebbs v. Smith, in which a woman's will left her estate "to the children and grandchildren of Mary Muntz." At the time of the woman's death, David—a grandchild of Mary Muntz—had not yet been born. He was *en ventre sa mere* and was born three days after the woman died. The court ruled that David was within the class of persons intended by the woman to inherit because her intent was to confer inheritance upon any child or grandchild of Mary Muntz, regardless of whether he had been born at the time of her death.[77]

But the cases get more complicated. What if Bill leaves his estate to his children, but one of them is not even *conceived* at the time of his death? How could such a thing even happen? It can happen, and it does. It is called posthumous conception, and it is made possible by the indefinite freezing of sperm, eggs, and embryos stored for artificial reproductive technology (ART) use. A recent case from New York illustrates the complexity of this area of the law. Several trust agreements were executed in 1969 in which the "issue" and "descendants" of Martin are granted interest in the trusts' principal after Martin passes away. Martin died in 2001, leaving only one son, Lindsay. Martin had another son, James, who contracted cancer and predeceased his father. At the time James died, he and his wife had no children. But because James knew he was likely to die from cancer, he decided to have some of his sperm frozen, instructing his wife to use it if she wanted to have children after his death. Three years after James died, his wife used the semen to conceive a child, James, Jr. Two years after that, she used more semen to conceive a second son, Warren. Should James, Jr., and Warren—who were not even conceived at the time Martin died—properly be considered Martin's "issue" or "descendants" under the terms of the trust?

The New York trial court answered this question yes. The court noted that recent statutory changes in New York limited inheritance to those individuals conceived during the decedent's lifetime. The purpose of excluding posthumously conceived children was to "ensure certainty in identifying persons interested in an estate and finality in its distribution."[78] Because posthumously conceived children could be born many years—perhaps even decades—after the decedent's death, the new statute recognized the difficulty in ascertaining the class of beneficiaries who take under a will in posthumous conception scenarios. In the interest of certainty and finality, therefore, the legislature opted to simply exclude posthumously conceived children. Other states have enacted similar statutes that limit the ability of posthumously conceived children to inherit. In California, for example, posthumously conceived children may inherit only if the parent has provided written consent to the posthumous use of their genetic material, designated a person to control its disposition, and the child must be conceived within two years of the parent's death.[79] Similar legislation has been enacted in Louisiana, where the posthumously conceived child must be born within three years of his parent's death.[80]

Unfortunately for the court in Martin's case, the revised New York law applied only to posthumously conceived children of the testator, not children of third parties. Martin's posthumously conceived grandchildren, as third parties, were simply not covered by the statute. The court began its analysis by correctly noting that James, Jr., and Warren were not *en ventre sa mere* because they were not only not in the womb at the time of their grandfather's death, but they were not even conceived. As the saying goes—albeit with a modern biotech twist—they were but frozen twinkles in their parents' eyes.

The court decided that basic property law principles should govern—namely, the intent of the donor. It concluded that if the "individual considers a child to be his or her own, society through its laws should do so as well. . . . Accordingly, in the instant case, these postconceived infants should be treated as part of their father's family for all purposes."[81]

The remarkable aspect of posthumous conception inheritance cases is that courts seem willing to permit posthumously conceived children to inherit, at least within certain limits. While some states have limited the number of years postdeath in which the conception must take place, the overall trend seems to be approving of the rights of the unborn, and even unconceived, to inherit. In order to do so, these posthumously born or conceived persons must be subsequently born. This mirrors the born alive rule often invoked in tort and criminal law. If born alive, posthumously born or conceived individuals may inherit, suggesting once again that the law recognizes at least the potentiality of the unborn, though this potentiality does not itself create vested legal rights unless and until birth occurs.

FROZEN EMBRYOS, BODIES, AND BODY PARTS

Baseball great Ted Williams has done it. *American Idol* judge Simon Cowell reportedly wants to.[82] Tens of thousands of embryos are doing it right now. What do they have in common? Cryonics—the freezing of tissues, body parts, or even whole bodies. Cryonics uses a process known as cryopreservation, which cools tissue to extremely low temperatures so that it can be thawed and revived in the future.

Modern cryopreservation techniques do not actually freeze the tissues, since freezing causes the water in the body to form ice, destroying cells in much the same way that ice destroys roads in winter. Instead of freezing, modern cryopreservation principally uses a process known as vitrification, in which chemical cryoprotectants—sort of like a specialized type of antifreeze—is pumped through the tissue in order to allow the use of much lower temperatures. Vitrification permits a slower and deeper cooling of the tissue, thereby preventing formation of destructive ice.[83]

Mainstream science scoffs at the use of cryonics for human bodies or body parts, dismissing it as fanciful science fiction. And so far, the mainstream scientists have it right: there has never been an instance of successful reanimation of any human body parts, much less whole bodies. Yet there are several cryonics institutes operating currently in the United States, with several hundred individuals cryopreserved, either in whole or in part. The most common (and least expensive) form of cryopreservation is called neuropreservation, meaning that only the head or brain is preserved. Neuropreservation is more common than whole body preservation, because it is substantially cheaper—in the $80,000 range—but it requires a rather large leap of faith because it is dependent upon future development of replacement bodies, whether through cloning, transplantation, or robotics. Whole body preservation is the most expensive—about $150,000 to $200,000 dollars—but ironically the least likely to succeed, since successful reanimation of large areas of tissue is exponentially more challenging. Although the costs of cryopreservation are very high, most people who choose it pay for it by listing the cryopreservation institute as a beneficiary of a life insurance policy, making it theoretically affordable for many people. The high costs are arguably justifiable, since cryopreservation not only requires specialized embalming immediately after death but continued maintenance and storage for potentially hundreds, even thousands, of years.

Cryopreservation of human bodies or parts is a growing business, considering that it is an industry built on little more than hope mixed with a dash of egotism. The hope is not entirely unreasonable. Cryonics has been used successfully on a few small mammalian organs like rabbit kidneys and frog and hamster hearts.[84] And for smaller biological materials that can vitrify much faster, cryopreservation has proven very successful. Semen, stem cells, oocyes, ovarian tissue, and early-stage human embryos created through in vitro fertilization (IVF) are all routinely cryopreserved.

As with any new technological development, the law has been rushing to keep apace, and there is presently little guidance on how to resolve difficult legal issues that arise with cryonic preservation. The foundational issue involving cryopreserved human tissue is the legal status of the frozen parts. Are frozen embryos, human bodies, or body parts persons, property, or something in between? If a person cryopreserves her brain, head, or whole body, is the person really dead, or simply "on hold"?

When it comes to cryopreservation of human bodies or parts, the law is a bit fuzzy. The Uniform Anatomical Gifts Act (UAGA), adopted by the majority of states, permits individuals to donate all or part of their body once they have been declared legally dead. Section 6 of the UAGA list three categories of persons or institutions that may become donees of human bodies or parts, only one of which potentially applies to cryopreservation institutes. Specifically, Section 6 allows a "hospital, physician, surgeon, or procurement organization" to receive a donation "for transplantation, therapy, medical or dental education, research, or advancement of medical or dental science."[85] Arguably, a cryopreservation institute is a "procurement organization" that receives human bodies or parts for "research, or advancement of medical . . .

science." The chief difficulty, however, comes from the definition section of the UAGA, which defines a "procurement organization" as "licensed, accredited, or approved under the laws of any state for procurement, distribution, or storage of human bodies or parts."[86] If a state's law does not specifically license, accredit, or approve a cryogenic preservation facility, the UAGA arguably does not permit such a facility to be a donee of human bodies or parts.

The definitional problem posed by the UAGA was litigated in California in the early 1990s. California regulators, worried about the sudden proliferation of cryopreservation facilities in the state, issued an opinion stating that such facilities did not qualify as donees under the state's Anatomical Gift Act. Both the California trial and appellate courts ruled against the state because the state's refusal to even consider approving cryopreservation facilities placed such facilities in a "Catch-22": they could not be donees because they were not approved procurement organizations, yet the state would not allow them to seek approval.[87] Unless and until the UAGA is amended to specifically address cryogenic facilities, additional state-by-state litigation will be needed to clarify the legal status of cryogenic facilities. Arguably, cryogenic institutes are functionally indistinguishable from cemeteries or mausoleums and could be required to abide by similar regulations relating to storage, maintenance, and record keeping. Whether states will go this path remains to be seen.

Another major legal obstacle to cryopreservation is hostility to the procedure, which manifests itself in various ways. One bizarre example is that of the Martinot-Leroys of France, a couple who firmly believed in cryonics and had been cryopreserved and stored in the basement of their Loire Valley chateau at a chilly minus eighty-five degrees Fahrenheit. After the couple had been entombed this way for several years, the top French administrative court ordered the Martinot-Leroys' son to either cremate or bury them, ostensibly on grounds of guaranteeing "public health and order."[88]

Or consider the case of Orville Richardson of Iowa, who executed a $50,000 neuropreservation contract a few years before his death. When he told his brother and sister about his intent to be cryopreserved, they adamantly objected. After Richardson died, his siblings quickly had him buried, failing to notify the cryopreservation facility of his demise. When the siblings had the chutzpah to demand refund of the $50,000 from the cryopreservation facility, it demanded Richardson's body be delivered for preservation. A lawsuit resulted, with an Iowa trial judge ruling in favor of the siblings.[89] The judge stated that the UAGA was inapplicable because another, recently enacted statute regarding disposition of remains controlled. Specifically, the new law lists those individuals who have the right to control the disposition of a person's remains. The first (and highest-ranking) decision maker is a "designee, or alternate designee, acting pursuant to the decedent's declaration."[90] The sixth-ranking decision maker is a "surviving sibling of the decedent, or, if there is more than one, a majority of the surviving siblings whose whereabouts are reasonably ascertainable."[91] Because Richardson had designated a cryogenics facility to take possession of his body after his death, it would seem that the new Iowa law allowed the cryogenics facility to trump Richardson's siblings. But the statute did not grandfather designations made prior to the effective date—July 1, 2008—so Richardson's 2004 designation of the cryogenics facility was ineffective.[92] The net result is that Richardson's final wish to be cryopreserved is not likely to be fulfilled.

On a more theoretical level, cryopreservation poses some thorny questions about the nature of death itself. Cryonics advocates unabashedly contend that cryopreserved individuals are not actually dead, even though the law may deem them so. One of the leading cryonics institutes in the United States, the Cryonics Institute in Michigan, states on its Web page that they prefer to call a cryopreserved person a "patient," because they "do not regard the cryopreserved person as being really 'dead.' "[93]

Cryopreserved individuals must be declared legally dead before they can be cryopreserved. Premortem cryopreservation would constitute suicide, and those who assisted them would be criminally liable for assisting their suicide. Even in the two states that permit assisted suicide—Oregon and Washington—a physician cannot assist with suicide by cryopreserving his patient; he can only prescribe a lethal dose of medication. An illustrative case exploring the relationship between cryopreservation and suicide and assisted suicide is Donaldson v. Lungren, decided by the California Court of Appeals in 1992.[94]

In Donaldson, the plaintiff, Thomas Donaldson, had an incurable, progressively worsening malignant brain tumor. His prognosis was grim. The tumor had caused seizures, speech problems, and weakness. His doctors told him it would lead to a persistent vegetative state and ultimately death. Donaldson wanted to be cryogenically preserved—prior to his legal death—so that he could preserve as much of his brain as possible and increase his chance of being successfully revived in the future. He went to court seeking a declaration of his right to premortem cryopreservation of his body, including the right to receive the assistance of others in doing so.[95] As the court of appeals put it, Donaldson sought a court declaration allowing him "to die in order to live."[96]

Although the *Donaldson* case was decided prior to the Supreme Court's decisions regarding physician-assisted suicide, the outcome would be no different today. The California Court of Appeals held that the state's interests in preserving human life, preventing suicide, and protecting the integrity of the medical profession were all sufficient reasons to outlaw assisted suicide. They also noted—as did the Supreme Court in its later physician-assisted suicide cases—that the states may rightly decide that all life is worth protecting, regardless of the quality of that life.[97] As such, California's prohibition against assisting suicide did not violate Donaldson's constitutional rights.

The *Donaldson* court noted that Donaldson had a right to take his own life, since California law (as with other states) no longer sought to add to such persons' pain by imposing punishment on those who tried unsuccessfully to kill themselves. So, at least in theory, a person desperate to cryopreserve their body before it deteriorates too badly—and before legal death occurs—could simply commit suicide (without third-party assistance) and prearrange to have a cryopreservation facility notified immediately thereafter. The problem with this approach is exemplified by a recent case from Florida.,

In December 2009, Michael Ned Miller was found dead in his apartment outside St. Petersburg, Florida. Prior to his death, Miller had signed a $150,000 contract with a cryonics institute to have his whole body preserved after his death. As is the typical case with suicides, however, the coroner ruled Miller's death suspicious and ordered an autopsy.[98] Autopsies take time and are generally incompatible with successful cryopreservation. And while an anatomical gift of one's body to a cryonics facility would normally give the facility the right to take possession of the donor's body upon his death, the UAGA says that the right of a medical examiner to conduct an autopsy is superior to the right of the donee to take the body.[99] So someone who wanted to cryopreserve his body in a physiologically "better" state by committing suicide (rather than waiting for legal death) would likely not have his desires fulfilled.

In Miller's case, the cryonics facility requested the coroner to turn over Miller's body. But the coroner refused, and the parties went to court. As would be expected given the language of the UAGA, the trial judge ruled in favor of the coroner, deeming his rights superior to that of the cryonics facility. After the trial judge's ruling, the cryonics facility negotiated with the coroner to minimize dissection of Miller's body so as to maximize the chances of an eventual cryopreservation. Undoubtedly, however, Miller's body will have deteriorated enough that his chances of successful cryopreservation (and future revival) will be materially reduced.

Intriguingly, these cryopreservation cases show that it is hard to have your last wishes honored, if your last wishes involve cryopreservation. The unanswered question is: why? Perhaps it is because the science is so slim that those who think cryonics is expensive snake oil paternalistically fight its implementation, believing they are protecting the dead from such shysters. Maybe it is because the "yuck" factor—the visualization of bodies or severed heads emerged in giant frozen tubes—makes us want to defy this bizarre Orwellian future. Or perhaps there is a hostility toward the potential of man-made resurrection generally, a theologically driven opposition to an invasion of the perceived domain of a higher creator.

There is also, from a lawyer's (and probably also from a doctor's) perspective, an innate desire to control death by defining it and issuing a formal and final declaration. If cryopreservation ever turns out to be something other than science fiction, there will be tremendous practical and theoretical legal issues to resolve. On a practical level, analogous to missing persons who have been "lost" for many years, the possessions of cryogenically revived persons will have been long distributed and could no longer be practically undone. Their professional licenses, if any, would have lapsed. Would they have the same right to practice such licensed professions, or would a significant span of time render them ineligible to continue practicing such professions? Would they have to start over, professionally speaking? Even if their prior lives did not involve practicing a licensed profession, the steady march of knowledge and technology would likely mean that they would no longer have any transferable skills that would enable them to earn a living. They would have no money, no property, and no skills.

More fundamentally, what would such future resurrection do to the legal identity of the person? Would such persons become "un-dead"? Or perhaps they were never really dead at all? As mentioned briefly before, the most ardent supporters of cryonics believe that those who are cryopreserved are not really dead. They advocate an "information theoretic" criterion of death, which asserts that death is the loss of one's memory and personality.[100] Such memories and personality reside somewhere in the brain—most likely the higher brain—so if the brain is cryopreserved, the logic goes, the person cannot be dead. Their memories and personality are still in there, waiting to be jump-started again.

Interestingly, this "information theoretic" criterion of death is not too far removed from the concept of death advocated presently as "higher brain" death (absent, of course, the cryopreservation angle). Under either a "higher brain" conception of death or an "information theoretic" one, death occurs when that portion of the brain responsible for thinking, feeling, and remembering has irreversibly ceased functioning. But if this portion of the brain resumes functioning, would this mean that death never really occurred? Indeed, if one uses present definitions of death—"irreversible" cessation of cardiopulmonary or whole brain function—the same issue is potentially raised. If someone who has undergone whole body cryopreservation is resurrected, both her heart and brain could potentially resume functioning, calling into question whether, by the current definition of death, death actually occurred. The bottom line is that: if cryonics ever becomes reality, the definition of death will need to be amended, most likely to recognize some state in between life and death—a state of "suspension" perhaps—that balances the pragmatic need for finality and the rights of the presently living against the pragmatic needs and rights of those who may be resurrected. What that in-between state would ultimately entail, I happily leave to future lawyers.

Frozen sperm, eggs, and embryos offer another glimpse into society's definition of life. Sperm and egg banks have become ubiquitous—a simple Web search will pull up numerous banks that allow you to search for that "perfect" donor by criteria such as hair or eye color, ethnicity, height, weight, and education level.[101] For a short time, there was even an "embryo bank" in San Antonio, Texas—called Abraham Center of Life—that combined donor egg and donor sperm to create embryos that were frozen and sold to willing infertile couples around the globe.[102] After less than a year in business, it voluntarily closed shop, claiming that it was "no longer cost effective" to operate.[103]

Even though you can no longer order embryos on the Web, you can still go to an in vitro fertilization (IVF) clinic and create an embryo for a small fortune. Once you have successfully created embryos, they can be transferred into the uterus for purposes of creating pregnancy or frozen indefinitely as insurance against initial transplantation failure. At present there are about four hundred thousand embryos in frozen storage—so-called "frosties"—in the United States alone.[104] In the last few years, some couples have begun putting their excess frozen embryos up for "adoption." It is estimated that over a thousand babies have been born this way.[105]

There are many legal issues relating to frozen embryos, but for present purposes, we will focus on whether these frosties are considered alive, dead, or something in between. The landmark case is Davis v. Davis, a dispute between a divorcing Tennessee couple who disagreed over the disposition of seven frozen embryos created by IVF prior to their divorce. By the time their case found its way to the Tennessee Supreme Court, both of the Davises had remarried. Mary Sue no longer wanted to use the frozen embryos herself, but instead wished to donate them to an infertile couple. Junior Davis objected, asserting that the embryos should be discarded.[106] The most challenging issue facing the *Davis* court was the legal status of these frozen embryos. Were they "persons" or "property" under the law?

In answering this question, the Tennessee Supreme Court looked principally to the U.S. Supreme Court's abortion jurisprudence, which draws an important distinction between pre-viable and post-viable unborn. Because viability was essential to the Supreme Court's abortion cases, the *Davis* court thought it important that "that stage of fetal development [post-viability] is far removed, both qualitatively and quantitatively, from that of the four-to-eight celled preembryos in this case."[107] The court did not feel comfortable classifying such early-stage, pre-viable embryos as "persons," recognizing that it would not only be inconsistent with the Supreme Court's abortion cases but also with some state statutory causes of action, such as wrongful death.

Also important was the pragmatic implication of finding such embryos to be legally cognizable persons: "Left undisturbed . . . afford[ing] preembryos the legal status of 'persons' and vest[ing] them with legally cognizable interests . . . would doubtless have . . . the effect of outlawing IVF programs in the state of Tennessee."[108] Although the *Davis* court did not elaborate on this point, presumably they were concerned about deprivations of life or liberty that could be claimed to result from indefinite frozen storage or the practice of discarding excess embryos.

Having decided that frozen embryos were not persons under the law, the *Davis* court next considered whether they could be considered a type of property. Here the court relied heavily on ethical standards promulgated by the American Fertility Society (AFS), which recommended an "intermediate position" between those who believe human embryos are full legal persons and those who believe they are no different from other human tissue. The AFS stated that this intermediate position "holds that the preembryo deserves respect greater than that accorded to human tissue but not the respect accorded to actual persons. The preembryo is entitled to greater respect than other human tissue because of its potential to become a person and because of its symbolic meaning for many people. Yet, it should not be treated as a person, because it has not yet developed the features of personhood, is not yet established as developmentally individual, and may never realize its biologic potential."[109]

Following the AFS guidance, the Tennessee Supreme Court concluded that "preembryos are not, strictly speaking, either 'persons' or 'property,' but occupy an interim category that entitles them to special respect because of their potential for human life."[110] As a result, the Davises' interest in their frozen embryos was "not a true property interest" but an "interest in the nature of ownership to the extent that they have decision-making authority concerning disposition" of them.[111]

If one looks at the *Davis* conclusion closely, it becomes apparent that the "interim" status of frozen embryos is not really interim at all. The court gives lip service to the fact that they are neither persons nor property and entitled to "special respect," but in the end it admits that the Davises, as the gamete donors who created the embryos, had an "interest in the nature of ownership" that entitled them to "decision-making authority concerning disposition." An ownership interest that permits the owner to control disposition is ownership, plain and simple. Courts can talk about special respect all they want, but it is meaningless if, at the end of the day, those who have created the embryo own and control it. The bottom line from *Davis* is that those who create frozen embryos have the right to dispose of them, no differently from other forms of property such as cars, jewelry, or furniture.

If the gamete donors are in disagreement and there is no contractual agreement regarding disposition in the event of divorce, the *Davis* court concluded that the interests of the parties should be balanced against each other, weighing the burdens that would accrue if their dispositional preference was not followed.[112] The court asserted that "the party wishing to avoid procreation should prevail assuming that the other party has a reasonable possibility of achieving parenthood by means other than the use of the preembryos in question."[113]

As an initial matter, one should question whether balancing interests in such a situation is appropriate or even possible. How can a court realistically weigh the benefits and burdens involved in becoming a parent, giving up a potential child for adoption, destroying a potential life, or not becoming a parent? Is there any principled, objective way to assign weight to these differing scenarios? Courts weigh things all the time; multifactorial balancing tests are ubiquitous. But they rarely weigh such deeply intimate and personal values for the simple reason that doing so can lead to wildly disparate results across courts, counseling that on such controversial subjects—where reasonable people often disagree—the balancing is better left to the legislature.

The *Davis* court's application of the balancing test is illustrative. Notice how the court presumes that these frozen embryos are fungible widgets. As long as the party wishing to use them for procreative purposes has a "reasonable alternative" for achieving parenthood—including adoption or procreation with another mate—the party wishing to avoid procreation should prevail and the frozen embryos should be destroyed.

This rationale implies that these frozen embryos are not particularly special, that Mary Sue Davis can, if she wants to become a parent, create embryos with someone else or, if this is not possible, satisfy her parental urge through adoption. There seems to be no recognition of the fact that these embryos may be, in the eyes of Mary Sue Davis, her children, the destruction of which could be emotionally devastating. Perhaps under the particular facts of *Davis*, the court assumed that such emotional devastation would not occur because Mary Sue was willing to put her embryos up for adoption by another couple. In the court's own words:

> Balanced against Junior Davis's interest in avoiding parenthood is Mary Sue Davis's interest in donating the preembryos to another couple for implantation. Refusal to permit donation of the preeembryos would impose on her the burden of knowing that the lengthy IVF procedures she underwent were futile, and that

the preembryos to which she contributed genetic material would never become children. While this is not an insubstantial burden, we can only conclude that Mary Sue Davis's interest in donation is not as significant as the interest Junior Davis has in avoiding parenthood. If she were allowed to donate these preembryos, he would face a lifetime of either wondering about his parental status or knowing about his parental status but having no control over it. He testified quite clearly that if these preembryos were brought to term he would fight for custody of his child or children. Donation, if a child came of it, would rob him twice—his procreational autonomy would be defeated and his relationship with his offspring would be prohibited.

There are some interesting value judgments inherent in the court's statement. First, consider how the court characterizes the burdens placed on Mary Sue if the embryos are destroyed: (1) there will be a burden of knowing that the IVF procedures were futile; and (2) a burden of knowing that the preembryos would never become children. There is no recognition of the possibility that Mary Sue's burden was not that the embryos "would never become children" but were in fact already her children. The court itself does not believe the frozen embryos are the moral equivalent of children—they had already determined that they were a type of property owned by the gamete providers. But the court's moral determination should not be imputed to Mary Sue in its balancing test. Mary Sue may well have a different set of moral values from the court, and it is her interests, not the court's, that are supposedly being balanced.

The court simply assumed that, from Mary Sue's perspective, the embryos were merely a type of property with a potential for life, nothing more. The point here is not that the embryos are or are not living persons—reasonable minds can disagree about that—but that the court seems unable to imagine that some parents in the position of Mary Sue Davis would think of them as such. It is conceivable that, for some people, destroying a frozen embryo results in the burden of feeling that they have lost their children—a loss that adoption or procreating with someone else could never replace. Recent studies have shown that a lot of couples who undergo IVF use "baby talk" when discussing their embryos, conceptualizing them as children, not just potential or future ones.[114] Even among those who decide to have their excess embryos destroyed rather than donated for research or adoption, some wish they had the option to hold a funeral-like ceremony during the thawing and disposal process.[115]

At the same time that the *Davis* court minimized Mary Sue's interests, it maximized the interests of Junior. The court says that Junior Davis "would face a lifetime of either wondering about his parental status or knowing about his parental status but having no control over it. . . . Donation, if a child came of it, would rob him twice—his procreational autonomy would be defeated and his relationship with his offspring would be prohibited." It is true that if the frozen embryos were donated to others for adoption, Junior Davis would probably never know whether his embryos were ultimately born. But is this burden any heavier than that borne by those who donate sperm and ova? Those who donate sperm and ova realize that they may have children "out there somewhere" whom they may never know. But a man who donates his sperm for IVF treatments with his wife probably never contemplates such a possibility. So it is a burden, and a substantial one at that.

But the court's unequivocal conclusion that his relationship with any such offspring would be "prohibited" is an overstatement. Nothing would prohibit Junior Davis from having a relationship with such offspring. And as adoption cases illustrate, individuals who want to find their biological parents have ways of doing so. In theory, then, it is possible that Junior Davis and his child could have a relationship, though whether or when that would happen is purely speculation.

We should also take a critical look at the *Davis* court's statement that donation of these frozen embryos would defeat Junior Davis's procreational autonomy. He has already created embryos with a woman (his ex-wife) and did so with the full intent (or hope) that they would one day be born and become his children. Once conception has occurred—even if the embryo is frozen— arguably, Junior Davis's right to procreational autonomy has been fully exercised. He has made his decision to procreate—he has in fact procreated—and so it seems odd for the *Davis* court to assert that donating these frozen embryos will "rob" him (or his ex-wife) of his procreational autonomy. If these frozen embryos had been implanted into Mary Sue's womb, it is true that *she* would have an additional constitutional right to decide whether to abort her pregnancy. But Junior's constitutional procreational rights ended at the time

of conception. Is the *Davis* court suggesting that because these frozen embryos were never implanted into a woman's womb, both the man and the
woman who created the embryo have an additional constitutional right—not
just an ordinary property law right—to destroy these embryos? If so, this is
an interesting and novel expansion of existing constitutional doctrine relating
to procreational rights, which previously have been understood to: (1) give
both men and women a right to avoid conception by using contraceptives
and sterilization procedures; and (2) give a pregnant woman the right to terminate a pregnancy (pre-viability), recognizing her liberty interest in controlling her own body. The *Davis* decision, however, at least implies something
further: that after conception and prior to implantation into a woman's body,
both the donors of the sperm and egg have a constitutional right to control
the disposition of the embryo they have created. Constitutionally, in other
words, the embryo "belongs" to them both, and a court presumptively should
not rule on disposition in such a way as to "impose" parenthood on either
one of them against their will.

The *Davis* court thus engages in some creative and novel logic in its attempt to maximize Junior's interests and minimize Mary Sue's. But what alternatives does a court realistically have when faced with such an intractable
dispute, in which there are arguably substantial burdens to be borne regardless of outcome? Is it best, as the *Davis* court suggested, to simply err on the
side of avoiding procreation? Or would it be better to err on the side of providing an opportunity for the embryos to fulfill their life potential? If embryos are a unique type of property entitled to "special respect," should this
create a presumption in favor of giving them a chance to be born? There is no
easy answer to this, but the question raises the possibility that there is a logical incongruity between the *Davis* court's pronouncement that embryos are
entitled to special respect and the court's subsequent method of balancing
the respective interests, which arguably denied such respect.

Courts asked to decide the legal status of frozen embryos after Davis v.
Davis have uniformly agreed that frozen embryos are a form of property that
is controlled by those who donate the gametes. The vast majority of cases
have stated that, like other forms of personal property, frozen embryos can
be the subject of presumptively binding contracts, specifying the couple's
wishes involving disposition in the event of divorce, death, or disagreement.[116]
A few jurisdictions have altered the approach slightly, enforcing advance di-

rectives for embryo disposition but also permitting either party to change his mind up to the point of use or destruction.[117] This approach recognizes that individuals may experience a change of heart from the time the original contract is made, voiding the contract if such a change occurs. These courts differ, however, regarding which analytical framework to employ once the original contract is voided. New Jersey opts to conduct a balancing test in this situation, much like the Tennessee Supreme Court in *Davis*.[118] Iowa opts to simply maintain the status quo, permitting the embryos to be frozen indefinitely.[119]

Only one state, Louisiana, has dissented from the embryos-as-property perspective. Specifically, in 1986, the Louisiana legislature enacted a special statute addressing the legal status of embryos created by IVF. The statute declares that an "in vitro fertilized human ovum is a biological human being"[120] as well as a "juridical person."[121] As such, the embryo "is not the property" of the physician, the IVF clinic, or the gamete donors, and it "cannot be owned by the in vitro fertilization patients who owe it a high duty of care and prudent administration."[122] Once the IVF embryo is created, the physician or IVF clinic is "directly responsible for [its] safekeeping."[123] If the couple undertaking IVF formally renounces their parental rights over the embryos, they are deemed available for adoptive implantation by other married (yes, married) couples.[124]

The Louisiana approach is a radical departure from that taken by most states. It declares the IVF embryo to be a person entitled to respect, meaning it cannot be discarded by those who created it. Destruction of a "juridical person" would violate the statutory rights the embryo possesses and constitute a breach of the "high duty of care and prudent administration" it is owed. And while the Louisiana statute does not explicitly forbid the indefinite freezing of IVF embryos, one wonders whether a future lawsuit may allege that such indefinite limbo could be found to breach this high duty of care.[125] The only legal option for parents who do not wish to use their frozen embryos may be to formally renounce their parental rights and allow the embryos to be put up for adoptive implantation. In a case such as *Davis*, where the couple disagrees about what to do, the statute specifies that the "judicial standard for resolving such disputes is to be the best interest of the in vitro fertilized ovum."[126] Accordingly, unlike most jurisdictions, Louisiana courts appear to operate with a strong presumption against permitting the destruction of IVF embryos.

As the frozen embryo cases illustrate, virtually all jurisdictions (with the notable exception of Louisiana) consider embryos created by artificial reproductive technology to be the personal property of those who created the embryo, special respect platitudes notwithstanding. Couples who create the embryos are free to use or dispose of them as they see fit, incentivizing the use of written contracts to express their wishes in advance. In general, courts will uphold these contractual agreements. Classification of ART embryos as property is consonant with the Supreme Court's abortion jurisprudence permitting them to be aborted (discussed in the next chapter). It also pragmatically enables important scientific research to take place, such as human embryonic stem cell research.

2

Constitutional Life

> We need not resolve the difficult question of when life begins. When those trained in the respective disciplines of medicine, philosophy, and theology are unable to arrive at any consensus, the judiciary, at this point in the development of man's knowledge, is not in a position to speculate as to the answer.
>
> —U.S. Supreme Court, Roe v. Wade (1973)

The U.S. Constitution is the supreme law of the land. It refers throughout to "persons" and "people" who are entitled to basic rights. Neither the state nor federal governments, for example, may deprive "persons" of life, liberty, or property without due process of law.[1] Given the variety of constitutional rights that explicitly or implicitly attaches to persons, the question arises: who qualifies as a constitutionally cognizable person?

The stakes in the constitutional debate are high. Unlike the ordinary statutes and common law discussed in the previous chapter, the Constitution establishes a guaranteed minimum, a floor of protection, below which no ordinary law can go. Because the Constitution is supreme law, any constitutional ruling that declared the unborn (or some subset thereof) to be persons within the meaning of the Constitution would reverberate throughout the country. It would not simply be a matter of shifting decision-making responsibility to the states, which could then opt to permit or outlaw abortion as they see fit. Instead, any state law allowing abortion—and possibly some types of contraception—would be presumptively unconstitutional, as it would deprive such persons of their constitutional rights. It might even result in new laws limiting a pregnant woman's right to engage in certain behaviors—such as smoking, drinking, or sports—that might pose a risk of harm to the "person" she is carrying within. In short, if the unborn are constitutionally cognizable persons, they presumably would be entitled to protection against harm, in much the same way as you or I. While the pregnant woman would be entitled to her own legal rights, any actions she took that would harm the "person" she was carrying potentially could be punished.

Preventing Pregnancy: Contraception

We begin with contraceptives, since there is a more complex association between contraception and abortion than most people realize. The modern array of contraceptives is mind boggling, especially considering that most of them have only existed since the early 1960s. Some of the more old-fashioned contraceptives, such as diaphragms and condoms, prevent conception by placing a physical barrier between sperm and egg. Newer ones, such as birth control pills, patches, and implants, use hormones to suppress ovulation or thicken cervical mucous, thereby reducing the ability of sperm to reach the egg and preventing conception from taking place. It is also possible that, in some cases, hormonal birth control methods or intrauterine devices (IUDs) may create a hostile environment inside the womb, making it difficult for an already fertilized egg to implant.[2]

A lot of terminology involving birth control has been driven by the abortion debate, including the definition of abortion and pregnancy itself. What is an abortion? Legally speaking, an abortion is an "artificially induced termination of a pregnancy for the purpose of destroying an embryo or fetus."[3] In order for something to be classified as an abortion, then, it must: (1) be artificially induced; (2) result in the termination of a pregnancy; and (3) be for the purpose of destroying an embryo or fetus. Numbers one and three differentiate abortion from spontaneous miscarriage or medical procedures that may unintentionally result in the death of an embryo or fetus. Number two—termination of a pregnancy—is the more complex and politically charged element of the abortion definition.

If abortion is the intentional termination of a "pregnancy," it is critical to define pregnancy with some precision. A drug or device that prevents a pregnancy from occurring in the first place is merely a contraceptive. But a drug or device that causes the termination of a pregnancy is an abortifacient. It is the word "pregnancy," then, that draws the line between contraceptives and abortifacients.

So when does pregnancy begin? Does a woman become pregnant when the sperm and egg unite—that is, when conception occurs? Or does a woman become pregnant about a week later, when the fertilized egg implants in the uterine wall? Earlier versions of *Black's Law Dictionary* define pregnancy as a condition that results from the fertilization of an ovum, existing from the time of conception until the delivery of the child.[4] The most recent edition of *Black's,* by contrast, contains no definition of pregnancy at all. Current medical dictionaries define pregnancy as having a developing embryo or fetus within the body.[5] These definitions comport with the idea—learned by virtually every teenager—that once sperm meets egg, the woman is pregnant.

There has been a steady movement in recent years, however, to define pregnancy more narrowly. The newer definition of pregnancy is one that begins at implantation, not conception. The debate over abortion played a large role in this definitional revision. If the newer definition of pregnancy is used, a pill or device that destroys a fertilized egg before it successfully implants in the uterine wall can be called a contraceptive because there is no "pregnancy." Both the American and British Medical Associations have embraced this definition for purposes of their abortion policies. They define abortion as induced termination of an "established pregnancy," which is then defined as postimplantation.[6] The medical associations' addition of the word "established" to qualify the word "pregnancy" implicitly acknowledges that pregnancy itself occurs prior to implantation, but it is only termination of an "established" (postimplantation) pregnancy that triggers invocation of the abortion label.

While this may seem to be splitting hairs, it has turned out to be an important battleground in the abortion debate. Hormonal birth control pills, patches, implants, and even the so-called "morning-after" pill (Plan B) all contain the same basic hormones (estrogen, progestin, or a combination thereof) that act primarily by preventing conception from occurring, and in some cases, affecting the lining of the uterus (endometrium) in a way that inhibits the implantation of a fertilized egg.[7] All of them may potentially cause an already-fertilized egg to die, though how often this occurs is not clear.[8] For those who believe that pregnancy begins at conception, these contraceptive methods could be considered potential chemical abortifacients.

By contrast, mifepristone (RU-486) is a chemical abortifacient regardless of whether one defines pregnancy as beginning with conception or implantation. RU-486 is a steroid that blocks the production of progesterone, a hormone important in pregnancy because it helps prepare the uterine wall to nourish the growing embryo. It tricks the body into thinking it is no longer pregnant, triggering menstruation and subsequent loss of an embryo that has already implanted itself in the uterine wall. Because RU-486 works to rid the body of an already-implanted embryo, it is admitted to be an abortifacient, even by pro-choice groups.[9]

With these definitions in mind, we can proceed to discuss how the Constitution protects an individual's right to use contraception. State laws prohibiting contraception—most notably in Massachusetts and Connecticut—had a rich history of litigation. The first lawsuit to reach a state supreme court was Commonwealth v. Gardner in 1938. In *Gardner*, the Supreme Judicial Court of Massachusetts considered a challenge to the constitutionality of a Massachusetts law that declared, "Whoever sells, lends, gives away, exhibits, or offers to sell, lend or give away . . . any drug, medicine, instrument or article whatever for the prevention of conception" commits a felony. The defendants in *Gardner* were a physician, a nurse, and two social workers who staffed the North Shore Mothers' Health Office, a nonprofit association that dispensed contraceptives to married women. They were convicted of violating the law and sentenced to pay a fine. They appealed their convictions, arguing that the statute allowed licensed physicians to prescribe contraceptives when, according to generally accepted medical practice, contraception was necessary to preserve the life or health of the mother. Alternatively, they argued that the statute violated their state and federal constitutional rights.[10]

The Supreme Judicial Court of Massachusetts denied all of these claims. With regard to the claimed exception for physician prescriptions, the court responded that under the plain language of the statute, no such exception existed. The statute's prohibition on sale or provision of contraception was "sweeping, absolute, and devoid of ambiguity."[11] Briefly addressing the constitutional claim, the court asserted that the law was designed to address "moral and social wrongs" and, as such, was a valid exercise of the state's police power, analogous to laws regulating the sale of intoxicating liquors.[12]

The U.S. Supreme Court denied review, "for the want of a substantial federal question," implying that there was no viable constitutional problem with the statute.[13] The *Gardner* decision effectively shut down all contraceptive clinics in Massachusetts and sent out a wave of uncertainty in states with similar laws.

In neighboring Connecticut, a similar legal battle had just begun. In 1939, one year after the decision in *Gardner*, two physicians and a nurse asked a trial judge to declare that Connecticut's anticontraceptive statute did not apply to physicians who prescribed contraceptives for their patients—the same argument that had failed in *Gardner*. The trial court's decision, in State v. Nelson, noted that there was a difference between the Massachusetts anticontraceptive statute and the Connecticut one: the former prohibited the sale or provision of contraceptives, whereas the latter prohibited their *use*.[14] Was it possible, therefore, that a physician could lawfully prescribe contraceptives that could not be lawfully used by his patients? Or would a physician who wrote such a prescription be guilty of aiding a violation of the antiuse law? The trial court in *Nelson* determined that, like the Massachusetts statute in *Gardner*, the plain language of the statute was sweeping, offering "no defense to a doctor facing prosecution for a violation of it."[15] Without such an exception, the trial judge felt compelled to address the constitutionality of the statute, concluding that "without these proper exceptions the statute is defective on . . . constitutional grounds."[16] The trial court did not elaborate on the constitutional basis for his conclusion.

The *Nelson* case was appealed to the Connecticut Supreme Court, which agreed that the statute contained no exception for contraceptives dispensed under a physician's prescription.[17] Unlike the trial judge, however, the Connecticut Supreme Court saw no constitutional problem with the statute, concluding that it was reasonable for the legislature to believe that contraceptive use was "inimical to the public welfare" and "injurious to public morals"[18] by encouraging nonprocreative sex and sexual activity outside marriage. There was no constitutional right, in the eyes of the Connecticut Supreme Court in 1940, to avoid procreation.

The next Connecticut case was filed shortly after *Nelson* by Dr. Wilder Tileston, a physician who was concerned that the health of three of his married patients was such that childbearing would endanger their lives. He filed a lawsuit seeking a declaration that the law was unconstitutional as applied to these particular patients—specifically, that prohibiting these married women from using contraceptives deprived them of their lives without due process of law. Tileston's case made it all the way to the U.S. Supreme Court, which decided, in a brief per curiam opinion, that Tileston lacked standing to bring suit on behalf of his patients. Because Tileston had not alleged that the statute violated any of his own personal rights, his lawsuit was dismissed, and the constitutional claims were not addressed.[19]

It was almost twenty years later, in 1961, that the Supreme Court faced another constitutional challenge to the Connecticut anticontraception law. In this case, a doctor, Lee Buxton, and three of his married patients—using the fictitious names Doe, Hoe, and Poe—sought a declaration that the statute was a violation of their due process rights under the Fourteenth Amendment. Specifically, the patients all claimed that having children would cause significant harm to either their lives or mental health, so denying them access to contraceptives deprived them of their substantive rights to life and liberty. Plaintiff Jane Doe alleged that she had a condition that could cause death if she became pregnant. Plaintiffs Paul and Pauline Poe claimed that, having suffered three miscarriages, another pregnancy would be psychologically disturbing. Plaintiffs Harold and Hanna Hoe had achieved pregnancy four times, but all four ended in miscarriage due to an Rh blood mismatching between the couple. They claimed that the prospects of producing a normal healthy child were highly unlikely. Dr. Buxton also claimed a separate substantive liberty interest to practice his medical profession without unreasonable state restraint. Once again, the Connecticut Supreme Court refused to create an exception from the operation of the statute and upheld the law as a valid measure to protect public morals.[20]

Dr. Buxton and his patients petitioned the U.S. Supreme Court for review of their constitutional claims. The Court's decision, Poe v. Ullman, was fractured, with five Justices voting to uphold the Connecticut Supreme Court and four Justices dissenting.[21] The five Justices who voted to uphold did so on technical, justiciability grounds, finding that there was no active controversy between the parties. They thought that, although the statute was still on the books, the "fact that Connecticut has not chosen to press the enforcement of this statute deprives these controversies of the immediacy which is an indispensable condition of constitutional adjudication. This Court cannot be umpire to debates concerning harmless, empty shadows."[22] Justice Brennan joined this plurality decision to provide the critical fifth vote upholding the Connecticut Supreme Court, asserting, "I am not convinced, on this skimpy record, that these appellants as individuals are truly caught in an inescapable dilemma. The true controversy in this case is over the opening of birth-control clinics on a large-scale: it is that which the state has prevented in the past, not the use of contraceptives by isolated and individual married couples. It will be enough to decide the constitutional questions urged upon us when if ever, the real controversy flares up again."[23]

Four dissenters in *Poe* were outraged at the technical side stepping of the constitutional issues raised by the case. Justice Douglas, writing for the dissenters, noted that the nonenforcement rationale of the majority disregarded the prosecution and conviction of the doctors and nurse in the *Nelson* case. Douglas asked, "What are these people—doctor and patients—to do? Flout the law and go to prison? Violate the law surreptitiously and hope they will not get caught? By today's decision we leave them no other alternative. . . . It is not the choice worthy of a civilized society. A sick wife, a concerned husband, a conscientious doctor seek a dignified, discrete, orderly answer to the critical problem confronting them. We should not turn them away and make them flout the law and get arrested to have their constitutional rights determined."[24]

Regarding the merits of the constitutional claims raised in *Poe*, the dissenters had slightly different visions. Justice Douglas believed that married persons' right to use contraceptives (and obtain the advice of doctors in doing so) emanated from a "right to privacy," implied in various constitutional provisions: "[W]hen the State makes 'use' a crime and applies the criminal sanction to man and wife, the State has entered the innermost sanctum of the home. If it can make this law, it can enforce it. And proof of its violation involves an inquiry into the relations between man and wife. That is an invasion of the privacy that is implicit in a free society."[25]

Justice Harlan wrote a separate dissent to state that the constitutional violation was not one of privacy but of substantive liberty guaranteed by the Fourteenth Amendment's Due Process Clause. He asserted, "This 'liberty' is not a series of isolated points pricked out in terms of the taking of property; the freedom of speech, press, and religion; the right to keep and bear arms; the freedom from unreasonable searches and seizures; and so on. It is a rational continuum which, broadly speaking, includes a freedom from all substantial arbitrary impositions and purposeless restraints."[26] Since the anticontraception law applied to married couples engaging in intimate relations within their own homes, Harlan concluded that it violated the fundamental right to liberty.[27]

The dissenters' views in *Poe* ultimately became critical for understanding the conceptual foundation underlying the Supreme Court's landmark contraceptive and abortion decisions. The contraception case, Griswold v. Connecticut, was penned by Justice Douglas and not surprisingly based on the same "right to privacy" Douglas urged in *Poe*. But by the time the Supreme Court recognized the right to abortion in Roe v. Wade, it was Justice Harlan's substantive liberty approach—not Justice Douglas's penumbral right to privacy—that became the conceptual basis for a constitutional right to abortion.

Before turning to abortion, we must finish the story of the constitutional right to contraception. After the *Poe* Court had dismissed the latest challenge to Connecticut's anticontraception law in 1961, supporters of contraception were reenergized the following year, when newly elected President John F. Kennedy appointed two Justices to the Supreme Court (his only two appointments). Byron White replaced Charles Evans Whittaker, who had voted with the *Poe* plurality that dismissed the case on a technicality, avoiding the constitutional issues. Arthur Goldberg replaced Felix Frankfurter, who penned the plurality in *Poe*. The replacement of these two Justices presented a potential new opportunity for consideration of the constitutional claims.

The case that ultimately made history was Griswold v. Connecticut, decided by the Supreme Court in 1965. In *Griswold,* the executive director of the Planned Parenthood League of Connecticut, Estelle Griswold, and Dr. Lee Buxton (the same doctor who was a plaintiff in the earlier *Poe* case) had opened a birth control clinic in New Haven, openly flaunting the law and hoping to trigger prosecution to force consideration of the constitutional issues. It worked. After only ten days in business, Griswold and Buxton were arrested. They were convicted as accessories for providing contraceptives and contraceptive advice to married persons and ordered to pay a fine of one hundred dollars each. Their convictions were affirmed by the Connecticut Supreme Court.[28]

The U.S. Supreme Court's majority opinion was penned by Justice Douglas, who took the same approach in his *Poe* dissent, finding a right to privacy implicit in what he called the "penumbras" and "emanations" of various provisions of the Bill of Rights, including the First, Third, Fourth, Fifth, and Ninth Amendments.[29] Applying this right to the Connecticut law, Douglas's majority concluded, "Would we allow the police to search the sacred precincts of marital bedrooms for telltale signs of the use of contraceptives? The very idea is repulsive to the notions of privacy surrounding the marital relationship."[30]

Justice Harlan concurred in the result, but he did not join Justice Douglas's opinion, writing separately to emphasize, as he did in *Poe,* that he thought the appropriate constitutional source for a right to use contraceptives was found in the substantive liberty of the Due Process Clause rather than a penumbral "right to privacy."[31] One of the new Kennedy appointees, Justice Byron White, also concurred separately to express the same belief that substantive due process, not penumbral privacy, should be the basis for the decision. Harlan's and White's reluctance to jump on the penumbral privacy bandwagon was likely based on its lack of a clear jurisprudential pedigree. No other decisions of the Court had acknowledged that such a right existed, and there was fear that the Court would be accused of "making things up" to reach the results it wanted. There was greater intellectual safety in the substantive liberty approach because it had a richer, more established history, harkening back to earlier twentieth-century decisions of the Court that had recognized liberties to marry and direct the upbringing of one's own children.[32]

Despite Harlan's and White's objections, the freedom to use contraceptives was based on a new, potentially broad "right to privacy." The big question after *Griswold* thus became: How far does this right to privacy extend? What are its definitional parameters? With regard to the specific right to use contraceptives, was it enjoyed only by married persons? The defendants in *Griswold,* after all, were married, and the principal concern expressed by the majority was the specter of "bedroom police" searching the marital bedchamber for signs of contraceptives. So what did this rationale imply for unmarried persons? Did they, too, have a constitutional right to use contraceptives in the privacy of their own bedrooms? The answer came seven years later, in the 1972 decision in Eisenstadt v. Baird.

In *Eisenstadt,* the defendant was convicted of violating a Massachusetts law that made it a felony to "give away . . . any drug, medicine, instrument or article whatever for the prevention of contraception," except by a physician or pharmacist who prescribed or furnished them to married persons.[33] The

Massachusetts law was revised in an attempt to conform to *Griswold,* allowing married persons, but not single persons, access to contraceptives. Eisenstadt was arrested for violating the law after he gave away a package of vaginal spermicidal foam to a single woman following his lecture on contraceptives at Boston University.[34]

A deeply divided Supreme Court, consisting of only seven members (Justices Rehnquist and Powell had not yet been sworn in), decided, in a six-to-one vote, that the Massachusetts law was unconstitutional. Precisely why it was unconstitutional was a matter of some difference of opinion. Justice William Brennan wrote the majority opinion, garnering the support of four of the seven voting Justices. The majority concluded that the law violated the Equal Protection Clause because it irrationally discriminated against single persons.[35]

Massachusetts attempted to justify the distinction between married and unmarried by asserting that the law was intended to discourage premarital sex, thereby protecting purity and encouraging self-restraint.[36] The *Eisenstadt* majority found this justification irrational, proclaiming, "It would be plainly unreasonable to assume that Massachusetts has prescribed pregnancy and the birth of an unwanted child as punishment for fornication, which is a misdemeanor under [Massachusetts law]."[37] It further concluded that there was no rational relationship between this objective—preventing premarital sex—and the statute, because the statute only banned contraceptives used "for the prevention of contraception." Contraceptives used for other purposes, such as preventing the spread of sexually transmitted disease, were sold legally and widely available throughout the state. Condoms, for example, were sold in pharmacies to married or unmarried persons. And married persons, who were able to obtain all contraceptives post-*Griswold,* could share those contraceptives with their unmarried paramours. The *Eisenstadt* majority concluded that "the Massachusetts statute is thus so riddled with exceptions that deterrence of premarital sex cannot reasonably be regarded as its aim."[38]

After concluding that the law violated equal protection, the *Eisenstadt* Court, in dicta, articulated a broad conception of the right recognized by *Griswold:* "It is true that, in *Griswold,* the right of privacy in question inhered in the marital relationship. Yet the marital couple is not an independent entity, with a mind and heart of its own, but an association of two individuals, each with a separate intellectual and emotional makeup. If the right of privacy means anything, it is the right of the individual, married or single, to be free from unwarranted governmental intrusion into matters so fundamentally affecting a person as the decision whether to bear or beget a child." The implications of this statement were enormous, particularly for the right to abortion.

Taken together, *Griswold* and *Eisenstadt* provide a constitutional right for all adults to access and use contraceptives. The right was extended to minors in 1977, in the case of Carey v. Population Services International.[39] *Carey* involved a New York law that criminalized the sale or distribution of contraceptives to anyone under the age of sixteen. A majority of the Court concluded, in a plurality opinion plus two separate concurrences, that the right to privacy extends to minors as well as adults. This was essentially a foregone conclusion, as the Supreme Court had ruled in 1976 that a state law requiring parental consent prior to a minor's abortion violated the minor's right to privacy.[40] The *Carey* plurality concluded that "[s]ince the State may not impose a blanket prohibition, or even a blanket requirement of parental consent on the choice of a minor to terminate her pregnancy, the constitutionality of a blanket prohibition on the distribution of contraceptives to minors is *a fortiori* foreclosed."[41] Since minors had a right to abortion, the *Carey* plurality thought it clear that the "lesser" right of contraceptive use necessarily followed.

The *Carey* decision brought contraceptive rights full circle, extending the right to anyone, whether married or unmarried, adult or minor. And as the plurality's rationale in *Carey* shows, there is a continuing close relationship between the right to use contraceptives and the right to terminate pregnancy.

Terminating Pregnancy: Abortion

The contraceptive cases did not explicitly recognize a right to abortion. They recognized a right to avoid pregnancy, not to terminate an existing one. But the contraceptive cases did imply, at least in dicta, that the right to privacy upon which they were based was broad enough to encompass an individual right to decide and control whether to bear or beget children. Moreover, since some contraceptives can act to prevent implantation of an already-fertilized egg, the right to use them arguably sanctioned the right to terminate a pregnancy, at least if pregnancy were defined as existing from the moment of conception.

The landmark case is Roe v. Wade, decided in 1973.[42] The case was filed by Jane Roe, the fictitious name of an unmarried pregnant woman who sought a declaration that the Texas statute prohibiting all abortions (other than to save the life of the mother) violated her right to privacy, as pronounced in *Griswold*. Roe's case was consolidated with that of a childless couple who wished to avoid pregnancy for medical reasons (though not life-threatening) and a practicing physician who wanted to provide abortions to his patients.[43] The Supreme Court, in a seven-to-two decision, ruled that "[t]his right of privacy, whether it be founded in the Fourteenth Amendment's concept of personal liberty and restrictions on state action, *as we feel it is,* or, as the District Court determined, in the Ninth Amendment's reservation of rights to the people, is broad enough to encompass a woman's decision whether or not to terminate her pregnancy."[44] The Court agreed that there was a right to privacy, but clarified that, unlike the independent, penumbral right on which the majority opinion in *Griswold* was based, the right was implicit in the word "liberty" in the Due Process Clause—the analytical approach advocated by the concurrences of Justices Harlan and White in *Griswold*.

The majority in *Roe* believed the right to abortion was a "fundamental" right, which means that courts must apply a standard called "strict scrutiny" to any law interfering with the right. Lawyers are routinely taught that this level of scrutiny is "strict in theory, but fatal in fact," because it begins with a presumption that the law is unconstitutional. To overcome this presumption, the government must convince the court that the law serves a "compelling" governmental interest and is "narrowly tailored" to further that interest.[45]

With the legal test decided upon, the case turned on the interest articulated by Texas to justify the ban on abortion. Texas argued that the law was designed to "recognize and protect prenatal life from and after conception."[46] The state, in other words, argued that: (1) life began at conception; (2) protecting life was a compelling governmental interest; and (3) the ban on abortion was necessary to protect this interest. Texas also asserted that the word "person" in the Constitution attached to living human beings. If human life begins at conception, therefore, the "persons" whose lives were protected by the Due Process Clause included the unborn, and any state law *allowing* abortion would be unconstitutional.[47]

The Supreme Court in *Roe* thus squarely faced the issue of when personhood begins, for it is one's status as a "person" that triggers constitutional rights, including the substantive right to life protected by the Due Process Clause. The Court acknowledged that the Constitution does not define "person," but it listed the various provisions in which the word appears, concluding that "in nearly all these instances, the use of the word is such that it has application only postnatally. None indicates, with any assurance, that it has any possible pre-natal application."[48] The Court also thought it important that, at the time the Constitution and Bill of Rights were ratified in the late eighteenth century, abortion was generally permissible, at least prior to the point of quickening (first discernible movement in the womb).[49] Historical legal allowance of early abortion at the time of ratification, combined with the fact that most constitutional references to "person" only make sense if the word is understood postnatally, persuaded the Supreme Court "that the word 'person' as used in the Fourteenth Amendment and elsewhere in the Constitution, does not include the unborn."[50]

Although the Court did not think the unborn could be constitutionally cognizable persons, it still had to consider whether the Texas statute could survive strict scrutiny by furthering a "compelling" governmental interest. Texas, you may recall, stated that the interest served by the abortion ban was the protection of prenatal life. The Supreme Court carefully avoided deciding whether "life" begins before birth, declaring, "We need not resolve the difficult question of when life begins. When those trained in the respective disciplines of medicine, philosophy, and theology are unable to arrive at any consensus, the judiciary, at this point in the development of man's knowledge, is not in a position to speculate as to the answer."[51]

The Court acknowledged, however, that the state has an interest in protecting "the potentiality of life" of the unborn, as well as in protecting the health of pregnant women. Both of these interests "grows in substantiality as the woman approaches term and at a point during pregnancy, each becomes 'compelling.'"[52] If the state's objective is to protect the health of the mother, the Court concluded that the "compelling" point is "at approximately the end of the first trimester" because, until that time, "mortality in abortion may be less than mortality in normal childbirth."[53] In other words, because first trimester abortion is as safe as being pregnant, prohibiting abortion during the first trimester logically cannot be necessary to protect the life or health of the mother. Reasonable regulations after the first trimester are permissible, so long as they are designed to ensure that the procedure is safe (for example, licensure of facilities and personnel). During the first trimester, however, *Roe* did not appear to permit any regulations of abortion at all.

What about the state's interest in protecting the potential life of the unborn? For this interest, the *Roe* majority drew the line at "viability"—the point at which the fetus "presumably has the capability of meaningful life outside the mother's womb."[54] The Court noted that because post-viability fetuses, by definition, are likely to survive independently of the mother, the state's interest in protecting their life is sufficiently compelling that it "may go so far as to proscribe abortion during that period, except when it is necessary to preserve the life or health of the mother."[55] After the point of viability (approximately six months' gestation at the time *Roe* was decided), therefore, the state may prohibit all abortions. But even in the post-viability phase, *Roe* recognized that the already-existing interests of the mother could trump those of her viable fetus, since she still had a right to abort when necessary to save her life or health.

The basic analytical framework of *Roe* remained intact until 1992, when the Supreme Court decided Planned Parenthood of Southeastern Pennsylvania v. Casey.[56] A majority of the Court in *Casey* explicitly reaffirmed the "essential holding" of *Roe,* including a right, grounded in the liberty interest of the Due Process Clause, to abort a pregnancy prior to the point of viability.[57] But the Court became deeply divided after that.

A plurality of the Court, led by Justice O'Connor, was willing to explicitly reject the trimester framework of *Roe,* focusing solely on viability.[58] The O'Connor plurality was also willing to uphold state regulation of pre-viability abortions—something *Roe* did not seem willing to do—so long as such regulations did not amount to an "undue burden" on the woman's right to choose.[59] The plurality attempted to clarify "undue burden" by declaring it "shorthand for the conclusion that a state regulation has the purpose or effect of placing a substantial obstacle in the path of a woman seeking an abortion of a nonviable fetus."[60]

The plurality's willingness to assess pre-viability abortion regulations using an "undue burden" standard signaled a retreat from the strict scrutiny regime of Roe v. Wade. It shifted away from traditional fundamental rights analysis and increased states' ability to regulate early abortions by imposing waiting periods, mandating the provision of information about abortion alternatives, and enacting other laws that do not pose a "substantial obstacle" to obtaining an abortion. The plurality's analytical framework implied that although there was still a constitutional right to pre-viability abortion, the right was no longer fundamental.

Justice Blackmun, the author of the majority opinion in *Roe*, understood the implications of the O'Connor plurality's opinion, arguing vehemently that the right to terminate pregnancy prior to viability was a "fundamental" right that required the application of strict scrutiny.[61] The four dissenters in *Casey* believed that "Roe was wrongly decided, and that it can and should be overruled."[62]

The net result of *Casey* was a hodgepodge of views about the nature of the right to abortion, though a majority still agreed that the right existed until viability. There was ardent disagreement about the status of this right— whether it was a "fundamental" right or not—and what judicial test should be applied. After *Casey*, however, the lower courts uniformly applied the "undue burden" standard, not strict scrutiny, to laws regulating pre-viability abortions. Effectively, then, *Casey* ushered in a subtle but significant shift in constitutional analysis of abortion laws.

Any uncertainty regarding the proper interpretation of *Casey* was put to rest in 2007, when the Supreme Court decided Gonzales v. Carhart.[63] In *Carhart*, four physicians challenged the constitutionality of the federal Partial Birth Abortion Act of 2003 (PBAA), which, as its name suggested, prohibited a type of abortion known as partial-birth abortion or intact dilation and evacuation (D&E). The Act made an exception when partial-birth abortion was "necessary to save the life of the mother, whose life was endangered by a physical disorder, physical illness, or physical injury."[64] This was not an exception for the health of the mother (such as mental health)—but only for her life.

Congress enacted the PBAA due to concern that intact D&E skirted the line between abortion and infanticide, since it was performed on second- and third-trimester fetuses that had been partially delivered outside the mother's body.[65] The Supreme Court in *Carhart* stated that the percentage of abortions performed using intact D&E was unknown, but it noted that between 85 and 90 percent of all abortions in the United States took place in the first trimester, using either RU-486 or vacuum aspiration.[66] Of the 10 to 15 percent of abortions that took place after the first trimester, doctors had various options available other than intact D&E, including ordinary D&E, hysterectomy (removal of the uterus), hysterotomy (C-section), and medical induction of labor.[67]

Ordinary D&E differs from intact D&E because, as the name suggests, intact D&E involves partial delivery of an intact fetus, with dismemberment or decapitation occurring once the fetus has been partially delivered beyond the cervix. Ordinary D&E, by contrast, involves dismemberment or decapitation of the fetus before any part of the fetus is delivered outside the cervix.[68] The "partial-birth abortion" prohibited by the PBAA was defined as when a physician "deliberately and intentionally vaginally delivers a living fetus until, in the case of a head-first presentation, the entire fetal head is outside the body of the mother, or, in the case of a breech presentation, any part of the fetal trunk past the navel is outside the body of the mother, for the purpose of performing an overt act that the person knows will kill the partially delivered living fetus."[69]

The federal trial and intermediate appellate courts in *Carhart* had ruled the PBAA unconstitutional because it failed to make an exception for the health of the mother and posed an undue burden on a woman's ability to choose abortion.[70] There was no doubt that Congress had the ability to ban post-viability abortions—that had been obvious since *Roe*. But since intact D&E was used during the second trimester—a large portion of which is before fetal viability—it was debatable whether the government's interests in protecting the pre-viable fetus's life were sufficiently weighty to ban a particular type of abortion procedure. To put it in *Casey* terminology, the question was whether prohibiting partial-birth abortion was an "undue burden" on a woman's right to pre-viability abortion.

The *Carhart* Court began its analysis by clarifying *Casey*. First, it reaffirmed that prior to viability, a state may not prohibit a woman from terminating her pregnancy. Second, it stated that prior to viability, a state may enact laws that "create a structural mechanism by which the State, or the parent or guardian of a minor, may express profound respect for the life of the unborn" so long as they do not impose an undue burden on the woman's right to choose.[71] Notice the subtle shift in language, from *Roe's* and *Casey's* references to the "potential" life of the unborn, to *Carhart's* reference to the "life" of the unborn. The implication is that the unborn are, in fact, living, not merely potentially so, though they are still not considered constitutionally cognizable "persons." While this may seem to be incongruous, there is a defensible rationale here, based on the difference between what it means to be "alive" in the biological sense, versus what it means to be a "person" under the Constitution. The difference, as *Roe* declared long ago, is that the word "person" in the Constitution does not refer to the unborn, though ordinary laws may consider the unborn to be alive and hence eligible for some legal protection.

The *Carhart* Court concluded that *Casey*'s undue burden standard balanced the state's interests, including protecting prenatal life, against the degree of burden that the law imposed on the woman's right to choose. Applying this balancing test to the PBAA, the *Carhart* majority thought the Act was based on the government's desire to "express profound respect for the life within the woman."[72] This government interest was weighed against the burden of prohibiting intact D&E, and the Court concluded that burden was relatively low, as the PBAA left open ample alternative abortion methods with "extremely low rates of medical complications," such as ordinary D&E.[73] It was the first abortion decision that sanctioned prohibition of a particular type of pre-viability abortion. In so doing, *Carhart* confirmed that the right to pre-viability abortion can no longer be characterized (as it was in *Roe*) as a fundamental right subject to strict scrutiny. Instead, the right still exists, subject to state regulations that do not rise to the level of an undue burden. In determining whether a particular state law amounts to an undue burden, *Carhart* tells us that the government's interest in protecting the unborn may sometimes trump a woman's right to choose a particular method of abortion.

Addressing the plaintiffs' other contention—that the PBAA was unconstitutional because it failed to provide an exception for the health of the mother (though it did contain an exception for her life)—the *Carhart* Court concluded that the medical testimony was conflicting as to whether it was ever medically necessary to perform partial-birth abortion to protect the health of the mother. The Court concluded that, in the face of such conflicting testimony, the legislature is free to choose among competing views, particularly since other safe alternative abortion procedures were still available.[74] It was the first time in the Supreme Court's abortion jurisprudence that it had allowed an abortion law to stand without an exception for the health of the mother—a result that the four dissenters found "alarming."[75]

The government's interest in protecting the unborn—including previable fetuses—has grown in jurisprudential significance from *Roe* to *Carhart*. In somewhat simplistic terms, the *Carhart* decision moves abortion jurisprudence in the direction of ordinary tort, property, and criminal laws that have increasingly valued prenatal life and punished acts that pretermit it. Constitutional law has taken a subtle but noticeable step toward enhancing government power to protect the life of the unborn and away from a right to choose termination without government interference. How far this trend will go remains to be seen, though it seems likely that government regulation of abortion will increase while the basic constitutional right to pre-viability abortions remains intact.

Continuing recognition of a right to terminate before viability also helps avoid creating conflicts with the Court's contraceptive jurisprudence. If the Supreme Court reversed course completely, no longer recognizing a right to abortion, it would create potential incongruity with *Griswold* and its progeny. Could individuals have a right to use contraception but not a right to terminate early-stage pregnancies? Perhaps not, since some contraceptives—including the most popular hormonal ones—may terminate an existing pregnancy by preventing implantation. If there is no constitutional right to abortion, in other words, it could imply that there is no right to use contraceptives that may potentially act as abortifacients. The Court could solve this dilemma by revising its contraception jurisprudence to define "pregnancy" as existing only after implantation, but until it did so, the constitutional right to use of some popular contraceptives could be thrown into doubt. Because the Supreme Court has continued to recognize a right to pre-viability abortions, however, there has been no pressure to address the controversial question about when pregnancy begins.

Abortion and the "Brain Life" Theory

Now that we have examined the most important Supreme Court decisions on abortion, it is intriguing to preview how those decisions comport with the legal definition of death, the topic explored in the remainder of the book. Death, as the next two chapters will examine, is statutorily defined as either an irreversible loss of cardiopulmonary function (that is, of the heart and lungs) or an irreversible loss of brain function. As we pondered in the introduction, if this is the definition of death, should our definition of life be its opposite? Should life and death, in other words, be antithetical concepts, so that life is defined as "not death"? If you say yes—that life and death are antonyms—

then this would mean that life exists whenever either (1) cardiopulmonary function or (2) brain function, exists. This conception of life, moreover, could (though would not necessarily) significantly change abortion and contraception jurisprudence.

In the early 1980s, a pediatrician named John Goldenring wrote a letter to the *New England Journal of Medicine* in which he advocated establishing symmetry between the definitions of death and life. More specifically, Goldenring proposed symmetry with the relatively new phenomenon known as brain death, calling his theory "brain life."[76] He expounded further on his theory in an article published in 1985, in which he asserted a fetus becomes a "human being" "at the point at which its brain begins to function."[77]

Goldenring is careful to state that he uses the term "human being" rather than "person" because he is trying to "make scientifically based definitions which are relatively 'value-free' and objective."[78] But he also acknowledges that a "person" is a "human being accorded full rights, protection and respect" and that his brain life theory "has implications for the definition of a 'person.'"[79] In drawing these distinctions, Goldenring is acknowledging the distinction drawn by the Supreme Court in its abortion jurisprudence— namely, that being "alive" is not necessarily the same thing as being a "person" entitled to the full panoply of legal rights. Even if we accepted Goldenring's definition of brain life, therefore, it would not necessarily mean that the word "person" in the Constitution would need to be redefined to include unborn fetuses that have brain life.

Goldenring marks the beginning of brain life (and hence status as a human being and possibly also as a person) at eight weeks' gestation. He compares the eight-week-old fetus to an eighty-year-old woman on a respirator. He states that the eighty-year-old woman "may be terminally ill, may not be able to survive without the respirator. But if that human being has a functioning brain, there is no doubt on the physician's part that he is dealing with a living patient."[80] He then asks us to consider the eight-week-old fetus, asserting, "It is inside the most advanced intensive care unit ever designed—the uterus. And it is being maintained by the most complex extracorporeal respirator known—the placenta." And at eight weeks, "a wealth of evidence indicates that the brain has begun functioning electrically." He concludes that "if a fetus is analysed [sic] in the same way as a born human, then at eight-weeks gestation with a functioning brain present, it is a living human being in the biological sense of that term."[81] Goldenring's brain life theory has garnered a good number of followers, though they differ wildly as to the point in time at which they pinpoint the beginning of brain life.[82]

Goldenring claims that his brain life theory is "unmatched in its logic and symmetry."[83] But upon closer inspection, the symmetry Goldenring understandably seeks to achieve is absent. He picks eight weeks because he says that it is at that point at which there is "no doubt" that *higher* brain function exists. The subcortical (brain stem) portions of the brain, he admits, are formed much earlier, at about four to five weeks' gestation.[84] Eight weeks is chosen, therefore, because it represents the point at which Goldenring believes the whole brain is capable of rudimentary function.

The problem is that brain life theory seeks to define life by reference to whole brain function, yet the definition of brain death acknowledges that partial brain function constitutes life. Think about it: a person is brain dead only if their entire brain stops functioning. So a person who has a functioning brain stem, yet no higher brain function, is not legally dead; she is in a vegetative state. If we wanted to try to visualize the difference between brain life and brain death, it would look something like this:

Functioning whole brain (cortical and subcortical) = brain life
Functioning part of the brain (cortical or subcortical) = not brain dead

As you can see, under the legal definition of brain death, having a part of your brain still functioning will mean that you are not dead. If we wanted to be truly symmetrical, therefore, we would have to define brain life as partial functioning of the brain, not the whole of it. Goldenring's brain life theory, by defining brain life as existing at eight weeks, when the *whole* brain is capable of rudimentary function, thus lacks symmetry.

This is not to say that achieving symmetry between the legal definition of brain death and a legal definition of life is impossible. We could also achieve symmetry by positing that since brain death is the loss of whole brain function, function of any part of the brain equals brain life. In Goldenring's view, for example, discernible brain stem function occurs at approximately four to five weeks. Once this partial brain function exists, symmetry would suggest that a fetus of four to five weeks' gestation is as alive as the eighty-year-old woman in a vegetative state, since both of them would have partial brain (brain stem) function. Goldenring's desired symmetry is potentially possible, but at a much earlier point in time than he realizes—four to five rather than eight weeks' gestation.

We could also achieve symmetry if the law defined brain death as death of the higher brain (which it currently does not), as it would mean that higher brain function is all that matters. As such, we could then define brain life as existing from the moment of ascertainable higher brain function. In this respect, the equation would look like this:

Loss of higher brain function = brain death
Presence of higher brain function = brain life

Here, you can see that it is the presence (or absence) of higher brain function that defines life or death, achieving the desired symmetry.

On a more theoretical level, however, despite the innate appeal of harmonizing the definitions of life and death, such harmonization may not produce the logical result desired. Goldenring asserts that one of the benefits of brain life is that it is "based on relatively objective rather than heavily evaluative criteria" for defining life such as conception or viability. But if we are seeking an objective indicator for the existence of life, we need to look elsewhere.

The votaries of brain life offer different moments in fetal development when they claim the brain begins functioning. Goldenring, for example, chooses eight weeks because it is at eight weeks that some intermittent discernible brain waves can be detected using electroencephalography (EEG). But EEG waves do not actually tell us that the brain is functioning, merely that some portion is emitting some electrical activity. And scientists can guesstimate when certain neural substrates come into existence, but there is really no objective way to test whether those portions of the brain are, in fact, working in the classic sense. How could a doctor tell, for example, whether a fetus's brain stem is functioning? In the context of brain death, brain stem function cannot be ascertained by EEG. The doctor must conduct bedside tests that elicit brain stem reflexes. The presence of these reflexes is the most reliable way to determine if the brain stem is functioning. But a doctor cannot test for these brain stem reflexes in the womb—he cannot shake the fetus's head vigorously side to side, shine a light in its eye, rub cotton across its eye, or pour cold water in its ear. Because the fetus is *in utero*, there simply is no way reliably to test its brain stem function.

As Chapter 4, "Brain Death" will discuss, the same problem plagues the diagnosis of brain death. One of the shortcomings of the concept of brain death is that there is no objective test for it. There are some objective tests for cerebral blood flow and EEGs that can aid the doctor in his diagnosis, but they are far from definitive. The diagnosis of brain death is therefore dependent on clinical (bedside) tests that are very difficult to interpret.

Equally troubling for brain life is that it fails to offer the kind of individualized assessment for the existence of life that brain death offers for the existence of death. The definition of brain death—irreversible loss of function of the entire brain—is applied on an individual, case-by-case basis. To declare brain death, the doctor must conduct a series of bedside tests over a period of time. If we wanted to be symmetrical in defining life and death, brain life would have to involve the same individualized assessment. It would require case-by-case bedside testing to determine whether the fetal brain is functioning. Brain life theory, however, does not seek to do this. Instead, it proposes a definition of life that irrebuttably presumes that all fetal brains function at X days' or weeks' gestation. Given the difficulty of determining whether a portion of the fetus's brain is functioning (and the wide variation in medical opinion as to what day or week such function begins), brain life is pragmatically unworkable.

A final problem with brain life theory is that it ignores cardiopulmonary death. Death, after all, may be declared either by traditional cardiopulmonary criteria or brain death criteria—irreversible loss of either function constitutes death. The symmetry supposedly created by brain life, therefore, could create symmetry only with brain death, not cardiopulmonary death. To achieve true symmetry, life would need to be defined as the presence of either cardiopulmonary function or partial brain function in the fetus. The embryonic heart begins to form at only three weeks after conception, though its distinctive four chambers do not exist until sometime between the fifth and eighth week postconception.[85] Where on this broad spectrum of development a "heart life" advocate would pinpoint the beginning of cardiopulmonary life is something I must leave to the medical profession.

After Conception or Pregnancy: Embryonic and Fetal Research

One of the most controversial issues related to the constitutional right to abortion is research conducted either on human embryos, human fetuses, or portions thereof, such as fetal tissue or human embryonic stem cells (hESCs). The two issues are related because, like contraception, a constitutional right to abortion (with its inherent rejection of constitutional "personhood" for the unborn) necessarily implies that there is no constitutional problem with research using unborn fetuses or embryos. Moreover, because abortion causes many embryos and fetuses to be discarded, researchers would like to be able to use them for research that may help cure diseases or further knowledge of the human body. Those who oppose abortion oppose such research, however, believing it dehumanizes the unborn and encourages a greater number of abortions by allowing women to rationalize that some good may come from termination.

The government has become involved in this moral debate by imposing restrictions on the use of federal dollars to fund such research. It has not chosen to go the additional step of prohibiting private research from occurring, however, possibly because of constitutional concerns regarding free expression.[86] So even when federal laws do exist, they relate only to research conducted using federal funding, not privately funded research. There are some state laws limiting fetal and embryonic research,[87] but at the federal level, there are no prohibitions per se. Instead, it is all about the Jacksons—that is, whether federal dollars will fund such research.

Federal funding of fetal research is readily available. After the Supreme Court's decision in Roe v. Wade, there was some hesitation about the effect abortion-on-demand could have on fetal research. Congress passed the National Research Act in 1974, creating a National Commission for Protection of Human Subjects and charging it with developing recommendations regarding the ethical conduct of human subjects research funded by federal dollars. The Act included a temporary moratorium on federal funding of fetal research until after the Commission completed its report.[88] The Commission recommended that the moratorium be lifted "immediately" following the issuance of its report.[89] The Secretary of the Department of Health, Education, and Welfare issued final regulations lifting the federal funding moratorium shortly thereafter, and funding has been uninterrupted since that time.[90] Current regulations require that all federally funded fetal research be approved by an Institutional Review Board (IRB), must not offer any inducements to terminate pregnancy, and must not permit researchers to have a role in any determination of viability or decision to abort.[91] Federally funded fetal research (1) must also provide the prospect of direct benefit to the pregnant woman or fetus; or (2) if no such benefit is possible, the research must be necessary to the development of "important biomedical knowledge" and the risk to the fetus can be no more than minimal.[92]

Research involving the use of fetal tissue for the specific purpose of transplantation into another living person is dealt with under a different law, though it, too, may be funded by the federal government. In 1988, the Reagan Administration imposed a moratorium on federal funding of research involving transplantation of fetal tissue from induced abortions, based on concerns that expanding therapeutic use for fetal tissue transplantation—for example, the transplantation of fetal brain cells into Parkinson's patients—would encourage more abortions. Five years later, however, the moratorium was lifted by an order of President Clinton.[93] Current law permits therapeutic transplantation of fetal tissue, whether from aborted or spontaneously miscarried fetuses, provided the pregnant woman provides written informed consent, does not know the identity of the recipient, and certain other procedural requirements are satisfied.[94]

Research on human embryos has faced much stiffer legal opposition than that on fetuses or fetal tissue. In 1996, Congress passed a law—called the Dickey-Wicker Amendment—forbidding federal funding of research in which human embryos are created or "destroyed, discarded or knowingly subjected to risk of injury or death greater than that allowed for research on fetuses" (that is, more than minimal risk).[95] This law effectively halted all federal funding of IVF and related artificial reproductive technology research, as well as research involving hESCs.

In his last months in office, President Clinton decided that while the Dickey-Wicker Amendment prohibited research that derived embryonic stem cells from a human embryo—because such derivation necessarily "destroys" the embryo—it did not prohibit research on such embryonic stem cells *after* the embryo had already been destroyed. Accordingly, the National Institutes for Health (NIH) promulgated final guidelines in August 2000 that authorized federal funding of hESC research using stem cells already derived from excess, leftover IVF embryos.[96]

Before any federal funds could be awarded for hESC research, however, the intervening presidential election ushered in a new administration. President George W. Bush immediately put the NIH guidelines on hold and ordered a review of the Clinton policy. In August 2001, President Bush announced a compromise between those who wanted full federal funding for hESC research and pro-life groups that opposed it entirely. The Bush compromise was to permit federal funding of hESC research on already-derived cells (as did the Clinton policy), but only on "pre-existing" cell lines that had been derived prior to his announcement on August 9, 2001.[97] Bush's policy, though it enabled federal funding for some hESC research, was quite limiting, as there were only thirty or so cell lines that were accordingly eligible for federally funded research.[98] It also created administrative challenges, requiring researchers conducting both publicly and privately funded hESC research to segregate their facilities and equipment.

Believing that hESC research was critical to finding cures and treatments for disease, many states responded to the relatively parsimonious federal funding of the Bush compromise by passing their own laws that offered billions of state dollars for hESC research. California, Connecticut, Maryland, Massachusetts, New Jersey, and New York, for example, have committed billions in state funds.[99]

After states stepped up to the plate to fill the perceived funding gap, another change in administrations brought another change in policy toward federal funding of hESC research. President Barack Obama's administration issued final guidelines in March 2009 to permit federal funding of hESC research using any hESCs derived from human embryos created using IVF but that are "no longer needed" for that purpose, provided minimum informed consent and other rules are satisfied.[100] The Obama administration's policy effectively reinstates the earlier Clinton policy.

The Obama policy suffered a setback in late August 2010. In Sherley v. Sebelius, the U.S. District Court for the District of Columbia issued a preliminary injunction prohibiting further federal funding of hESC research. The court believed that Obama Administration's policy violated the Dickey-Wicker Amendment, concluding:

> [T]he language of the statute reflects the unambiguous intent of Congress to enact a broad prohibition of funding research in which a human embryo is destroyed. This prohibition encompasses *all* "research in which" an embryo is destroyed, not just the "piece of research" in which the embryo is destroyed. Had

Congress intended to limit Dickey-Wicker to only those discrete acts that result in the destruction of an embryo, like the derivation of ESCs, or to research on the embryo itself, Congress could have written the statute that way. Congress, however, has not written the statute that way, and this Court is bound to apply the law as it is written. . . . ESC research is clearly research in which an embryo is destroyed. To conduct ESC research, ESCs must be derived from an embryo. The process of deriving ESCs from an embryo results in the destruction of the embryo. Thus, ESC research necessarily depends upon the destruction of a human embryo. Despite defendant's attempt to separate the derivation of ESCs from research on ESCs, the two cannot be separated.[101]

As of the time this book was written, the U.S. Court of Appeals for the D.C. Circuit had issued an administrative stay of the trial court's decision "to give the court sufficient opportunity to consider the merits of the emergency motion for a stay. . . ." The appellate court cautioned, however, that the administrative stay "should not be construed in any way as a ruling on the merits of that motion."[102] The net effect is that the Obama Administration's expanded federal funding of hESC research will continue, pending the outcome of the litigation, unless the appellate court decides to lift its administrative stay.

The critical legal question posed by *Sherley*—whether the Obama Administration's policy violates the Dickey-Wicker Amendment—is an intriguing question of statutory interpretation for which there is no easy answer. The Obama policy (like the Clinton policy that never went into effect) is based on a distinction between "derivation" and post-derivation "research" on hESCs— a distinction that matters only if the Dickey-Wicker Amendment's prohibition on "research in which a human embryo or embryos are destroyed" refers to the discrete act(s) of research that occurs after the discrete act of derivation. If the "research" refered to in Dickey-Wicker refers to the larger *process* in which hESC research takes place, then it is logical to conclude that derivation is a necessary part of that hESC research, and therefore prohibited by the Amendment. In the words of the *Sherley* trial court:

Derivation of ESCs from an embryo is an integral step in conducting ESC research. Indeed, it is just one of many steps in the "systematic investigation" of stem cell research. Simply because ESC research involves multiple steps does not mean that each step is a separate "piece of research" that may be federally funded, provided the step does not result in the destruction of an embryo. If one step or "piece of research" of an ESC research project results in the destruction of an embryo, the entire project is precluded from receiving federal funding by the Dickey-Wicker Amendment. Because ESC research requires the derivation of ESCs, ESC research is research in which an embryo is destroyed.[103]

What did Congress intend when it used the word "research" in Dickey-Wicker? Did it mean to refer to a process, one early part of which involves the destruction of a human embryo? Or did it mean to refer only to the process that occurs *after* a human embryo has already been destroyed—in other words, after derivation? Eventually, the courts will provide an answer. But even if the federal appeals courts (including possibly the Supreme Court) eventually concurs with the trial court's broader conception of "research" as encompassing all of its component parts, Congress can have the last word if it chooses. Dickey-Wicker is a statute; it can, like all other statutes, be amended or discarded by future Congresses.

If the federal courts conclude that hESC "research" includes derivation—and therefore constitutes research that destroys a human embryo under Dickey-Wicker—Congress is free to change its mind about Dickey-Wicker. It could refuse to attach Dickey-Wicker to future health appropriations bills. Alternatively, if discarding Dickey-Wicker wholesale is politically unpalatable, Congress could revise it to provide a specific exception for hESC research while still prohibiting other forms of research involving the destruction of a human embryo. So while the *Sherley* litigation raises interesting questions about congressional intent in drafting Dickey-Wicker back in 1996 (before scientists had even been able to derive and culture stable hESC cell lines), the last word on the legality of federal funding for hESC research is likely to come from Congress, not the *Sherley* case.

Given the scientific community's belief in the vast potential of hESC research to yield remarkable diagnostic and treatment advances, it is doubtful that Congress will be willing to halt all federal funding for all hESC research—which is the net effect of the trial court's decision in *Sherley*. It seems inevitable, in other words, that Congress will eventually be asked to clarify its intent with regard to federal funding of hESC research, and equally likely that its answer will be some degree of endorsement of federally funded hESC research. If the 2010 mid-term elections return one or both houses of Congress to Republican control, the result may be that Congress expresses a preference for something analogous to the Bush policy, which represented a political compromise allowing some federal funding of hESC research, but only using stem cell lines that had already been created. This approach attempted to more clearly segregate federal funding of hESC research from the embryo-destroying act of derivation, though it significantly limited the number of cell lines that could qualify for federally funded research. If Congress exercises its right to have the last word, some type of political compromise seems inevitable.

Despite all of the political back-and-forth on embryonic and fetal research, the law seems to have arrived at a point of relative acceptance for both. This acceptance reflects the legal view—found in both constitutional and ordinary laws—that embryos and fetuses are not entitled to the same legal rights as those who have been born. They may have some interests deserving of protection, but those interests are not the same as yours or mine.

In this particular chapter, we have explored the meaning of life within the context of our Constitution. What we have found is that the Supreme Court has steadfastly declined to speculate about when life begins. Our Constitution simply offers no guidance on this intractable issue. The meaning of life, in this sense, is a debate better suited for medicine, ethics, philosophy, or theology than law. But what our Constitution does say is that "persons" and "people" are entitled to certain rights. And the Supreme Court was duty bound to answer: who is a "person" within the meaning of the Constitution? The answer it has provided, in its contraceptive and abortion jurisprudence, is that the word "person" or "people" refers only to the born, not the unborn. This basic decision has made it possible for ordinary laws permitting contraception, abortion, and fetal and embryonic research to exist.

3

Cardiopulmonary Death

The true color of life is the color of the body, the color of the covered red, the implicit and not explicit red of the living heart and the pulses.

—Alice Meynell, *The Color of Life and Other Essays* (1896)

What is death? It is death that marks the critical moment when one's last will and testament becomes effective, when charges of murder or manslaughter become salient, or when life insurance contracts must be satisfied. But when, exactly, does the law declare that the grim reaper has taken us?

A conservative answer would be that death can be declared only on evidence of decomposition, for only then can we be sure that we have crossed the point of no return. But putrefaction can take days to set in, and it seems a poor proxy for death when compared to quicker ways, such as tests to determine whether certain "vital" functions have been irreversibly lost. As a result, the law has never required evidence of putrefaction prior to a declaration of death; although decay is an inevitable process after death, it has never marked death itself.

But which vital function should the law use as its proxy for death? Heartbeat? Breathing? Kidney function? Liver function? Brain function? Arguably, each of these biological functions is vital because, upon their loss, the body as a whole will begin to break down, and if these functions are not restored, the entire organism will eventually fail. They each represent, in their own way, biological points of no return. Putrefaction ineluctably will follow some time later. Arguably, therefore, any of these vital functions, when irreversibly lost, could provide a logical legal proxy for death.

The definition of death developed by the common law was relatively simple: death occurred when one stopped breathing. Respiratory function was the hallmark of death for many reasons. First, it was easy for anyone, even nonphysicians, to check for respiration. A mirror or feather could be placed under the nose. The chest could be observed for rising and falling. Second, respiratory cessation was not generally reversible. Cardiopulmonary resuscitation (CPR) techniques were not invented until the nineteenth century and were not widely known until the twentieth century. A person who stopped breathing was unlikely spontaneously to start breathing again. Third, an irreversible loss of respiratory function was preceded or quickly followed by the loss of cardiac function. And until the modern era, it was widely believed that the heart, not the brain, was the seat of thought and emotion. Aristotle, for example, asserted in the fourth century B.C., "The seat of the soul and the control of voluntary movement—in fact, of nervous functions in general—are to be sought in the heart. The brain is an organ of minor importance."[1] Heart-centric biology continued for many centuries. Indeed, the historical importance of the heart to our concept of life is evident in numerous phrases we still use to describe emotions and personality, such as "heartbroken," "heartache," "heavyhearted," "bighearted," "heartless," or "my heart's not in it."

Yet respiratory loss is not without its faults as the proxy for death. Various conditions can cause a temporary loss or severe curtailment of respiratory function, leading to false positive diagnoses of death. Individuals who have been submerged in cold water for long periods of time or who have overdosed on barbiturates, for example, can have such shallow respiration that it cannot not be easily detected, leading to an inaccurate diagnosis of death.[2] The problem of improper death diagnoses became so profound that the Victorians positively panicked about premature burial.[3] They devised complex mechanisms to allow the prematurely buried to escape from their coffins or inserted tubes in their coffins so they could shout out to passersby above.[4] The perfection and mass production of the stethoscope in the 1850s gave doctors a powerful new tool to aid in the diagnosis of death. Diagnosis thereafter shifted from respiration only to heartbeat and respiration combined. By focusing on two vital functions rather than just one, physicians allayed fears of premature burial and refined scientific understanding of death.[5]

Cardiopulmonary death is still recognized as death in all states. The Uniform Determination of Death Act (UDDA), a widely adopted model statute, offers one definition of death as the "irreversible cessation of circulatory and respiratory functions."[6] Indeed, despite modern legal recognition of brain death as an alternative means to diagnose death, the vast majority of deaths are still diagnosed using the traditional cardiopulmonary criteria.[7]

Since the early 1990s, there has been a resurgence in interest in cardiopulmonary death, fueled by an increasing need for organ donors. This newfound interest in cardiopulmonary death is ironic, given the fact that expanding the definition of death to include brain death was motivated in large part by a perceived need to increase the number of available organ donors. Yet brain death's promise with regard to organ donation has not been entirely realized. Individuals are still reticent to become organ donors, and arguably the recognition of brain death has exacerbated this problem. Brain death, moreover, is not common enough to be a panacea for the shortage of organs. In a world where there are far more waiting recipients than available organs, refocused attention on cardiopulmonary death was perhaps inevitable.

Donation After Cardiac Death

Renewed hope for expanding the supply of available organs has come from a practice known as donation after cardiac death (DCD). Under the most commonly used form of DCD, referred to as "controlled" cardiopulmonary death, a patient on life support who does not satisfy the definition of brain death (for example, a patient in a persistent vegetative state) is weaned from life support, leading to cardiac arrest within a short period of time. Because the DCD patient is not brain dead, the only legal way to harvest her organs is to invoke a controlled cardiopulmonary death, grounded in the concept of patient autonomy to refuse unwanted medical treatment. Because courts have acknowledged that incompetent patients enjoy the same right as competent patients to refuse unwanted treatment, family or other legally recognized surrogate decision makers are permitted to decide whether the incompetent patient would want life support terminated; if so, these surrogate decision makers can authorize such termination, permitting traditional cardiopulmonary death to occur. Once cardiopulmonary function fails, the patient is declared dead, and organ harvesting is begun. The speed with which all of this occurs has led ethicist Arthur Caplan to label DCD "snatch and grab."[8]

Some experts have suggested that if DCD is widely implemented, it could increase the number of available organ donors by 20 to 25 percent.[9] Such a drastic increase in organ donation, however, would likely include another form of DCD that is not widely practiced today, called "uncontrolled" cardiopulmonary death. With uncontrolled DCD, organs are harvested from individuals who suffer cardiopulmonary failure outside the hospital setting as a result of heart attacks, automobile accidents, gunshot wounds, or other traumatic events. Unlike controlled DCD, cardiopulmonary death that occurs outside the hospital setting is uncontrolled, necessitating that consent to harvest organs be obtained relatively quickly after the cardiopulmonary death occurs. And at least in theory, as with controlled DCD, an individual with a valid organ donation card who suffers a heart attack on the street could, after unsuccessful resuscitation attempts, have his organs harvested without the need for any additional family or surrogate consent.

The vast untapped source of potential organ donors represented by uncontrolled cardiopulmonary death has recently led New York City to announce plans, modeled on a similar program in Spain, to begin a pilot project for special "rapid organ recovery" ambulances. These ambulances would be dispatched after the "normal" ambulance. Once on the scene, the paramedics in the normal ambulance would begin resuscitation efforts. If resuscitation failed, cardiopulmonary death would be declared, the paramedics in the organ recovery ambulance would take over, and efforts to preserve the organs would begin. The organ recovery ambulance would then quickly transport the body to the hospital, where organ harvesting would take place.[10]

At first blush, one might wonder what all the fuss surrounding DCD is all about. After all, what is so controversial or novel about pulling the plug, waiting for cardiopulmonary death to occur, and then harvesting their organs? Or for that matter, what is troubling with what New York is planning—attempting normal resuscitation outside the hospital setting, failing, declaring cardiopulmonary death, and then quickly initiating procedures to preserve organs for possible harvesting back at the hospital? The devil, as they say, is in the details.

Early cadaveric transplant donors were technically DCD donors, but this is only because legal recognition of brain death had not yet occurred, necessitating that all patients be declared dead by traditional cardiopulmonary criteria after disconnection from life support.[11] Once brain death became accepted, the overwhelming majority of organ donors have been those declared brain dead.[12] The medical community has developed a strong preference for harvesting organs from brain-dead patients because, unlike DCD donors, brain-dead donors are still breathing (with mechanical assistance) at the time the organs are harvested. Organs retrieved from brain-dead donors are full of oxygen up until the moment of removal, making them more viable—and viable for longer periods of time—for transplantation.[13] Because DCD organs are less fresh, DCD is believed to pose a higher risk of transplant failure.

Irreversibility

The critical question thus becomes: How long should transplant surgeons wait before removing an organ via DCD? How much time, in other words, should pass between the last sign of cardiopulmonary function and the removal of organs? When can we confidently say that the loss of cardiopulmonary function is "irreversible" as required by law? The shorter the time period, the higher the chance of transplant success. But a shorter time period creates ethical and legal doubts about whether the donor's cardiopulmonary failure is genuinely irreversible—and hence, whether the donor is truly dead. The answer, as it turns out, is not legally prescribed and varies significantly from institution to institution.

No case law or statute has ever attempted to decide how many minutes must elapse after heartbeat and breathing stops before a person can be declared dead. Instead, the law has preferred to punt this difficult question to the medical profession, adopting language that requires "irreversible" cessation of cardiopulmonary functions.[14] How to interpret the word "irreversible" is left to treating physicians, provided they abide by accepted medical standards.[15] One of the first health care institutions to adopt a formal DCD protocol was the University of Pittsburgh Medical Center in 1992. Under the Pittsburgh protocol, a non-brain-dead patient is, with family consent, disconnected from life support. Once cardiac arrest occurs, the physicians wait for two minutes before declaring cardiopulmonary death.[16] After cardiopulmonary death is declared, organ harvesting begins immediately. After only two minutes of cardiopulmonary cessation, is it appropriate to conclude that the patient is legally dead, or should we wait a bit longer, to make sure he will not take another breath?

The Pittsburgh protocol's two-minute rule skirts the line of legality, raising a question as to whether two minutes is sufficient to constitute irreversible cardiopulmonary function loss under accepted medical standards. Unfortunately, the medical profession's standards do not provide any clear answers. At the present time, Pittsburgh's two-minute rule appears to fall on the aggressive end of a rather wide range of professional protocols regarding DCD. Relevant are the recommendations of the Society of Critical Care Medicine and a 2009 draft proposal of the Australian Organ and Tissue Donation and Transplant Authority, which embrace a range approach, waiting a minimum of two minutes, but no more than five minutes, before declaring death and beginning the organ harvesting process.[17] More conservatively, both the Institute of Medicine and the Canadian Council for Donation and Transplantation have recommended that physicians wait at least five minutes before initiating organ removal.[18] New York City's plan for special organ recovery ambulances likewise would instruct paramedics not to begin organ preservation procedures until five minutes after the normal paramedics declared cardiopulmonary death.[19] The Maastricht protocol used in Europe is more conservative still, requiring a ten-minute standoff prior to harvesting DCD organs.[20]

As could perhaps be expected over time, Pittsburgh's two-minute rule has not emerged as the minimum amount of time that some medical professionals are comfortable waiting before declaring cardiopulmonary death. A protocol implemented in 2004 by the Denver Children's Hospital, for example, required a wait of only seventy-five seconds before beginning the removal of hearts from infant DCD donors.[21] The question becomes: As health care institutions adopt shorter and shorter waiting periods for the declaration of cardiopulmonary death, at what point do they cross the line of legality? How short of a waiting period, in other words, is too short to constitute irreversibility of cardiopulmonary function as required by law?

Published empirical evidence indicates that resuscitation of cardiopulmonary function is possible for ten to fifteen minutes following asystole.[22] So a seventy-five-second wait, two-minute wait, or even five-minute wait before declaring cardiopulmonary death seems premature by comparison. Yet no institutional policy or professional standard has advocated waiting for fifteen minutes before declaring cardiopulmonary death in the context of DCD. Why not? The primary justification seems to be that although cardiopulmonary death is normally reversible for up to fifteen minutes, the meaning of "irreversible" cardiopulmonary function is an ethical concept that must be considered in specific context. Tom Tomlinson explains it in the specific context of DCD:

> An essential element of the present [DCD] context is that the non-heart-beating donor . . . has volunteered to donate organs only after exercising his right to refuse any further life-prolonging treatments, including treatments aimed at resuscitation from cardiopulmonary arrest. To refuse to withdraw the life-prolonging respirator therapy or to institute other life-prolonging treatments would be a violation of the donor's wishes and of his rights, and so not ethically acceptable. . . . Therefore, to ignore those possibilities in making the determination of death takes all due account of our obligations to the donor's interests, and so does no violence to the requirement of irreversibility once that requirement is properly understood. A [DCD] donor . . . who arrests and has been reliably determined to have lost the capacity for auto-resuscitation is properly determined to be "irreversibly" dead, despite the remaining possibilities of medical resuscitation.[23]

Because a DCD donor by definition does not want any further medical intervention to sustain his life—and certainly not resuscitation—Tomlinson argues that it is both ethically and legally permissible to declare cardiopulmonary death whenever the donor has "lost the capacity for auto-resuscitation."

Tomlinson's argument about the meaning of irreversibility is consistent with the legal concept of patient autonomy, particularly the autonomy to refuse unwanted medical treatment. After all, if a patient has a right to refuse unwanted medical treatment, it follows that he has the right not merely to pull the plug but to refuse subsequent attempts at resuscitation. The fact that resuscitative efforts, if begun, could succeed within fifteen minutes of asystole should not be relevant for purposes of deciding whether the loss of cardiopulmonary function satisfies the legal requirement of irreversibility. The possibility of restoring cardiopulmonary function, in other words, is legally irrelevant because considering it would eviscerate the patient's right to refuse treatment.

But discounting the possibility of resuscitation does not entirely solve the problem of timing for cardiopulmonary death in the DCD context. If we agree that the law should not consider whether resuscitation is possible for the DCD donor, we still must decide how long doctors should wait before declaring cardiopulmonary death in this particular context. On the one hand, one could argue that no waiting period should be necessary, since the DCD donor (or their surrogate) has refused any life-sustaining treatment, including resuscitation. So why wait at all? In the context of controlled DCD, why not go ahead and harvest the organs immediately after shutting off the ventilator or other life support? In some sense, no waiting period is a logical extension of Tomlinson's ethics and autonomy-centered definition of irreversibility. If the goal is ensuring ethical behavior that is consistent with the legal right to refuse unwanted treatment, it would seem both ethical and legal to allow organ harvesting without a waiting period.

Yet there is another problem here, which arises not by virtue of the irreversibility requirement but by the other language of the Uniform Determination of Death Act. Recall that the UDDA defines cardiopulmonary death as the "irreversible cessation of circulatory and respiratory functions." So it is not just irreversibility that must be satisfied, but also "cessation of circulatory and respiratory functions." In other words, the law demands that doctors wait at least until the heart and breathing have stopped. So pulling the plug and immediately harvesting organs is not a legal option. Legally, we must at least wait for the cardiopulmonary functions to stop. But once those functions have stopped, should any additional waiting periods be legally required? If there has been proper documentation of cardiopulmonary cessation, is the cessation necessarily irreversible (given the context)? The answer must be no.

The reason that some waiting period is necessary, even in the context of controlled DCD where it is clear that the patient does not want any further medical treatment (including resuscitation) and cardiopulmonary function is documented as nonexistent, is that nature may intervene. Specifically, once life support is disconnected and cardiopulmonary function stops, it is possible—and indeed not unheard of—that the patient spontaneously may begin breathing again. There is, in other words, a short period of time in which autoresuscitation is possible. Although the patient may not want wish to be resuscitated, resuscitation may naturally occur anyway.

If a patient autoresuscitates, the law will not permit doctors to intervene and stop this renewed natural breathing. The law will permit doctors to withdraw life support, but it will not permit doctors actively to stop naturally occurring life sustaining functions.[24] Once a patient has begun breathing on his own again, it would be considered homicide for a doctor to intervene and smother the patient. If autoresuscitation occurs, doctors must respect this function and let nature run its course. The patient's family is not required to consent to any additional life-sustaining medical interventions—such as ventilator support—but doctors cannot actively intervene to stop natural functions from occurring. They must wait until cardiopulmonary function fails once more, and the appropriate waiting period must be satisfied to ensure that no further autoresuscitation occurs.

But how long must we wait to ensure that autoresuscitation will not occur? The answer to this question may require that we draw a distinction between uncontrolled and controlled DCD. With uncontrolled DCD, the donor by definition suffers cardiopulmonary loss outside the hospital setting, such as after an accident or a heart attack. In these uncontrolled settings, a significant waiting period is inherent and may not need to be legally specified.

Think about it: assume you are on the tennis court when you are struck with a massive heart attack. Assume further that you live in New York City, which has a fleet of special ambulances to recover organs in uncontrolled, extrahospital situations such as this. The normal paramedics arrive on the scene, and they begin efforts to resuscitate. After all resuscitative efforts fail, you are declared dead using cardiopulmonary criteria. Now the special organ recovery ambulance team immediately takes over, prepping your body for possible organ transplantation and rushing you to the hospital.

The transportation to the hospital will take several minutes at least. Once at the hospital, organ retrieval cannot begin unless and until the hospital has obtained proper legal authorization. By the time proper authorization has been documented, it has presumably been many minutes since your cardiopulmonary function ceased. Since normal resuscitative efforts were tried and failed, the cardiopulmonary cessation is reasonably viewed as irreversible. In an uncontrolled DCD scenario such as this, the waiting period between the cessation of cardiopulmonary function and the removal of organs is much lengthier than it would or could be in a controlled DCD context. A reasonable waiting period, in other words, seems inherently built in.

Controlled DCD is another story. With controlled DCD, consent is obtained to withdraw unwanted life-sustaining medical treatment. Following withdrawal, cardiac failure typically occurs within a few minutes. A waiting period is then required to confirm that the loss of cardiopulmonary function is irreversible, so that death can be declared and organs harvested. The $6 million question, therefore, is how long of a wait is long enough to provide reasonable assurance that the loss of cardiopulmonary function is indeed irreversible?

Presumably, enough time must pass such that autoresuscitation is no longer reasonably possible. The Pittsburgh protocol's two-minute waiting period was justified on grounds that two minutes was the maximum time period beyond which no documented autoresuscitation has occurred.[25] Stuart Youngner has claimed that the data relied upon by Pittsburgh was "seriously flawed" because of small sample size and the disparate purpose underlying the collection of the data.[26] Joanne Lynn has argued that data regarding the timing and incidence of autoresuscitation is virtually nonexistent, leading to an unacceptable possibility that a two-minute wait will prove erroneous in some cases, allowing doctors to "tak[e] organs from persons who are not dead."[27] Similarly, James Bernat has asserted that "the brief absence of heartbeat and breathing is highly predictive of death in this context, but . . . at the time the organs are being procured in the Pittsburgh protocol, death has not yet occurred."[28] Norm Fost is even more blunt, stating, "the DCD protocol pretends that patients are dead at the time organs are taken out. They're not."[29]

Concerns about the possibility of autoresuscitation after a two-minute waiting period seem to have been validated in a recent incident reported in France. Shortly after France initiated pilot DCD projects, a shocking story was reported in June 2008, buried deep inside a smattering of newspapers across the world. A forty-five-year-old man had a heart attack and was rushed to the nearby hospital, where resuscitation efforts took place for ninety minutes. He was declared dead using cardiopulmonary criteria, and preparations were begun for organ retrieval. He "came alive" in the operating room, and after a significant time in intensive care, fully recovered.[30] The French hospital's ethics committee report following the incident revealed that other physicians "spoke of situations in which a person whom everyone was sure had died in fact survived after reanimation efforts that went on much longer than usual."[31] Anecdotal evidence such as this suggests that assertions that auto-resuscitation is not possible after two minutes (or even five minutes) may be overstated and that further research is warranted.

Do Not Resuscitate Orders

The law's insistence on irreversibility of cardiopulmonary loss essentially mandates the use of modern resuscitative techniques and technology unless the patient (or her surrogate) declines such resuscitative efforts. The irreversibility requirement thus effectively creates a presumption in favor of using resuscitative techniques and technologies—a presumption that may not always be wise, efficient, or consistent with a patient's own preferences. In many instances, conditions and diseases that previously would have resulted in permanent loss of cardiopulmonary function (and hence, death) no longer do so, as medical advances often allow us to reverse the loss of these vital functions.

One attempt to counter the intrusion of medical technology has been the development and widespread use of do not resuscitate (DNR) orders. A DNR order does what its name suggests—it orders that if a patient needs cardiac or respiratory resuscitation, none should be given. The usual legal presumption is *against* providing medical care without patient consent, yet in the context of a potentially lethal situation in which consent is impracticable (for example, cardiac arrest), the law presumes that the dying patient would *want* medical care. A DNR order, when it is entered, alters this usual presumption, allowing an affirmative order not to resuscitate to be entered in the patient's medical chart. Most states have laws permitting individuals to have special DNR bracelets that notify emergency medical personnel (either within or outside the hospital setting) that a DNR order is in effect. Even without such bracelets, however, DNR orders can be placed on a patient's medical chart in certain instances.

Legally, DNR orders walk a very fine line. On the one hand, patients clearly have a right to refuse unwanted medical treatment, and DNR orders reflecting the patient's desires are an effective means to effectuate this important right. On the other hand, a patient's desire regarding resuscitation is not always evident, leaving family members and physicians to make decisions on the patient's behalf. In this vast gray area, physicians' subjective values and preferences may dominate, as family members and other surrogate decision makers acquiesce, perhaps all too happy to leave the difficult decision making in other hands.

Two particularly delicate legal issues surround the use of DNRs. First, there is considerable confusion regarding the appropriate scope of DNR orders. A DNR could be interpreted as prohibiting all aggressive treatment of the patient, not just cardiopulmonary resuscitation (CPR). In this sense, a DNR order is a broad command to withdraw all medical care even before cardiac or respiratory arrest, providing only comfort care until death occurs. Alternatively, a DNR order could be interpreted more narrowly as refusing only CPR itself, allowing all other medical interventions until the moment of cardiac or respiratory arrest.[32] And, of course, there is always the possibility that a DNR order could be intended to mean something between these two extremes, allowing some specific forms of intervention prior to cardiac arrest, but not others.

The laws of the various states do not generally resolve the ambiguity in the appropriate scope of a DNR. One exception is Ohio, which adopted a law in 1998 that recognizes two distinct kinds of DNR orders: "DNR Comfort Care" and "DNR Comfort Care–Arrest."[33] The former—DNR Comfort Care—is the broader DNR order, refusing all care other than comfort care from the moment of the order's execution. The latter—DNR Comfort Care–Arrest—is the narrower one, refusing all care other than comfort care, but only after the patient experiences cardiac or respiratory arrest. Most state laws, however, are not so clear in distinguishing among the kinds of DNR orders. As a result, there is little to no uniformity in their interpretation.

A second delicate issue implicating DNRs occurs when a physician believes that resuscitative attempts for an incompetent patient would be "futile," but family members disagree. The futility doctrine shares conceptual roots with DNR orders, but branches out significantly farther. Rather than simply not resuscitating a patient who goes into cardiac arrest, the futility doctrine permits a doctor to withdraw all life-sustaining treatment even in the absence of cardiac arrest or other life-threatening emergency. Take the case of Emilio Gonzales, a toddler born with a terminal neurometabolic disorder called Leigh's disease. After arriving at the hospital, Emilio was placed on a respirator and a feeding tube inserted. His young mother wanted his care continued, but his doctors concluded that doing so would be futile. They gave his mother ten days to find another hospital to take Emilio, or he would be removed from life support. Sound far-fetched? It is not. Emilio's plight was real.[34]

Futility cases such as Emilio's are the conceptual flip side of right-to-die cases. In right-to-die cases, one or more loved ones ask the providers to terminate life support so that the patient can die. Right-to-die cases are about patient autonomy—namely, the right to refuse unwanted treatment, to be free from intrusive medical technology that violates one's own sense of dignity and values. In futility cases, by contrast, it is the physicians who wish to terminate life support, despite objections by loved ones who want care continued. Futility cases do not involve the autonomy of the patient but rather the autonomy of the physicians. Why should we care about the autonomy of the physicians? Because physicians, it is argued, take an oath to "do no harm." Providing care that is futile can be harmful because it presents risks without any likely patient benefit. And futile care wastes scarce medical resources. Who says that a patient should get all treatments they demand, especially when their care is being paid for by the government or subsidized by other insured individuals? The time and resources that go into providing futile care could be reallocated to uses that are more beneficial to society at large.

In situations where the patient or their loved ones insists on continued provision of care—including life-sustaining care such as CPR—but the provider thinks it is futile, who should have legal authority to decide? For those of you who answered "the patient or their loved one," think again. This is one area of the law in which patient autonomy has been scaled back.

The difficulty is where to draw the line between patients' rights, physicians' rights, and society's rights. The initial query—how do we define "futile" care?—is impossible to answer in any objective way.[35] One person's futile care is another person's beneficial care. Age, income, social status, educational attainment, world views, gender, race, religious views, diagnoses, and prognoses can make a difference in the real-world application of futility.[36] If a standard, objective definition of futility cannot be agreed upon, does this

mean that providers have no ability to unilaterally deny futile care—that patients' or surrogates' treatment demands must always be satisfied? The cautious legal answer that has emerged in the last two decades is no.

The law's approach to futility is evolving rapidly. One salient legal source
is the Uniform Health Care Decisions Act (UHCDA), a model law promulgated in 1993 that has been adopted by eleven states.[37] Under the UHCDA,
health care providers may refuse to comply with a request for "medically ineffective health care" or care that is "contrary to generally accepted health-
care standards applicable to the health-care provider or institution."[38] The
UHCDA permits a provider to refuse any treatment—not just cardiopulmonary resuscitation—if the provider thinks it would be futile, even if the patient or their surrogate adamantly insists on such treatment. The UHCDA
does require, however, that the provider inform the patient or surrogate of
their unilateral decision to refuse treatment, continue providing care "until a
transfer can be effected," and make reasonable efforts to assist with such
transfer.[39] If transfer cannot be obtained (which is often the case in futility
situations), the UHCDA does not provide any further guidance. Implicitly,
however, if a transfer cannot be effectuated after reasonable efforts, the provider is legally authorized to unilaterally refuse treatment, including life-
sustaining treatment such as cardiopulmonary resuscitation.

Individual state statutes vary wildly. Some state laws are considerably
narrower than the UHCDA, addressing only providers' specific obligation to
provide CPR if the patient or patient's surrogate requests it. If the patient is
incompetent or there is no surrogate able or willing to make a DNR decision
on the patient's behalf, these statutes permit the physician to enter a DNR
order unilaterally.[40] Other states are more aggressive than the UHCDA. One
of the shortcomings of the UHCDA is that it does not provide a remedy in
the situation where transfer to another facility cannot be obtained. Some
states have filled this gap, enacting futility statutes that give providers an explicit legal trump card, allowing them to withhold or withdraw life-sustaining
care if another facility cannot be found that is willing to accept transfer.

The first statute of this sort was enacted by Texas in 1999. Under the
Texas Advance Directives Act, a physician is authorized to refuse treatment—
even life-sustaining treatment—for any patient, even if the patient or his
surrogate requests it or the patient's advance directive expresses a desire for
continued treatment. In such circumstances, the physician's refusal to treat

is referred to an institutional committee for review. If the committee agrees that continuation of care is inappropriate, the physician must make a reasonable effort to help locate another physician or facility willing to accept transfer. If a willing provider cannot be found within ten days, the patient's life-sustaining care can be terminated.

If a transfer facility can be located, the patient is responsible for paying the costs of transfer.[41] Patients or their surrogates may ask a court to extend the ten-day period, but such an extension may be granted "only if the court finds, by a preponderance of the evidence, that there is a reasonable expectation that a physician or health care facility that will honor the patient's directive will be found if the time extension is granted."[42] Any physician, person acting under direction of a physician, or health care facility that complies with the statutory procedures for unilateral refusals to treat is broadly immunized from all civil, criminal, and licensing sanctions.[43]

The Texas law is remarkable in many ways. First, it avoids the sticky problem of defining futility, offering instead a process-based, extrajudicial mechanism for resolving disputes between providers and patients about the propriety of treatment. Second, it gives tremendous power to both physicians and ethics committees to decide which care is "inappropriate" in any given context. If the physician and committee are in agreement, their decision to stop life-sustaining care is unassailable, either by the patient, their loved ones, or the courts. Not surprisingly, a study conducted after the first two years' experience with the Texas law found that of forty-seven futility cases referred by physicians to ethics committees, the committees agreed that care should be terminated in forty-three (91 percent) of those cases.[44] Third, it places substantial financial hurdles in the path of patients who wish care continued, forcing them to locate another facility, pay for any transfer, and pay for the costs of hiring a lawyer and going to court to try to get an extension if transfer cannot be effected within ten short days. These burdens create strong incentives to acquiesce to termination of life support—undoubtedly one goal the law was designed to accomplish. As Robert Fine wrote recently, "Some dying patients receive three to six times as much treatment as others without having better outcomes. Many physicians are trying to be more thoughtful about end-of-life resource expenditures, but it is difficult to steward resources ethically when families demand unlimited treatment for dying patients. Texas law encourages cultural change toward the communitarian value that no one has unlimited claim on the community; the resulting savings might not be 'trivial.'"[45]

The net result may indeed be more expeditious, less expensive, nonjudicial resolution of futility disputes between providers and patients, but this result comes at a significant cost to due process, patient autonomy, and respect for differing values about life. The Texas law effectively mandates a one-size-fits all "communitarian" conception of the value of life—a conception that says that if the relevant "community" (consisting of physicians and ethics committees) thinks continuing your life is inappropriate, that community has the power to end your life. There is no ability to obtain judicial review regarding the propriety of the "community's" determination. It is final, unless you can somehow convince another facility to accept a transfer (good luck). In this scenario, a life can be deprived with little to no due process of law. True, patients' surrogates are permitted to attend the ethics committee meeting,[46] though there is no explicit mention of their being provided the simple courtesy of being heard. Ethics committees are dominated by providers, with only a few slots reserved for general community members, who are often lawyers. Having served on a hospital ethics committee, I can attest to the fact that they reflect a provider-based culture regarding life-sustaining care that is different from that of most ordinary Americans. As Robert Truog has cogently observed, ethics committees are poor substitutes for courts and juries of our peers.[47] Texas stands as a shining example of what can happen when the right to become the obligation to die, and when communitarian values are permitted to trump individual ones.

You may recall that the genesis of DNR orders was a desire to enable individuals to "fight back" against the onslaught of medical technology that threatened to keep them alive against their will. They were devised to empower individuals to resist cardiopulmonary resuscitation and the specter of subsequent mechanical life support. DNR orders were one small but important way of allowing individuals to control their own treatment destiny, to have their treatment reflect their own individualistic preferences and values.

But as the UHCDA and Texas Advance Directives Act show, DNR orders have morphed from an individualistic, autonomy-based tool to refuse CPR into a much broader one, giving physicians power to overrule individual preferences and implement explicit end-of-life rationing. What started out as autonomy-driven has now become communitarian-driven, designed to further the collective values of the dominant provider culture. It is this set of values that helps explain why, in the debate over health care reform, fears about "death panels" for elderly Medicare beneficiaries were so ubiquitous and impassioned (even if misinformed). The futility doctrine, now commonly in place via either law or formal or informal hospital policies, represents a potential long-term threat to the hard-won right of patient self-determination.

DCD and Brain Death

A somewhat ironic objection to all proposed DCD waiting periods is that they are insufficient to establish an irreversible cessation of the patient's brain function. While this may seem irrelevant in the context of DCD—which hinges on a determination of cardiopulmonary, not brain, death—critics have suggested that the continuation of brain function in DCD patients is nonetheless potentially relevant.

You may recall that under the UDDA, death is defined as the irreversible cessation of either cardiopulmonary or brain function. The legal definition is disjunctive: irreversible cessation of either type of function will suffice to establish that death has occurred. A person with a working brain who lacks cardiopulmonary function is dead, as is someone with functioning heart or lungs whose brain has stopped working. In the case of DCD, therefore, it would seem relevant only to consider whether the patient has experienced an irreversible loss of cardiopulmonary function, rendering the functional status of his brain inapposite.

Yet there is something eerie about declaring a person dead whose brain may still be functioning unaided. In the context of traditional cardiopulmonary death, a person suffers, say, a heart attack and after many minutes of unsuccessful resuscitative measures, death is called. In this typical scenario, we are confident that the person's cardiopulmonary function has been irreversibly lost. We are also confident that his brain function has been irreversibly lost, because after a few minutes without cardiopulmonary function, brains simply cannot work. The demise of the brain, in the face of irreversible loss of cardiopulmonary function, is inevitable and irreversible, because loss of cardiopulmonary function will inevitably lead to loss of integration of the organism as a whole.

With controlled DCD, by contrast, there is loss of cardiopulmonary function, but it is irreversible only because providers have chosen not to restore it. The brain of a controlled DCD patient will accordingly die within a few minutes—just like with traditional cardiopulmonary death—but the death of the brain in controlled DCD is not a byproduct of loss of integrative functioning; instead, it is the byproduct of a decision to end cardiopulmonary life support.

The President's Commission that recommended the legal recognition of brain death asserted that brain death was needed because the technology to artificially maintain cardiopulmonary function had interfered with our ability to detect death. More specifically, the President's Commission claimed that a disjunctive death statute (such as the UDDA) merely "reinforce[s] the concept of death as a single phenomenon—the collapse of psycho-physical integrity."[48] The Commission asserted that cardiopulmonary cessation was "merely evidence for the distintegration of the organism as a whole"[49] that was the true hallmark of death.

If the Commission's vision is correct, it raises troublesome issues regarding the legality of controlled DCD. If the UDDA's disjunctive approach is meant merely to offer alternative evidentiary indicators of death rather than alternative definitions of death itself, then what matters is not whether one or the other type of evidence (cardiopulmonary loss or brain loss) exists, but whether, once one such type of evidence exists, the definition of death itself has been satisfied. More specifically, if the definition of death is the "collapse of psycho-physical integrity" or "disintegration of the organism as a whole," as the President's Commission claimed, arguably a DCD patient may not, after a two- or five-minute waiting period, meet this definition. A person whose cardiopulmonary function ceased only two or five minutes ago will likely still have some degree of continuing brain function. As Winston Chiong has pointed out, five minutes of asystole would likely cause serious destruction of higher brain structures, but the lower brain (brain stem) would still be functioning.[50] A patient under such circumstances has not yet suffered holistic disintegration and certainly not collapse of psycho-physical integrity. If the UDDA truly represents a unitary definition of death with alternative indicia, declaring a controlled DCD patient dead after only five minutes of cardiopulmonary cessation could be premature.

As Tom Tomlinson has pointed out, renewed interest in DCD "forces us to make a choice between heart and head."[51] He astutely asks, "Is the [DCD] patient dead because his heart has stopped beating? Or is he alive because his brain is still working?"[52] Answering these questions requires us to decide whether the UDDA reflects an understanding of death that is definitionally unitary or binary, a decision that has not been previously necessary. If we decide that death is indeed a unitary concept, the pragmatic implication may be that DCD cannot be legally practiced, as the short waiting periods that permit successful organ harvesting inevitably mean that the patient has not yet suffered the requisite holistic distintegration. On the other hand, if we decide that death is a binary concept, DCD presumably will both continue and flourish.

DCD, Hearts, and the Double Effect

DCD faces other conceptual problems. For example, can DCD satisfy the legal requirement of irreversibility when the organ being harvested is the heart? Can we say, with a straight face, that a DCD patient has suffered an irreversible loss of cardiopulmonary function when his heart stops working, we remove it from his chest, transfer it to a waiting recipient, where it starts functioning again? Does this imply that the DCD donor's loss of heart function was, in fact, reversible?

One possibility is that the legal requirement of irreversibility refers to the donor alone, and presumably the excised heart had irreversibly ceased functioning at the time it was harvested. The fact that the donor's heart was successfully restarted in the body of the recipient should not cause us to doubt this fact, as irreversibility should be viewed contextually. In the context of the donor, therefore, the heart has irreversibly stopped for the simple reason that neither the donor nor his family wishes to attempt restarting it.

But there are critics such as Robert Veatch who assert that, among other reasons, DCD has not yet become accepted for heart transplants because "if a heart is restarted, the person from whom it was taken cannot have been dead according to cardiac criteria. Removing organs from a patient whose heart not only can be restarted, but also has been or will be restarted in another body, is ending a life by organ removal."[53] Under this view, employing DCD to harvest hearts constitutes murder.

While Veatch is correct that DCD is not widely used to harvest hearts (whether due to concerns about criminal prosecution or simply because hearts are more sensitive to ischemic injury), it is not unheard of. For example, the Denver Children's Hospital clinical trial, mentioned briefly before, used DCD to harvest hearts from three infant donors. The first infant's heart was harvested after waiting three minutes after cardiopulmonary cessation; the other two hearts were removed only seventy-five seconds after cardiopulmonary cessation.[54]

Were the infants involved in the Denver Children's Hospital protocol legally dead only three minutes or seventy-five seconds after their hearts stopped? Although all three infants suffered from severe brain injuries, none of them was brain dead.[55] After such short waiting periods, would it be fair to say that they had lost holistic integration? Or were their functioning, albeit severely damaged, brains evidence that they were still alive? Is the fact that their donated hearts resumed healthy function in the donee evidence that their initial loss of function was reversible?

A couple of facts may be salient in answering these difficult questions. First, because infants are more malleable in general, this may mean that a longer waiting period would be appropriate for DCD involving infants, whether of hearts or other organs. There may be wisdom in waiting a bit longer than seventy-five seconds to be reasonably certain that the infant's heart will not autoresuscitate. Second, the use of certain drugs with DCD implies that thinking or feeling patients may be subjected to organ harvesting, creating an impression that DCD is some form of euthanasia. Drugs such as heparin, fentanyl, lorazepam, and Regitine are sometimes administered to facilitate organ retrieval. Heparin, which is perhaps the most widely used, is a blood thinner that keeps blood from clotting and facilitates blood flow through the organs as long as possible. Fentanyl is a synthetic opioid used for pain management that is many times more potent than morphine. Lorazepam is a sedative and muscle relaxant that is widely prescribed to treat anxiety. Regitine is a blood pressure medicine that is used to relieve stress during surgical procedures and helps perfuse organs with blood.

While one can see that heparin and Regitine help facilitate successful organ transplantation, the use of fentanyl and lorazepam are more troubling. As pain and anxiety medications, they are presumably used to reduce any potential pain and anxiety experienced by the DCD organ donor. Because DCD patients by definition are not brain dead, their use implies that DCD donors may experience some reaction to the pain or anxiety associated with organ removal.

The use of fentanyl and Regitine have also raised eyebrows, however, because their use may hasten the death of DCD donors.[56] This is the so-called "double effect," in which a drug is administered that alleviates pain or other adverse symptoms in a patient but presents the known possibility that it can speed up a patient's death. Normally, the law accepts the double effect as an unavoidable consequence of the medical profession's desire to alleviate suffering.[57] Since the doctor's intent is to relieve pain or other unpleasant symptoms, the administration of a drug that might secondarily hasten the patient's death is considered legally innocuous.

Use of potentially death-hastening drugs in the context of DCD is particularly troubling to some who observe that, unlike most situations in which such drugs are administered, the goal of DCD is to cause the death of a patient so that their organs can be harvested.[58] When a powerful opioid is administered to a terminal cancer patient to lessen her pain, the double effect may be ethically acceptable because there generally is no reason to question the basic assumption that the treating physician would not wish to cause the death of her patient. Given the potential difference of the physician-patient relationship under DCD, one might wonder whether providing potentially death-hastening drugs impermissibly crosses the line between intending to alleviate pain and intending to hasten death so that the freshest organs possible can be obtained. If the public were widely aware that such drugs are administered during DCD, it could result in a perception that DCD skirts the line of euthanasia.

A recent case reported in California suggests that the temptation to use drugs to hasten death in the context of DCD may occur. In late January 2007, a twenty-six-year-old mentally retarded patient named Ruben Navarro suffered a cardiac arrest. He was taken to Sierra Vista Regional Medical Center in San Luis Obispo and put on life support.[59] After obtaining family consent, the hospital agreed to attempt controlled DCD.[60]

The transplant surgeon brought in to harvest Navarro's organs provided large quantities of sedatives and narcotics when Navarro's heart did not stop as quickly as expected. After Navarro still did not die thirty minutes after being weaned from life support, the organ retrieval was called off due to concerns that the organs were no longer viable. Navarro was returned to the intensive care unit of the hospital and died of cardiopulmonary death about seven hours later, without donating his organs.[61]

State prosecutors filed felony charges against the transplant surgeon, asserting that his provision of the narcotics and sedatives was an attempt to hasten Navarro's death to harvest his organs.[62] The transplant surgeon asserted that he did not intend to cause Navarro's death, only to ease his suffering because his death after removal from life support was prolonged. A jury ultimately acquitted the transplant surgeon of a single felony charge of abuse of a dependant adult.[63]

The surgeon's acquittal in the Navarro case illustrates how difficult it is to determine whether the administration of potentially death-hastening drugs was merely an instance of an innocent double effect or a more nefarious effort to speed up the patient's death. Trying to pinpoint motive is always difficult, as multiple motivations are plausible in most situations. The physician who participates in DCD, like the surgeon in the Navarro case, may well be motivated by appropriate desires to either relieve the patient's suffering or effectuate their (or their family's) wish to die and donate organs. Regardless of how the question of motive is resolved in any particular double effect case, its ubiquity—perhaps particularly in the context of DCD—highlights the potential for abuse and the need for clearer legal line drawing in such delicate situations.

Despite concerns that have been raised, DCD seems to be flourishing, fueled in large part by pragmatic needs. There is tremendous pressure to find new sources of organ donors, and DCD vents some of this pressure. Assuming DCD is preceded by full and informed consent of the families, it provides a mechanism for allowing some good to come of very tragic circumstances. And whatever one may think about the nature of hearts or holistic notions of death, the people closest to these donors do not consider themselves either victims or murderers. Nonetheless, because DCD does present opportunities for abuse, there is a real risk that horror stories publicized in the media could cause some individuals who would otherwise consider organ donation to balk at DCD in the future. Those involved in DCD, therefore, would be well advised to adopt waiting periods as long as possible, though ascertaining this outer limit will necessitate further research regarding the maximum time periods that are consistent with successful transplantation.

As Good As Dead?

In the attempt to obtain greater clarity and perhaps reduce the potential for abuse, some prominent ethicists and physicians are now advocating the abandonment of the dead donor rule (DDR), thereby allowing vital organs to be donated before the donor's death. Robert Truog, for example, advocates discarding both the DDR and brain death. Jettisoning the DDR alleviates the need for brain death, it is argued, because brain death was conceptualized as a way to increase the number of available organs.[64] Once it becomes legally acceptable to harvest organs from individuals who are not yet dead, returning to the traditional cardiopulmonary definition of death becomes both possible and desirable. Norm Fost likewise argues that the DDR should be abandoned, though he appears to disagree with Truog's position that brain death should also be abandoned. Fost's position is bolder, in the sense that he unabashedly maintains that "many thousands" of patients are already having their organs removed before they are dead, based on physicians' rationalization that such patients are "as good as dead" anyway.[65] Because Fost believes the DDR has been honored in the breach, he sees no reason to cling to it in the face of apparent public acquiescence to predeath donation.

Abandoning the dead donor rule faces many challenges, both conceptually and pragmatically. Conceptually, it would necessitate public acceptance of the notion that it is ethical to remove organs from an individual who is not yet legally dead. Recent surveys reveal that only about one-third of Americans think it would be acceptable to remove organs from living patients.[66] But some advocates of abandoning the DDR think this sort of data is inaccurate or misleading and that the public may be much more receptive to discarding the DDR than is commonly believed. In particular, they point to a recent survey about death and its relationship to organ transplantation that described several scenarios, one of which was as follows: "A 22/70 [these are two alternate ages that were varied by surveyors] year-old is in the hospital. This patient is also on machines that keep the heart and lungs working. This patient's brain is so severely damaged that they will never recover. They will not wake up, will not eat on their own, and will never breathe on their own. However, there are still some brain waves left."[67] The description is of an individual who is not brain dead, because there are "some brain waves left." But the individual is severely disabled and ventilator-dependent. When faced with these facts, the majority (57.2 percent) of respondents thought the patient was dead. Of those who thought the patient was dead, virtually all of them (95.6 percent) stated that they would be willing to donate this patient's organs. Of those who correctly believed the patient was alive (42.8 percent), a surprisingly healthy minority (45.7 percent) expressed a willingness to donate the patient's organs.[68]

Norman Fost concludes from this survey that "the hypothesis that a majority of the general public would be alarmed if organs were removed from a living patient with profound brain damage is not supported by these data."[69] In other words, most Americans would accept taking vital organs from an incompetent living donor, thus dispensing with the DDR. Yet such characterization of the data is overly aggressive. Because a clear majority of respondents thought the patient was legally dead, it is unreasonable to conclude that they support abandoning the DDR. The more pertinent group of respondents is those who thought the patient was still alive yet nonetheless were willing to donate the living patient's organs (45.7 percent). But it is useful to put this population of respondents in overall context: in this scenario, describing a severely brain-damaged, ventilator-dependent individual, only 264 out of 1,351 respondents—less than 20 percent—indicated a willingness to donate the organs of what they believed to be a living person.[70] Twenty percent is not insignificant, but it is far from a majority. The survey thus does not seriously undercut the conclusion that a majority of the public still supports the DDR.

More compelling than the debate about public acceptance is a conceptual argument on which some proponents of abandoning the DDR rely. It has been suggested that dispensing with the DDR will better respect patient autonomy by permitting individuals who are comfortable donating their organs prior to death to do so. If such individuals are going to die soon anyway, why not allow them to control their own destiny and die as a result of organ harvesting, enabling them to give the gift of life to others? Why not let something good come out of something that is otherwise inevitable and awful?

Patient autonomy is undoubtedly a value that most people (myself included) hold dear. But neither society nor law accepts that patient autonomy is limitless. For example, the most autonomy-centric laws involving medical care are found in Oregon and Washington, which permit physicians to assist suicide by writing lethal prescriptions for competent, terminally ill adults. Yet even these laws do not allow physicians to commit the final act that directly leads to the patient's death, nor do they allow physicians to assist with the suicide of an incompetent patient or a patient who can reasonably be expected to live more than six months.

The kind of physician-assisted suicide that is sanctioned in Oregon and Washington leaves the final act up to the patient. They can choose whether or not to swallow the fatal pills, and in many instances, data indicates that they exercise their autonomy by opting not to do so.[71] If the DDR were discarded, by contrast, the final act leading to the patient's death would be an act of the physician, not the patient. Patient autonomy has not been extended so far as to allow a third party to commit the final act.

Some of the fears associated with DDR abandonment could be allayed by carefully limiting the population to which the DDR no longer applies. But attempting to selectively abandon the DDR creates pragmatic problems of its own. Who exactly, among the living population, should be permitted to donate life-sustaining organs? Truog suggests two categories of patients who should be allowed to make such lethal donations: (1) individuals who are permanently unconscious and have an advance directive that indicates their desire to donate organs in such a situation; and (2) competent individuals who request withdrawal of life support and can be expected to die shortly thereafter. Fost adopts a different approach, stating that the present debate about abandoning the DDR should center around "incompetent patients who are imminently dying and about whom there is unanimity—among family and providers—that discontinuing treatment and allowing death to occur is in the patient's interest." He further stipulates that the "paradigm case is the patient in a permanent vegetative state" (PVS) and that the "strongest case" in this instance is when the PVS patient had "consented to such a donation while still competent."[72]

There are two categories of patients identified by both Fost and Truog who would be permitted to provide lethal donations: (1) those diagnosed as PVS; and (2) those diagnosed as terminally ill. Permitting PVS patients to provide lethal donations has broad implications. Abandoning the DDR for PVS patients would implicitly endorse a higher brain conceptualization of personhood, implying that individuals without a fully functioning higher brain are not fully alive or entitled to the same legal protection. Abandoning the DDR for PVS patients would thus permit higher brain advocates to accomplish something that the law has steadfastly refused to do: end the life of PVS patients for the sole utilitarian purpose of filling the need for more organs.

Truog explicitly states that he would permit such withdrawal only in the face of a valid advance directive; Fost does not. Advance directives would help ensure that the act that causes the patient's death—removal of vital organs—comports with the patient's wishes, thereby respecting patient autonomy. The law accepts that advance directives can be used in other contexts, such as turning off a ventilator, without being characterized as euthanasia. So why should not a similar rationale justify permitting lethal donation for PVS patients? The reason, as explained by the Supreme Court in Vacco v. Quill, is that honoring a patient's wish to refuse unwanted life support does not cause the patient's death. Instead, in such a situation, the patient's death is caused by the underlying disease or condition that gave rise to the use of the life-sustaining technology in the first place.[73] The life-sustaining technology is keeping the patient alive, and the patient has a right to refuse such treatment and experience a natural dying process.

Could the same logic be applied to the context of abandoning the DDR for PVS patients? If such patients have an advance directive indicating they would want to donate their organs before they are legally dead, why not let them do so? Causation is again the answer. In the context of abandoning the DDR, the question is not whether the patient may refuse unwanted life-sustaining treatment—they always may. Instead, the question is: What can doctors do once the life-sustaining treatment has been removed? Must they wait until the patient has died (cardiopulmonary loss), or can they go ahead and harvest the patient's organs before death has occurred? Proponents of abandoning the DDR advocate the latter, permitting doctors to remove the patient's organs without waiting for cardiopulmonary death to occur. Under such circumstances, the transplant surgeon would be committing an act (removal of organs) that causes the death of the patient. This is clearly euthanasia, and the question is therefore whether we, as a society, are willing to sanction it (at least for certain categories of people) so long as there is an advance directive. Are we comfortable, in other words, allowing physicians to commit an act that kills us, so long as we have consented in advance to be killed in this manner? Thus far, the answer to this question has been no.

Regarding terminally ill patients, some would limit this right to terminal patients who are competent. Others, such as Fost, would extend the right to incompetent terminal patients, provided there is unanimity among family and providers that permitting an early death is in the patient's "best interests." This would allow third parties (family and providers) to agree to end the life of a terminal patient if they all agree it is for the best.

Extending the right to incompetent patients is disconcerting because it could allow family and physicians to euthanize unconscious, terminally ill patients who do not have advance directives indicating a desire to provide lethal donation. Absent clear and convincing evidence that such donation comports with the patient's wishes, allowing donation under such circumstances would be antithetical to patient autonomy. Those who support this position might argue that terminal patients may experience severe and chronic pain that is not properly managed, so early death could be in the patient's best interests. In the vast majority of cases, however, pain can be managed with proper dosage and provider knowledge. More fundamentally, is the possibility of pain sufficient to conclude that such patients are better off dead? If you answer this question yes, you should realize that such a position accepts euthanasia based on third parties' judgments about another individual's quality of life.

Perhaps another justification for allowing third parties to authorize lethal donation of an incompetent, terminal patient's organs is that such patients are going to die soon anyway, so the benefit they derive from giving the gift of life would outweigh the cost of dying early. Limiting lethal donations to *competent* terminally ill patients at least has the advantage of respecting patient autonomy by ensuring that the patient herself has made such a cost/benefit determination. Permitting third parties to make the best-interests determination has no similar virtue, allowing third parties to weigh the costs and benefits on behalf of incompetent patients. While it is true that courts routinely use the best interests test to permit withdrawal of life support for incompetent patients, doing so permits only the withdrawal of treatment so that the patient can die. The best interests test is not currently used to authorize third parties to actively terminate a patient's life, as would be the case with lethal donation.

In a broader context, it is worth pondering whether limiting lethal donations to either populations—PVS patients or terminally ill ones—is possible. Is there any principled reason why we should not also allow lethal donation from those who are suffering from nonterminal disorders such as Alzheimer's, Parkinson's, Huntington's, or general dementia? Like PVS patients, such individuals can suffer serious cognitive impairment and may, in the eyes of some, have little to no quality of life. Why would PVS patients be permitted to undergo lethal donation whereas individuals with other types of serious permanent cognitive impairment would not? And why stop with cognitive disabilities? Arguably, individuals with severe physical disabilities can also suffer greatly and should be allowed to die so that others may live full, productive lives.

The slope here is realistically slippery. Legal acknowledgement of the utility of lethal donation for some patients implies that it is all right to terminate some "low-value" lives early so that others may live. Once the door is opened for legal euthanasia of PVS or terminally ill patients, rationing based on other forms of disability is no longer conceptually off the table, at least for those who have lost competency, and potentially for competent individuals as well. Are we willing to change the legal rules to enable early organ harvesting because some patients are so "out of it" (PVS or suffering from other cognitive impairments) or at death's door (terminally ill)? Are some patients, in other words, "as good as" dead?

The central legal questions posed by cardiopulmonary death are precipitated by one overarching desire: organ harvesting. Most people die from cardiopulmonary death, not brain death. This fact alone incentivizes finding ways to call cardiopulmonary death quicker so that the greatest number of fresh, viable organs can be harvested. Accordingly, hospitals have devised DCD protocols that allow organs to be harvested after a couple of minutes of asytole. Special organ recovery ambulances are being experimented with to see if more transplantable organs can be obtained when individuals collapse from cardiac arrest outside a hospital. Some ethicists and physicians are even advocating dispensing with the dead donor rule altogether. The question for the law is how to ensure that cardiopulmonary death organ donors have truly experienced "irreversible" cessation of cardiopulmonary function. Alternatively, the law may ultimately decide that "irreversible" cardiopulmonary loss is just too demanding a standard, necessitating an exception permitting organ harvesting prior to cardiopulmonary death. Whichever path the law ultimately takes—adhering to the dead donor rule or discarding it—one thing seems clear: there is pressure to call cardiopulmonary death sooner so that viable organs can be donated to those who desperately need them.

4

Brain Death

I think, therefore I am.

—René Descartes, *Principles of Philosophy* (1644)

Medical technology has both saved and enslaved us. It saves us from death in a mind-boggling number of ways. Yet precisely because it can reverse the previously irreversible, it also keeps us alive when it may not seem morally, ethically, or rationally appropriate to do so. This has created a unique modern legal question: can we disconnect this life-sustaining technology at some point—that is, pull the plug? The law's attempt to answer this question has given rise to two parallel legal developments, both of which have the net effect of allowing life-sustaining care to be terminated: (1) the recognition of patient autonomy to refuse unwanted medical care; and (2) statutory reforms that expand the definition of death to include brain death. The first of these two developments—recognizing a right to refuse unwanted care—will be explored in detail in the following chapter. The second one—expanding the definition of death to include brain death—will be explored now.

In the mid-twentieth century, a perfect storm of medical technology began brewing, the effects of which we are still grappling with today. Physicians successfully began transplanting healthy vital organs from donors who had died under the traditional cardiopulmonary definition of death. By the late 1960s, transplantation techniques had been refined sufficiently that the possibility of saving thousands of lives was transformed into a probability—if only a way to obtain a large quantity of fresh, oxygenated organs could be found.

About the same time that organ transplants were becoming feasible, there was an explosion of methods and machines that enabled our hearts, lungs, and other vital organs to continue functioning even when our brains (or at least parts of our brains) did not. Ventilators, heart-lung machines, pacemakers, dialysis, and stomach tubes could now substitute for previously irreplaceable bodily functions. Interventions to restore breathing and heart-beat, such as cardiopulmonary resuscitation (CPR), defibrillators, and the Heimlich maneuver, became commonly practiced. We could, in short, be saved from cardiopulmonary death in an astonishing number of instances.

In most instances, modern technology restores life with little or no disability. The organ or pacemaker recipient can resume a relatively normal life. A dialysis patient can run a marathon. But there is a darker side to these medical miracles. The intended beneficiaries of medical technology can become its victims, trapped in an artificially maintained existence that seems undignified and perhaps even cruel. Many thousands of individuals whose breathing and respiration are restored slip into varying degrees of unresponsiveness—a coma or vegetative state—ranging from transient to permanent. Some may recover consciousness fully, some partially or intermittently, and some not at all. Predicting who will fall into which category is difficult. Doctors can provide well-educated guesses, but unexpected recoveries do sometimes occur, and the person labeled as permanently unconscious may not really be.

So which of these individuals, if any, should be declared legally dead? Their hearts and lungs still function, either spontaneously or with the assistance of modern technology. Under the traditional cardiopulmonary definition of death, therefore, all of them are alive. But does it make sense to classify all of these technology-dependent individuals as living? Could we not reconceptualize death to classify at least some of these individuals as dead—breathing corpses, if you will? Why waste thousands of dollars and scarce medical resources on such patients, especially those who are unlikely to ever regain consciousness? Why not save them from the potential indignity of a long, drawn-out death, while simultaneously creating an opportunity to save others in desperate need of replacement organs?

The solution devised to solve these pragmatic problems is called "brain death." The label is somewhat misleading, however, since various proponents and critics of brain death have used the same phrase to mean very different things, all of which will be explored in this chapter. Suffice it to say, for present purposes, that "brain death" refers to an irreversible loss of functioning of all or part (depending on the definition being used) of the human brain, as determined by various clinical observations or diagnostic tests.

The impetus for discovering, defining, and implementing brain death as a legal concept was medical technology. It was not just the development and widespread availability of ventilators, but the concomitant progression and success of various organ transplantation techniques, that ignited the passionate call for legal reform. The chances for successful organ transplantation are increased if the donated organs are as fresh—oxygenated—as possible. An organ removed from someone who has died in the traditional way (cardiopulmonary cessation) is not ideal for transplantation because the organ has been deprived of oxygen from the time of declaration of cardiopulmonary death to organ removal, a period that can make a significant difference in the organ's viability.[1] By contrast, an organ removed from a body in which the heart and lungs are still functioning is much fresher, since the organ will suffer no oxygen deprivation prior to its removal.

If the law insisted on clinging to the traditional cardiopulmonary definition of death, the benefits potentially reaped from organ transplantation would have been limited. If death were defined only as cardiopulmonary death, then a patient whose breathing was being maintained on a ventilator would be alive, and harvesting his organs would be a crime. To harvest the freshest organs possible, therefore, it became imperative that the legal definition of death be expanded. The medical community needed legal permission to declare an individual with a beating heart dead. The emerging concept of brain death filled this void.

As you can imagine, most people do not really understand brain death (indeed, many medical professionals do not either, as will be discussed below). They do not understand that a brain-dead patient who becomes an organ donor will remain pink, warm, breathing, and with a beating heart while his organs are being removed.[2] Perhaps, on some level, we can justify this widespread ignorance as for the best. Knowledge of the particulars of brain death and its relation to organ transplantation can be deeply disconcerting. If donors or their families really understood all of the particulars, the number of donations might drop significantly. Emotionally, for most people, there is a distinction between removing organs from someone whose heart and breathing have stopped and removing them when the person is still rosy-cheeked, breathing, and with a beating heart. The concept of brain death requires that we accept the latter patient as a corpse—a dead person whose heart, lung, and other bodily functions continue. This is the essence, and difficulty, of brain death.

Since the late 1960s, the view of the medical establishment worldwide has been that brain death and death are synonymous, and little criticism of this view was voiced or tolerated. But in the last decade, critics of brain death have been emboldened by advancing medical knowledge that undermines the assumed certainty of brain death as both a concept and a clinical diagnosis. The critics of brain death generally fall within one of two camps: those who think the extant definition of brain death is too conservative and those who reject brain death altogether. The former camp believes that brain death should be liberalized to encompass a greater number of individuals—specifically, those who have lost only partial (cerebral) brain function. The latter camp asserts that brain death, however defined, is conceptually incoherent, and accordingly advocates for a return to the traditional cardiopulmonary definition of death. But before we consider the views of brain death's critics, let us examine what, exactly, brain death is.

Recognizing Brain Death

The original movement toward recognizing brain death occurred in the late 1950s. In 1959, a group of Belgian physicians published an article describing "death of the nervous system" for unconscious patients whose cardiopulmonary function was being maintained by respirators.[3] Later the same year, French physicians coined the term "coma dépassé" (beyond coma) to describe respirator-dependent patients who appeared to be caught in a twilight zone between life and death.[4] These individuals had, by all previously normal accounts, a living, functioning body, yet isoelectric (flat) electroencephalograms (EEGs) that measured no discernible brain activity.[5]

The Belgian and French researchers' public discussion triggered more extensive examination of the phenomenon. In the United States, a substantial move toward recognizing brain death came in February 1968, when the Board of Medicine of the National Academy of Sciences (NAS) issued a report that endorsed the identification of donors for heart transplantation when there was "evidence of crucial and irreversible damage and imminent death" of the donor.[6] These criteria seemed to suggest that a heart could be removed prior to a declaration of death, yet undoubtedly the NAS board was trying, albeit in a crude way, to identify brain dead donors, who could provide the freshest hearts to recipients undergoing this risky new procedure.

A more explicit endorsement of brain death came later in 1968, when an Ad Hoc Committee of the Harvard Medical School issued a report that established criteria for what the committee (unfortunately) termed "irreversible coma":

1. *Unreceptivity and Unresponsivity.* There is a total unawareness to externally applied stimuli and inner need and complete unresponsiveness. . . . Even the most intensely painful stimuli evoke no vocal or other response, not even a groan, withdrawal of a limb, or quickening of respiration.

2. *No movements or breathing.* Observations covering a period of at least one hour by physicians is adequate to satisfy the criteria of no spontaneous muscular movements or spontaneous respiration or response to stimuli such as pain, touch, sound, or light.

3. *No reflexes.* . . . [T]he absence of elicitable reflexes. The pupil will be fixed and dilated and will not respond to a direct source of bright light. . . . Ocular movement (to head turning and to irrigation of the ears with ice water) and blinking are absent. . . . Swallowing, yawning, vocalization are in abeyance. Corneal and pharyngeal reflexes are absent. As a rule, the stretch of tendon reflexes cannot be elicited. . . . Plantar or noxious stimulation gives no response.

4. *Flat Electroencephalogram.* Of great confirmatory value is the flat or isoelectric EEG.[7]

The Harvard criteria for brain death (as they have come to be known) are still widely used today, despite some minor modifications that have been made over time.[8] What is critical to understanding the Harvard criteria, however—as well as coma dépassé—is that they describe a situation that today would be referred to as "whole" brain death, meaning all functions of the entire brain—upper (cerebrum) as well as lower (brain stem) regions—have ceased.

Whole brain death is distinguishable from "higher" brain death, which refers to death of the cerebrum (the classic squiggly "gray matter"). The cerebrum is the portion of the brain that maintains and controls the content of our thoughts, memories, and feelings.[9] It is the cerebrum, therefore, that many believe provides the capacity for conscious thought—the essence of personhood, if you will.[10] Individuals who suffer death of the higher brain are thus referred to as in a "vegetative" state because their capacity for reason and emotion has been destroyed. The most widely publicized cases in recent years—Karen Ann Quinlan, Nancy Cruzan, and Terri Schiavo—have all involved individuals who suffered from higher brain, not whole brain, death. But when medical professionals or lawyers speak of brain death, they mean whole brain death, not higher brain death. This is so simply because, thus far, whole brain death has been the only definition of brain death endorsed by legal regimes worldwide, including the United States. Following publication of the Ad Hoc Committee's criteria, it became clear that, if the medical community considered an individual with a nonfunctioning brain to be a corpse, the legal definition of death needed to be updated to reflect this new understanding.

The first legal move towards recognizing brain death came in Kansas, which in 1970 enacted a statute modeled on the Ad Hoc Committee's criteria. The statute offered two alternative definitions of death, causing much confusion and concern. It articulated the traditional cardiopulmonary definition of death, but it alternatively defined death as "an absence of spontaneous brain function."[11] Immediately after defining brain death, the statute declared, "Death is to be pronounced before artificial means of supporting respiratory and circulatory function are terminated and before any vital organ is removed for purpose of transplantation."[12]

The confusion engendered by the Kansas statute was attributable to the above-quoted sentence, which seemed to necessarily link brain death with organ transplantation. The conundrum was observed by Capron and Kass, who acknowledged that if X were *not* an organ donor, the only way he could be declared dead under the Kansas statute would be if he met the traditional cardiopulmonary definition of death. By contrast, if X *were* an organ donor, he could be declared dead if his brain stopped functioning.[13] The apparent use of a different definition of death for organ donors versus non–organ donors was particularly troubling, opined Capron and Kass, in the situation where X, an organ donor, is declared brain dead but then the potential organ recipient, Y, dies before X's organs have been removed. Since there is no longer an identified available recipient for X's organs, must X be declared alive again? Because the brain death definition appeared to have been adopted solely with organ transplantation in mind, the answer, to Capron and Kass, seemed to be yes.[14]

In response to the confusing duality of the Kansas statute, Capron and Kass proposed a model statute that embraced the two definitions of death— cardiopulmonary and whole brain—but specified how the two definitions interrelated. Specifically, the Capron-Kass model stated that death was "an irreversible cessation of respiratory and circulatory functions. In the event that artificial means of support preclude a determination that these functions have ceased, a person will be considered dead if . . . he has experienced an irreversible cessation of total brain functions."[15] Under this approach, brain death could be declared for anyone, whether or not an organ donor, but only if the traditional cardiopulmonary definition of death could not be used because cardiopulmonary function was being artificially maintained. The Capron-Kass model was embraced, with minor modifications, by the American Bar Association (ABA), the American Medical Association (AMA), and the National Conference of Commissioners on Uniform State Laws' Uniform Brain Death Act (UBDA).[16]

Unfortunately, the net result of this initial round of legal reform was a patchwork quilt that often contained a statute defining death as brain death, while simultaneously leaving in place the old common law definition of death (cardiopulmonary cessation). As a result, some courts expressed confusion as to whether the later-in-time brain death statutes unintentionally voided the earlier common law cardiopulmonary definition of death.[17] It accordingly became apparent that there was a need for a single, uniform statute defining death.

Defining Brain Death: The UDDA

In 1980, ten years after enactment of the original Kansas statute, the National Conference of Commissioners on Uniform State Law, with the approval of

AMA, ABA, and a President's Commission[18] (of which Capron was executive director), agreed upon the Uniform Definition of Death Act (UDDA), a model statute that, in the ensuing years, has been substantially adopted in all fifty states. The UDDA defines as dead anyone who "has sustained either (1) irreversible cessation of circulatory and respiratory functions, or (2) irreversible cessation of all functions of the entire brain, including the brain stem."[19] There are thus two distinct paths to death under the UDDA. A person can be declared dead when *either* cardiopulmonary function or brain function irreversibly cease. The definitions appear to stand independently, with no necessary relationship between them. A person whose heart irreversibly stops is dead, even if his brain continues to function for a short time. Likewise, a person whose brain irreversibly stops functioning is dead, even if his heart continues to function for a while. Once the point of irreversible functioning of either cardiopulmonary or brain functions has been reached, legal death exists.

There are a couple of important but potentially confusing aspects to the UDDA's definition of brain death. First, the UDDA accepts only death of the whole brain, not just the higher brain (cerebrum). As David Lamb puts it, the UDDA's definition of brain death is the "physiological equivalent of anatomical decapitation."[20] The problem with requiring the "entire brain" to cease functioning is that the "entire" brain technically includes not just the cerebrum and brain stem but also such things as the basal ganglia, cerebellum, and thalamus—all portions of the brain that may continue functioning despite death of the cerebrum and brain stem.

Defenders of whole brain death argue that the UDDA's reference to "all functions of the entire brain, including the brain stem" should be interpreted as placing significance on the word "functions" rather than the word "entire." This appears to be the position taken by the President's Commission, which suggested that continued activity in *de minimus* portions of the brain would not preclude whole brain death under the UDDA. Specifically, the President's Commission stated, "In measuring *functions,* physicians are not concerned with mere *activity* in cells or groups of cells if such activity (metabolic, electrical, etc.) is not manifested in some way that has significance for the organism as a whole. . . . Tests that measure cellular activity are thus relevant to the determination of death only when they forecast whether missing functions may reappear."[21] The commission's report thus emphasizes that

brain "functions" must cease, although the term "functions" is not synonymous with cellular "activity" that may continue after all brain functions have
ceased.

A related interpretive approach to whole brain death has been articulated
by neurologist James Bernat, who asserts that whole brain death should be
understood as occurring when all "clinical" functions of the brain have
ceased.[22] He has explained that whole brain death "does not require the cessation of functioning of every single neuron. . . . Permanent cessation of the
clinical functions of the entire brain, therefore, remains the best criterion of
death."[23] Bernat's approach is presumably designed to limit whole brain death
to those situations in which clinical—and by this he means bedside—tests
uniformly suggest an absence of brain stem function.[24] These bedside tests
for brain stem function will be discussed in greater detail in a moment, but
for now, suffice it to say that they are susceptible of ambiguity and variation
(as Bernat acknowledges).[25] Nonetheless, Bernat's principal point seems to be
that if these bedside tests for brain stem function are properly performed and
uniformly negative, whole brain death should be declared despite the fact
that some *de minimus* portions of the brain (whether higher or lower) continue to function. He takes this position despite its apparent conflict with the
UDDA's requirement of "irreversible cessation of all functions of the entire
brain, including the brain stem," and indeed, in the same article, he ironically
praises the UDDA as a "useful statute" with "unambiguous wording."[26]

Bernat is correct when he characterizes the UDDA as "unambiguous." If
one utilizes a plain language analysis, the UDDA's definition of brain death as
"irreversible cessation of all functions of the entire brain, including the brain
stem" unequivocally mandates three determinations: (1) irreversibility; (2) of
all functions; (3) of the entire brain. Whether one likes it or not, this is a very
conservative statute, allowing brain death to be declared only when all three
prerequisites are satisfied. All functions of the entire brain must have irreversibly ceased—not most functions of most of the brain, and certainly not "clinical" functions of the brain as measured merely by conducting bedside tests
of brain stem reflexes.

Bernat has suggested that the absence of a *de minimus* exception in the
text of the UDDA was merely "for the sake of brevity" and that language in
the commission's report endorses his interpretation of the statute.[27] Though
Bernat's interpretation may be both pragmatically useful and normatively

desirable, it is not consistent with the cautious language or intent behind the UDDA. The President's Commission's report itself does not differ or retreat from the model act's requirement that "all functions of the entire brain" must irreversibly cease. The report's language emphasizes and attempts to clarify what the commission intended when it referred to "all functions" of the brain by distinguishing between brain "functions"—all of which must irreversibly cease—and brain "activity," which may continue at the cellular (nonfunctional) level even after all functioning has ceased. In the words of the report:

> The phrase "cessation of *functions*" reflects an important choice. It stands in contrast to two other terms that have been discussed in this field: (a) "loss of activity" and (b) "destruction of the organ."
>
> Bodily parts, and the subparts that make them up, are important for the functions they perform. Thus, detecting a loss of the ability to function is the certain aim of diagnosis in this field. After an organ has lost the ability to *function* within the organism, electrical or metabolic *activity* at the level of individual cells or even groups of cells may continue for a period of time. Unless this cellular activity is organized and directed, however, it cannot contribute to the operation of the organism as a whole. Thus, cellular activity alone is irrelevant in judging whether the organism, as opposed to its components, is "dead."[28]

The commission's report thus clarifies that brain "functions" are not the same as cellular "activities," but it does not go so far as to suggest that the model act's requirement that "all" functions should be interpreted to mean "most" or "some" or "clinical."

Even assuming (for the sake of argument) that the commission's report language supports Bernat's position, it should not trump clear statutory text. The commission's report—like all committee reports, such as congressional committee or conference reports—was written principally by the staff of the commission, not its individual members. Busy committee members rely upon staff to write up the report that accompanies the text of their proposals, and they often will only briefly look over a draft report before it is published.

It is not uncommon for subtleties in report language to go unnoticed by committee members.

The law recognizes the potential disjunct between the intentions of the actual committee members (the drafters of the statute) and the intentions of the committee staffers (the drafters of the accompanying report) and understandably prefers the former over the latter. Conflicts between statutory text and legislative history are not uncommon, and when they occur, there is a strong presumption that the plain language of a statute expresses the intent of its drafters, and this may be rebutted only in rare and exceptional circumstances.[29] Put another way, "[W]hen the statute's language is plain, the sole function of the courts—at least where the disposition required by the text is not absurd—is to enforce it according to its terms."[30] Applying this presumption means that the UDDA's definition of brain death as "irreversible cessation of all functions of the entire brain, including the brain stem" should be implemented according to its plain language, since requiring complete brain death is not "absurd" but in fact consistent with the intentionally conservative approach taken by the drafters of the UDDA.[31]

A second interesting aspect of the UDDA is that it requires that whole brain death be "irreversible," a shibboleth that is perhaps better understood as an artistic interpretation of numerous facts than a fact by itself—in other words, more subjective than objective. The commission's report accompanying the UDDA does little to help clarify the ambiguity of the irreversibility requirement, other than stating that it is designed to keep the law up-to-date, allowing individuals to be declared "alive" if or when medical technology advances to the point where "all functions of the entire brain" cease but can be reversed, perhaps by futuristic brain regenerators or mechanical brain substitutes.[32]

There have been serious criticisms of the irreversibility requirement, mainly from those who question whether cessation of brain function can ever be definitively deemed irreversible. Paul Byrne, for example, argues that unlike physical destruction of the brain by something like crushing or burning, an intact head with brain matter inside has potential for some brain function, no matter how small or unlikely.[33] Byrne's point appears to be true on more than just a theoretical or philosophical level. Numerous reports have confirmed that patients who are clinically determined to be whole brain dead may exhibit variable neuroendocrine and intracranial autonomic nervous system (ANS) functions, such as regulation of blood pressure, insulin secretion, urination, and growth.[34] Similarly, some intermittent electrical brain activity, as measured by an EEG, may occur even after a diagnosis of whole brain death.[35] The possibility of continued sporadic brain functions therefore suggests an alarming conclusion: neither the death of the "entire" brain, nor the "irreversibility" of its demise, can be established in many situations. Accordingly, under the UDDA (as well as the laws of many other countries that have similar statutes), death should not be declared; yet it routinely is.[36]

So why does the medical community seem to give a wink and a nod to the legal demand for "irreversible" cessation of functioning of the "entire" brain? How can death be declared for a patient who still exhibits (or may exhibit, if given time) some small, discernible brain activity? The rationalizations are moral, pragmatic, and scientific.

On a moral level, many in the medical community—like those in the community at large—believe that it is not unethical to remove life support and harvest the organs of an individual who has lost most (but not necessarily all) of the functions of the brain.[37] This moral position dovetails with that of the pragmatist, or utilitarian, who sees little benefit in using scarce medical resources to artificially maintain someone who has only minimal evidence of brain function. And of course the individual with only minimal brain functioning likely possesses healthy organs that can be transplanted to save the lives of many others.

On a scientific level, those who support the current approach to whole brain death argue that the concept of death reflects a holistic view of mind-body integration—that is, death means death of the "organism as a whole" rather than death of the "whole organism." Viewed this way, both the traditional cardiovascular definition of death, as well as the modern whole brain definition of death, should be understood and interpreted in a manner consistent with this integration concept.

The integrationist approach initially received widespread acceptance in the medical community[38] because it was believed that a patient who experienced whole brain death could be artificially sustained for only a short period of time—typically only a few hours or at most a few days. Death of the whole brain was inevitably followed by death of the "organism as a whole," even in the face of vigorous application of life support.[39] If death is understood as the "point of no return" when critical integrative bodily functions fail, then death of the whole brain, like cardiopulmonary death, is death.

In recent years, however, new evidence has weakened the previously incontrovertible linkage between whole brain death and death of the organism as a whole. In over 150 cases reported in medical journals, patients who were declared whole brain dead continued biological integration for weeks, months, or—in one remarkable published case of a child who had contracted meningitis—over fifteen years.[40] These brain-dead patients "lived" a long time, and despite their diagnosis of brain death, continued numerous bodily functions that are often associated with living organisms, including the metabolism of nutrition and excretion of waste, regulation of temperature, maintaining electrolyte balance, functioning immune response, continued growth, and the production of sperm and eggs.[41] In several reported cases, brain-dead women have been artificially maintained for prolonged periods to gestate fetuses until a point of viability outside the womb—a bizarre situation in which legally dead mothers' corpses are being used as incubators.[42]

The continuation of integrative functions in brain dead patients has led some physicians to retract their earlier support for the concept of brain death. Notable among them is Alan Shewmon, a neurologist who has concluded that, precisely because a lack of integrated functioning of the organism as a whole provides the appropriate concept of death, he no longer views whole brain death as death. To Shewmon, the "point of no return" for bodily integration is the "sustained cessation of circulation of oxygenated blood," which he surmises takes twenty to thirty minutes in most cases.[43] Shewmon essentially reembraces the traditional cardiopulmonary definition of death, adding some clarification regarding the latency period required for a declaration of irreversible cardiopulmonary loss and explicitly rejecting any formulation of brain death.

For some, Shewmon's argument for a return to cardiopulmonary death represents a step backwards, at least from the perspective of expanding the availability of organ transplants. Shewmon defends his approach, however, by asserting that legal recognition of brain death "was in retrospect quite unnecessary, even for the utilitarian purposes [organ procurement] which historically inspired it."[44] He refers specifically to the recent resurgence of donation after cardiac death (DCD), in which organs are procured immediately following a declaration of traditional cardiopulmonary death.[45]

The growth in acceptance and performance of DCD, combined with expansion of possibilities for xenotransplantation (that is, using organs from other species such as pigs or primates) and living organ donation[46] have perhaps eased some of the pressure to vigorously defend the conceptual basis of whole brain death. Accordingly, Shewmon's call to reembrace the traditional cardiopulmonary definition of death has not been isolated. For at least the past two decades, higher brain proponent Daniel Wikler has asserted that whole brain death "makes less sense" than either cardiopulmonary death or higher brain death, because "defenders of the whole-brain definition of death have yet to make a convincing case, at the conceptual level, for equating loss of all brain function with the end of life."[47] More recently, Robert Truog urged abandonment of brain death and return to cardiopulmonary death,[48] declaring that "[t]here is nobody in the world of philosophy and bioethics who thinks brain death is a coherent concept."[49]

Compounding the challenges faced by whole brain death is a lingering lack of public understanding about what, exactly, brain death is. In a recent survey conducted by Laura Siminoff and colleagues, over 98 percent of individuals had heard of the phrase "brain death," yet only one-third understood that brain dead patients were legally dead.[50] A 2007 study conducted in Brazil likewise suggests that when individuals are given a scenario in which the word "death" is substituted for the words "brain death," their willingness to donate organs decreases by 20 percent. The researchers concluded that the drop-off in donations was due either to the individuals' lack of understanding, or lack of acceptance, of brain death as death.[51]

The public's inability to grasp the complexity of brain death is understandable. While the law itself is demanding and relatively clear—"irreversible cessation of all functions of the entire brain, including the brain stem," in the words of the UDDA—the medical community's implementation of this legal standard has not been consistent with the law's cautious approach, instead accepting diagnoses of brain death in situations in which some functions may indeed remain. The reason this is not resolved by litigation is because the UDDA also says that "[a] determination of death must be made in accordance with accepted medical standards." This language provides sufficient wiggle room to redefine "all functions of the entire brain" by disregarding some indicators of continued function. All of this is perhaps pragmatically understandable, as the diagnosis of whole brain death is complex, resource-intensive, and time-consuming. There is tremendous pressure to find a happy medium—the magical point where *enough* of the brain is dead that most members of the medical community (and the lay public) can continue to accept brain death. How, then, is a diagnosis of whole brain death made?

Diagnosing Brain Death

Even assuming that society can agree on a definition of brain death and its conceptual basis, one impediment still looms large: a lingering doubt as to whether brain death can be accurately diagnosed. If we lack faith in the ability of medical professionals accurately to diagnose brain death, we will worry about false positives (that is, individuals being declared dead when they really are not). If the risk of false positives becomes too high in the eyes of average citizens, acceptance of brain death, as both a conceptual and legal matter, will diminish over time.

Those who defend the concept of brain death have repeatedly insisted that no one has ever recovered after a "proper" diagnosis has been made. For example, the chairman of a Chicago-area hospital ethics committee, a physician, recently declared, "There is no controversy regarding when brain death occurs. That sentence is unimpeachably true. The criteria for brain death (synonymous with 'whole brain death' to include both the cerebral hemispheres and the brainstem) when properly applied have never resulted in anyone recovering after being declared brain dead."[52] Physician-ethicist Robert Truog of Harvard Medical School likewise recently proclaimed—confidently omitting qualifiers such as "accurate" or "proper"—that "there has never been a single case of a patient diagnosed as brain dead who has recovered consciousness."[53]

Unfortunately, such absolute confidence in the reliability of brain death diagnoses is unwarranted. Misdiagnoses have been made, though they rarely filter through to the news media. In 2007, the *Los Angeles Times* ran a front-page story about forty-seven-year-old John Foster, who was diagnosed as brain dead by two physicians at a Fresno, California, hospital. Preliminary preparations to harvest his organs began, when his daughter (a nurse) insisted that a third doctor, a neurosurgeon, be consulted. The neurosurgeon concluded that Foster was not brain dead. The daughter said that the physicians were "waiting like vultures, waiting for someone to die so they could scoop them [his organs] up." When asked to comment about the case, the chairman of the ethics committee of the American Academy of Neurology said that it was "one of those things that is pretty spooky when it happens."[54]

A similar story emerged in 2008, when twenty-one-year-old Zach Dunlap suffered traumatic brain injury after an ATV accident. The doctors in the Wichita Falls, Texas, hospital where he was taken declared him brain dead after conducting both clinical and diagnostic tests for brain activity. Zach heard the doctors pronounce him dead, but could do nothing to tell them they were wrong. Because Zach's driver's license indicated that he was an organ donor, an organ recovery team was flown in by helicopter and a nurse was instructed to begin preparing Zach for the harvesting procedure. Fortunately for Zach, his two cousins, both nurses, were in the room at the time. One of them had misgivings about the brain-death diagnosis, so he pulled out a pocket knife and ran it along the bottom of Zach's feet. Zach's feet responded, but the attending nurse said it was just a spinal reflex. Zach's cousin then dug a fingernail under one of Zach's nails, and Zach responded in pain, pulling his hand away and across his body. The attending nurse agreed that this was a sign of life, and preparations for organ harvesting were stopped. Five days later, Zach opened his eyes. And forty-eight days after being admitted to the hospital, Zach went home, substantially recovered.[55] Surprisingly, no major newspaper in the country reported Zach's story, though it did appear on national television.

Fortunately for John Foster and Zach Dunlap, a nurse-relative was savvy enough to notice telltale signs of life and bold enough to second-guess the diagnosing physicians. Not all patients are so fortunate. How many others have been wrongly diagnosed? We simply do not know, though cases like Foster's and Dunlap's are undoubtedly the exception rather than the rule. The rate of misdiagnoses of brain death is not known, so it is hard to say with any certainty whether the rate of false positive diagnoses of brain death is within an acceptable range. Indeed, as we have seen, just *admitting* the possibility of a misdiagnosis is hard for many in the medical community. To gauge the possibility of this frightening phenomenon, it is helpful to spend some time outlining how brain death is typically diagnosed.

As an initial matter, unlike cardiopulmonary death, which can often be pronounced by nonphysicians such as nurses or physician assistants (PAs),[56] licensed physicians must declare brain death in the overwhelming majority of states.[57] In the vast majority of jurisdictions, any licensed physician, regardless of specialty, can make a determination of brain death. Only a handful of states require that the physician declaring brain death have any sort of specialized training in brain-related fields such as neurology or neurosurgery.[58] As a result, in most brain-death situations, the physician who declares brain death has no special expertise in neurology. David Greer and colleagues recently confirmed this fact in a survey of the top fifty neurology and neurosurgery institutions in the United States (as assessed by *U.S. News and World Report* rankings)—presumably the most sophisticated institutions capable of making a brain-death determination—finding that only 42 percent required that a neurologist or neurosurgeon be involved in the diagnosis of brain death.[59] The researchers concluded that "[g]iven a technique with some complexity as well as potential medical-legal implications, we found it surprising that more institutions did not require a higher level or more specific area of expertise."[60]

Moreover, in the majority of states, the law does not require a second opinion; the opinion of one physician is sufficient for a legally binding diagnosis of brain death.[61] In Greer's survey, 71 percent of the top U.S. neurology and neurosurgery institutions required multiple exams to diagnose brain death, yet only 44 percent required that the examinations be performed by different physicians.[62]

The difficulty with diagnosing whole brain death goes beyond identifying suitably trained physicians. It also includes the difficulty of determining precisely which diagnostic tests should be performed. In the United States (unlike several other countries),[63] the law does not typically specify which diagnostic tests should be performed in order to declare death. This is true of cardiopulmonary death as well as brain death. Cardiopulmonary death thus can be diagnosed by various methods, such as checking for a pulse, placing a mirror or feather under the nose (indicating respiration), winding a thread tightly around a finger to check for swelling and discoloration (indicating circulation), or more commonly today, using higher-tech methods such as a heart monitor or stethoscope. The law does not mandate that any of these specific tests be employed, instead giving discretion to the medical professional to choose among available accepted diagnostic methods.

The same is true of brain death. In the United States, state laws generally defer to the medical profession regarding the method used to diagnose brain death. The UDDA, for example, states that "[a] determination of death must be made in accordance with accepted medical standards."[64] It does not specify what those "accepted medical standards" are, leaving the medical profession great latitude to articulate and implement practices that fall within a relatively wide range of accepted behavior. One notable exception to the general rule of professional deference is the state of New Jersey, which has enacted a statute requiring the promulgation of specific regulations to define more precisely what "currently accepted" medical standards are, including the criteria, tests, and procedures acceptable for a diagnosis of whole brain death.[65]

In addition to the Harvard Ad Hoc Committee's criteria for determining brain death (which is still considered by many to be the "gold standard" of diagnosis),[66] in 1994 the American Academy of Neurology (AAN) issued practice guidelines for the determination of brain death,[67] and both of these sets of guidelines certainly should reflect currently accepted medical standards. Unfortunately, like the Ad Hoc Committee's criteria, there is no legal requirement that physicians conform to the AAN guidelines. Indeed, Greer's recent survey of the top fifty U.S. neurologic institutions shows that there is disturbingly wide variability in adherence to various aspects of these guidelines.[68]

The general failure of the law to specify how brain death must be diagnosed is surprising, given the complexity of the diagnosis itself and the wide variation in practice among physicians who routinely diagnose it. Brain death, after all, is a much more subtle determination than cardiopulmonary death, and it involves more ambiguous situations. Unlike, say, checking a pulse, there is no simple, relatively fail-safe test for brain function. Although people seem to yearn for a magical machine that would conclusively confirm brain death without the need to resort to the more variable diagnostic tool known as the doctor, this unfortunately does not exist. Diagnosing brain death, when done correctly, involves a series of clinical (bedside) tests conducted over a period of time, sometimes supplemented with the use of confirmatory technologies where they are available and deemed appropriate.

One of the more commonly used of these confirmatory technologies is the electroencephalogram (EEG), which involves placing of electrodes on various portions of the head to detect electrical activity in the brain. A normal EEG shows waves of electrical activity in the brain; a flat (isoelectric) EEG is potentially indicative of brain death. The criteria developed in 1968 by Harvard Medical School's Ad Hoc Committee, for example, recommended using an EEG to confirm brain death.[69] Physicians still routinely defend EEGs as providing useful confirmation of whole brain death.[70] Indeed, a 2008 "Patient Page" published by the *Journal of the American Medical Association* and designed to be distributed to patients confidently proclaimed that "if brain death is present, the EEG will show no activity."[71]

The EEG is readily available and noninvasive, which may help explain its popularity, but there are serious doubts regarding its usefulness in determining whole brain death.[72] EEGs require extensive training to perform appropriately, and false positives and false negatives are not uncommon.[73] EEGs are subject to contamination from the electrical activity of other electronic devices such as respirators and monitors, and require specific sensitivity settings, accurate placement of the electrodes, and adequate monitoring time.[74] False positive electrocerebral silence may also be caused by shock and drug intoxication, particularly sedatives.[75]

These performance challenges aside, the EEG suffers from two significant weaknesses as a diagnostic aid for whole brain death. First, a substantial minority of individuals who are diagnosed as whole brain dead may, indeed, continue to register some electrical activity in the brain.[76] This should strongly suggest that "irreversible cessation of all functions of the entire brain" has not yet occurred and that a diagnosis of whole brain death cannot yet legally occur. Yet the medical literature is replete with case reports of brain death diagnosed despite such continued electrical activity.[77] The rationale seems to be that because brain death is principally a clinical, bedside diagnosis, the physician is never required to conduct confirmatory objective tests (such as an EEG) unless the bedside tests are inconclusive or inconsistent. If a physician makes the "mistake" of ordering an EEG despite having already made a positive bedside diagnosis of brain death, the physician should feel free to disregard the confirmatory test(s) suggesting continued function of the brain.[78] The second major shortcoming of the EEG's diagnostic value for whole brain death is that the EEG can detect only cerebral (higher brain) activity; it has no value in determining brain stem (lower brain) function.[79] Properly performed, a flat EEG thus has value in diagnosing coma or higher brain death—a vegetative state—but considerably less in diagnosing whole brain death, which by definition requires irreversible cessation of the lower brain (brain stem) as well.

Another measurement commonly used to assist with the diagnosis of brain death is cerebral blood flow (CBF), an assessment of the amount of blood (and hence, oxygen) that is reaching the brain. It is commonly accepted that a lack of blood flow for ten to fifteen minutes will cause death and liquefaction of the brain.[80] CBF is tested in various ways, usually involving the injection of a radioactive dye or isotope into the bloodstream and subsequent use of nuclear imaging techniques such as angiography (x-ray), positron emission tomography (PET) scans, and cerebral perfusion scintigraphy (CPS), which reveals whether the radioactive material flowed into the brain. A noninvasive method, Doppler sonography, has also been touted as having predictive value for whole brain death.[81]

Not all methods of testing CBF, however, can test blood flow to the brain stem (lower brain), and so like EEG, their value in assessing whole brain death is limited. Radionuclide angiography, for example, is relatively inexpensive and widely used, but can only assess blood flow to the higher brain.[82] Similarly, Doppler sonography is inexpensive and noninvasive, but it only assesses blood flow to the higher brain and is subject to false positives if the examiner is not well trained in its specific use for brain death diagnosis.[83] CPS and PET scans, by contrast, can evaluate blood circulation through the brain stem, but are much more costly than radionuclide angiography and therefore much less commonly used.[84] Likewise, four-vessel cerebral angiography, which involves direct injection of radioactive material into the brain, can test blood flow to the brain stem, but it is not commonly used in the United States because it is expensive, invasive, and potentially destructive of potential donor organs.[85]

Perhaps the most potent criticism of CBF testing is the same criticism associated with EEG—namely, the evidence of continued function even after a clinical diagnosis of brain death. Consider this: if cessation of blood flow to the brain means brain death (or at least is indicative of imminent brain death), this should necessarily imply that the opposite is also true—that is, that continued flow of blood into the brain indicates that the brain is *not* yet dead. Surprisingly, however, this is not the case. As with continued positive EEGs, physicians have asserted that an individual can (and should) be declared brain dead even in the presence of CBF tests that indicate continued blood flow to the brain.[86] The acceptance by some physicians that continued cerebral blood flow or electrical activity as measured by an EEG does not necessarily rule out a diagnosis of whole brain death is both counterintuitive and disturbing. Although perhaps motivated by a sincere belief that continuing to care for such patients is futile, it is hard to accept that positive results from supposedly objective tests of brain function could be effectively disregarded when they do not confirm the physician's subjective belief that a patient is brain dead. A disturbing hypothesis is that these confirmatory diagnostic tests (such as EEG and CBF) are hailed as objective confirmation of brain death when they confirm a prior clinical diagnosis of brain death, yet dismissed as false positive indicators of life when they do not.

A logical conclusion is that these technological confirmatory tests for brain death are of little value, regardless of whether they are used to confirm or reject a clinical diagnosis. This is somewhat ironic, since the concept of brain death itself is a byproduct of medical technology. It is medical technology that caused us to reconceptualize death to include brain death, yet it is medical technology that ultimately fails to give us confirmation of brain death's existence. In making an accurate diagnosis of whole brain death, therefore, doctors must rely more on clinical (bedside) observations, using old-fashioned judgment, attention to subtlety, and patience. Of critical importance are tests for spontaneous breathing and reflexes that are controlled by the brain stem.

Tests to determine whether a patient can still breathe on her own—so-called apnea tests—are considered an essential component of any attempt to diagnose whole brain death. Under the voluntary practice guidelines issued by the AAN, apnea is tested by disconnecting the ventilator for approximately eight minutes, looking for respiratory movements during that time, and testing the levels of oxygen and carbon dioxide that exist in the arteries just before the ventilator is reconnected. If the patient's carbon dioxide (pCO_2) levels exceed 60 mm Hg—or greater than a 20 mm Hg increase over the baseline carbon dioxide level—the apnea test is considered positive, and the diagnosis of brain death is supported. If the patient's carbon dioxide levels are lower than 60mm Hg, or if any respiratory movements are noted during the ventilator's disconnection, the test is considered negative.[87]

Despite the AAN's relatively specific guidelines, there is significant variability in the degree to which apnea tests are conducted. This variation is potentially dangerous, since turning off the ventilator, if not performed skillfully, may further harm the patient (most notably by causing cardiac arrhythmia and sudden drop in blood pressure). Indeed, one prominent commentator has lamented that "apnea testing has often been conducted without adequate precautions."[88] Greer's survey of the top fifty U.S. neurologic institutions confirmed that while apnea testing was required in all institutions except one, there was a disturbing variation in methodology:

> Of concern was the variability in the apnea testing, an area with the greatest possibility for inaccuracies, indeterminate testing, and potentially even danger to the patient. This included variability for temperature, drawing of an ABG [arterial blood gas] prior to testing, the proper baseline pCO_2, and technique for performing the test. Although a final pCO_2 level was commonly stated (most often 60 mm Hg), specific guidelines in a situation of chronic CO_2 retention, clinical instability, or inconclusive testing were commonly lacking. A surprising number (13%) of guidelines did not specify that spontaneous respirations be absent during the apnea test.[89]

Similar conclusions have been drawn by researchers who have surveyed apnea testing in other countries, including the United Kingdom and Singapore.[90] A recent study conducted by neurologist Eelco Widjicks of the Mayo Clinic revealed that, of eighty countries studied, only 59 percent required apnea testing using a target pCO_2 value.[91] In the 41 percent of countries that did not use a target pCO_2 value, approximately half required no apnea testing whatsoever, while the other half simply required disconnection from the ventilator alone without the need for any blood gas measurement.[92]

The variation documented in apnea testing has also been documented in another essential aspect of brain death diagnosis: clinical testing of brain stem reflexes. Perhaps the most widely tested and predictive of the brain stem reflexes is the pupillary reflex. The reflex is tested by shining a bright light into the eyes to see if the pupil dilates in response to the light. A nonreacting pupil (not merely an enlarged pupil) is strongly suggestive of whole brain death.[93] Another predictive reflex is the oculocephalic reflex ("doll's eyes" reflex), in which the patient's head is moved rapidly from side to side. A patient with a normal oculocephalic reflex will move her eyes in the direction opposite of the head turn; a brain-dead patient's eyes will move in the same direction as the head turn.[94] A slightly more complicated but reliable indicator of whole brain death is the oculovestibular reflex, which is tested by pouring ice water into the ear (the "cold caloric" test). If the reflex is present, the eyes will slowly move towards the irrigated ear.[95] Despite its predictive usefulness, the oculovestibular reflex is "often neglected in the routine neurological examination even of a comatose patient."[96] In those instances in which the vestibular reflex is tested, it is not unusual for the cold caloric test to be performed incorrectly.[97]

Other brain stem reflexes worthy of testing include the corneal reflex, or blinking response, in which a small piece of cotton is brushed over the eye to induce blinking; the audio-ocular reflex, in which hands are clapped loudly to see if the patient blinks; the swallowing reflex, in which water is placed on the tongue to see if the patient swallows; the cough reflex, in which suction is placed in the back of the throat to see if the patient coughs; the gag reflex, in which the pharynx is touched to see if a gag is produced; and the jaw jerk reflex, in which a thumb is placed on the patient's chin and pressed slightly to see if the muscles that close the jaw contract.[98]

The challenges faced by a physician testing these brain stem reflexes involve time, availability, and ambiguity. The greater the number of absent brain stem reflexes, the greater the assurance of the accuracy of a brain-death diagnosis, particularly when these clinical observations are confirmed by technological tests such as angiography or CPS. But of course not all brain stem reflexes are routinely tested. Sometimes, in the heat of the moment, the physician simply forgets to test certain reflexes. For example, in a study of patients declared brain dead at Los Angeles County General Hospital, researchers discovered that the corneal reflex was not documented in the patient's charts in an astounding 43 percent of cases.[99] Some brain stem reflex tests are difficult to interpret, such as the doll's eye (oculocephalic) reflex.[100] Others cannot be accurately tested under certain situations, such as when an intratracheal tube has been inserted, preventing testing of the cough or gag reflexes. And sometimes physiological phenomenon render testing unreliable, such as a dry throat hindering tests of the gag or swallowing reflexes, obstructions (for example, ear wax) hindering cold caloric testing of the oculovestibular reflex, or a spinal injury impeding testing of the oculocephalic reflex. Moreover, these reflexes tend to come and go, being present at one testing session, absent at another.[101] Testing therefore should ideally occur over a period of time, on several occasions, and results should be uniformly negative. Yet this ideal is rarely achieved.

If we lack confidence in the ability of physicians accurately to diagnose whole brain death, its continued acceptance as legal death may be in serious jeopardy. It seems the more we learn about the human brain, the less we know about the way it functions and its relationship to the rest of the body. What seemed incontrovertible ten or twenty years ago is being challenged with each new study. New doubts about the conceptual basis and diagnosis of whole brain death are requiring us to reconsider whether it is, as Alan Shewmon called it, a "bioethical sacred cow that must be reserved at all costs."[102] Or is it possible that we are on the verge of a new era, in which whole brain death will be discarded? If such a new era is indeed on the horizon, what will emerge to take whole brain death's place? The three choices available seem to be: (1) reembracing cardiopulmonary death as the exclusive definition of legal death; (2) retaining brain death, but narrowing it by defining it as death of the brain stem only; or (3) retaining brain death, but expanding it to refer to death of the higher brain, rather than the whole brain. The possibilities and problems posed by cardiopulmonary death have already been explored, so we will now examine the brain stem and higher brain death options.

"Lower" Brain (Brain Stem) Death

The argument in favor of replacing whole brain death with brain stem death is that the latter will inevitably lead to the former. A person whose brain stem dies, in other words, has lost the capacity to sustain function of the higher brain. Death of the brain stem is death, in the words of David Lamb, because it is the equivalent of decapitation.[103] Relatedly, Christopher Pallis defends brain stem death by asserting that all attempts to define death—including cardiopulmonary death—are grounded in the recognition that death of the brain stem inexorably leads both to a loss of consciousness (higher brain death) as well as of cardiopulmonary function (cardiopulmonary death).[104] The notion of brain stem death is thus touted as a panacea, capable of satisfying virtually anyone's conception of death. If death of the brain stem will cause both irreversible loss of consciousness (higher brain death) as well as apnea (ability to breathe), the argument goes, then brain stem death should satisfy both those who believe death means loss of the capacity for consciousness as well as those who believe it means the loss of cardiopulmonary capacity.

But of course proponents of cardiopulmonary death and higher brain death have not found solace in the concept of brain stem death. The higher brain proponents may admit that brain stem death inevitably results in higher brain death, but they do not wish to wait so long for death to be declared. If death means the loss of capacity for consciousness, why should we have to wait until the brain stem dies before death is declared? Higher brain death can occur much sooner than brain stem death—and indeed, those in vegetative states may never experience brain stem death at all. Moreover, as Daniel Wikler argues, focusing solely on death of the brain stem is misplaced because it makes the declaration of death hinge on a function that is technologically replaceable, much like cardiopulmonary function.[105] In recent years, emerging evidence has confirmed Wikler's assertion about the ability of technology to replace the homeostatic functions of the brain stem. As discussed in the previous section on whole brain death, patients diagnosed as whole brain dead (which by definition includes those without a functioning brain stem) have been artificially maintained for weeks, months, and even years.[106]

Cardiopulmonary death proponents likewise find no satisfaction in the linkage between brain stem death and irreversible apnea. Loss of cardiopulmonary function, after all, is what matters to the proponents of cardiopulmonary death. And it does not matter that cardiopulmonary function is being maintained artificially. As discussed earlier, it is the continuation of function itself that matters, not the artificial maintenance of the function—otherwise individuals with pacemakers or paralyzed individuals dependent upon ventilators would be considered dead. Precisely because cardiopulmonary function *can* be maintained—even after brain stem death—the proponents of cardiopulmonary death are not willing to embrace mere brain stem death as death.

Brain stem death also fails to satisfy those who are willing to accept the concept of brain death, but who wish to define it conservatively, so as to err, whenever possible, on the side of life. This is likely why jurisdictions in the United States adopted, through the UDDA, whole brain death rather than brain stem death. Whole brain death recognizes the critical integrative role of the brain stem, but it also mandates death of the higher brain as well. So while it is true that death of the brain stem will cause death of the higher brain, it is not until both portions cease functioning that we in the United States are willing to declare brain death.

The cautious approach evidenced by whole brain death has been followed by all countries that recognize brain death, with the notable exceptions of the United Kingdom and Israel. The United Kingdom's acceptance of brain stem death dates back to the 1970s.[107] Israel's embrace of brain stem death is much more qualified and recent, dating from a 2008 law designed to increase organ donation. Because most Orthodox and Conservative Jews do not accept brain death as death, there was great opposition in Israel to any attempt to legally recognize brain death. The compromise ultimately reached was that brain stem death could be recognized as death, but only in those situations in which the individual is an organ donor, and then only if the family does not object to the declaration of brain death. In cases where the family does object, the law makes it clear that the patient may declared dead only by reference to the traditional cardiopulmonary definition of death.[108]

The brain stem approach allows doctors to diagnose brain death without any need to perform confirmatory tests such as EEG or CBF, since most of these tests are not capable of ascertaining brain stem function anyway.[109] In brain stem jurisdictions, therefore, there is a greater emphasis on correct clinical (bedside) diagnosis, including testing for apnea and brain stem reflexes. But as we saw in our discussion of whole brain death, these clinical tests are sometimes difficult to administer and susceptible of wide variation in use and methodology. These shortcomings are of course not unique to countries that use a whole brain death definition; similar difficulties have been documented in Great Britain as well.[110]

"Higher" Brain Death

Some of the most forceful criticisms of the whole brain death approach have been voiced by those who support brain death as a concept but prefer a definition that centers upon cessation of functioning of the higher brain (cerebrum) rather than the entire brain. While a higher brain approach has not been adopted by the legal system of any country in the world, its proponents remain vocal and numerous.

The central idea behind higher brain death is that the higher brain, or cerebrum (or more specifically still, the cerebral cortex), is the locus of individual emotions, thought processes, and hence, personality. A loss of higher brain functioning, therefore, is the equivalent of a loss of life in the most pragmatic sense: a person who cannot think or emote is no longer "really" alive. The higher brain formulation of brain death thus necessarily hinges upon a judgment about the value, or quality, of a life without higher brain capacity. Most people would probably not *want* to go on living in such a vegetative state; they would prefer that all medical treatment be stopped so that they could die with dignity.

But notice what I just said: They would not want to "go on living" and would want to "die with dignity." This reveals an important distinction, one that is too often overlooked: there is a difference between defining *death* and defining *individual rights*. Many fail to grasp (or at least acknowledge) this distinction, because though it is of importance to legal analysis, it is not a particularly sexy topic when one is trying to make larger philosophical, ethical, or moral arguments about the nature of death itself. The critical point for our discussion of the law of death, however, is that how we legally define death is a question that can (and should) be analyzed separately from how we define our legal right to refuse medical care. The organization of this book reflects this important analytical bifurcation, with separate chapters discussing the definitions of death and the nature of individuals' right to refuse treatment.

Statements such as X would not "want to live like a vegetable" and should therefore be declared legally dead commit the sin of deriving a false conclusion from a true premise. It is probably true that most people today (at least those in Western countries) would not want to "live like a vegetable." They would not want their bodies to be artificially maintained when their higher brain has ceased functioning. If they could not think or feel, most people would not see the sense in continuing to live.

Advance directives such as living wills and health care powers of attorney typically reflect this preference, stating that in the event of incompetence, the patient does not want to have any "life-sustaining" or "life-prolonging" procedures provided. Advance directives thus come into play when a patient is deemed incompetent to make her own medical decisions—and, of course, a person who is unconscious (whether due to coma, vegetative state, or brain death) is necessarily incompetent. These advance directives are an attempt to effectuate an individual's right to refuse unwanted medical care, not an attempt to define death itself. Advance directives state that if A happens (loss of capacity to make my own medical decisions), I would like to exercise my right to B (withdraw unwanted medical care). They do not say that if A happens (loss of capacity to make my own medical decisions), I want to be declared legally dead. To the contrary: they implicitly recognize that as a prerequisite to withdrawing life support, the patient must necessarily be *alive*. Advance directives thus seek to effectuate an individual's right to refuse unwanted medical care; they do not pretend to provide a legal definition of death for all.

Conflation of the two legal issues—the definition of death and a right to refuse unwanted medical care—is common, perhaps because advocates of higher brain death also generally support liberalization of the right to refuse treatment to include a more general "right to die." If a person has a right to refuse life-sustaining treatment, the argument goes, he should also have a right to receive the assistance of a third party (for example, a physician, nurse, or loved one) in achieving the desired goal of dying. If one embraces higher brain death, therefore, one would believe that the appropriate response of the medical providers or loved ones of a higher brain-dead patient would be either to take active measures to stop the patient from breathing (for example, placing a pillow over the head) or to simply bury the breathing corpse. There would be no need to disconnect a ventilator in many instances, since higher brain-dead patients still have functioning brain stems that may enable them to breathe without mechanical assistance. The boldest proponents of higher brain death are unapologetic about this necessary implication. Roland Puccetti, for example, has declared, "[I]f the notion of burying a breathing corpse is repulsive, then I suggest we stop it from breathing."[111]

Advocates of higher brain death would not consider stopping the breathing of a higher brain-dead patient to be an act of euthanasia for the simple reason that such a patient, in their view, is not alive. After all, one cannot euthanize someone who is already dead. And Puccetti is correct in his observation that burying a breathing corpse should not be morally repugnant if we accept the concept of higher brain death, since individuals who have dead cerebrums may have intact brain stems and hence, spontaneous respiration. But for most people, the thought of asking health care providers to take active measures to either (1) stop a patient's spontaneous breathing or (2) ignore the breathing and proceed with burial is deeply disturbing. Puccetti may have intellectually and morally accepted the pragmatic consequences of higher brain death, but I doubt most ordinary citizens have, even if they believe that "personhood" is embodied in the higher brain.

So we are faced with a fascinating disjunct. One the one hand, most people think "personhood" goes when the higher brain goes. On the other hand, most people are not prepared to accept higher brain death as the legal definition of death. While these two statements may seem hopelessly incompatible—perhaps even irrational—a reconciliation can be surmised. Higher brain death, if accepted, necessarily hinges upon a belief that the higher brain-dead patient's quality of life is no longer sufficient to classify them as living. Their capacity for personhood—thinking and feeling—has been destroyed. The rest of their bodies may be functioning, but is there really anyone at home? To a higher brain-death proponent, the answer is of course no. There is no "person" any longer, so why not simply declare them dead?

But perhaps, in the minds of some people, a higher brain-dead patient should not be declared dead because of the subjectivity inherent in the determination. If a person can be declared dead when he lacks the capacity to experience the "essence" of life—thinking and feeling—then we had better be prepared (as a legal and ethical matter) to offer reasonable ways to verify this state of being. More specifically, if a loss of "personhood" is the conceptual basis for death, how can society implement this concept in an objective way? There is, after all, no real "test" for personhood.

Proponents of higher brain death have responded by asserting that the core concept behind higher brain death is consciousness, not personhood.[112] One of the leading proponents of the higher brain approach, Robert Veatch, has argued that "the debate over personhood is irrelevant" because higher brain death requires only "irreversible cessation of the capacity for consciousness"[113] Veatch selects the "capacity for consciousness" as his marker for higher brain death instead of "all higher brain function," or "all cerebral function" because he acknowledges that, as with the UDDA's reference to "all functions of the entire brain," there will often be *some* small degree of cerebral or higher brain function intact, as evidenced by EEG or other diagnostic tests. He also recognizes that specific legal reference to the brain itself—a biological structure—may become outdated because "in theory some really significant functions such as consciousness might some day be maintainable even without a cerebrum—if, for example, a computer could function as an artificial center for consciousness."[114] Under Veatch's higher brain formulation, it is the capacity for consciousness that matters, regardless of whether that capacity is biologically or mechanically generated. To paraphrase Descartes, "I [can] think, therefore I am."

Veatch defends his consciousness-centered definition of brain death by asserting that it "provides a bright line" to distinguish between those individuals who have integrated mind-body functioning and those who do not.[115] His conceptual starting point is what he calls the "classical Judeo-Christian notion" that life exists when there is mind-body integration—a self-conscious soul, seated in the mind, that animates its host body—and this leads him to the conclusion that "when, and only when there is the capacity for organic (bodily) and mental function present together in a single entity is there a living human being."[116] Presumably, then, according to Veatch, a body without a capacity for consciousness, or a capacity for consciousness without a body, would be dead, since it takes body plus mind (and by "mind" he means a capacity for consciousness) to equal life.

Veatch's conceptualization of life (and hence, his conceptualization of death) is problematic for several reasons. First, it is not clear what degree of bodily or cerebral functions must be absent before the necessary mind-body integration fails and hence, death occurs. Take, for example, the classic brain-in-a-jar hypothetical. If we could remove a person's brain from his body, place it in a jar, and sustain both the bodily and brain functions artificially (delivering oxygenated blood, and so forth), is there a living person anymore? If so, which entity constitutes the living person: The brainless body? The bodyless brain? Both?

Proponents of higher brain death have generally asserted that the brain in the jar, not the brainless body, is a living person entitled to all the rights that go along with that status.[117] If the brain in a jar constitutes a living person, then the human body is superfluous; its total loss will not strip a person of his living status. Yet under Veatch's formulation of higher brain death, it is the integration—the continued interdependency—of the body and the capacity for consciousness that constitute life. A brain in a jar, even if thinking like mad, would presumably not qualify as a living person, since the mind-body integration is clearly absent.

If mind-body integration is our basis for conceptualizing life, to what extent do we tolerate malfunction of either body or mind? At what point of severity, in other words, does physical or mental disability destroy mind-body integration sufficient to declare a person dead? If X is a quadriplegic, is there sufficient mind-body integration for X to be alive? Or does X only need a functioning head (eyes, ears, nose, and so forth)? Veatch may believe that the hypothetical brain in a jar could be classified as a living person if we could somehow create a mechanical substitute for the human body—perhaps robotic eyes and ears, arms and legs. This would be a logical conclusion for higher brain adherents, since it essentially recognizes the centrality of continued consciousness to life, while simultaneously admitting that physical disability (whether minor or major) will not strip individuals of their living status.

Second, Veatch's formulation of higher brain death has deeply problematic implications for those who suffer from mental disability. This weakness, of course, is not unique to Veatch: all higher brain death formulations must deal with this criticism. Take, for example, our brain-in-a-jar hypothetical, but reverse it—that is, assume there is a functioning body without a functioning brain. More specifically, since we are discussing higher brain death, we must assume that our hypothetical patient has a functioning body *and* lower brain (brain stem) but not a functioning higher brain. In the eyes of a higher brain proponent, a functioning body without a functioning higher brain (or capacity for consciousness) is of course dead.

But how much loss of higher brain function is required? All? Most? A critical portion thereof? If a patient has some *de minimus* higher brain functioning, would we still consider him alive? According to Veatch's "capacity for consciousness" approach, *de minimus* cerebral functioning would be ignored and death could be declared. Indeed, Veatch states that he intentionally chose a "capacity for consciousness," rather than "higher brain functions" or "cerebral functions" as his definition for brain death, in part because the latter two would not allow death to be declared when there are "isolated cerebral functions that most would not want to count" in assessing brain death.[118]

Veatch claims that his "capacity for consciousness" definition is *less* susceptible to the slippery slope than whole brain death by pointing out (correctly) that whole brain proponents "are already sliding along the slippery slope" by allowing a diagnosis of whole brain death in the face of evidence of continued brain function.[119] He also points out that the medical community's apparent agreement to "count" brain stem reflexes as indicative of brain function, but *not* to count spinal reflexes, is arbitrary because "[a]t most there are gradual, imperceptible gradations in complexity between the reflexes of the first cervical vertebra and those of the base of the brain stem."[120] He concludes that "[w]hatever principle could be used to exclude the spinal reflexes surely can exclude some brain stem reflexes as well."[121]

Veatch's assertion on this point may have merit in a biological sense, but not a legal one (at least not as the law currently stands). It may well be that distinguishing between spinal and brain stem reflexes is arbitrary because of the integration of the neurological system as a whole. But as a legal matter, it is clear that distinguishing between spinal and brain stem reflexes is permissible—even required. Whole brain death laws and brain stem death laws refer to death of the "brain," not death of the neurological system as a whole. If the medical community has determined that certain reflexes are mediated by the brain stem, this qualifies such reflexes as brain function, and they accordingly must be tested and found nonexistent before either whole brain or brain stem death can be legally declared. The law, in short, has already drawn this line between brain stem and spinal reflexes. While one may argue that the law should be changed to include the latter as well as the former, this does not mean that distinguishing the two, under current law, is sliding down a slippery slope. The slope legally ends, in other words, at the brain stem; no further sliding would be legal.

But while Veatch and other higher brain proponents may claim that their approach is less susceptible to the slippery slope than the whole brain or brain stem approaches, they do not address with any degree of specificity where they believe the line between life and death should be drawn in patients with higher brain damage. Are mentally retarded individuals "dead"? Are senior citizens with dementia disorders such as frontotemporal lobar degeneration (FTLD) or Alzheimer's "dead"? What about individuals with degenerative neurological disorders such as Huntington's or Creutzfeldt-Jakob disease? Are anencephalic infants (born without higher brains) "dead"?

Presumably, the answer is that the first three—mentally retarded, seniors with dementia, and those with degenerative neurological disease—are not dead because they still have at least some limited capacity for consciousness. But it is not clear why (or even if) these types of individuals have *enough* of a capacity for consciousness to count them among the living. In theory, at least, some of these individuals could reach a point where their capacity for consciousness is sufficiently diminished that Veatch and other higher brain proponents would no longer classify them as alive, particularly if they (or their families) had consented to donation of their organs. Indeed, as Veatch admits, determining whether someone has a capacity for consciousness "involves fundamentally nonscientific value judgments."[122] So why not classify at least some of these patients as dead, when their capacity for consciousness is so very limited, and their death could mean life for many others?

Most proponents of higher brain death do not publicly profess willingness to go down the slippery slope when it comes to mental retardation, dementia, or degenerative neurological diseases. But when it comes to anencephaly—a rare and fatal condition in which babies are born without all or significant portions of their higher brain—the higher brain proponents' pragmatism seems to have gotten the better of them.

Anencephaly is a rare condition in which the neural tube (the early brain and spinal cord) of a fetus fails to close properly within the first month of gestation. The head of an anencephalic baby (if born) will be substantially open, not covered by bone or skin. An anencephalic infant will have some portion of a lower brain (brain stem), however, so it accordingly may breathe on its own and otherwise maintain bodily integration, usually only for a few hours or days. Anencephaly exists in approximately eleven of every one hundred thousand births in the United States, though it is believed that the true incidence of anencephaly is underreported.[123]

Under the whole brain definition of brain death, anencephalic infants are living persons because they have at least a portion of their brain stem functioning. They do not satisfy the cardiopulmonary definition of death, because they are either capable of breathing on their own or can be artificially ventilated. Since anencephalic infants are alive under current law, their parents cannot donate their organs until cardiac arrest (and hence, cardiopulmonary death) occurs. By the time cardiopulmonary death occurs, the viability of the anencephalic infant's organs has substantially deteriorated.

Higher brain proponents, as well as some parents of anencephalic infants, have argued that adhering to the dead donor rule in this specific context does not make sense. Why should we wait for cardiac arrest to declare death when the anencephalic infant has no hope for consciousness and will inevitably die within a short time? Would it not make more sense to either declare these infants to be dead (despite their intact brain stem) or alternatively to make an exception to the dead donor rule, thereby allowing their organs to be harvested? One possible way to bring some meaning to the hopeless condition of these infants, the argument goes, is to allow them to give the gift of life to other children who desperately need healthy organs. This can only be accomplished effectively if anencephalic infants' organs are harvested prior to either whole brain death or cardiopulmonary death.

In the late 1980s, Loma Linda University Medical Center in California pioneered an ambitious program to use anencephalic infants as organ donors. The Loma Linda protocol called for sustaining the anencephalic infants on a respirator, allowing their organs to remain fresh. But sustaining the babies on a respirator made it impossible for brain death to occur in a timely manner, since the brain stem remained fully oxygenated. The devised alternative—delaying life-support measures until brain stem death appeared imminent—caused the infant's organs to deteriorate too much as the infant struggled to breathe. The costs of supporting these infants was substantial, and the vast majority of attempts at organ donation failed, mostly because once life support was begun, the infants never progressed to whole brain death. The Loma Linda program was discontinued after less than one year.[124]

The Loma Linda experience highlights the challenges posed by the current legal definitions of death. Loma Linda was trying to save lives and satisfy parents desirous of donating their infants' organs, but it had to walk a very fine line between accomplishing these worthy goals and satisfying the law. They were stuck between the proverbial rock and hard place, unable to harvest organs after cardiopulmonary death and unable to harvest organs after whole brain death. But the ethical implications of the experiment reverberated throughout the United States. While other medical centers have made similar attempts, none have been successful.

Loma Linda's failure did not deter those who believed that simply allowing these infants to die, without harvesting their organs, represented a failure of modern medicine. If the organs of anencephalics could not be successfully harvested under current law, perhaps the law needed to be changed. This was the position taken by the American Medical Association in the mid-1990s, when it formally endorsed organ donation by anencephalic infants prior to their death, effectively carving out an exception to the dead donor rule.[125] Public outcry against the AMA's position was so strident that a little over one year later, in December 1995, it rescinded its position.[126]

Recent advances in organ transplantation techniques have reduced the need for infant organ donors, and the declining incidence in anencephaly (partially due to an awareness of the benefits of taking folic acid prior to and during pregnancy) has likewise lessened the pressure to find ways to harvest organs from anencephalic infants. For now, it seems, the debate about whether to change the law to facilitate such donation has ebbed.

But the fundamental theoretical question remains: should individuals with no higher brain function (like anencephalic infants) be considered legally dead? For the higher brain proponents, the answer is yes. Indeed, anencephalic infants represent the paradigmatic case for recognizing higher brain death: not only do they lack a capacity for consciousness, they lack the physiological structure that makes consciousness possible. There is no need, with an anencephalic infant, to perform EEGs or CBF tests. There is no subtlety to the diagnosis of a loss of consciousness, because there is no cerebrum capable of functioning at all.

Opponents of higher brain death see anencephalics as representing the proverbial camel's nose. If anencephalics are not living persons (or alternatively, if alive, should be considered as "exceptions" to the dead donor rule), then why not also extend this rationale to infants with related cephalic disorders such as exencephaly (in which the brain is located outside the skull) and microencephaly (in which the head is very small)? Or why limit the rationale to infants with cephalic disorders? Why not also include those in a persistent vegetative state (PVS) who, by definition, no longer have a functioning higher brain? And while we are at it, why not also include those who suffer from disorders of dementia, such as Alzheimer's and Parkinson's, whose cognitive capacity has essentially died or substantially diminished?

Slippery slope concerns aside, it is difficult for many to swallow a mandatory legal definition of death that would seem so coldly utilitarian. When one sees an anencephalic infant—or demented senior citizen or PVS patient—one cannot help but instinctively acknowledge that they are alive. They may not have a high quality of life, but their basic humanity, despite severe disability, seems undeniable. It is this instinctive reaction to their biological functioning that ultimately prevents higher brain death from being widely accepted as a legal definition of death.

One final difficulty with higher brain death is worthy of mention. Even assuming we could agree on a definition of personhood or consciousness that would demarcate the dead from the living, it may not be satisfied by death of the higher brain. The lower brain (brain stem) is more important to consciousness and emotions than higher brain proponents would like to admit. For example, the 1981 President's Commission report accompanying the UDDA stated, "It is not known which portions of the brain are responsible for cognition and consciousness; what little is known points to substantial connections among the brain stem, subcortical structures and the neocortex. Thus the 'higher brain' may well exist only as a metaphorical concept, not in reality."[127]

If the lower brain is indeed important to the processing of thoughts and emotions, higher brain death, as a concept, is knocked off its philosophical foundation. A person with a functioning brain stem could have a rudimentary capacity for consciousness, rendering it somewhat odd for a higher brain proponent to argue that the person should nonetheless be declared dead. Presumably, higher brain votaries could escape the conundrum by arguing that some *de minimus* capacity for consciousness does not mean that consciousness exists, but once again we are left with a definition of death that appears to be sliding down a very slippery slope, in which the underlying concept of death (personhood or capacity for consciousness) has been ignored for the sake of reaching a result subjectively perceived as "correct."

Choice in Death?

As we have seen, current law provides two distinct definitions of death. The traditional definition of death—cardiopulmonary death—is still recognized and, indeed, is the basis for declaring death in the vast majority of cases. Brain death—legally defined as death of the whole brain—is resorted to in those tragic situations in which an individual's heartbeat and breathing are maintained by technology, but the patient has suffered massive brain damage. Because these patients represent both a strain on limited medical resources and an attractive source of donor organs, there is pressure to disconnect life support and scrape some ray of hope from an otherwise hopeless landscape. Not all people, however, accept the concept or trust the medical community's implementation of brain death. Many of these objectors, such as Orthodox Jews, base their objections on religious beliefs. Many others, however, just plain object.

Do we have a choice in how our death is declared? In most instances, the answer is no. There are a couple of notable exceptions. In New Jersey, a statute specifies that individuals may not be declared brain dead if brain death contravenes their "personal religious beliefs."[128] In such a case, death may be declared only when cardiopulmonary death occurs. Similarly, in Israel, brain stem death may be declared, but only if the family does not object. If an objection is voiced, death may occur only upon irreversible cardiopulmonary cessation.[129] The brain death opt-out laws of both New Jersey and Israel were motivated by a desire to accommodate religious objections to brain death. Neither one is intended to benefit those whose objections are ethical, scientific, or simply personal (for example, the "yuck" factor).

For the vast majority of us, whose religions voice no specific objection to brain death, we have no choice. If our brain dies, we will be declared dead, whether we like it or not. The law, after all, is designed for society as a whole. Very rarely (if ever) are we given the chance to "opt out" of laws that we find objectionable. Robert Veatch has argued forcefully for the adoption of "conscience clauses" such as the one adopted by New Jersey, with the notable difference that he would expand its availability to those who object to brain death as incompatible with their philosophical, not just religious, convictions.[130]

There is merit to Veatch's call for conscience clauses. Some argue that if we allow X to define his own death as cardiopulmonary death, we must also allow X to define death as higher brain death, severe dementia, or the loss of a finger. This is a rational argument, and it recognizes that, at some point, allowing individuals to customize their own laws results in anarchy. After all, each of us lives in an organized society; we are not just a random bunch of individuals. Our ability to sustain a government is severely compromised if each of us can customize our own unique legal definition of death. If individual customization were permitted, there would undoubtedly be confusion in the administration of justice. It would be exceedingly difficult to determine when to pay off life insurance policies, charge perpetrators for murder, and distribute property to heirs. So whether one views this as a societal harm that justifies the limitation on autonomy or merely as a pragmatic limitation to the full realization of autonomy itself, it seems reasonable to conclude that individual customization of death would not be realistically achievable.

But this is not to say that conscience clauses should not be given serious consideration, at least within limits. If we agree that the balance should generally be struck in favor of individual autonomy, then laws that give individuals a choice among existing definitions of death are rationally defensible. In theory, we could allow individuals to select from the four main definitions that have been widely discussed and embraced: (1) cardiopulmonary death, (2) whole brain death, (3) brain stem death, and (4) higher brain death. Explicit legal endorsement of the availability of these choices would more meaningfully effectuate the constitutional and common law rights to autonomy and privacy that already underlie our acceptance of advance directives.

Oddly, legal recognition of advance directives and the right to refuse medical treatment have created a conceptualization of autonomy as a one-way street that flows only in the direction of death. If you do not wish to have life-sustaining treatment provided, advance directives and/or the right to refuse medical treatment can step in and allow you to die. If you think that living like a "vegetable" (higher brain death) is not a life worth living, the law has provided these mechanisms to implement your preferences.

Yet the opposite side of the coin is not true: neither advance directives nor the right to refuse treatment will let individuals opt out of the mandatory imposition of a legal definition of death that they find deeply objectionable. If an individual is diagnosed as brain dead, no advance directive in the world can stop the medical professionals from pulling the plug. The law declares the brain-dead person dead. There is no further obligation to render any care, no matter how abhorrent the idea of pulling the plug may be, either to the patient or his family. Neither the right to refuse medical treatment nor advance directives can give an individual the autonomy to choose a definition of death that excludes whole brain death. In this particular instance, individual autonomy has been subsumed by a legal rule that imposes death.

Legal recognition of advance directives and the right to refuse medical treatment (topics that will be discussed in detail in the next chapter) are good first steps towards recognizing individual autonomy when it comes to death, but they stop short of full autonomy. It is therefore salient to ask: why not finish the job by making the autonomy complete, allowing individuals to choose their own definition of death, or at least to choose from among the four most commonly accepted ways to define death? If one wishes to be even more cautious, one could simply allow individuals to opt out of brain death (as is currently permitted in some states for religious reasons), since it is brain death that seems most controversial and objectionable to some. It would be

relatively easy to permit individuals to choose from among the four definitions or to opt out of brain death, using such things as advance directives or
indicators on driver's licenses. But the medical community has concluded
that only cardiopulmonary cessation or whole brain death is death, the legal
community has concurred, and the law has imposed this definition of death
upon us all, whether we like it or not.

5

Constitutional Death

[T]he wise man will live as long as he ought, not as long as he can. . . .
He always reflects concerning the quality not the quantity, of his life.
As soon as there are many events in his life that give him trouble and
disturb his peace of mind, he sets himself free. . . . He does not regard it with fear, as if it were a great loss; for no man can lose very
much when but a driblet remains. It is not a question of dying earlier
or later, but of dying well or ill.

—Seneca, *Moral Epistles* (c. 62–65 AD)

The Constitution does not speak of death or the dead. It
speaks of persons and people, and gives those persons various rights. Persons
are entitled, for example, to be free from governmental deprivations of "life,
liberty, or property, without due process of law."[1] The due process guarantee
implies that government may exact life as punishment, so long as due process
is provided. Additionally, the Eighth Amendment prohibits cruel and unusual
punishment, which has been interpreted to allow the death penalty in certain
situations.[2] Death, therefore, is constitutionally sanctioned as a penalty for
crime.

Beyond the death penalty, however, the Constitution relates to death in
its guarantees of liberty and privacy. So the question becomes: Do these
rights encompass the right to commit suicide? And if so, does the right to
commit suicide include the additional right to enlist the aid of others in
doing so?

As an initial matter, it is useful to explore terminology, which is often jumbled and imprecise when discussing asserted rights related to dying. First, there is suicide, defined as the intentional act of killing one's self. Assisted suicide, by contrast, occurs when a third party provides the means by which another commits suicide. For example, if Mary obtains poison from David (that David knows Mary will use to kill herself), drinks it, and dies, then David has engaged in assisted suicide. When the assisting party is a physician, assisted suicide is referred to as physician-assisted suicide (PAS). If Mary obtains a lethal prescription from Dr. David (that Dr. David knows Mary will use to kill herself), takes it, and dies, then Dr. David has engaged in PAS.

Euthanasia can be committed by either a physician or layperson, but its distinguishing hallmark is that the euthanizer takes a more direct, active role in causing the person's death. A doctor who euthanizes a patient, for example, may inject the patient with a lethal dose of pentobarbital or morphine. Euthanasia is sometimes bifurcated into voluntary euthanasia, in which the patient asks the third party to end her life, and involuntary euthanasia, in which the third party ends the patient's life without the patient's prior consent.

A related concept is withdrawal of life-sustaining care, including artificial hydration and nutrition. When life-sustaining care is withdrawn, there is no extraneous substance—such as a pill, intravenous drug, or bullet—that causes the patient's death. Instead, withdrawal of life-sustaining care is just that—withdrawal of medical intervention that is keeping the patient alive, such as a respirator, feeding tube, or dialysis machine. The medical intervention is stopped, and the patient is allowed to die of the underlying disease or condition.

Those who advocate for a constitutional "right to die" are referring either to assisted suicide, PAS, or euthanasia, as the law has long recognized a right to withdraw life-sustaining care. The right-to-die movement seeks not merely a right to take one's own life (as this is an option that is always available), but a right to seek assistance from a third party in achieving this goal. The third party's role can be either passive, as in assisted suicide or PAS, or active, as in euthanasia.

The Legality of Suicide, Assisted Suicide, and PAS

Suicide has been consistently condemned throughout history. There have been groups within societies—such as the Stoics and Epicureans in ancient

Greece and Rome—who believed that suicide was an acceptable way to exit life.[3] The opening quote of this chapter, for example, comes from Seneca, a famous Roman Stoic who touted the value of suicide. After plotting unsuccessfully to kill the Emperor Nero, Seneca was forced to kill himself, an event quixotically relayed by Tacitus in the *Annals of Imperial Rome*. Seneca's suicidal act was anything but ideal, quick, or pain free, requiring several deep cuts in his wrists and behind his knees, consumption of poison, and finally, immersion in a warm bath that suffocated him.[4]

English common law considered suicide to be "self-murder," a felony committed against the king and society at large. William Blackstone revealed that, to be convicted of suicide at common law, the defendant "must be of years of discretion, and in his senses, else it is no crime."[5] The fascinating implication is that suicide could be a rational decision—undertaken by someone "in his senses." If the defendant's suicide was the product of mental illness, it was not a crime. Blackstone clarified his meaning further:

> But this excuse ought not to be strained to that length, to which our coroners' juries are apt to carry it, viz. that the very act of suicide is an evidence of insanity; as if every man who acts contrary to reason, had no reason at all; for the same argument would prove every other criminal non compos, as well as the self-murderer. The law very rationally judges, that every melancholy or hypochondriac fit does not deprive a man of the capacity of discerning right from wrong; which is necessary, as was observed in a former chapter, to form a legal excuse. And therefore, if a real lunatic kills himself in a lucid interval, he is a felo de se as much as another man.[6]

A couple of points are worth noting about Blackstone's description of the insanity exception to suicide. First, notice how he tells us that, even back then, juries were apt to acquit defendants in suicide cases by liberally invoking the insanity exception (to a degree Blackstone finds objectionable). This suggests that punishment for suicide was often avoided. Second, the insanity exception was designed to relieve criminal responsibility only for the most egregious and clear-cut cases of irrational behavior resulting in suicide. Truly crazy behavior, in suicide as elsewhere in the criminal law, was a valid defense, because it established that the defendant lacked the requisite mental state to support a conviction. In the specific context of the crime of suicide, however, the allowance of an insanity defense implies that "rational" suicide was both possible and criminal. Ironically, in modern times, it is this very concept of rational suicide—not the insanity-driven suicide considered excusable under common law—that forms the basis for efforts to recognize a right to die.

One likely reason that juries during Blackstone's day were taking advantage of the insanity exception was that punishment for suicide was harsh, consisting of forfeiture of the suicide's property and an ignominious burial, usually under the crossroads of a public highway.[7] In 1651, the Common Bench in England, in the case of Hales v. Petit, explained that one who intentionally kills himself has violated the natural law of self-preservation, offending society as a whole and providing an "evil example."[8] The court also noted that, since the person who commits suicide cannot be punished by the court, the only pragmatic way to exact retribution for the crime was to confiscate his property.[9]

The common law's punishment for suicide seems severe by modern standards. To take away the property of one who committed suicide—and to deny them a proper burial in addition—tainted and harmed the innocent family members who presumably already suffered enough. But as E. P. Evans has demonstrated, it is difficult for modern minds to comprehend the nature of criminal punishment underlying these penalties. The premodern world was full of superstitions. There were devils in disguise everywhere, possessing animals, inanimate objects, and people. The widespread belief that evil was to blame for bad events led to somewhat ridiculous results, at least in modern eyes. Criminal punishment was viewed as a means to exact revenge and achieve expiation for evil.[10] This retributive focus of criminal law—referred to as *lex talionis*—had biblical (and even prebiblical) roots.[11] The Old Testament's vision of punishment (and hence, law) was a literal, tit-for-tat response to evil. The Book of Exodus, for example, says "If any harm follows, then you shall give life for life, eye for eye, tooth for tooth, hand for hand, foot for foot, burn for burn, wound for wound, stripe for stripe."[12] Similarly, Leviticus proclaimed, "Anyone who kills an animal shall make restitution for it, life for life. Anyone who maims another shall suffer the same injury in return: fracture for fracture, eye for eye, tooth for tooth; the injury inflicted is the injury to be suffered."[13]

One English embodiment of *lex talionis* was the deodand, an object for-feited to God after it caused a person's death. An animal that killed someone, a cart that ran over someone, or a tree that fell on someone all became deo-dands under English law, forfeited and often ritualistically sacrificed to atone for their sins, combat the evil behind the death, and appease God.[14] This no-tion of deodand puts the common law's punishment of suicide into perspec-tive. The forfeiture of the suicide's property was not intended to punish the innocent family members left behind, but instead to "prescribe an adequate atonement for a grievous offence, and in seeking to accomplish this main purpose, [the English judges] ignored the effect of their actions upon the for-tunes of the heirs or deemed it a matter of minor importance."[15] Likewise, ignominious burial of a suicide at the crossroads of a public highway (the symbol of the crucifix) was intended to ensure that the evil that had pos-sessed the body was dispersed.[16]

Beginning in the late eighteenth and early nineteenth centuries, however, American states began relaxing the common law's severe sanctions, due to a "growing consensus that it was unfair to punish the suicide's family for his wrongdoing."[17] In states that have incorporated the common law, however, some courts have concluded that the withdrawal of punishment does not mean that suicide is no longer a crime; it remains a crime, albeit without pun-ishment.[18] The modern attitude toward attempted suicide is that it, too, should not be punished as a crime, since someone who unsuccessfully at-tempts suicide is mentally unstable, necessitating empathy, therapy, and coun-seling, not jail time.[19]

It is not appropriate to characterize the American decriminalization of suicide and attempted suicide as reflecting some larger societal acceptance of suicide. Instead, the rationales proffered by courts for decriminalization sug-gest a pragmatic response to the ineffectiveness of criminal sanctions. As the Supreme Court of North Carolina reasoned, "So it must be conceded that suicide may not be punished in North Carolina. But in our opinion this fact does not change the criminal character of the act. . . . Suicide is none the less criminal because no punishment can be inflicted. It may not be indictable because the dead cannot be indicted. If one kills another, and then kills him-self, is he any less a murderer because he cannot be punished?"[20]

Assisted suicide stands in stark contrast to suicide and attempted suicide. While criminal law may have abandoned punishment for the suicidal person himself, the same cannot be said of the third party who assists a suicide. Dr. Jack Kevorkian's conviction in 1999 for second degree murder for fatally injecting Thomas Youk is a famous illustration. All states consider assisted suicide to be either a species of homicide or a distinct crime of its own.[21] Two states—Oregon and Washington—have special statutes that permit PAS, though they do not allow laypersons to assist with a suicide.[22] Euthanasia—where the third party commits the final act—is likewise universally condemned in the United States as some degree of homicide. Other countries, such as the Netherlands and Belgium, permit euthanasia under certain circumstances.[23]

In addition to the criminal penalties that may attach to suicide or its assistance, tort law is often invoked to impose civil monetary damages for acts causing the suicide of another. For states that still recognize suicide as a common law offense, the commission of the crime may operate as a bar against tort recovery, on the theory that someone who participates in an illegal act cannot be rewarded for it, though this rule is not universally followed.[24] In the majority of states, tort recovery is permitted for suicide, with the most common theory being negligence—specifically, that the defendant's negligent conduct caused delirium or insanity in another person that led to that person's suicide.[25] If the individual is sufficiently lucid to control his suicidal impulse, the suicide will be deemed an independent, intervening cause of death that relieves the defendant of liability. But if the defendant's acts create a delirium, whereby the decedent cannot understand the nature of his acts, or causes an irresistible impulse for the decedent to kill himself, a finding for the plaintiff will be sustained. The core idea is that the defendant's acts must actually cause the suicide; it cannot be the result of a preexisting, independent desire to die.

A recent example of the majority approach is Stafford v. Neurological Medicine, Inc., in which Robert Stafford sued a neurologist and neurology practice after his wife, Pauline, committed suicide. A couple of days before hanging herself in their home, Pauline had seen a copy of an insurance form that the defendants had incorrectly filled out, stating that she had a cancerous brain tumor. Stafford claimed that the defendants' negligence caused her to commit suicide. A jury agreed, awarding Stafford $200,000 damages. The trial judge took away the jury's verdict, finding for the defendants. On appeal, the U.S. Court of Appeals for the Eighth Circuit reinstated the jury's verdict, concluding that there was ample evidence from which the jury could find that defendants' negligent act created irresistible impulse for Pauline to kill herself.[26]

As *Stafford* illustrates, suicide, though decriminalized as to the person wishing to end his own life, is still considered a social wrong deserving of compensation, if for no other reason than it involves a tragic (and often avoidable) loss of life. The majority approach—which allows tort recovery for suicides due to delirium or insanity—authorizes recovery for suicidal acts that would not be considered criminal suicide under the common law. Recall that under the common law, suicide was criminal only if the person was "in his senses." A delirious or insane person, according to Blackstone, was not guilty of the crime of suicide because he could not form the requisite criminal intent. Modern tort recovery, by contrast, generally permits recovery when the defendant's acts cause the decedent to *become* delirious or insane. In this sense, modern tort law provides compensation for self-inflicted deaths that are not (or were not) considered to be criminal at common law. On some level, this should not be surprising, since civil law often provides compensation for acts that do not rise to the level of crimes. It also implies a broadening, rather than contracting, view of suicide as a cognizable wrong, and an attendant shifting of legal focus from the public (criminal) to private (civil) spheres. Suicide may no longer be a crime due to the pragmatic and ethical difficulty of imposing punishment, but the continued legal recognition of the crime of assistance with suicide, combined with broad tort recovery for acts that cause suicide, suggests that suicide is still considered a wrong.

The Right to Refuse Unwanted Medical Treatment

If suicide is wrong, why do individuals have a legal right to refuse medical treatment, even when it will cause their death? Is refusing life-sustaining treatment functionally the same as suicide? The law considers them to be distinct, though as we will see, the line between suicide and refusing life-sustaining treatment is a thin line indeed.

One of the most significant ways in which the Constitution relates to death is the right to refuse unwanted medical treatment. Under the common law, a physician who performed any operation or act upon his patient's body without the patient's consent committed an intentional tort—specifically, a form of trespass or battery.[27] An action for medical battery is still viable today in most states, on the theory that the physician-patient relationship is a consensual one, necessitating patient consent prior to initiating treatment.[28] In a recent decision of the Pennsylvania Supreme Court, for example, a triable case of battery was made out against a urologist who surgically implanted a penile pump prosthesis in a patient who had consented only to a different, revascularization procedure.[29]

Medical battery is thus like any other battery: a nonconsensual touching, except it is committed by a physician rather than a layperson. The theory underlying all types of battery is that the individual has a right to decide who may touch his body. The U.S. Supreme Court acknowledged this right in Union Pacific Railroad Co. v. Botsford, in which the plaintiff sued a railroad for negligence after she hit her head on the upper berth of a sleeping car. The railroad wanted to force the plaintiff to submit to a physical examination in order to confirm the nature and extent of her injuries, but Botsford objected, arguing that she could not be forced to submit to an examination of her body without her consent. The trial court agreed with Botsford, and the railroad appealed to the Supreme Court. The Supreme Court agreed with the trial judge, declaring,

> No right is held more sacred, or is more carefully guarded, by the common law, than the right or every individual to the possession and control of his own person, free from all restraint or interference of others, unless by clear and unquestionable authority of law. As well said by Judge Cooley, "The right to one's person may be said to be a right of complete immunity: to be let alone. . . . The inviolability of the person is as much invaded by a compulsory stripping and exposure as a blow. To compel anyone, and especially a woman, to lay bare the body, or to submit it to the touch of a stranger, without lawful authority, is an indignity, an assault, and a trespass."[30]

Fifty years after *Botsford,* in 1941, a deeply divided Supreme Court did an about-face, enforcing a newly enacted Federal Rule of Civil Procedure (Rule 35) that required that parties to civil lawsuits submit to physical or mental examinations when such examinations are relevant and supported by good cause. A five-Justice majority, in Sibbach v. Wilson, concluded that *Botsford's* reliance on the right to bodily privacy was a mere common law right, subject to statutory modification, and that Rule 35 had the same legal force as a statute.[31] A four-Justice dissent, penned by Justice Frankfurter, argued that the right recognized in *Botsford* was "not a survival of an outworn technicality. It rested on considerations akin to what is familiarly known in the English law as the liberties of the subject. To be sure, the immunity that was recognized in the Botsford case has no constitutional sanction. It is amenable to statutory change. But the 'inviolability of a person' was deemed to have such historic roots in Anglo-American law that it was not to be curtailed 'unless by clear and unquestionable authority of law.' "[32] The dissent concluded that since the physical and mental examinations contemplated by Rule 35 invaded the common law right of bodily privacy, Congress was required to act more clearly, by reenacting it through separate legislation.[33]

The Court's decision in *Sibbach* reveals something potentially important for our analysis of the right to refuse unwanted medical treatment: the *Sibbach* Court unanimously agreed that a right to bodily privacy existed, preventing any nonconsensual touching by a third party, whether layperson or medical provider. This right, however, emanated from the common law and was accordingly subject to legislative modification. It was not considered to be a constitutional right by any of the *Sibbach* Justices.

CONSTITUTIONALIZING THE RIGHT TO REFUSE TREATMENT: THE *CRUZAN* CASE

Botsford and *Sibbach* are important to understanding the Supreme Court's hesitation in declaring a constitutional "right to die" in the 1990 decision in Cruzan v. Director, Missouri Department of Health.[34] Nancy Beth Cruzan was twenty-five years old when she left a bar late one night, got into her old Dodge Rambler, and drove off the road. She was not wearing her seat belt and was thrown from the vehicle, landing face down in a ditch. Paramedics arriving on the scene administered CPR, restoring her heartbeat and breathing. But Nancy's brain had been deprived of oxygen for at least fifteen minutes, and she slipped into a coma. After about three weeks in a coma, Nancy progressed to a vegetative state. She was able to take some food orally, but not enough to maintain her health, so her husband authorized the insertion of a gastronomy tube.[35]

Four years later, Nancy's parents (her husband had since divorced her) petitioned a Missouri trial court to allow them to discontinue her feeding and hydration. The trial court agreed with the parents, finding that Nancy had a fundamental right under both the Missouri and U.S. Constitutions to withdraw medical treatment, including artificially provided nutrition and hydration. The Missouri Supreme Court reversed, recognizing a common law (but not constitutional) right to refuse treatment but concluding that termination of life-sustaining treatment for incompetent patients like Nancy required "clear and convincing evidence" that it comported with her own values and preferences. The only evidence regarding what Nancy would have wanted under such circumstances was a "somewhat serious" conversation with a housemate, in the year prior to her accident, that if she ever became injured or ill, she would not want to continue living unless she could live a halfway normal life. Given the paucity of evidence regarding what Nancy would do if she were competent to say so, the Missouri Supreme Court decided that termination of life support was inappropriate.[36]

The U.S. Supreme Court granted review of the case to answer the question of "whether Cruzan has a right under the United States Constitution which would require the hospital to withdraw life-sustaining treatment from her under these circumstances."[37] As it turned out, it was a question the Court had a difficult time answering. The five-Justice majority opinion, written by Chief Justice William Rehnquist, upheld the Missouri Supreme Court, holding that Missouri's decision to require "clear and convincing evidence" before terminating nutrition and hydration for incompetent patients was constitutionally permissible.[38]

The antecedent question—whether patients like Nancy had a constitutional right to withdraw life-sustaining treatment—was delicately avoided. The Supreme Court ambiguously stated that "[t]he principle that a competent person has a constitutionally protected liberty interest in refusing unwanted medical treatment *may be inferred* from our prior decisions."[39] After briefly discussing those prior decisions, the Court declared, "Although we think the logic of the cases discussed above would embrace such a liberty interest, the dramatic consequences involved in refusal of such treatment would inform the inquiry as to whether the deprivation of that interest is constitutionally permissible. *But for purposes of this case we assume* that the United States Constitution would grant a competent person a constitutionally protected right to refuse lifesaving hydration and nutrition."[40]

The *Cruzan* majority's language is remarkable. It assumes, without actually deciding, that there is a constitutionally protected liberty interest—grounded in the Due Process Clause—that permits individuals to refuse medical treatment, including life-sustaining treatment, and further including nutrition and hydration. In one swoop, the Court simply assumes away the critical question posed by the case. This bizarre behavior leads one to wonder: Why merely "assume" such a right exists, only for purposes of the present case? Why not instead *declare* that it exists? By failing to be more declarative, the majority opinion caused a cloud of doubt to form, leaving lawyers, academics, and medical providers scratching their heads over the carefully chosen, amorphous language.

Another remarkable aspect of the *Cruzan* majority's language is its subtle, but critical, limitation of the assumed right to competent persons. The assumed right to refuse treatment, in other words, did not extend to incompetent persons such as Nancy Cruzan. The Court was extremely careful to avoid any implication that such a constitutional right survived incompetency, saying:

> Petitioners [Cruzan's parents] go on to assert that an incompetent person should possess the same right in this respect as is possessed by a competent person. . . . The difficulty with petitioner's claim is that in a sense it begs the question: An incompetent person is not able to make an informed and voluntary choice to exercise a hypothetical right to refuse treatment or any other right. Such a "right" must be exercised for her, if at all, by some sort of surrogate. Here, Missouri . . . has established a procedural safeguard to assure that the action of the surrogate conforms as best it may to the wishes expressed by the patient while competent. Missouri requires that the evidence of the incompetent's wishes as to the withdrawal of treatment be proved by clear and convincing evidence. The question, then, is whether the United States Constitution forbids the establishment of this procedural requirement by the State. We hold that it does not.[41]

Again notice the majority's waffling language, describing the right as "hypothetical" and placing the word "right" within quotation marks, emphasizing its undecided status. Beyond this, notice that the Court has not agreed with the notion that any such right to refuse unwanted treatment extends to incompetent patients like Nancy. Instead, the Court arduously avoids the issue by converting it from, "Do incompetents also have such a right?" to "May states enact procedures to protect the rights of incompetents?" This is an important intellectual move for the *Cruzan* Court to make, as it allows the majority to continue shifting focus away from the right itself to the ability of states to protect vulnerable incompetent patients. It is as if the Court were saying, "We'll assume the right to refuse unwanted treatment exists, at least as to competent persons. As to incompetent persons, we need not decide whether they also have this right, since Missouri has given them the right but enacted procedural safeguards to ensure that the right is exercised appropriately. There is nothing constitutionally wrong with Missouri enacting such procedures to protect incompetent people."

The Court then analyzed Missouri's interests in protecting the rights of incompetent people such as Nancy and other vegetative patients. It noted that Missouri's heightened evidentiary standard protected the right to "life" guaranteed by the Due Process Clause, providing more demanding proof before incompetents' lives could be ended by withdrawal of medical treatment.[42] In the eyes of the *Cruzan* majority, therefore, the case involved not merely the word "liberty" in the Due Process Clause, but also the competing word "life." In Missouri's attempt to balance both the liberty of patients to refuse unwanted treatment and the right to governmental protection of life, the majority believed the clear and convincing evidence rule was constitutionally permissible. Because Nancy Cruzan and other incompetent patients cannot tell the courts what they want, the Missouri approach ensured that, when the evidence was unclear regarding their wishes, the law would err on the side of protecting their lives.

One of the five Justices who joined the majority opinion in *Cruzan* was Justice Sandra O'Connor, who penned a separate concurrence to "clarify" why she agreed that a constitutionally protected liberty interest to refuse treatment "may be inferred" from the Court's prior decisions.[43] Specifically, O'Connor relied on the Court's prior Fourth Amendment cases, which have invalidated some forcible intrusions into a criminal suspect's body as constituting "unreasonable" searches and seizures. For example, O'Connor cites *Schmerber v. California*, a case in which the police ordered a blood sample taken to test the blood alcohol level of an individual involved in a car accident who appeared inebriated and smelled of alcohol.[44] The defendant, Schmerber, raised numerous constitutional objections to the forcible testing of his blood, including due process and the Fourth Amendment.

Regarding Schmerber's Fourth Amendment claim, the Court asserted that the "overriding function of the Fourth Amendment is to protect personal privacy and dignity against unwarranted intrusion by the State" and agreed that the blood test was a "search" within the meaning of the Amendment.[45] The Court excused the officer's failure to obtain a warrant prior to the blood test, concluding that the body's metabolism of alcohol created an emergency situation that threatened the destruction of critical evidence of intoxication.[46] Moreover, given that the blood test involved "virtually no risk, trauma, or pain" and was performed by a physician in a hospital setting, the *Schmerber* Court concluded that the search was reasonable under the Fourth Amendment.[47]

Another Fourth Amendment case cited by O'Connor in her *Cruzan* concurrence is Winston v. Lee, a case involving a state's request to surgically remove a bullet lodged in the collarbone of a robbery suspect. The *Winston* Court agreed that the proposed surgery constituted an unreasonable search and seizure, concluding that on balance, the risk and invasive nature of the surgery outweighed the state's need for the evidence, since there was "substantial additional evidence" that the defendant was the robber.[48]

O'Connor's reliance in *Cruzan* on the Court's Fourth Amendment jurisprudence is misplaced. The Fourth Amendment is not the same as the Due Process Clause, which was the basis of Cruzan's constitutional claim. The Fourth Amendment states, "The right of the people to be secure in their persons, houses, papers, and effects, against unreasonable searches and seizures, shall not be violated. . . ." By its plain terms, then, the Fourth Amendment grants all persons a right to be secure in their "persons" against unreasonable searches and seizures. There is no need for an inferential leap here: the right to bodily security in the event of governmental searches and seizures is express, and the standard for ascertaining the violation of that right is clearly articulated ("unreasonable"). Implying a similar—or even broader—right to bodily security in the word "liberty" of the Due Process Clause is more challenging, requiring the Court to not only ascribe meaning to the generic term "liberty" but also to articulate a standard for determining when such liberty has been infringed.

This is not to say that no such substantive liberty exists. Rather, my point is simply that borrowing the Fourth Amendment's right to protection against unreasonable searches and seizures as the basis for recognizing a right to refuse medical treatment under the Due Process Clause is a bit like borrowing sugar to build a house. Sugar is necessary for baking cookies, but it will not help with home construction. Likewise, Fourth Amendment case law is obviously necessary for understanding the meaning of the specific language of the Fourth Amendment, but it tells us nothing about the substance of the word "liberty" as it appears in the Due Process Clause. It is for this reason, presumably, that the *Cruzan* majority, unlike Justice O'Connor, never mentioned the Court's prior Fourth Amendment case law.

Fortunately, there are salient due process cases to help guide consideration of an asserted liberty to refuse medical treatment. Perhaps the earliest case attempting to define the parameters of liberty in the context of forced medical treatment is the Supreme Court's 1905 opinion in Jacobson v. Massachusetts.[49] *Jacobson* involved a Massachusetts law that allowed cities and towns to require mandatory, free vaccination of adults when "necessary for the public health or safety." Pursuant to this statute, the city of Cambridge adopted a regulation requiring smallpox vaccinations for all residents over the age of twenty-one. Jacobson refused to be vaccinated, citing concerns about the risks involved in vaccinations generally. He claimed, among other things, that the statute violated his right to liberty under the Due Process Clause. Specifically, Jacobson asserted that forced vaccinations were "hostile to the inherent right of every freeman to care for his own body and health in such a way as to him seems best; and that the execution of such a law against one who objects to vaccination, no matter for what reason, is nothing short of an assault upon his person."[50]

The *Jacobson* Court denied that forced vaccination per se violated an individual's liberty, stating, "[T]he liberty secured by the Constitution of the United States to every person within its jurisdiction does not import an absolute right in each person to be, at all times and in all circumstances, wholly freed from restraint. There are manifold restraints to which every person is necessarily subject for the common good. . . . Real liberty for all could not exist under the operation of a principle which recognizes the right of each individual person to use his own, whether in respect of his person or his property, regardless of the injury that may be done to others."[51] Because mandatory vaccination was necessary to protect the community from "an epidemic of disease which threatens the safety of its members," the *Jacobson* Court concluded that no infringement of constitutional liberty had occurred under these circumstances.[52]

The *Jacobson* opinion does not deny the existence of a liberty to choose which medical treatments to which one submits, but it counsels that such a liberty must give way when necessary to protect the safety of the community. Because the individual's exercise of liberty—refusing vaccination—presents a reasonable risk of harm to others, it is outweighed by the state's interest in protecting them. Such externally harmful exercises of liberty thus fall outside the ambit of due process protection.

A trilogy of forced treatment due process cases from the 1950s and 1960s are likewise instructive. Recall that the *Schmerber* (blood alcohol test) case involved both Fourth Amendment and due process claims. We have already learned that the Supreme Court denied Schmerber's Fourth Amendment claim, but it denied his due process claim as well. In doing so, the Court relied exclusively on its earlier decision in Breithaupt v. Abram, another drunk driving accident case involving forcible blood withdrawal from an arrestee. Breithaupt had argued that forcing him to submit to a blood test while unconscious "shocked the conscious" and therefore violated his liberty under the Due Process Clause.[53] The only factual difference between *Breithaupt* and Schmerber's situation was that Breithaupt was unconscious at the time blood was drawn and therefore had no chance to object. The *Schmerber* Court found this difference irrelevant, concluding (as had the *Breithaupt* Court), that the blood withdrawal did not deprive the defendant of liberty as guaranteed by due process.[54]

The standard Breithaupt argued should be invoked to analyze due process claims—state action that "shocks the conscious"—came from an earlier case, Rochin v. California, that is also useful for understanding liberty in the context of forced medical treatment. In *Rochin,* the police received a tip that someone at Rochin's house was selling narcotics. They went to Rochin's house, found him in the bedroom, and saw two capsules lying on the nightstand next to his bed. Rochin grabbed the capsules and swallowed them. The police tried to force Rochin's mouth open to extract the capsules, to no avail. They took Rochin to a nearby hospital, where they ordered doctors to pump Rochin's stomach against his will. The capsules containing morphine were recovered, and Rochin was convicted of violating California's drug laws.[55] Rochin challenged his conviction, arguing that the police officers' conduct violated his rights under the Due Process Clause.

Unlike *Breithaupt* and *Schmerber,* which concluded that due process had not been violated, the *Rochin* Court unanimously found a violation. In reaching this conclusion, the *Rochin* Court asserted, "This is conduct that shocks the conscience. Illegally breaking into the privacy of the petitioner, the struggle to open his mouth and remove what was there, the forcible extraction of his stomach's contents—this course of proceedings by agents of government to obtain evidence is bound to offend even hardened sensibilities. They are methods too close to the rack and the screw to permit of constitutional differentiation."[56] Under the totality of these circumstances, the *Rochin* Court thought that the "sense of justice" protected by the Due Process Clause had been violated.[57]

The *Rochin-Breithaupt-Schmerber* trilogy echoes the vision of liberty first articulated in *Jacobson*. All four cases suggest that, while there may be a liberty interest in refusing unwanted medical treatment or intervention, the interest is not absolute but is necessarily tempered when it harms others or the legitimate interests of society at large. This interpretation is bolstered by more recent cases involving involuntary commitment and forced administration of psychotropic medications for prisoners. For example, in Youngberg v. Romeo, the Supreme Court acknowledged that involuntarily committed individuals retain "liberty interests in safety and freedom from bodily restraint" yet cautioned that "these interests are not absolute." In determining whether state actions infringe liberty interests, the *Youngberg* Court stated, "In determining whether a substantive right protected by the Due Process Clause has been violated, it is necessary to balance the liberty of the individual and the demands of an organized society. In seeking this balance in other cases, the Court has weighed the individual's interest in liberty against the State's asserted reasons for restraining individual liberty."[58] Similarly, in Washington v. Harper, the Court agreed that a state prisoner had "a significant liberty interest in avoiding the unwanted administration of antipsychotic drugs under the Due Process Clause of the Fourteenth Amendment."[59] Yet in upholding the state law permitting forcible administration, the *Harper* Court agreed that an individual's liberty interests must be weighed against competing state interests.[60]

The due process cases do not establish a liberty interest *simpliciter* to do what one wishes with one's own body, but they do establish that, under the right set of facts, an individual's liberty to decide what medical treatments to undergo can outweigh the state's asserted interests. As the *Cruzan* majority stated, a liberty interest to refuse unwanted medical treatment can be reasonably inferred, though it must be balanced against the state's interests in any given case. Global predictions as to outcome are therefore exceedingly difficult to make, as each assertion of liberty, as well as each assertion of state reasons for restricting it, will vary from case to case. Indeed, this point was made by the *Rochin* Court: "We are not unmindful that hypothetical situations can be conjured up, shading imperceptibly from the circumstances of this case and by gradations producing practical differences despite seemingly logical extensions. But the Constitution is 'intended to preserve practical and substantial rights, not to maintain theories.'"[61]

The difficulty of articulating *per se* rights, in the context of a balancing test, may help explain why the *Cruzan* Court merely assumed the existence of a liberty interest in refusing medical treatment, focusing its energy instead on the state's reasons for restricting that liberty. After all, why bother declaring that individuals have a liberty to do X, when you believe that X is outweighed by the state's interests in Y and Z? Under such circumstances, it is intellectually smoother to avoid X altogether and go straight to Y and Z. Moreover, the *Cruzan* majority may have avoided making a declarative statement about a liberty to refuse unwanted medical treatment because doing so would open a rather large can of worms. If the Court declares (rather than assumes) a right to refuse unwanted medical treatment, even when life-sustaining, would it also be reasonable to assume that this right implies a right to kill yourself—in other words, a right to die? Even if this right would need to be balanced against competing state interests, the acknowledgment of the right itself would ignite a wave of litigation to discover the right's logical end. For example, one of the first questions to be resolved regarding the assumed right to refuse medical treatment was whether it survived incompetency.

EXTENDING THE RIGHT TO INCOMPETENT PATIENTS

Once patients become incompetent and can no longer tell us whether they want continued treatment, can surrogates make the decision on their behalf?

If so, who qualifies as a proper surrogate? A court-appointed guardian? A family member? A close friend?

While Justice Rehnquist's majority opinion in *Cruzan* carefully side-stepped these questions, there arguably was a majority of Justices—four dissenters, plus Justice O'Connor in concurrence—that agreed that a liberty to refuse unwanted medical treatment survived incompetency.[62] Justice O'Connor, holding the balance of power between two competing pluralities, was outspoken on the means to effectuate the right on behalf of incompetent patients. In her words, "I also write separately to emphasize that the Court does not today decide the issue whether a State must also give effect to the decisions of a surrogate decisionmaker. In my view, such a duty may well be constitutionally required to protect the patient's liberty interest in refusing medical treatment."[63] It is clear from this statement that Justice O'Connor believed the liberty to refuse medical treatment should extend to incompetent individuals, since permitting surrogates to make treatment decisions "may well be constitutionally required" to effectuate this right. O'Connor expressed particular concern that some states did not allow surrogate decision making, permitting only living wills to be used as evidence of the incompetent patient's wishes. Since most people do not write living wills, O'Connor reasoned that an incompetent patient's right to refuse medical treatment would often be frustrated by such parsimonious policies. O'Connor offered a specific solution: "Such failures [to effectuate the incompetent person's right to refuse treatment] might be avoided if the State considered an equally probative source of evidence: the patient's appointment of a proxy to make health care decisions on her behalf."[64]

O'Connor's suggestions sparked a frenzy of legislative activity to recognize durable health care powers of attorney. In the event that individuals did not take advantage of durable powers of attorney, state legislatures also enacted default surrogate decision-making statutes, referred to as "family consent" statutes. Family consent statutes establish a hierarchy of surrogate health care decision makers in the event an individual has become incompetent and has not made any advance directive. The spouse is usually first in the hierarchy, followed by adult children, parents, adult siblings, and then other close family members or close friends.[65]

Assuming a surrogate decision maker can be identified to decide whether an incompetent patient wishes to forego life-sustaining treatment, the more difficult question is what standard the surrogate should apply in making her decision. Most statutes and case law state that, as far as possible, the surrogate should make her decision based on what the patient would have chosen if she were competent.[66] This approach is referred to as "substituted judgment." Substituted judgment works well when there is clear evidence regarding the patient's desires. But when the evidence is sparse, there is pressure for courts to defer to the surrogate's decision. In the Terri Schiavo case, for example, there was little evidence regarding what Terri would have wanted. She was only twenty-seven years old when she collapsed from cardiac arrest. She had no living will or health care power of attorney. The only evidence adduced at trial regarding her wishes came from Terri's mother; a friend of Terri; her husband, Michael Schiavo; Michael's brother; and Michael's sister-in-law. Terri's mother and friend testified that Terri had made statements about another famous vegetative patient, Karen Ann Quinlan, indicating that Terri would not want to have her feeding tube removed.[67] Michael Schiavo was the one who petitioned the court for removal of life support; he was also the sole heir of Terri's sizable estate (won as a result of a lawsuit brought by Michael against her physician). Michael, together with his brother and sister-in-law, testified that Terri had previously stated on several occasions that she did not want to be "hooked to a machine" or want to live like her grandmother, who had been in intensive care.[68]

Despite the conflicting and relatively sparse evidence regarding Terri's wishes, trial judge George Greer ruled that there was "clear and convincing evidence" that she would want her feeding tube removed. In affirming Judge Greer's conclusion, the Florida appellate court said:

> In the final analysis, the difficult question that faced the trial court
> was whether Theresa Marie Schindler Schiavo, not after a few
> weeks in a coma, but after ten years in a persistent vegetative state
> that has robbed her of most of her cerebrum and all but the most
> instinctive of neurological functions, with no hope of a medical
> cure but with sufficient money and strength of body to live in-
> definitely, would choose to continue the constant nursing care
> and the supporting tubes in hopes that a miracle would somehow
> recreate her missing brain tissue, or whether she would wish to

permit a natural death process to take its course and for her
family members and loved ones to be free to continue their lives.
After due consideration, we conclude that the trial judge had
clear and convincing evidence to answer this question as he did.[69]

Unfortunately, this was decidedly *not* the "difficult question that faced the
trial court." The question was not whether Terri would choose these specific
indignities and burdens versus burdening her family members so that they
could be "free to continue their lives." Instead, the legal question was whether
there was clear and convincing evidence that she would prefer death to life
under these circumstances. If there was any doubt at all (which there most
assuredly was, given the paucity of evidence), she was to be kept alive.

The error in the Schiavo case, therefore, was one of disregarding the pur-
posefully demanding nature of the clear and convincing evidence rule. Indeed, it seems obvious from reading the passage above that the Florida Court
of Appeals had decided that no person in Terri's position would want to go
on living. In essence, it *presumed* that a patient in a persistent vegetative state
(PVS) would prefer death to life—a clear defiance of the clear and convincing
evidence rule, which is designed to err on the side of life.

The Schiavo case, unfortunately, brought out the worst in both the right-
to-life and right-to-die movements. Terri became a pawn of ideological extremes, resulting in shameful spin and abuse of the legal process by all parties.
Her name has become so divisive that one can hardly mention her case without triggering accusations or suspicions of allegiance to one ideological camp
or another. But in the middle of this political circus was a young woman, severely neurologically disabled, who had never really thought much about
what it might be like to be in a PVS. While many of us would undoubtedly
not want to go on living in such a condition, the law in Florida nevertheless
established a presumption that, absent clear and convincing evidence, a person should go on living. The difficulty with the Schiavo case, from my perspective as a lawyer who cares about process as much (or more) than results,
is that this legal presumption was essentially ignored. The substituted judgment standard, which was supposedly used in Schiavo's case, was perverted
in a way that should disturb anyone, regardless of their political leanings.

In situations such as Terri Schiavo's, where a surrogate does not know
what the patient would want—either because the specific situation in which

the patient finds herself was not contemplated or because the patient expressed ambivalence—the usual legal approach is to make a decision according to the patient's "best interests."[70] The best interests test requires a court to balance the benefits and burdens of continuing life support, inherently necessitating the consideration of the patient's quality of life.[71] This cost-benefit balancing test does not work well, if at all, for patients like Terri Schiavo who are in a PVS. This is because PVS patients, by definition, do not have any awareness of themselves or their surroundings. As such, PVS patients experience no pain, so there are no real burdens associated with keeping them alive, other than burdens borne by third parties—burdens which are not supposed to be considered legally relevant. Courts in this situation have accordingly expressed hesitation in applying the best interests test to PVS patients, suggesting that, if there is insufficient evidence regarding the patient's preferences, PVS patients should be kept alive.[72]

Suicide, Assisted Suicide and Euthanasia

Once a constitutional right to refuse medical treatment was established and statutorily (or constitutionally) extended to incompetent patients, the next legal frontier was the true "right to die"—not merely the right to stop intrusive life-sustaining medical interventions, but the right to commit suicide, to engage in an affirmative act that ends your own life. The right to suicide does not involve the pulling of plugs or tubes that are keeping you alive but the right to do something such as shoot, hang, or suffocate yourself, or swallow deadly pills. And if you cannot (or will not) take these acts yourself, the right to die may be extended further, to permit third parties to pull the trigger, hold down the pillow, or inject the deadly drug.

THE RIGHT TO COMMIT SUICIDE

We have already learned that in most states today, suicide is no longer a crime. But there are still a handful of states that retain criminal punishment for attempted suicide and, despite the inability to punish a successful suicide, still consider suicide to be a crime.[73] It is possible, therefore, that in states that still criminalize suicide and attempted suicide, a claim could be made that such laws interfere with constitutional rights. Because the constitutional right to refuse unwanted medical treatment recognized in *Cruzan* is conceptually moored to the common law right to control your own body, the right to commit suicide is arguably included. If your body truly belongs to you—subject to the caveat that you cannot use it to harm others—it seems logical that, assuming you are competent, you have the right to harm yourself, even to the point of death.

Some might argue that the act of suicide is not a purely internal use of one's body, as suicide harms other people, such as spouses, children, and other family members. Yet none of these loved ones' interests are harmed by your death. As Justice Brennan's dissent in *Cruzan* recognized (which garnered the support of Justices Marshall and Blackmun), the death of an individual neither improves nor harms the legal interests of others.[74] It is true that minor children and spouses may suffer financially as a result of a suicide. But they do not have a property interest in the continued receipt of their loved one's salary or other earnings. If you died of natural causes, you could devise your entire estate to charity, and your family would have no recourse, assuming your will is valid. So there may be some loss here, but it is not the type of loss that would normally justify governmental interference with individual liberty. Others may argue that suicide results in external emotional harm, but as I have argued elsewhere, this conception of external harm is also too tenuous to justify state infringement of liberty. Virtually anything we do can cause emotional harm to others, but it does not legitimately permit government to restrain our liberty. If it did, there would be very few areas of individual liberty left. Could the government enact statutes preventing us from breaking up with lovers because it would hurt their feelings, perhaps deeply? Could the government punish us for hanging up on people, calling them mean names, or failing to return phone calls, assuming these acts stop short of creating a reasonable threat of violence? Surely not. Even in the absence of a First Amendment right to free speech, a free government that recognizes liberty would not permit such infringements of that liberty. These types of actions might offend others, but they should not give rise to legally cognizable claims absent evidence of a harm (or a reasonable threat thereof) to others. Emotional harms are simply too subjective and ubiquitous to constitute a proper basis for restricting constitutionally protected liberty interests.[75]

But even assuming one disagrees with this conception of the proper scope of government power and believes such emotional or financial harms should be legally cognizable, this would not automatically mean that government could proscribe suicide. As the *Cruzan* decision made clear, the assumed liberty interest in refusing medical treatment is not absolute, nor is it a fundamental right necessitating strict scrutiny. Instead, it is an interest that must be balanced against competing state interests. So the salient question becomes: What state interest could outweigh your liberty to kill yourself? If you find your own life unbearable and conclude that death is preferable to life, what interest does government have in trumping your choice?

The right to suicide was lurking in the background of the *Cruzan* decision, even though the case technically involved only the right to discontinue life-sustaining medical treatment. As we have discussed, the majority opinion in *Cruzan* may have chosen to "assume" and "infer" the existence of a liberty interest in refusing medical treatment, rather than declare it outright, to avoid opening the Pandora's box of suicide-related rights. Justice Brennan's three-vote dissent in *Cruzan* seemed willing to accept a broader right to commit suicide, declaring that "the State has no legitimate general interest in someone's life, completely abstracted from the interest of the person living that life, that could outweigh the person's choice to avoid medical treatment."[76] While Brennan was careful to qualify his statement by referencing the "person's choice to avoid medical treatment," the introductory paragraphs seem absolute: a state's interests in preserving life cannot be abstracted from the interests of the person living that life. Presumably, if a person feels she no longer has an interest in continued life, the state could not second-guess her. This interpretation is reinforced by Brennan's additional assertion that "the State's general interest in life must accede to Nancy Cruzan's particularized and intense interest in self-determination in her choice of medical treatment. There is simply nothing legitimately within the State's purview to be gained by superseding her decision."[77] The implication is that the state's interest in life qua life can be no greater, or weightier, than the individual's own interest in that life.

Justice Stevens provides a fourth possible vote for the idea that the right to refuse treatment implies a right to commit suicide. He states, "The more precise constitutional significance of death is difficult to describe; not much may be said with confidence about death unless it is said from faith, and that alone is reason enough to protect the freedom to conform choices about death to individual conscience."[78] Yet elsewhere Stevens is careful to emphasize that Cruzan was in a PVS, which he characterizes as a state of mere bio-logical persistence, devoid of meaningful life.[79] He attempts to distinguish refusing medical treatment for an incompetent PVS from suicide, stating, "Even laws against suicide pre-suppose that those inclined to take their own lives have *some* interest in living, and indeed, that the depressed people whose lives are preserved may later be thankful for the State's intervention. . . . Not so here."[80]

Notice that Stevens does not say that suicidal individuals actually have an interest in continued life or that states may protect such an interest by pro-hibiting suicide. He merely acknowledges that suicide laws presuppose an interest in continued life, though he does not think such an interest actually underlies Missouri's law regarding withdrawal of life support. Indeed, Ste-vens makes it clear that he thinks Missouri's ulterior motive in the *Cruzan* case was to define life itself, implementing a religious belief that life is de-fined by mere biological existence, beginning from the moment of concep-tion: "It is not within the province of secular government to circumscribe the liberties of the people by regulations designed wholly for the purpose of es-tablishing a sectarian definition of life."[81]

Justice Scalia's concurrence in *Cruzan* asserts that the dissents of both Brennan and Stevens implicitly sanction a constitutional right to commit sui-cide. He says:

> For insofar as balancing the relative interests of the State and the individual is concerned, there is nothing distinctive about accept-ing death through the refusal of "medical treatment," as opposed to accepting it through the refusal of food, or through the failure to shut off the engine and get out of the car after parking in one's garage after work. Suppose that Nancy Cruzan were in precisely the condition she is in today, except that she could be fed and di-gest food and water *without* artificial assistance. How is the State's "interest" in keeping her alive thereby increased, or her interest in deciding whether she wants to continue living reduced? It seems to me, in other words, that Justice Brennan's position ultimately rests upon the proposition that it is none of the State's business if a person wants to commit suicide. Justice Stevens is explicit on the point.[82]

Scalia's position on a constitutional right either to refuse medical treatment or commit suicide is unequivocal: "[T]he Constitution has nothing to say about the subject. To raise up a constitutional right here we would have to create [it] out of nothing (for it exists neither in text nor tradition)."[83]

The constitutional status of a right to commit suicide was impossible to ascertain from the fractured opinions in *Cruzan*. Although there was a five-vote majority opinion in the case, the majority was intentionally silent on the nature, extent, or even definitive existence of a right to refuse medical treatment, leading to much speculation on important ancillary issues such as the right to commit suicide, or the right to do so with the assistance of others.

The Court tried to end the speculation about a constitutional right to commit suicide in a pair of cases decided in the summer of 1997: Washington v. Glucksberg and Vacco v. Quill. *Glucksberg* was a lawsuit initiated by four physicians, three terminally ill patients, and Compassion in Dying, a right-to-die advocacy organization. The *Glucksberg* plaintiffs sought a declaration that a criminal statute prohibiting assisted suicide infringed the liberty interest of competent, terminally ill adults to commit PAS. *Quill* was a companion case filed by three New York physicians and three terminally ill patients who asked the Court to declare New York's assisted suicide law unconstitutional on the basis of the Fourteenth Amendment's Equal Protection Clause. Their argument, in brief, was that prohibiting PAS while simultaneously allowing withdrawal of life-sustaining treatment constituted irrational discrimination by the state.

The Supreme Court unanimously rejected the plaintiffs' claims in both *Glucksberg* and *Quill,* finding that the states' prohibitions of assisted suicide violated neither due process nor equal protection. The majority opinions in both cases were penned by Chief Justice Rehnquist, with the support of four additional colleagues: Justices Kennedy, O'Connor, Scalia, and Thomas. As had been the case with the five-vote majority opinion in *Cruzan,* the majority opinions in both *Glucksberg* and *Quill* were muddied considerably by a separate concurrence penned by Justice O'Connor. The remaining four Justices on the Court all agreed with the end result—that it was constitutional to prohibit assisted suicide—but they varied considerably in their explanation as to why. As Yale Kamisar once aptly observed, the *Glucksberg* opinion in particular "may be the most confusing and the most fragile 9–0 decision in Supreme Court history."[84]

We should begin by examining Justice Rehnquist's majority opinions in both cases. In *Glucksberg*—the substantive liberty case—Rehnquist's opinion described the right being asserted as "a right to commit suicide which itself includes a right to assistance in doing so."[85] In ascertaining the constitutional status of this asserted right, the majority began by invoking history, finding that "for over 700 years, the Anglo-American common-law tradition has punished or otherwise disapproved of both suicide and assisting suicide."[86] Because of this history, the *Glucksberg* majority concluded that any liberty interest in engaging in PAS was not "deeply rooted in this Nation's history and tradition" so as to warrant status as a fundamental right. As such, the Court declined to invoke strict scrutiny, instead applying rationality review, which presumes the law constitutional unless the citizens challenging the law can provide it is not "rationally related to legitimate government interests."[87]

The *Glucksberg* majority's initial decision to deny fundamental rights status (and strict scrutiny) was outcome determinative. Rationality review is notoriously deferential; laws subject to rationality review are rarely overturned. The *Glucksberg* Court concluded that Washington had several legitimate interests in prohibiting assisted suicide, including the interest in preserving human life, protecting vulnerable citizens, and protecting the integrity and ethics of the medical profession.[88] It determined that a ban on assisted suicide bore a rational relationship to all of these legitimate goals.

Regarding the equal protection challenge involved in *Quill*, Chief Justice Rehnquist's majority took substantially the same approach. Because the New York prohibition on assisted suicide did not burden a fundamental right (as *Glucksberg* had decided) or target a class of persons that had been historically discriminated against (a so-called "suspect" class), the *Quill* majority applied rationality review. The question was therefore whether it was rational for a state such as New York to allow individuals to refuse life-sustaining medical treatment while simultaneously prohibiting assisted suicide. The majority in *Quill* concluded that this distinction between the *Cruzan* right to refuse unwanted treatment and the right to PAS was rationally based on principles of (1) causation; and (2) intent.

The causation difference perceived by the *Quill* majority between refusing life-sustaining care and PAS was that, in the former, the patient "dies from an underlying fatal disease or pathology; but if a patient ingests lethal medication prescribed by a physician, he is killed by that medication."[89] In recognizing the distinction between "letting die" and "causing death," the majority opinion in *Quill* adhered to a long-standing legal distinction between acts of omission and commission.

The difference in intent between refusing life-sustaining treatment and PAS was more subtle, as the *Quill* majority thought that the physician who pulls the plug or feeding tube "intends or may so intend, only to respect his patient's wishes and to cease doing useless and futile or degrading things to the patient when [the patient] no longer stands to benefit from them."[90] Similarly, the *Quill* majority thought that the aggressive use of painkillers at the end of life "may hasten a patient's death, but the physician's purpose and intent is, or may be, only to ease his patient's pain."[91] The so-called "double effect" of large quantities of painkillers—they kill the pain but also hasten death in some cases—was ascribed a single, noncriminal intent, distinguishing it from PAS, in which the *Quill* Court concluded the physician "must necessarily and indubitably intend primarily that the patient be made dead."[92] While such fine distinctions in state of mind—called *mens rea*—may seem like hairsplitting, they are a critical basis for much of criminal law. A negligent mindset is distinguished from a reckless, knowing, or intentional one. They are difficult lines to draw, to be sure, but they are drawn all the time. In the eyes of the *Quill* majority, it was rational for New York to conclude that a doctor who pulls the plug at the patient's (or surrogate's) request does not intend to cause the patient's death. Although death will likely and foreseeably result, the doctor does not have the specific intent to kill. Because such *mens rea* distinctions are a rational basis for drawing lines in criminal law, the Supreme Court in *Quill* concluded that New York's decision to criminalize PAS, but not withdrawal of life support, comported with equal protection.

One of the challenges posed by *Glucksberg* and *Quill* is that, although Chief Justice Rehnquist's opinions gained five votes, Justice O'Connor once again (as in *Cruzan*) joined the majority but wrote a separate concurrence. O'Connor's concurrence was given a stamp of approval by Justice Ginsburg, who agreed with the outcome "substantially for the reasons stated by Justice O'Connor in her concurring opinion," as well as by Justice Breyer, who concurred separately but believed "Justice O'Connor's views, which I share, have greater legal significance than the Court's [majority] opinion suggests."[93] Given O'Connor's crucial centrist role and the endorsement obtained by two of her colleagues, her concurrence deserves close examination.

O'Connor began by stating, "I join the Court's opinions because I agree that there is no generalized right to 'commit suicide.'"[94] But of course a generalized right to commit suicide was not really the issue before the Court—the right of competent, terminally ill patients to commit suicide with the help of a physician was the issue. With regard to this narrower issue, O'Connor equivocated: she saw "no need" to decide whether a competent individual "experiencing great suffering has a constitutionally cognizable interest in controlling the circumstances of his or her imminent death."[95] She implied, however, that such a liberty interest could be identified with the right set of facts, but those facts were not present in either *Glucksberg* or *Quill*. The barrier to considering such a liberty claim was posed by the fact that, in both Washington and New York, "a patient who is suffering from a terminal illness and who is experiencing great pain has no legal barriers to obtaining medication, from qualified physicians, to alleviate that suffering, even to the point of causing unconsciousness and hastening death."[96]

O'Connor suggests that because adequate pain relief was legally available to the patients litigating *Glucksberg* and *Quill*, they could not establish a constitutional claim to a death without "great suffering." In other words, she was willing to entertain the notion that the word "liberty" in the Due Process Clause includes a liberty to choose PAS in order to avoid a painful death, but these particular plaintiffs could not make such a claim because their states imposed no legal burdens to obtaining adequate pain relief. Justice O'Connor thus implied that a future case, filed by plaintiffs from a state *with* such legal burdens, could come out differently.

There are several perplexing aspects to Justice O'Connor's rationale. First, many states have enacted intractable pain statutes that are designed to encourage the liberal use of painkillers to control pain.[97] Even in states without intractable pain statutes, there are no specific legal barriers to physicians prescribing adequate pain medication. There are sometimes bureaucratic requirements for triplicate forms and record keeping when prescribing controlled substances, but these are not designed to stop legitimate prescriptions for pain management, only illegitimate prescriptions written for purposes of drug diversion. Some providers do fear that writing too many prescriptions for narcotics and other controlled substances will trigger scrutiny by state medical boards and law enforcement, and they are correct about that. But even assuming such scrutiny occurs, it does not mean that such legal efforts

are attempts to place barriers in the path of those seeking legitimate pain relief. They are, instead, unfortunate side effects of a "war on drugs," a war
against recreational, not medicinal, drug use.

More fundamentally, O'Connor's concurrence in *Glucksberg* and *Quill* in-
timates that there may be a constitutional liberty to be free from pain, at least
for those who are terminally ill. Justice Stevens's concurrence in *Glucksberg*
seems to agree with this conception, stating that the plaintiffs' liberty interest
was even stronger than Nancy Cruzan's because "they were suffering con-
stant and severe pain. Avoiding intolerable pain and the indignity of living
one's final days incapacitated and in agony is certainly 'at the heart of the
liberty . . . to define one's own conception of existence, of meaning, of the
universe, and of the mystery of human life.' "[98] Indeed, this asserted "liberty
from pain" seems increasingly to be the focus of the right-to-die movement.
Kathryn Tucker, director of Legal Affairs at Compassion in Dying (now
Compassion and Choices) and lead counsel in the *Glucksberg* and *Quill* cases,
has boldly asserted, "Justices O'Connor and Breyer appear to have answered
a question that the parties had not actually posed, and have recognized that
there is a constitutional right to adequate pain medication. Efforts to establish this right more firmly can be anticipated."[99]

But is the right to PAS really driven by a desire to alleviate pain? If the first
decade of experience with PAS in Oregon is any indication, the answer appears to be no. According to data collected by the Oregon Public Health Division, only 5 percent of Oregonians who died by PAS in 2008 were concerned
about or actually experienced inadequate pain control.[100] Similarly, a 2007 survey of relatives of Oregonians who had made formal PAS requests asked
them to rate, from 1 to 5—1 being "not at all important" and 5 being "very
important"—various reasons for the family member's PAS request. The survey revealed that "[n]o physical symptoms experienced at the time of the request [for PAS] were rated higher than 2 on the 1–5 scale. In most cases, future
concerns about physical symptoms were rated as more important than physical symptoms present at the time of the request."[101] An additional survey,
published in 2009, employed the same 1–5 scale, but surveyed the individuals
themselves, not their families. Specifically, the researchers asked fifty-six Oregonians who had requested PAS from their doctors or information about it
from Compassion and Choices to rank the reasons for wanting physician aid
with suicide, and the results revealed that "[p]hysical symptoms experienced

at the time of initial interest . . . were much less important; pain, shortness of breath, fatigue, confusion, and loss of bowel and bladder control were all rated at a median of 1. In contrast, all physical symptoms that the patient anticipated in the future were rated at a median of 3 or higher."[102] The highest median-scoring reasons (with a median score of five) for seeking PAS—according to both the family members' and patients' surveys—were wanting to control the circumstances of their own death, fear of a future poor quality of life, fear of future pain, fear of a future inability to care for themselves, and a fear of future loss of independence.[103] It is simply inaccurate to conclude, based on the Oregon experience, that pain itself justifies or motivates PAS. If anything, the data indicates that it is worry, anxiety, and fear that drive these decisions, a disconnect with the perceptions of PAS revealed by the Justices in *Glucksberg* and *Quill*.

Even if pain were actually important to PAS—and a prerequisite for the exercise of the right—we should ponder the theoretical implications of recognizing a constitutional right to be free from pain at the time of death. Would the right be properly conceptualized as a right to *die* without pain or a right to *live* your remaining days without pain? Kathryn Tucker's post-*Glucksberg* statement that some of the Justices had "recognized that there is a constitutional right to adequate pain medication" seemed to suggest the latter, though perhaps she was not being particularly careful in her choice of words. Either formulation, however, presumably implies something about a death "with dignity"—the right to die / live your remaining days without pain, because pain deprives you of your dignity.

There would be numerous difficulties with defining and cabining a "pain-free death" or "pain-free existence at the end of life." Is there any particular reason why a constitutional liberty to be free from state-imposed pain would be limited to the terminally ill? Why should they, and not others, enjoy this liberty? Is there something about impending death, in other words, that triggers the liberty interest in being pain free? While it is true that many terminally ill individuals suffer from intractable pain, it is equally true that many nonterminally ill individuals do as well. Pain is not the exclusive domain of the dying. If the interest is one of freedom from pain while still living, it should be an interest enjoyed by all citizens equally. If the interest is one of freedom from pain while dying, then the shibboleth limits the interest to dying yet fails to articulate a rational basis why such a liberty interest springs to life after only receiving a terminal diagnosis but not before. If one has a liberty interest in being free from pain at the threshold of death—if being pain free is essential to one's dignity—it is hard to understand why one would not have the same liberty interest throughout one's life.

Even assuming we could somehow limit the right to the terminally ill, the implications are enormous. Would state laws (other than those prohibiting PAS) that limit a terminally ill person's access to pain relief be unconstitutional? Would terminally ill patients, for example, have a constitutional right to smoke marijuana for pain relief? Would they have a constitutional right to use heroin, morphine, or other controlled substances? The two plaintiffs in a recent Supreme Court case, Gonzales v. Raich, suffered from chronic conditions that caused intractable pain that could not be managed by legal medicines.[104] As the trial court put it, "Traditional medicine has utterly failed these women. . . ."[105] So the plaintiffs filed a lawsuit seeking a declaration that using marijuana on the recommendation of their physicians would be legal. Unfortunately, for reasons unrelated to constitutional concepts of individual liberty, the *Raich* plaintiffs lost, leaving them with no legal access to pain relief through marijuana.

If there is a constitutional right to have a pain-free death, however, the outcome could change. Presumably the government in such a case would argue that controlled substances laws serve sufficiently important interests (combating addiction, for example) to outweigh a terminally ill patient's right to die / live their remaining days free from pain, but who can predict whether these state interests would prevail? A good deal would depend on whether the right to die / live one's remaining days free from pain is characterized as a fundamental right or a mere liberty interest. If the former, controlled substances laws would be presumptively unconstitutional as applied to the terminally ill.

In addition to these pragmatic concerns, we should critically examine the notion that dying or living your remaining days free from pain constitutes a "death with dignity." The assumption is that pain inherently robs one of dignity. But why stop at pain and suffering (which are essentially synonyms)? Why not also extend such a liberty to those who are suffering from "distress," a word that addresses purely psychological suffering, unmoored to pain? Would individuals in distress also have a right to assisted suicide so that they can die with dignity? Presumably so. Indeed, in 1998, an international conference of doctors and nurses who support the right to die issued the Zurich Declaration, which made it clear that the right to die with dignity would belong to anyone suffering "severe and enduring distress," not merely those who experience pain.[106] Under this reformulation, a terminally ill person whose pain was being well managed would still have a right to assisted suicide, on the basis that emotional, economic, or family burdens would cause severe and enduring "distress."

Even if the right to die with dignity somehow could be limited to those who are experiencing pain, not merely distress, we must realize that the pain rationale would create problems of its own. The death-with-dignity argument assumes that dignity can be obtained through medical intervention—that somehow, the physician's magic pills will erase or minimize the ravages of our bodies and minds caused by cancer, ALS, Parkinson's, or other infirmities. But dignity is a state of mind with which others perceive us, not a personal physical state. To be "dignified" means to be esteemed, respected, or poised.[107] Respect and esteem—dignity—is a mindset formed by others who observe our courage, honesty, and perseverance in the face of adversity. It is an odd use of language to argue that dignity necessitates recognition of a constitutional right to bypass the natural, albeit sometimes difficult, journey to death's door. As Leon Kass has cogently observed, "Dignity is not something which, like a nose or a navel, is to be expected or found in every living being. In principle, it is aristocratic. It follows that dignity, thus understood, cannot be demanded or claimed; for it cannot be provided and it is not owed. One has no more *right* to dignity—and hence to dignity in death—than one has to beauty or courage or wisdom, desirable though these may be."[108]

Even if we should conclude that the government is obliged and able to bestow upon us a "death with dignity," it is worth pondering whether the same government has an equal obligation to bestow upon us a *life* with dignity as well. If "liberty" includes a right to achieve some semblance of dignity through the medical provision of a pain-free death, it may also include a right to achieve dignity through a life equally free from pain and suffering. If ensuring dignity at death is the government's responsibility, dignity during life is an equal, if not greater, responsibility. Dignity, in short, would be an entitlement—an affirmative human right owed to us by government, effectuated by guarantees to such things as education, health care, food, housing, and pain medication. Admittedly, this is the vision of government found in many modern constitutions, but it is not the vision of government reflected in our own. The U.S. Constitution principally provides negative, not affirmative, rights—areas of "no government power," where citizens are at liberty to follow their own consciences and pursue their own visions of happiness. In this sense, liberty is an entitlement, but not in the modern, socialistic sense. It is a word embodying the concept of freedom from government, not a mechanism to demand government provision of basic needs. Liberty, in other words, does not come from government; it comes from its absence.

A right to "die with dignity"—defined as freedom from pain and suffering—would pose numerous analytical challenges. The difficulties of defining and containing the right would be enormous. The courts would be asked to make up a right virtually out of whole cloth, with little to guide them other than their own subjective preferences and values. But this does not mean that such a right does not, or should not, exist. It means, instead, that a firmer, more conceptually grounded foundation must be identified for such a right. In this sense, the *Cruzan* majority may have been correct: if the right to refuse medical treatment is moored to the common law concept of bodily autonomy, then it makes sense, *Glucksberg* notwithstanding, for a right to assisted suicide to be moored to it as well. The implication would be, as it has been from *Jacobson* on down, that individuals have a right to use their bodies, so long as doing so does not injure others. This liberty interest would be just that—a liberty interest, not a fundamental right—and it would need to be balanced against competing state interests.

In conducting the balance of an individual's liberty to die with dignity, the state's interest in preserving life would be the weightiest interest on the other side of the balance. But would it be sufficiently weighty to trump the individual's liberty interest? There is merit to the notion that the state's interest in preserving life *simpliciter* is too rigid. A state's interest in preserving life should not be abstracted from the particular context of the life sought to be preserved. In this sense, the state's interest in preserving the life of a terminally ill person is relatively weak, as compared to the state's interest in preserving the life of someone who is not terminal. Viewed this way, a liberty interest could be devised and limited to terminally ill individuals.

A trickier question is whether such a liberty interest could be limited to competent patients. Faced with an argument for extending the liberty interest to incompetent patients, the state would assert an interest in preventing vulnerable, incompetent individuals from abuse. Undoubtedly, this state interest is quite strong. But *Cruzan* poses conceptual problems, as a majority of the Court—though not the official majority led by Justice Rehnquist—seemed to assume that a right to refuse life-sustaining medical treatment survived incompetency.

If this is a correct interpretation of *Cruzan,* it is difficult to see why the right to refuse treatment should survive incompetency, whereas the right to death with dignity should not. The state's interest in protecting vulnerable groups is equally weighty in both contexts. An incompetent person is an incompetent person. It should make no difference whether the incompetent person's surrogate wishes to pull the plug versus provide a lethal injection. Either way, the result will be death, and an erroneous determination regarding the patient's preferences would be irreversible. But the various concurrences in *Cruzan* imply that the state's interest in protecting vulnerable groups is insufficient to trump the liberty interest itself. If there is a right to die with dignity, therefore, it will prove difficult to limit it to competent individuals only.

After *Glucksberg* and *Quill:* The Legal Battle Continues

After *Glucksberg* and *Quill,* the opportunities for winning Supreme Court recognition for a right to die were reduced dramatically, and this will remain the case, at least until the Court's composition changes significantly. Justice Sandra O'Connor—the centrist who brokered a compromise between dueling liberal and conservative pluralities in *Cruzan, Glucksberg,* and *Quill*—retired from the Court in 2006 and was replaced with Chief Justice John Roberts. The new center of the Court is occupied by Justice Anthony Kennedy, who joined Chief Justice Rehnquist's majority opinions in *Cruzan, Glucksberg,* and *Quill.* Because Justice Kennedy was supportive of these decisions, it seems safe to say that a majority of the present Supreme Court is not amenable to revisiting them.

There is one post-*Glucksberg* case, however, that may portend a change in substantive due process analysis—one that could provide a foundation for future right-to-die cases. In Lawrence v. Texas, decided in the summer of 2003, the Supreme Court ruled that a Texas law prohibiting homosexual sodomy violated the liberty interest protected by the Due Process Clause.[109]

Significantly, the majority opinion in *Lawrence* was written by Justice Kennedy, who holds the balance of power in the current Supreme Court.

In *Lawrence*, Justice Kennedy's majority concluded that consenting adults have a liberty interest to engage in private, consensual sexual conduct. The prohibition on homosexual sodomy, said the Court, touches "the most private human conduct, sexual behavior, and in the most private of places, the home. The statutes do seek to control a personal relationship that, whether or not entitled to formal recognition in the law, is within the liberty of person to choose without being punished as criminals."[110] The Court was careful not to describe this liberty as a fundamental right, instead content to characterize it as a simple liberty interest. As such, the court implicitly applied mere rationality review—a standard that normally results in the challenged law being upheld. But in *Lawrence,* the majority concluded the law was not supported by a rational basis, stating, "The Texas statute furthers no legitimate state interest which can justify its intrusion into the personal and private life of the individual."[111]

The *Lawrence* Court never even cited *Glucksberg*. The analytical framework used in *Glucksberg* to resolve claims involving substantive due process was simply ignored. Unlike the *Glucksberg* Court, the *Lawrence* Court minimized the importance of historical legal treatment of the asserted right, declaring that "history and tradition are the starting point but not in all cases the ending point of the substantive due process inquiry."[112] The tone in *Lawrence* was decidedly progressive, implying that recent legal treatment and trends were more important than ancient legal traditions. The *Lawrence* majority concluded that the Framers of the Fourteenth Amendment "knew times can blind us to certain truths and later generations can see that laws once thought necessary and proper in fact serve only to oppress. As the Constitution endures, persons in every generation can invoke its principles in their own search for greater freedom."[113]

The analytical framework employed by *Lawrence*—combined with the fact that the majority opinion was penned by Justice Kennedy—could suggest that the continuing validity of *Glucksberg* is questionable. As Yale Kamisar has pointed out, however, there are some critical differences between *Glucksberg* and *Lawrence* that could make this conclusion too rash.[114] First and foremost, *Lawrence* involved a law that targeted a politically vulnerable group (homosexuals), creating concern within the Court that the sodomy prohibition was motivated by inappropriate discriminatory animus. Laws prohibiting assisted suicide, by contrast, apply equally to all citizens, raising no concerns about discriminatory motives. Indeed, one of the strongest arguments put forth by New York and Washington in support of their assisted suicide bans was that they were designed to *protect* vulnerable groups from terminating their lives early due to financial pressures, lack of access to care, or social discrimination or stigmatization.

Second, unlike *Lawrence,* there is no emerging consensus or awareness that prohibiting PAS is antithetical to basic concepts of individual liberty. While it is true that Oregon and Washington have enacted laws allowing PAS, this is far from evincing a societal consensus or even an emerging trend. The vast majority of states still have laws that consider assisted suicide to be a felony. And of the two state supreme courts—Alaska and Florida—that have addressed state constitutional challenges to PAS post-*Glucksberg,* both have rejected those challenges unequivocally.[115]

Third, the state's interests in prohibiting PAS are arguably much stronger than in prohibiting homosexual sodomy. Indeed, in *Lawrence,* the only state interest in prohibiting homosexual sodomy was morality. While three dissenters in *Lawrence*—led by Justice Scalia—clearly thought morality alone was a sufficiently legitimate basis for criminalizing homosexual sodomy, Kennedy's majority saw things differently.[116] Laws that prohibit assisted suicide, by contrast, do not rest on mere moral condemnation. They rest on the interest in preserving life, protecting vulnerable groups, and protecting the ethics and integrity of the medical profession, none of which were implicated in *Lawrence.*

But the truth is that, if the center of the Supreme Court shifts, *Lawrence* may provide an analytical framework for rejecting *Glucksberg* and recognizing a constitutional right to PAS. Indeed, by rejecting the primacy of historical legal treatment of the asserted right and elevating the importance of modern trends, *Lawrence* frees the Court from a presumption of unconstitutionality, creating intellectual wiggle room to recognize a liberty interest in a future case. If more and more states enact statutes allowing PAS, a critical mass may eventually be reached that creates sufficient political cover for the Court to reconsider *Glucksberg.*

For the time being, however, the right-to-die movement has shifted its attention from federal constitutional claims to state litigation and legislation. All of the action, so to speak, is now taking place within the laboratory of the states. In this regard, the most significant post-*Glucksberg* development has been the passage of state laws in both Oregon and Washington that legalize PAS.[117] Under both statutes, competent, terminally ill adults (age eighteen or older) may request a lethal prescription from a licensed physician. The patient's request must be made both orally and in writing, signed by two witnesses, and the request must be orally repeated at least fifteen days after making the initial oral request. A second consulting physician must examine the patient and confirm the diagnosis and voluntary nature of the request. If either the attending or consulting physician believes the patient is suffering from depression or other psychological disorder that causes impaired judgment, they must refer the patient to counseling, and the lethal prescription cannot be provided until the depression or disorder no longer impairs judgment. If there are no issues of impaired judgment, the lethal prescription may be provided at the expiration of the fifteen-day waiting period.

Because the Washington statute only went into effect in 2009, there are not yet any published data on its use. The Oregon law, by contrast, has been in effect for over a decade. In that ten-year period, the number of individuals who have died using lethal prescriptions has tripled. In 2008, the most recent year for which data is available, eighty-eight lethal prescriptions were obtained, and sixty Oregonians died by lethal prescription.[118] Eighty percent of individuals taking the lethal prescriptions had been diagnosed with cancer.[119] There were no reported awakenings or other complications associated with taking the prescriptions.

One aspect of the Oregon and Washington laws worth noting is that they do not require pain as a prerequisite for obtaining a lethal prescription. An individual must simply be an adult diagnosed as being terminal, which is defined as an incurable disease that "will, within reasonable medical judgment, produce death within six months."[120] As discussed earlier, data indicates that, in fact, pain is not a motivating factor in most patients' decision to seek PAS. Indeed, one of the first individuals to die using the Oregon law was a woman in her mid-eighties named Helen, who had breast cancer that had metastasized to other parts of her body. Helen was not confined to her bed or experiencing substantial pain. She was still able to keep her own house clean and tidy. But Helen was afraid of her future, so she asked her physician for a lethal prescription. He turned her down, and she sought help from another physician, who also refused because he concluded she was suffering from depression. Helen's husband then called Compassion in Dying (now Compassion and Choices) and was given the name of a physician who would help her. The third physician agreed to prescribe Helen's lethal prescription, and shortly after the expiration of the fifteen-day waiting period, Helen drank the barbiturate-laced syrup and died.[121]

Was Helen's case an example of how the Oregon law worked or how it failed? The first two doctors she consulted refused to provide her with a lethal prescription; one did so because she was suffering from depression. The law does not prohibit this sort of "shopping around" for a willing provider. Once a willing doctor is located, a consulting confirmation is required. But neither the first nor second doctors are required to be notified of previous doctors' refusals, nor are they required to have any prior relationship with the patient. Moreover, even if earlier doctors express concerns about the patient's depression or other psychological disorder, they are not required to share these concerns with later doctors.

More importantly, under the Oregon law, depression alone is not a legitimate basis for denying PAS. It is only if the attending or consulting physician believes the patient may be suffering from depression that causes "impaired judgment" that the mandatory requirement for counseling referral is triggered.[122] Depression alone does not mandate a referral to counseling, only depression that results in impaired judgment. And although the statute says that physicians who believe such impaired judgment exists "shall" refer the patient for counseling, there are no penalties attached for a failure to do so. Indeed, physicians are immunized from civil and criminal liability, as well as professional disciplinary action, if they merely act with subjective "good faith" under the act.[123] Perhaps this explains why, in 2008, only two out of the sixty individuals (3.3 percent) who ingested a lethal prescription had been referred to counseling.[124]

In theory, then, there could be a substantial number of patients suffering from depression that obtain and take lethal prescriptions in Oregon. A study published in 2008 suggests this may be the case. After providing standardized assessments to Oregonians who had requested PAS from their doctors, one in four was determined to be suffering from clinical depression.[125] The study's authors concluded that "current practice of the Death with Dignity Act in Oregon may not adequately protect all mentally ill patients, and increased vigilance and systemic examination for depression among patients who may access legalized aid in dying are needed."[126]

A troubling case study from Oregon is that of Kate Cheney, an eighty-five-year-old woman with stomach cancer. Although Kate's first physician refused to provide her with a lethal prescription, he agreed to refer her to a second doctor, who upon examination, referred her to a psychiatrist. The psychiatrist concluded that Kate lacked "the very high level of capacity required to weigh options about assisted suicide."[127] But Kate's daughter, Ericka, became angry. She told a reporter for the *Oregonian*, "For me to sit there and witness someone coming in here with all their intellectual acumen and making a judgment call on my mother, it just incensed me."[128]

Kaiser Permanente, Kate's health insurance company, agreed to a second psychological consultation. The psychologist insisted on interviewing Kate alone, but Ericka requested that the interview be audiotaped.[129] The second psychologist concluded that Kate's "choices may be influenced by her family's wishes and her daughter, Ericka, may be somewhat coercive."[130] Nonetheless, the second psychologist concluded that Kate had the capacity to weigh her options and make an informed choice. Given the various medical opinions regarding Kate, the ethics director of Kaiser asked to meet with her. He concluded that she was indeed competent and acting free of coercion.[131] Kate thereafter received her lethal prescription.

After Kate had held on to the lethal prescription for a while without using it, one day Ericka and her husband decided they needed a break from the burdens of caring for her and sent her to a nursing home for a week. After bringing her home, Kate asked for her lethal pills. "When would you like to do this?" her son-in-law asked. "Now," replied Kate. Kate's family broke open the capsules and dumped them into a bowl of applesauce. They handed the bowl to Kate. Kate ate every drop. They opened a bottle of wine and toasted, clinking glasses with Kate. Within an hour, Kate was dead.[132]

Was Kate's death voluntary or coerced? Should it matter that two consulting psychologists expressed concerns about coercion? Should it matter that the final decision was made by a managed care administrator with a clear financial conflict of interest? Kate's death undoubtedly would save money.[133] Perhaps a third opinion should have been sought in light of the uncertainty of the two prior psychologists' reports. Perhaps a guardian should have been appointed, or a court hearing should have been required to determine Kate's competency and assess her psychological state to ensure compliance with the statute. We will never know whether Kate took the lethal prescription willingly or if she did it because she was coerced into believing she had become too much of a burden on her family. We do know that, in the decade of experience with Oregon, over 38 percent of individuals who took lethal prescriptions expressed concerns about becoming a burden on their family or caregivers.[134]

The PAS statutes in effect in Oregon and Washington are not perfect. It is worth considering whether additional safeguards, or perhaps even mandatory court intervention, should be required in certain cases. But they do seem to indicate, overall, that the sky is not falling. While the number of lethal prescriptions tripled between 1998 and 2008, the percentage of total deaths that are due to PAS is extremely low. And of the individuals who actually obtain lethal prescriptions, only about 60 percent take them, suggesting that, for many individuals, the law is more about providing a means to retake control over one's life in the face of otherwise uncontrollable illness or disease. The law is not perfect, but it does not seem to have transformed society or resulted in rampant abuses.

The Oregon and Washington statutes have not been the only important post-*Glucksberg* development regarding PAS. A couple of important post-*Glucksberg* court cases illustrate the new judicial strategy of the right-to-die movement. On the last day of 2009, the Montana Supreme Court handed down a decision in Baxter v. State, ruling that physicians who assist their competent, terminally ill patients with suicide will be able to claim consent to a subsequent charge of homicide.[135] The *Baxter* decision, in essence, decriminalizes physician-assisted suicide, making Montana the third state in the United States to permit PAS, and the only state to do so via judicial decision.

Robert Baxter, the main plaintiff, was a retired truck driver who had a form of terminal leukemia. He had been undergoing chemotherapy, which caused various difficult symptoms, including chronic fatigue, infections, night sweats, nausea, swollen glands, digestive problems, and pain and discomfort. Baxter wanted to obtain a lethal prescription from his doctor so that he could die at a time and in a manner of his own choosing. Baxter was joined in his lawsuit by four Montana physicians who treated terminally ill patients and by the right-to-die advocacy group Compassion and Choices.

The *Baxter* plaintiffs asserted that competent, terminally ill patients and their physicians have a right, under the Montana Constitution, to "aid in dying," the phrase they used to refer to PAS. They sought a declaration that the Montana homicide statutes were inapplicable to them and an injunction against enforcement of the statutes. Embedded within these claims were two distinct assertions: (1) the Montana Constitution grants the right to PAS to competent, terminally ill adults; and (2) the Montana homicide statutes are inapplicable to physicians who commit PAS because they commit the death-causing act with the patient's consent. The former is a constitutional question; the latter, a question of statutory interpretation.

The trial judge in *Baxter* opted to tackle the state constitutional claims. She denied the state equal protection claim, concluding that individuals who die as a result of refusing or withdrawing life-sustaining medical treatment are not similarly situated to terminal patients seeking PAS. The trial judge reasoned that the "difference between the two classes lies in the difference in the character of the act sought. The citizen who chooses to refuse life-sustaining treatment is entitled to do so based on the right to be free from an intrusion on his or her bodily integrity without the individual's consent. What that individual seeks is essentially a negative act—that the physician refrain from action or curtail action already taken, which permits nature to take its course. Baxter, however, seeks an affirmative act from his physician intended to hasten death."[136] This causation rationale was one of the bases (along with the intent rationale) of the Supreme Court's rejection of a federal Equal Protection Clause challenge in Vacco v. Quill.

But the trial court's agreement with the U.S. Supreme Court ended there. The rest of the opinion was devoted to a belief that the Montana Constitution's guarantee of privacy was violated by a prohibition on PAS. The Montana right to privacy, reasoned the trial judge, encompassed a "concept of personal autonomy with regard to bodily integrity."[137] This right was implicated by a prohibition on PAS because "[t]he decision as to whether to continue life for a few additional months when death is imminent certainly is one of personal autonomy and privacy. . . . [It is] perhaps the most intimate and personal choice of all—the choice of when and how to end one's life."[138] Recognizing that the U.S. Supreme Court in both *Glucksberg* and *Quill* had refused to conceptualize privacy this broadly, the trial judge correctly noted that these decisions did not bind interpretations of state constitutions and that the Montana constitutional right to privacy was broader, protecting "the right to determine the most fundamental questions of life," including the right of a competent, terminally ill person to "choose to end his or her life."[139]

Having decided that the Montana right to privacy included the right of terminally ill patients to kill themselves, the trial judge in *Baxter* turned to whether this right also included a right to "obtain assistance from a medical care provider in the form of obtaining a prescription for lethal drugs to be taken at the time of the patient's choosing."[140] Here, the judge invoked a very interesting analogy—that of abortion. She noted that prior Montana Supreme Court precedent had concluded that a woman's right to abortion included the right to obtain assistance from a health care provider.

The State argued that abortion was distinguishable because abortion was a legal (indeed, U.S. constitutional) right. The trial judge responded that suicide itself was legal in Montana—or more precisely, in her words, suicide was "not legally prohibited."[141] Since both abortion and suicide were legal, therefore, the judge in *Baxter* concluded that both could be legally aided with the help of a physician. Physician-assisted suicide, like abortion, necessarily requires physician involvement. They both involve a "right to make medical judgments affecting her or his bodily integrity and health in partnership with a chosen health care provider free from governmental interference."[142]

The trial court in *Baxter* concluded that "the method of effecting the patient's death with dignity would *require* the assistance of his medical professional."[143] Without a physician to assist with suicide, a terminally ill patient "may be forced to kill himself sooner rather than later" because the progression of his disease might make it impossible for him to kill himself later on, and the means chosen to commit suicide "would most likely occur in a manner that violates his dignity and peace of mind, such as by gunshot or by an otherwise unpleasant methods, causing undue suffering to the patient and his family."[144]

The court's reasoning is fascinating on many levels and is worthy of closer examination. First, we should examine the analogy between abortion and PAS. Justice Souter mentions the same analogy in his concurrence in *Glucksberg*:

> The analogies between the abortion cases and this one are
> several. . . . Like the decision to commit suicide, the decision to
> abort potential life can be made irresponsibly and under the influ-

ence of others, and yet the Court has held in the abortion cases that physicians are fit assistants. Without physician assistance in abortion, the woman's right would have too often amounted to nothing more than a right to self-mutilation, and without a physician to assist in the suicide of the dying, the patient's right will often be confined to crude methods of causing death, most shocking and painful to the decendent's survivors. . . . [T]he good physician is not just a mechanic of the human body whose services have no bearing on a person's moral choices, but one who does more than treat symptoms, one who ministers to the patient.[145]

One of the odd results of this rationale is that both Justice Souter and the trial judge in *Baxter* are trying very hard to limit the right to assisted suicide to *physician*-assisted suicide by arguing that physician involvement in suicide is normatively desirable since shocking or gruesome means will not be employed and patients can delay death until the last possible minute. Such mandatory physician involvement in death is ironic, to say the least, given that the right-to-die movement has been built upon the notion of restoring autonomy and dignity by demedicalizing death. Somehow we are supposed to now believe that doctors are critical to ensuring our autonomy and dignity, whereas they have been portrayed as the enemy of these goals in the context of the right to refuse unwanted medical treatment.

But even if one accepts this dichotomy—that doctors are the problem in the context of refusal of treatment, but the salvation in the context of assisted suicide—we should still question whether, as the *Baxter* trial judge assumed, doctors are "required" to effectuate a right to commit suicide. In comparing PAS to abortion, Justice Souter argued that the right to abortion had to include a right to physician-provided abortion because otherwise, women would have no other option than self-mutilation. This is generally still true today, with the exception of very early pregnancies that can be safely and effectively aborted using mifepristone (RU-486). But can the same be said of suicide, or assisted suicide? Must a doctor be involved to safely and effectively commit suicide? Must a doctor even be involved to ensure that suicide is pain free?

Suicide is the eleventh leading cause of death in the United States, with over thirty-three thousand suicides each year.[146] The most common method of suicide for males is firearms (56 percent), whereas the most common method for females is poisoning (40.3 percent).[147] It is impossible to know what percentage of these suicides is painful versus pain free. Carbon monoxide poisoning—an odorless, tasteless and nonirritating gas—can cause death quickly and with minimal or no pain. Suicide by carbon monoxide can be accomplished by sitting in a closed garage with the car running or turning on a gas oven—or one can simply buy carbon monoxide in a canister (a method used several times by Dr. Jack Kevorkian).[148] Most patients with chronic pain have a sufficient quantity of powerful narcotics on hand to accomplish suicide without the need to resort to physician assistance.

The necessity, therefore, of physician involvement is overstated. But there is something about having a physician assist with suicide that is comforting. If individuals know that they can enlist the aid of a doctor, it eases their worry about devising a pain-free and foolproof means of committing suicide. The doctor will know what to do, and the doctor will make sure it works. On a deeper level, a physician's involvement lends an air of legitimacy to suicide that it would otherwise lack. A suicide accomplished by inhaling carbon monoxide or taking an overdose of pills is viewed as sad, pitiful, and perhaps even creepy. I will never forget that when I was a child, the father of one of my neighborhood friends, a police officer, had committed suicide by shooting himself in the head in his garage. I could never walk through or past that garage without getting the chills and an overwhelming sense of sadness and empathy for my friend and her mother. So while there is no real necessity for physicians to assist with suicide, there are undoubtedly dignity benefits that flow from physician assistance, both to the suicide and his family.

The trial judge's constitutional ruling in *Baxter* was vacated by a deeply divided Montana Supreme Court. The Montana Supreme Court opinion, which garnered five out of seven justices' support, avoided the constitutional issues by resolving the case on the basis of statutory interpretation. Specifically, the majority took the other option presented in the plaintiffs' complaint—that physicians who assist their competent, terminally ill patients commit suicide through the use of lethal prescriptions do not violate the Montana homicide statute. Moreover, the *Baxter* majority decided that physicians under such circumstances could invoke the statutory consent defense, since their patients had consented to the act of the physician that caused their death.

To understand the *Baxter* reasoning, one must know a little bit about Montana law. The Montana statute defines homicide as an act that "purposely or knowingly causes the death of another human being."[149] Another section of the statute establishes a generic consent defense to crimes, stating that the "consent of the victim to conduct charged to constitute an offense or to the result thereof is a defense."[150] The law further specifies four exceptions to the consent defense, the fourth of which was applicable to *Baxter*. It provides that the consent defense is inapposite when "it is against public policy to permit the conduct or the resulting harm, even though consented to."[151] The question of statutory interpretation facing the Montana Supreme Court in *Baxter* was whether PAS was "against public policy" of the state.

The *Baxter* court reviewed prior decisions construing the "public policy" exception, finding that the common thread was a determination that consent could not be invoked to excuse violent, peace-breaching conduct, such as domestic violence or other assault. It concluded, "[T]he act of a physician handing medicine to a terminally ill patient, and the patient's subsequent peaceful and private act of taking the medicine, are not comparable to the violent, peace-breaching conduct that this Court and others have found to violate public policy."[152] Moreover, because the Montana legislature had enacted statutes recognizing the right of physicians to pull the plug on life-sustaining medical treatment, the court thought that this evinced a "long-standing, evolving, and unequivocal recognition of the terminally ill patient's right to self-determination at the end of life" so that it would be "incongruous to conclude that a physician's indirect aid in dying [through PAS] is contrary to public policy."[153]

The majority opinion in *Baxter* garnered five justices' support, but four of those justices concurred as a separate group. In this separate concurrence, they agreed that the statutory interpretation of the consent defense was correct. But they stated that the Montana legislature needs to "step up to the plate" and decide whether it agreed with the court's interpretation of that statute.[154] Because the decision was based on statutory, not constitutional, interpretation, the Montana legislature was free to rewrite the homicide statute to explicitly disallow the consent defense for PAS. The four concurring justices suggested that the legislature should promptly evaluate the court's interpretation, as the "logic of the Court's opinion is not necessarily limited to physicians."[155] In other words, because the consent defense was theoretically available to anyone who assists with another's suicide, laypersons (not just physicians) who assist with suicide might be able to claim immunity from homicide.

One could argue that the court would consider layperson-assisted suicide (LAS) to be against the "public policy" of the state in a way that PAS is not. But this would be a challenging argument, since the *Baxter* rationale was based on two notions: (1) PAS is not violent or peace-breaching; and (2) the state's recognition of the right to refuse unwanted medical treatment evinces a policy of recognizing a broad right to self-determination at the end of life. LAS does not seem to be inherently different in kind than PAS, in the sense that it, too, is not a typical act of aggression or violence. And if there is a right to self-determination at the end of life, then it should not matter whether the means of exercising that right involves assistance of a layperson rather than a physician. It seems likely, therefore, that the four concurring justices' concerns about the implications for LAS may come to fruition absent statutory amendment.

The *Baxter* decision is a preview of the litigation strategy of right-to-die advocates. Since *Glucksberg* and *Quill* effectively closed the door on federal constitutional claims, the right-to-die battle will be waged primarily in state courts, invoking state constitutional and statutory claims. Another intriguing example is litigation filed in late 2009 in Connecticut, in Blick v. Office of the Division of Criminal Justice. In *Blick*, two Connecticut physicians filed a lawsuit seeking a declaration that the Connecticut assisted suicide statute does not prohibit PAS. On the surface, the claim seems analogous to the plaintiffs' claim in *Baxter*. But the *Blick* claim is more aggressive, asserting that the word "suicide" in the assisted suicide statute does not include "aid in dying" (defined by the plaintiffs as PAS). The challenge is thus to the very definition of suicide itself—that the "choice of a mentally competent terminally ill individual for a peaceful death as an alternative to a dying process the patient finds unbearable does not constitute 'suicide.'"[156] If the Connecticut courts agree with this argument, it could send shock waves throughout the country, opening the door for similar litigation in the many states with specific laws prohibiting assisted suicide.

Though this new wave of litigation does not involve federal constitutional claims, it nonetheless has significant potential to reshape the legal landscape. These lawsuits endeavor to capitalize on judicial reticence to tackle constitutional issues, focusing instead on discrete but critically important statutory language. They illustrate how the line is beginning (and will continue) to blur between PAS and LAS. Although the lawsuits focus exclusively on PAS, acceptance of the arguments raised in such cases will likely lead to litigation to recognize LAS as well. In the *Blick* case, for example, the connection between PAS and LAS is even more overt than in the *Baxter* case. The Compassion and Choices press release accompanying the *Blick* lawsuit recounts the story of Hunt Williams, an elderly Connecticut man who assisted his terminally ill friend's suicide by cleaning, loading, and carrying his gun. Williams was tried and convicted of violating the assisted suicide law, but was sentenced to only one year of probation. The press release quotes Williams as saying, "I faced ten years in prison because my friend, John Welles, could not get from his physician the aid in dying that he needed. John Welles should not have had to shoot himself. John was dying of cancer and should have been able to have his doctor prescribe medication to ease his dying."[157]

The implication, of course, is that if Connecticut had not been so foolhardy as to interpret the word "suicide" as including PAS, laypersons such as Williams would never need to assist with suicide. This may or may not be true; it is hard to know what impact the legal availability of PAS would have on the incidence of LAS. There do not appear to be any data out of Oregon, for example, that would provide insight on this question. Undoubtedly, a good number of persons who would otherwise (1) not commit suicide, (2) commit suicide alone, or (3) commit suicide with the help of friends will turn instead to PAS when it is legalized. Yet there presumably would be others who would opt against PAS for various reasons, such as the lack of access to a doctor, reticence to get strangers involved, or a desire to avoid the second opinions, waiting periods, and other bureaucratic hurdles associated with legalized PAS. So it is an overstatement to claim that legalizing PAS will eliminate LAS.

More subtly, there is an implication in the *Blick* press release that LAS, like PAS, is acceptable, understandable, and (presumably) legally excusable behavior. Hunt Williams's prosecution was not invoked to contrast "good" PAS with "bad" LAS—quite the contrary. His case was used to illustrate how good, compassionate people are being inappropriately targeted for criminal punishment for providing "aid in dying" to terminally ill friends. The gravamen of the *Blick* lawsuit is that the word "suicide" should no longer be interpreted to include PAS. And if "suicide" can be redefined to exclude PAS, there is no logical reason why it cannot be redefined to exclude LAS as well.

The litigation discussed in this chapter illustrates one thing rather well: courts have a difficult time grappling with the relationship between the Constitution and death. Perhaps this is because death, whether in the context of capital punishment, the refusal of life-sustaining medical treatment, or assisted suicide, is an area fraught with complex and varied personal emotions and values. Asking a single judge, or a panel of judges, to tell us whether amorphous language in the Constitution grants us a "right to die" or a "right to die with dignity" or a "right to determine the manner and timing of our own death" or whatever phraseology one wishes to use, may be asking too much of our least democratic branch of government. Although there is arguably a liberty interest in controlling one's own body, including the right to commit suicide and perhaps seek another's aid in doing so, the disparate views expressed in court decisions thus far undermines confidence in courts' ability to shepherd this right well, particularly without extensive help from legislatures. Given the intense emotions and wide variety of views on these subjects, due respect for democratic processes and pluralism should counsel us to resolve these issues whenever possible through the legislative, not judicial, branch. In this manner, the people can express their collective preferences, effectuating an affirmative opt-in for these goals, as has been the experience in Oregon and Washington.

Explicating societal preferences for death-related rights through the legislative process avoids the interminable litigation that would be necessary to ascertain the parameters of such rights. Case-by-case adjudication is slow, unpredictable, and can result in inconsistent or fractured opinions. The advantage to legislative determination is that statutes can define and limit rights in a way that courts simply cannot, providing a stable, unified, and detailed set of rules regarding the who, what, where, when, and how of the rights so defined. Statutes, for example, can draw a clear line in the sand between PAS and euthanasia, PAS and LAS, competent and incompetent patients, or terminal or nonterminal status. And if those statutory lines prove unworkable, the legislature can redraw them relatively easily. Courts, by contrast, are poorly equipped to draw, maintain, or erase such lines.

6

Not Dead Yet

Here is the test to find whether your mission on earth is finished. If you're alive, it isn't.

—Richard Bach, *Illusions: The Adventures of a Reluctant Messiah* (1997)

Death of the whole brain is accepted as legal death. But what happens when our brains are severely and permanently damaged, yet still have some minimal degree of function? If discernible brain function remains, no legal declaration of death is supposed to ensue. But there are legal procedures—explored in the previous chapter, such as advance directives and the invocation of the right to refuse unwanted treatment—that allow death to occur short of whole brain death. These alternatives to whole brain death create pressure to terminate life support for those who suffer from massive brain injuries. The costs associated with their health care are enormous. The emotional suffering experienced by their loved ones is immense. Their brain damage is irreversible in the vast majority of cases. Even if they do recover some degree of awareness, their quality of life will be significantly diminished.

High profile cases such as Terri Schiavo, Nancy Cruzan, and Karen Ann Quinlan illustrate such pressure and the public's continued ambivalence over legal alternatives to whole brain death. Because severely brain-damaged individuals are not yet legally dead, it is important that providers, family members, and policy makers understand the nature of these patients' conditions in order to appropriately weigh available legal options and agree upon an appropriate course of care. Unfortunately, recent evidence reveals significant misunderstanding among both providers and the public about the various disorders of consciousness.

Differentiating Disorders of Consciousness

Brain disorders such as coma, the vegetative state, and the minimally conscious state all involve a degree of unconsciousness, though they fall on different points of a broad spectrum. The word "coma," for example, is derived from the Greek *koma,* meaning "deep sleep." A patient in a coma is unconscious and lacks any sleep-wake cycle. She appears to be sleeping all the time, with eyes closed and an inability to be awakened by external stimuli such as light or noise. Comas range from mild to severe, and their duration varies considerably. Some individuals will emerge from a coma, regaining normal consciousness; others may fall into a vegetative state; still others will die.

The Vegetative State

Coma patients who fall into a vegetative state (VS) will open their eyes but not evince any consciousness. It is this state of intermittent wakefulness-without-awareness that differentiates the comatose from the vegetative patient. In 1994, the five largest neurological societies in the United States formed a Multi-Society Task Force (MSTF) to explore the definition and prognosis of the vegetative state. They agreed that when a vegetative state lasts for more than one month, it is referred to as a "persistent" vegetative state (PVS)—a condition that the MSTF estimates encompasses between fourteen thousand to thirty-five thousand patients in the United States.[1] When PVS endures for more than a year for traumatic brain injury patients—such as those who have been in automobile or sporting accidents—or for more than three months due to nontraumatic injury, the vegetative state is generally labeled as "permanent."[2] Once a VS patient is determined to be permanently vegetative, many providers consider continued medical maintenance of the patient to be futile and may begin advocating termination of life support.[3]

The MSTF defined VS as a condition of "complete unawareness of the self and the environment accompanied by sleep wake cycles, with either complete or partial preservation of hypothalamic and brain-stem autonomic functions."[4] The MSTF definition thus requires three separate conditions: (1)

complete unawareness of the self and the environment; (2) sleep-wake cycles; and (3) complete or partial preservation of hypothalamic and brain stem autonomic functions.

Numbers two and three are uncomplicated. Sleep-wake cycles can be observed with no special medical training. And the preservation of all or some hypothalamic and brain stem autonomic functions is evident by continuation of functions regulated by these portions of the brain, including maintenance of body temperature and breathing without assistance. But the first criterion of VS—complete unawareness of self and environment—is notoriously difficult to determine, even for a skilled physician.

Awareness of self and environment is a rough proxy for the existence of consciousness. Consciousness—or more specifically, its absence—is hard to pin down, since there is no machine or laboratory test that can definitively tell us whether a person is aware of either herself or her surroundings. A determination of unconsciousness thus requires careful, repeated bedside examinations involving the administration of various stimuli—such as pain, light, or noise—to observe whether the patient can respond in a sustained, reproducible, and purposeful way.

The MSTF admits that there is a "biologic limitation to the certainty of this definition since we can only infer the absence of conscious experience in another person. A false positive diagnosis of a persistent vegetative state could occur if it was concluded that a person lacked awareness when, in fact, he or she was aware."[5] Bedside tests to gauge response to stimuli are, in other words, reliable only when the patient is physiologically capable of responding. As the MSTF further elaborated, the risk of PVS misdiagnosis is heightened "because of confusion about the terminology used to describe patients in this [vegetative] condition, the inexperience of the examiner, or an insufficient period of observation."[6]

The MSTF's concerns about misdiagnosis appear to be well founded. Several published studies have confirmed a startlingly high rate of misdiagnosis of PVS. In 1993, for example, a study conducted by Nancy Childs and colleagues examined forty-nine patients who had been diagnosed as being either in a coma or PVS. The research team carefully evaluated each patient using accepted standard definitions of coma and PVS. They determined that 37 percent of patients diagnosed as being in a coma or PVS were, in fact, capable of exhibiting behavior indicative of consciousness. The most commonly missed clinical signs of consciousness were responses to commands and purposeful visual fixation or tracking.[7] The authors surmised that misdiagnosis was caused by "confusion over terminology" or "lack of extended observation for behavioral evidence of cognitive awareness by qualified personnel."[8] They further suggested that because behavioral responses in coma or PVS patients are often slow or erratic, "health care providers may discount the reports of responses seen by family or other caregivers. If untutored in assessment of consciousness, the physician examining the patient briefly on rounds may not see signs of awareness."[9]

A similar study of PVS patients was published in 1996 by Keith Andrews and colleagues at the Royal Hospital for Neurodisability in London. Andrews's team studied the admission records of forty patients who had been diagnosed as vegetative and were more than six months' postinjury. Patients were given daily occupational therapy sessions for six weeks to determine whether they were capable of responding to commands or questions by using a buzzer switch or looking at named objects.[10] For patients who were blind or visually impaired, the therapists would speak the letters of the alphabet, and patients could operate the buzzer when the therapist spoke the desired letter. Any observed evidence of consciousness was confirmed by at least two members of the research team. Of the forty PVS patients, seventeen—43 percent—were capable of exhibiting awareness and consequently had been misdiagnosed,[11] a misdiagnosis rate remarkably similar to that reported three years earlier by Nancy Childs's study. The seventeen patients whose signs of consciousness had been missed, moreover, had been misdiagnosed for relatively long periods of time, with seven of the seventeen misdiagnosed for more than one year, and three between four and seven years.

One novel finding of the Andrews study was that 65 percent of the misdiagnosed patients (eleven patients total) were severely visually impaired or blind, a problem that the researchers found troubling, "since clinicians making the diagnosis of the vegetative state place great emphasis on the inability of the patient to visually track or blink to threat."[12] Because eleven out of the seventeen misdiagnosed patients could not see, standard bedside tests that relied too heavily on visual response to stimuli were poor predictors of awareness. Perhaps even more disturbing, the Andrews study noted that, in most cases, the inappropriate PVS diagnosis had been made by a neurosurgeon, neurologist, or rehabilitation specialist, whom the researchers asserted "could have been expected to have experience of the vegetative state."[13]

One would hope that the diagnosis of PVS has improved significantly since the Childs and Andrews studies of the mid-1990s. A 2009 study by Caroline Schnakers and colleagues, however, suggests that such hope is not warranted. Schnakers's team studied forty-four patients diagnosed as vegetative by the consensus of treating providers using standard clinical behavioral tests. The research team assessed each patient using a standardized neurobehavioral rating scale called the JFK Coma Recovery Scale-Revised (CRS-R), which was used because of its sensitivity in distinguishing VS patients from those who have some minimal consciousness.[14] The researchers found that eighteen out of the forty-four patients—41 percent—exhibited signs of awareness and had been misdiagnosed as vegetative. As with the Childs study, the most common missed indicator of awareness was visual fixation or pursuit.[15] Schnakers's team concluded that "[d]espite the importance of diagnostic accuracy and advances in the past 15 years, the rate of misdiagnosis among patients with disorders of consciousness has not substantially changed."[16]

The difficulty of accurately diagnosing the vegetative state is also exhibited by the reported cases of so-called PVS "miracles." Perhaps the most well-known and documented case is that of Terry Wallis, an Arkansas man who in 1984, at the age of nineteen, was involved in a serious car accident that rendered him unconscious. When Wallis exhibited no improvement after one year, his physicians told his parents that he was PVS and there was little hope for recovery.[17] The Terry Wallis Fund Web site recounts the story:

> Doctors cautioned the Wallis' [sic] [about Terry's grunts and movements]. These reactions, they said, were pure illusion. Terry's "responses" were nothing more than behavior hiccups, leftover neurological impulses from a once-healthy brain. Ghosts in a broken-down machine. No matter how convincingly Terry seemed to "be there" every now and then, he was—in fact— utterly incapable of cognition. The doctors made themselves very clear on this point: the man the Wallis had once known as a loving husband and son was gone. Furthermore, the medical community assured the Wallis' that any attempts at rehabilitating their son would prove useless.[18]

Despite this hopeless prognosis, nineteen years after his car accident, Wallis spontaneously uttered the word "mom" upon seeing his mother enter the room.[19] His recovery has continued to this day.

Wallis's story has engendered much controversy within the medical community. The consensus seems to be that Wallis had at some point emerged from PVS and became minimally conscious, though when this emergence occurred is far from clear. Undoubtedly, at some point in his nineteen-year journey toward exhibiting consciousness, Terry Wallis became conscious, though he was unable to exhibit it behaviorally for some time. But what is equally clear is that in 1984, when Wallis was injured, the medical community had not recognized a distinct condition known as the "minimally conscious" state. Disorders of consciousness in the mid-1980s were relatively black and white; there was no conceptualization of consciousness as a spectrum with infinite gradients. If a patient was unconscious, there were only a handful of recognized possible diagnoses, the most common of which were coma and VS. The difference between coma and VS was marked by the VS patient's open eyes and sleep-wake cycle, characteristics that Wallis possessed. Accordingly, under the state of medical knowledge as it existed in 1984, Wallis was considered vegetative. When his vegetative state endured for well over one year, he was classified as permanently vegetative.

Researchers anxious to explain Wallis's regained ability to speak have studied his brain using state-of-the-art scanning technology. The scans indicate that Wallis's brain continues to show neurological improvement, though they reveal widespread injury to the nerve fibers (axons).[20] The researchers speculate that Wallis's brain has somehow been able to sprout new nerves—a process called axonal regrowth—a phenomenon that previously had been documented in monkeys.[21] Why Wallis's brain was able to regrow critical nerve connections, and other severely brain-injured patients are not, is still unknown.

Wallis's story highlights another odd phenomenon in PVS recovery stories generally: a perceived need by the medical community to defend the incontrovertible nature of PVS diagnosis (and its concomitant hopeless prognosis) by confidently asserting that such recoveries involve unfortunate and rare incidents of misdiagnosis.[22] In Wallis's case, for example, physicians look back at Wallis's recovery with twenty-twenty vision and try to explain it using modern terminology.[23] A 2006 editorial by neurologist Eelco Wijdicks

in the *Mayo Clinic Proceedings* illustrates this phenomenon. In it, Wijdicks crit-
icizes a 1995 documentary about Wallis aired by the Discovery Health Chan-
nel that suggested Wallis was in PVS, asserting, "I suspect that any neurologist
who views the home video segments included in the Discovery Health Chan-
nel documentary will note that Wallis was not in PVS before his improvement. He looks about and responds quickly to his family. Although Wallis
was not in PVS, it is unclear what state he was really in because he was not
repeatedly examined by a neurologist."[24]

In what year these "home video segments" were taken is unclear. If they
were taken near the time of the 2005 documentary, Wijdicks may be correct
that a neurologist at that time would (or should) have immediately recognized that Wallis was no longer PVS but instead minimally conscious. Yet this
ex post rationalization substitutes current knowledge about disorders of consciousness for the state of medical knowledge upon which Wallis was initially
diagnosed in 1984. Because there were no formal criteria for diagnosing the
minimally conscious state until 2002, any neurologist examining Wallis would
have been hard-pressed to diagnose Wallis as anything other than PVS for
many years after his injury. Wijdicks's editorial nonetheless proclaims, "To
say that the case of Wallis is evidence of meaningful clinical improvement in
a case of PVS is a simplistic generalization. To say instead that PVS is often
overdiagnosed because the clinical state is uncommon and few physicians
have the skill to examine patients appropriately seems a more reasonable
conclusion."[25]

Wijdicks's logical fallacy—a fallacy that he is far from alone in
embracing—dismisses the possibility of PVS recovery by recharacterizing
a patient as something other than PVS. This fallacy blames the treating
physician using the power of perfect hindsight: the treating physician made
an unfortunate mistake, missing behavioral signs of consciousness; the treating physician was not trained in neurology; the treating physician did not
retest the patient enough; the treating physician should have obtained a second or third opinion, and so forth. Discounting PVS recoveries as unfortunate cases of misdiagnoses—even when doing so requires resorting to perfect
hindsight—is supposed to reassure us that we can still trust physicians when
they tell us a loved one is in a permanent vegetative state from which they
will not recover. Yet far from offering us reassurance, the medical community's reflexive offhand dismissal of any PVS "miracle" story as nothing more

than another case of misdiagnosis should highlight, not minimize, the shaky foundation upon which PVS diagnoses rest.

Ex post classification of Wallis as minimally conscious cannot change the fact that he was a severely neurologically disabled person who was written off by his health care providers as beyond hope for nineteen long years. Yet he beat the odds, somehow clawing his way back to consciousness and an ability to exhibit it to others. Wallis's parents could have initiated proceedings to terminate his life support—as many families understandably do under such circumstances—but they did not. His case stands as an example of what can go wrong all too often. It also stands as an example of the incredible potential of the human brain to heal itself if given enough time, offering some hope for loved ones who hesitate to terminate life support despite strong incentives to do so.

Terry Wallis's recovery may be the most recent and well-documented story, but it is not the only one. There have been a relatively steady stream of PVS recoveries, some better documented than others, although they are still quite rare. There's the story of Patricia White Bull, who slipped into what the media amorphously described as "unresponsive to the world . . . [in a] catatonic state"[26] and "near coma, eyes open but recognizing nothing," while delivering her fourth child.[27] In late 1999, after sixteen years of no behavioral signs of consciousness, Bull suddenly began speaking. She continues to speak and make gains in rehabilitation.

Another recovery story is that of Donald Herbert, a Buffalo fire fighter who suffered brain injury in 1995 when a burning building collapsed on his head. Herbert's consciousness level, like that of Terry Wallis, has been subject to some hindsight revision,[28] though given the time period of his injury, it is safe to say that he was treated by providers for many years as being in a vegetative state.[29] It was not until 2002—seven years after Herbert's accident—when anyone surmised that he might retain a slim reed of consciousness. At that time, a young Pakistani-trained doctor, Dr. Jamil Ahmed, assumed care for Herbert. After examining Herbert over an extended period of time, Dr. Ahmed concluded that Herbert was "close to the vegetative state" and initiated a new course of care. Ahmed began experimenting with various combinations of drugs, some of which have been credited as responsible for Herbert's unusual recovery.[30] Herbert's consciousness fluctuated until his death from pneumonia in 2006.[31]

Another widely publicized case is that of Gary Dockery, a Tennessee police officer who in 1988 was shot in the head when responding to a call. Dockery was described variously in media reports as being in a "coma-like state,"[32] "persistent vegetative state," or "locked-in state."[33] He was unable to move, talk, or feed himself, though media reports suggest that Dockery could occasionally respond to questions using eye motions, suggesting the possibility of some degree of consciousness.[34] After seven and a half years in this state, Dockery developed life-threatening pneumonia and, while being prepared for surgery to remove the fluid from his lungs, he suddenly began talking.[35] He talked incessantly with his family for eighteen hours before returning back to a mostly unresponsive, silent state. He died in April 1997.[36]

There are some additional well-publicized cases that are worthy of brief mention because they represent the most frightening aspect of a PVS misdiagnosis—namely, its potentially deadly combination with a successful petition to remove life support. The right to refuse unwanted medical treatment may be exercised by incompetent patients through the petition of certain third parties such as family members, court-appointed guardians, or other statutorily recognized proxies. But what happens if an appropriate third party petitions for removal of life support from a PVS patient who has been misdiagnosed?

The salient question in such cases is whether the patient would want to continue life support. In other words, if the patient were competent, what would they tell us they wanted to do under the circumstances? Would they tell us to discontinue their life support? Ascertaining the patient's desires requires a court to consider the relevant context, including the patient's diagnosis and prognosis. It is conceivable that a patient who is diagnosed as PVS might wish to discontinue life support (due to the inherently poor prognosis that goes along with such a diagnosis), whereas the same patient might want to continue life support if diagnosed with a less dire condition involving some minimal degree of consciousness. The diagnosis therefore can (and should) make a difference in the legal outcome of a petition to remove life support.

But diagnosing PVS is notoriously tricky because of its inherent reliance on behavioral tests for consciousness. So mistakes inevitably will be made. In most instances, a misdiagnosis of PVS will mean a foregone opportunity to rehabilitate or communicate with a patient. In other cases—how many can only be speculated—a misdiagnosis of PVS can lead to termination of life support, and hence death of a patient who was in fact conscious to some degree. The cases of Carrie Coons, Haleigh Poutre, and Jesse Ramirez illustrate the potential for such errors and stand as cautionary tales.

In 1988, eighty-six-year-old Carrie Coons suffered a massive stroke. She was diagnosed by two separate physicians as being in a PVS.[37] About four months after her stroke, Coons's sister, Edith Gannon, asked a court to remove her feeding tube and allow Coons to die.[38] At the hearing, Gannon presented expert testimony of a nationally recognized specialist in geriatrics, who evaluated Coons and testified that her vegetative state was irreversible.[39] The trial judge granted the request to remove Coons's feeding tube. A couple of weeks later—before the tube was removed—Coons regained consciousness. She was able to speak and eat soft food by mouth, though it is unclear if she was ever lucid enough to be considered competent.[40] The trial judge vacated his order to terminate life support, and Coons lived for another two and a half years.[41]

A similar mistake almost led to tragic consequences for Haleigh Poutre, an eleven-year-old girl in Massachusetts who had been so severely beaten that she lost consciousness. Only nine days after Haleigh was admitted to the hospital for her injuries, the state's Department of Social Services petitioned to disconnect Haleigh's respirator and feeding tube, asserting that Haleigh was in a vegetative state with no chance of recovery.[42] After a hearing at which testimony was provided by a court-appointed guardian and two medical experts (who disagreed as to whether removal was appropriate), the trial court issued an opinion concluding that Haleigh's "dignity and quality of life would be most respected by withdrawing both the ventilator and feeding tube."[43]

In an odd turn of events, Haleigh's stepfather, who had been charged with abuse that led to Haleigh's condition, petitioned the state's supreme court to reverse the trial court's withdrawal order, perhaps realizing that Haleigh's death could elevate the charges against him to murder.[44] The Massachusetts Supreme Judicial Court upheld the trial court's order, clearing the way for Haleigh to die, concluding that Haleigh "is in an irreversible and permanent coma, with the least amount of brain function that a person can have and still be considered alive."[45]

Although the court's use of language is rather loose, its reference to a "permanent and irreversible coma" and minimal brain function is descriptive of higher brain death with retained brain stem function—that is, a PVS. One day after the state supreme court's ruling, state officials revealed that Haleigh had begun to show some purposeful responses indicative of consciousness.[46] Haleigh subsequently recovered enough to give statements to the police regarding her abuse, leading to her stepfather's conviction for child abuse.[47] Having once effectively been given up for dead, Haleigh is still alive and rehabilitating today.

The case of Jesse Ramirez is the most recent near-death mistake. In May 2007, Jesse and his wife Rebecca were riding in their SUV when Jesse suddenly lost control and crashed. Jesse was diagnosed by doctors as being in a vegetative state, but Rebecca survived with only minor injuries.[48] Only nine days after the accident, Rebecca asked Jesse's providers to remove his feeding tube and transfer him to a hospice so that he could die.[49] The providers complied, and Jesse's food and water were discontinued. Jesse's siblings and parents vehemently disagreed with Rebecca's decision, believing her judgment might have been clouded by the couple's rocky marriage. The family sought permission from an Arizona trial court to reinsert Jesse's feeding tube, winning a temporary reprieve pending the outcome of mediation between the family and Rebecca.[50] As the mediation effort was taking place, Jesse regained consciousness. He has since divorced his wife and begun the long road to rehabilitation. He insists that he would not have wanted to die by starvation.[51]

Jesse's story sparked intense debate within Arizona about the appropriateness of statutes that permit family members to make life support decisions for patients who lack advance directives. The culmination of Arizona's debate is a new law, dubbed "Jesse's law," that creates a presumption that patients would not want their feeding tubes withdrawn. Specifically, the law prohibits withdrawal of nutrition and hydration unless a court finds, by clear and convincing evidence, that the patient: (1) is in "an irreversible coma or . . . a persistent vegetative state that is irreversible or incurable"; and (2) manifested an intent (while competent) to refuse artificial nutrition and hydration in the event he was diagnosed as being in an irreversible coma or PVS.[52] There is a strong presumption, in other words, that PVS patients would not want to die by starvation.

The stories of unexpected recovery should counsel humility and caution before abandoning treatment for those faced with a PVS diagnosis. While it is undoubtedly true that many diagnoses of PVS are accurate and result in very poor prognoses, there seems to be more doubt, ambiguity, and hope than the medical community is willing to admit, preferring instead to employ hindsight to rediagnose patients who have recovered. As the cases of Carrie Coons, Haleigh Poutre, and Jesse Ramirez illustrate, there is a potential for loved ones (or guardians) to pull the trigger too quickly, petitioning for withdrawal of life support based on early bedside evaluations that can provide only a rough snap shot of the patient's prognosis.

There seems to be a collective misimpression that PVS is a certain diagnosis with certain prognosis, when in actuality it is a difficult diagnosis, susceptible of substantial rates of misdiagnosis, with a prognosis that is difficult to state with certainty. As the Terry Wallis, Patricia White Bull, Gary Dockery, and Donnie Herbert cases show, even patients who have been in a PVS for long periods of time are potentially capable of recovering, perhaps due to very slow regrowth of axons in the brain. Predicting who among the PVS population has such potential is obviously difficult, but it is likely to be the focus of important future study. Until then, the best we can say with confidence is that misdiagnosis is too common, recoveries happen but occasionally, and extreme caution should be exercised before granting petitions to remove life support. The handful of states, like Arizona with "Jesse's law," that impose a higher evidentiary burden for granting petitions to withdraw life support have probably struck the right balance, erring on the side of life in all but the clearest of cases.

LOCKED-IN SYNDROME

Patients who suffer from locked-in syndrome (LIS) do not actually suffer from a disorder of consciousness, but their symptoms are sufficiently similar to several consciousness disorders that they are often misdiagnosed as being PVS. If consciousness is imagined as a spectrum, the LIS patient is on one far end, clearly within the realm of consciousness. A person in LIS is aware of his environment and has intact cognitive ability, but he suffers from complete or near-complete paralysis of voluntary muscles, rendering him substantially unable to respond to any stimuli. Some locked-in patients are able to move their eyes to a certain degree, allowing some caregivers to realize, over time, that the patient is aware of his surroundings. Others are completely paralyzed, a state referred to as "total" locked in syndrome.

Even if an LIS patient is not totally locked-in, spotting her eye movement is not easy, and some LIS patients have been misdiagnosed for years as PVS.

Perhaps the most famous locked-in patient is Jean-Dominique Bauby, former editor-in-chief of *Elle* magazine, who by using blinks of his left eyelid wrote a moving book called *The Diving Bell and the Butterfly*. Another example is Julia Tavalaro, who was diagnosed as PVS for six years before a speech therapist noticed that her eyes seemed to evince awareness of her surroundings. Like Bauby, Tavalaro wrote a poignant book about her experience, *Look Up for Yes*, using eye movements. More recently, in late 2009, a Belgian man, Rom Houben, was discovered to be fully conscious and in LIS after being misdiagnosed and treated as permanently vegetative for a startling twenty-three years.[53]

No statistics are kept on how many patients suffer from locked-in syndrome. No one knows how many LIS patients are misdiagnosed as PVS. What is known is that because the definition of PVS hinges upon a patient's unawareness of self and the environment—which can only be tested by seeing if the patient can respond to external stimuli—there is a potential for misdiagnosing LIS patients as vegetative, particularly if the patient is totally locked in.[54]

The MSTF suggested that brain scans could potentially differentiate locked-in patients from vegetative patients by revealing higher metabolic levels in the locked-in patients.[55] The existence of a lowered regional cerebral metabolic rate for glucose with PVS patients is well established.[56] But there is only one published small-scale study that compares the brains of seven PVS patients with three locked-in patients (the study that the MSTF relied on), and it does suggest that locked-in patients have notably higher cerebral glucose metabolic rates than vegetative patients.[57] To what extent physicians are employing such scans to ascertain whether their patients are locked in versus vegetative is unclear, but the relative rarity of these tests to assess vegetative patients[58]—for which much more evidence exists—suggests that their use among locked-in patients is similarly rare.

Another potential, remarkably creative means for differentiating total LIS patients from vegetative patients measures changes in the patient's salivary pH. Because the pH of saliva is notably different when one imagines "milk" versus "lemon," research has shown that accurate yes/no communication can be achieved with total locked-in patients who are told to imagine lemon for "yes" or milk for "no."[59] Even more futuristically, scientists are making significant strides in the refinement of brain computer interface (BCI) technology that reads a patient's brain waves and translates their thoughts via computer, potentially allowing locked-in patients not merely to communicate but also to operate computers, wheelchairs, or other machinery.[60]

THE MINIMALLY CONSCIOUS STATE

The role of technology has not been limited to differentiating the conscious from the unconscious. It has been the driving force behind a revolution in understanding about consciousness itself. Advanced neuroimaging techniques have revealed that consciousness is not a simple binary of consciousness versus unconsciousness. Instead, there appears to be a broad and virtually infinite spectrum of consciousness. And contrary to traditional understanding, many (or perhaps even most) severely brain-damaged patients fall somewhere in the middle of the spectrum, between full consciousness (for example, LIS) and zero consciousness (for example, VS). These patients occupy a vast gray area (no pun intended), experiencing intermittent or fluctuating pockets of consciousness. The medical community has long known that compromised consciousness can result from age-related dementia and disorders such as Alzheimer's, Creutzfeldt-Jakob, and Huntington's diseases. But in recent years, advanced neuroimaging techniques have begun to reveal that other types of patients, including some patients previously categorized as completely unconscious (vegetative), occupy the twilight zone of consciousness. Two intriguing examples are akinetic mutism (AM) and the minimally conscious state (MCS).

Akinetic mutism is described by the MSTF as "a rare syndrome characterized by pathologically slowed or nearly absent bodily movement and loss of speech. Wakefulness and self-awareness may be preserved, but the level of mental function is reduced."[61] As with the vegetative state, AM may result after any event that causes brain lesions, including strokes, degenerative disease, car accidents, or other head trauma. There is a range of AM, with the most severe cases involving complete lack of movement or speech and unresponsiveness to commands, and milder cases exhibiting some movements or ability to respond. The most severe cases of AM may be misdiagnosed as vegetative because of the patient's immobility and inability to respond to commands. A well-trained provider should be able to distinguish AM from VS, however, by the patient's ability to engage in visual tracking.[62] Yet because AM patients can track objects with their eyes, severe cases of AM are susceptible of misdiagnosis as locked-in syndrome.[63]

A condition closely related to akinetic mutism—and indeed, perhaps indistinguishable from it—is the minimally conscious state. MCS was first formally defined in 2002 by a work group of health care providers as "a condition of severely altered consciousness in which minimal but definite behavioral evidence of self or environmental awareness is demonstrated."[64] The MCS patient's consciousness is minimal, transitory, and inconsistent. Such patients seem to drift in and out of awareness, with no clear pattern or consistently reproducible behavior. It is estimated that somewhere between 112,000 and 280,000 individuals in the United States are in a minimally conscious state.[65]

In metaphorical terms, the mind of the MCS patient is a light bulb that randomly switches on for short periods of time. The mind of a PVS patient is, by contrast, a burned-out bulb, incapable of switching on. And the locked-in patient is the opposite—a light bulb that is constantly switched on, though total paralysis renders the LIS patient physiologically unable to exhibit awareness other than perhaps an ability to move the eyes.

To make a diagnosis of MCS, the patient must demonstrate, on a reproducible or sustained basis, an ability to either follow simple commands, provide verbal or nonverbal yes/no responses to questions, verbalize distinct words, or demonstrate purposeful behavior such as reaching for objects, tracking objects with the eyes, or providing appropriate responses, such as smiling or crying, to emotional content.[66] MCS patients' abilities to engage in such acts are, by definition, fleeting and inconsistent, though they are reproducible and sustainable for the particular moment during which clinical testing occurs.

The definition of MCS appears to be relatively indistinguishable from akinetic mutism, as both conditions hinge upon some behavioral evidence of awareness that can include such things as following simple commands, gestural or verbal responses, reaching for objects, and visual tracking. Indeed, if visual tracking is present, it is exceedingly difficult to distinguish between AM and MCS based on the medical definitions. Both conditions lie somewhere in the middle of the consciousness spectrum; both require some minimal, reproducible behavioral manifestation of consciousness; and both have varied etiologies resulting in brain lesions. The Aspen Neurobehavioral Conference Workgroup that initially defined MCS acknowledged that akinetic mutism is likely to be indistinguishable from MCS, concluding that "until these diagnostic ambiguities can be resolved by future research, the above definitions [of MCS] should be applied to all patients whose behavior fails to substantiate higher levels of consciousness."[67] The end result seems to be that AM is now considered a subset of MCS that cannot be reliably diagnosed as a distinct disorder, suggesting that it may not be the "rare" and distinct disorder originally defined by the MSTF in the mid-1990s. The minimally conscious state thus appears to be a blanket term encompassing any patient who has an ability to exhibit purposeful responses. A patient in MCS is not constantly conscious (unlike the locked-in patient), but has fluctuating, unpredictable moments in which a skilled clinician, present at the right time, may be able to elicit behavior evincing awareness.

Like those in a vegetative state, some patients do unexpectedly emerge from a minimally conscious state. One recent example is Sarah Scantlin, a woman who, at age eighteen, was hit by a drunk driver, suffering extensive brain damage. Scantlin entered a minimally conscious state, able to visually fixate and occasionally respond to yes or no questions by blinking her eyes.[68] After twenty years in MCS, Sarah suddenly began speaking, shocking her caregivers and family. She continues to improve her speech and is working toward rehabilitation.[69]

Another case illustrates the progressive but also potentially cyclical nature of disorders of consciousness. A woman in Colorado, Christa Lilly, suffered a heart attack in 2000, slipped into a coma, and was eventually diagnosed as persistently vegetative.[70] But then Lilly briefly went in and out of consciousness on four different occasions, leading to her eventual reclassification as minimally conscious.[71] In 2007, after spending over six years in PVS/MCS, Lilly began speaking again—this time for three days, talking, eating, and laughing with friends and family—before inexplicably lapsing back into a minimally conscious state.[72] Whether, when, or for how long Lilly will ever emerge again is anyone's guess.

The next frontier for MCS research is identifying individuals who are unable to physically respond at all—due to complete motor paralysis, perhaps combined with blindness or deafness—but who retain fleeting moments of awareness. Unlike total locked-in patients, who are permanently conscious, these patients have only sporadic consciousness and should therefore be classified as MCS, yet if they are unable behaviorally to exhibit awareness, they will be diagnosed as vegetative. Is it possible that some patients now diagnosed as vegetative have a rudimentary awareness that they cannot physically exhibit? Could their minds have intact pockets of memories, such as family members, familiar voices, music, or places? Is it possible that some of these patients can hear what goes on around them—at least on occasion—and therefore be considered "aware" of themselves or their environment?

The answer appears to be a cautious maybe. In the last decade, scientists have begun exploring whether imaging tools such as functional magnetic resonance imaging (fMRI) or positron emission tomography (PET) could reveal preserved auditory or cerebral processing. PET scans involve the injection of radioactive chemicals into the body, which are then absorbed by the body. The rate of absorption yields a three-dimensional image of specific organs or tissues and their rates of blood flow, oxygen absorption, or glucose metabolism, thus providing physicians with a snapshot into the functioning of those organs or tissues. Functional MRI is, like traditional MRI, an imaging tool that does not require the use of radiation, instead using magnetic fields and radio frequency pulses to yield images of organs or tissues. Functional MRI is dramatically different from traditional MRI. Traditional MRI brain scans provide a snapshot of the brain's function in a still state. Functional MRI, by contrast, applies stimuli—such as familiar voices, music, nonsense noise, or specific information—while the patient is in the fMRI machine and scans the brain as it responds to the stimuli. The fMRI images can indicate whether the patient can process various types of auditory stimuli, respond more significantly to familiar voices or sounds, or follow commands mentally. Functional MRI, in other words, can provide our first neuroimaging glimpse of the brain in "real time" as it processes information.

The Functional Neuroimaging Revolution

The use of PET and fMRI has sparked a revolution in thinking about the brain and disorders of consciousness. These new functional imaging technologies have created controversy within the medical community concerning their validity, usefulness, and ethical use with patients in locked-in, minimally conscious, and vegetative states. If these technologies indicate that severely brain-damaged individuals retain greater awareness of their surroundings than previously assumed, does this suggest that more aggressive treatment should be provided or that withdrawal of life support is not ethically warranted? Or does it suggest the opposite—that patients' awareness of their dire predicament should make family or providers more open-minded about ending their suffering by terminating life support?

Functional neuroimaging techniques ultimately may be used to communicate with previously noncommunicative patients, allowing scientists to literally read such patients' minds. Such potential communication would create its own host of ethical and legal questions, including reconsideration of competency for some who have previously been categorized as incompetent to make their own health care decisions. If such technologies can render communication possible, must they be used in order to ascertain the patient's treatment preferences? If the patient wants to continue treatment, including aggressive rehabilitation, must such expensive care be provided, even if the provider thinks such rehabilitative efforts are futile?

One of the first published functional neuroimaging studies came in 2004, when Melanie Boly and colleagues used PET scans to determine if the brains of either vegetative or minimally conscious patients might indicate brain processing of clicking sounds, which could imply a potential ability to hear. The study involved five MCS patients, fifteen PVS patients, and eighteen healthy control subjects. The researchers discovered that for both the MCS and PVS patients there was activation in the outer layers of both hemispheres of the brain, in areas believed to be responsible for processing hearing. The MCS patients exhibited broader brain activation than the PVS patients, however, suggesting to the researchers that the MCS patients experienced "a more elaborate level of [auditory] processing."[73]

Another 2004 study, conducted by Laureys and colleagues, used PET scans on a forty-two-year-old male MCS patient and seemed to confirm Boly's findings regarding the hearing potential of MCS patients. Specifically, the Laureys experiment used PET scans to compare the extent of brain activation when the patient was provided meaningless noise versus sounds of an infant crying and the patient's own name. It revealed that the MCS patient's brain was activated much more widely in response to the infant's cries, and even more so to his own name, than to the meaningless noise.[74]

While the early PET scan studies were both important and promising, the explosion of fMRI onto the scientific scene was a game changer. One of the first published studies came in 2005, when Schiff and colleagues used fMRI to study brain response to auditory and tactile stimulation in two MCS patients as compared to seven healthy controls. They discovered that MCS

patients' brains responded in "remarkably similar" ways to the control subjects, both with regard to light touching of both hands as well as narratives of
familiar events presented by familiar persons.[75]

More surprisingly, similar findings have been made in PVS (rather than
MCS) patients. Specifically, a study published in 2005 by Adrian Owen and
colleagues used both PET and fMRI to evaluate a thirty-year-old PVS patient,
"KA." The scans revealed that KA's brain retained the potential for processing
semantically ambiguous sentences such as "there were dates and pears in the
fruitbowl." Owen concluded that KA's brain scans "yielded compelling evidence for high level residual auditory processing in the PVS patient."[76] More
significantly, Owen concluded that the results suggested that "some level of
speech comprehension is preserved in this patient; the different activation
patterns observed could not simply be due to the perception of sounds in
general as the basic acoustic properties of the stimuli were well matched
across conditions."[77] Owen's research was remarkable and controversial because he asserted not merely that PVS patients had the neurological capacity
to process sounds but the additional capacity to *understand* them—a thesis
that contradicts the very definition of PVS itself.

Owen's study of KA was bolstered by a study published the following
year by Austrian researchers led by Wolfgang Staffen. Staffen's study used
fMRI to examine the brain reaction of a fifty-year-old PVS patient to his own
name versus another name. Similar to the brain reactions of three healthy
control subjects, the PVS patient exhibited higher brain activity upon hearing
his own name as opposed to another name, a phenomenon which Staffen
concluded "requires the ability to perceive and access the meaning of words."[78]

While the results of the Owen and Staffen studies were promising, they
were potentially only outlier cases, providing snap shots of single PVS patients. In 2007, Di and colleagues published a larger-scale, three-month fMRI
study of eleven patients, seven of whom were diagnosed as vegetative and
four of whom were MCS. They took scans of the patients' response to hearing their own names spoken by familiar voices. Like both Owen's and Staffen's
studies, Di's research revealed that all of the vegetative patients showed some
cerebral activation within auditory regions of the brain, with three showing
"significant" activation and two others showing "widespread" activation extending to higher areas of the brain.[79] Di's study also revealed that, at three
months post-scanning, the two VS patients whose fMRI showed widespread

higher level activation began to exhibit clinically observable signs of consciousness and were recategorized as MCS. They asserted, "In our opinion, these two patients were already MCS during fMRI scanning but behavioral signs of consciousness could (even using the best clinical assessments available) only be shown 3 months later."[80] Di concluded that fMRI could be used as a better tool than bedside tests to differentiate MCS from VS patients.[81]

A study similar in scale to that of Di's was published in 2007 by Martin Coleman and colleagues, who studied fourteen patients, seven of whom were diagnosed as being in a vegetative state, five of whom were MCS, and the remaining two of whom were severely brain damaged but unambiguously conscious. The researchers used fMRI to measure brain activity of the patients in response to a hierarchy of five different degrees of auditory stimulation: (1) no noise; (2) scanner-type nonsense noise; (3) intelligible noise; (4) low ambiguity sentences (for example, "There was 'beer' and 'cider' on the kitchen shelf"); and (5) high ambiguity sentences (for example, "There were 'dates' and 'pears' in the fruit bowl").[82] The study found that "while some patients did not show any significant responses to the auditory stimuli, others, including patients clinically diagnosed as being in a VS, showed significant auditory, speech perception and semantic responses that were anatomically appropriate and comparable to the results of healthy volunteers."[83] They concluded that the findings "suggest that a small number of patients with a diagnosis of VS may retain islands of residual cognitive function that cannot be observed using methods that rely on the patients' ability to make overt motor responses."[84] Of the seven VS patients in the study, three showed "some evidence of intact speech processing abilities."[85] Interestingly, by contrast, only two of the five MCS patients exhibited similar evidence of auditory processing.[86] Like Di, Coleman acknowledged that the VS patients who evidenced speech processing capability could potentially be more properly classified as MCS; but unlike Di and his colleagues, Coleman's group concluded that "[t]he favoured opinion is that these results do not change the diagnosis of the patients" because "responses measured with functional brain imaging only provide 'neural correlates' of critical cognitive processes and such data are insufficient to conclude that the brain areas activated in normal participants are necessary for successful performance."[87] Objective indicators of continued function of certain portions of the brain known to be associated with speech comprehension, in other words, do not necessarily mean that such comprehension is actually occurring. Yet Coleman further explained that "although intact speech comprehension is not necessarily entailed by our observations, our data is most parsimoniously explained by assuming that certain neural responses to speech do provide evidence for intact comprehension."[88]

Coleman and colleagues published another, larger study of forty-one patients two years later in 2009, including twenty-two VS patients and nineteen MCS patients. Using a hierarchical speech processing paradigm similiar to the 2007 study, Coleman found that nineteen patients (46 percent) showed significant response both to sound versus silence and to meaningful speech (both low and high ambiguity sentences) versus unintelligible noise.[89] Of these nineteen patients, seven were VS and twelve were MCS,[90] yielding significant response rates of 32 percent for all VS patients and 63 percent for all MCS patients. Like the 2007 study, however, these response rates may imply only that these patients are capable of processing sound and speech; they do not tell us whether they have any conscious ability to understand the sound and speech being provided.

Coleman recognized this limitation, conducting additional brain scans to see if any of the patients would respond appropriately to high ambiguity sentences that could indicate an intact ability to differentiate (and hence, comprehend) words. Of the nineteen patients who responded significantly to sound and speech, four of them (two VS patients and two MCS patients) exhibited an ability to process high ambiguity sentences, leading the researchers to conclude that, for the two vegetative patients, there was "strong evidence that some aspects of speech comprehension, and thus, higher order function, are preserved despite absent behavioural markers."[91] They also noted that evidence of such awareness suggested that these two vegetative patients had been misdiagnosed, although they had both been evaluated extensively in specialist centers, "suggesting that even specialist teams employing appropriate behavioural tools can sometimes fail to detect evidence of higher order function."[92] The results led the researchers to suggest that fMRI would be a good adjunct to standard bedside tests of consciousness, not merely for ensuring an accurate diagnosis but also as a valuable prognostic tool, since seven out of eight VS patients who had progressed to MCS at the six-month follow-up mark were those who had exhibited significant response to both sound and speech.[93]

While these early functional neuroimaging studies prove that the neuronal structure for auditory processing is intact and functioning in some MCS and VS patients, they only inferentially support the possibility of actual comprehension (and hence consciousness). The biggest unanswered question, therefore, is whether vegetative patients (who by definition are completely unconscious) may have not only a physiological capacity to process auditory information but can actually do so. Is there, in other words, a way to prove that a vegetative patient can actually understand what they are hearing?

Initial compelling evidence came in late 2006, from a study published by Adrian Owen and colleagues, who studied a single, twenty-three-year-old female vegetative patient using fMRI. The young woman had been involved in a car accident and diagnosed as being in a vegetative state. At five months post-injury, Owen used fMRI to confirm that she evidenced brain activity consistent with the potential for speech comprehension. But the next step of the study was novel: researchers asked the young woman to perform two mental imagery tasks during an fMRI scan: (1) imagine playing a game of tennis; and (2) imagine moving through all of the rooms of her house, beginning at her front door. Remarkably, the parts of her brain responsible for engaging in mental imagery lit up, revealing "neural responses [that] were indistinguishable from those observed in healthy volunteers performing the same imagery tasks in the scanner."[94] Owen concluded that the results "confirm that, despite fulfilling the clinical criteria for a diagnosis of vegetative state, this patient retained the ability to understand spoken commands and to respond to them through her brain activity, rather than through speech or movement."[95] The scientists asserted that the fMRI results indicated "a clear act of intention, which confirmed beyond any doubt that she was consciously aware of herself and her surroundings."[96] If this VS patient is capable of processing information and using it to respond to commands, it implies that she is consequently aware of her surroundings, despite previous clinicians' diagnoses of a vegetative state.

Owen's groundbreaking research may have much larger implications. Although his initial mental imagery study was limited to a single patient, a larger-scale study of twelve healthy volunteers seems to support his assertion that commanding a patient to imagine performing specific tasks triggers brain activation in specific, identifiable portions of the brain. In a study published in 2007 by Melanie Boly and colleagues, researchers used fMRI to ascertain whether healthy individuals told to imagine certain things would trigger predictable, consistent brain responses. Boly's research also sought to determine whether blinded researchers looking at the fMRI images could accurately predict which imagination task the subjects were asked to undertake. In the first phase of the study, the healthy subjects were asked to imagine four different things for thirty seconds while inside the fMRI machine: imagine moving through your house, starting at the front door; imagine singing "Jingle Bells" at the top of your lungs; imagine playing tennis, hitting the ball very hard as if during a competitive game; and imagine the face of a familiar relative, focusing on the specific facial features one by one. [97] After looking at the fMRI scans that followed these four mental imagery tasks, the researchers determined that the spatial navigation task (imagine moving through your house) and the motor imagery task (imagine playing tennis) yielded the most robust evidence of activation of specific areas of the brain.

In the second phase of the Boly experiment, subjects alternated between the spatial navigation and motor imagery tasks (with rest intervals in between) in a randomized order chosen by a computer and unknown to the researchers. Based on predefined criteria identifying the areas of the brain affected by the two tasks, the researchers then looked at the blinded fMRI scans and predicted whether the subjects had been asked to engage in either spatial navigation or motor imagery tasks. Such differentiation was made with 100 percent accuracy.[98] Boly's study confirmed Owen's earlier assertion that volitional brain activity—and thus consciousness—can be reliably ascertained using fMRI scans. It also refuted critics of Owen's study who argued that such imagery tasks measured only reflexive, unthinking responses to commands.[99] As the study's authors noted, thirty-second imagery tasks that consistently activate specific areas of the brain "would confirm that a patient has understood the instructions and has voluntarily performed the task."[100]

Boly's research suggests that fMRI potentially can be used to read the minds of healthy individuals. Owen's study of a single PVS patient likewise suggests that patients presently diagnosed as PVS may not only be able to hear what is spoken to them but also to process what is heard in an appropriate and meaningful way. Further studies are warranted to learn whether Owen's single PVS patient is atypical or representative of vegetative patients generally. If Owen's work is replicated on a larger scale with VS patients, it would imply that a subset of patients currently diagnosed as vegetative are not really vegetative at all. More specifically, it would suggest that a portion of VS patients are at least minimally conscious, though they are incapable of exhibiting their consciousness in any behavioral way. It would also presumably warn the medical community that bedside tests for consciousness—the present gold standard—may be substantially underinclusive, identifying consciousness for only a portion of those patients who still possess some degree of consciousness.

If future research confirms Owen's findings, there will be tremendous pressure to make fMRI technology available, to train health care professionals in its reliable use, and to use fMRI scans to facilitate more accurate diagnoses. More accurate diagnoses, in turn, would presumably result in more accurate prognoses and plans for care, including rehabilitation. Equally important from a legal perspective, if objective neuroimaging techniques can confirm consciousness, they potentially could be used to facilitate communication, at least on a simple yes/no basis. For example, an individual who is unable to behaviorally exhibit consciousness could be asked to imagine playing tennis when she wishes to answer yes to a question, or to imagine walking through her house when she wishes to answer no.

If neuroimaging can be used to establish communication with individuals previously assumed to be unconscious, it would have far-reaching implications not only for such individuals' own quality of life but also for their legal rights. If reliable communication can be established, such individuals would be highly analogous to totally locked-in patients—severely physically disabled but with a sufficient degree of consciousness to grant them legal rights. If deemed to be competent, such patients would have the right to decide whether to continue or terminate life-sustaining treatment, including ventilation, nutrition, and hydration. Legal alternatives to whole brain death that are currently invoked to terminate life support for such patients—such as health care proxies, family consent statutes, and medical futility determinations by providers—could not be used to contradict an articulated contrary wish of the competent patient. The patient, in short, would be in control of his own body, fulfilling the concept of autonomy that is the conceptual foundation of the right to refuse medical treatment.

But is such communication really possible or just science fiction? Recent studies intimate that unlocking the communicative potential of currently

noncommunicative patients is edging closer to reality. In 2009 Monti and colleagues used fMRI to study twenty healthy volunteers and one MCS patient,
presenting them with a sequence of twenty-six monosyllabic words in two
different phases. In the first phase, subjects were told to relax and listen to the
words. In the second phase, subjects were told to count mentally the number
of times a preidentified target word was detected. The purpose of presenting
the words in two different phases was to ascertain whether subjects could
maintain instructions though a period of time and ultimately adopt, on command, a different "mind-set" during the counting phase, exhibiting their
brain's ability to fire up when target words were heard.

Not surprisingly, fMRI scans of the healthy volunteers exhibited specific
patterns of brain activation upon hearing the target words, confirming previous studies of working memory and target detection. What was surprising,
however, was that the MCS patient's brain "exhibited an extremely similar set
of activations."[101] As a result, the researchers concluded:

> [I]t is difficult to interpret these results without accepting that the
> [MCS] patient retained several types of cognitive ability. In par-
> ticular, the patient must have retained sufficient linguistic pro-
> cessing to comprehend the instructions, the ability to maintain
> information through time, and the ability to monitor incoming
> stimuli. . . . [It] also indicates that the patient could willfully
> adopt, on command, different "mind-sets" as a function of condi-
> tion. Furthermore, he must have been capable of voluntarily as-
> signing, in a top-down fashion, saliency to words (i.e., the targets)
> that would otherwise be "neutral" and logically incapable of elic-
> iting such activation automatically. Remarkably, none of these
> cognitive abilities was apparent when the patient was tested at the
> bedside.[102]

Monti and colleagues' most remarkable study to date was published in
early 2010. Their specific task was to use the same basic research paradigm,
targeting a large group of vegetative and MCS patients to ascertain: (1)
whether they could willfully modulate their brain activity to respond to spatial navigation commands (for example, imagine moving through your house)
and/or motor imagery commands (for example, imagine playing tennis); and

(2) whether reliable communication could be established with such patients by using simple yes/no autobiographical questions (for example, "Is your father's name Alexander?"). This study essentially picked up where Monti's previous studies had left off, expanding the number of patients to confirm the prevalence of the ability to respond to commands, and exploring whether such an ability could be used to establish communication.

The study consisted of fifty-four patients, twenty-three of whom were diagnosed on admission to the study as being in a vegetative state and the remaining thirty-one of whom were minimally conscious. All fifty-four patients were scanned using fMRI while being instructed to perform both the motor imagery and spatial imagery tasks, with rest periods in between. Of these fifty-four patients, five of them (9.25 percent) indicated response. Four of the five responders responded to both the motor imagery and spatial imagery tasks; the fifth responded only to the motor imagery task. Remarkably, of the five responders, four had been diagnosed as vegetative; only one had been diagnosed as MCS. All five of the responders had suffered traumatic brain injury rather than anoxic injury (for example, disease or stroke). This data suggests that for an important minority of vegetative patients whose injuries are due to trauma, there is a realistic possibility that an ability to hear and respond appropriately to commands—that is, at least rudimentary awareness—exists. Indeed, of the thirty-three patients who had suffered traumatic (not anoxic) brain injury, 15 percent (five out of thirty-three)—a rather remarkable percentage—responded to one or both of the imagery tasks, suggesting an ability to willfully modulate their brain activity.

Contrary to their vegetative diagnosis, which presupposes no awareness of self or surroundings, some light still seems to be shining within these patients' severely damaged brains. In the words of the researchers, "[I]n a minority of cases, patients who meet the behavioral criteria for a vegetative state have residual cognitive function and even conscious awareness."[103] This initial phase of the Monti study thus confirmed what Adrian Owen had published several years ealier, in his single fMRI case study of KA: that some subset of vegetative patients are not truly vegetative, yet there is no clinical (bedside) way to discover their awareness.

It was the second phase of the Monti study, however, that broke new ground, suggesting for the first time that fMRI could be used to establish reliable communication with an unconscious patient. In this second phase, the researchers selected one of the five responders to undergo additional fMRI scans, in which six yes/no autobiographical questions were asked. The patient was instructed to use one of the specific imagery tasks if the answer to the question was yes, and the other imagery task if the answer was no. To confirm the accuracy of this mode of fMRI communication, the researchers used the same technique on sixteen healthy control subjects. The fMRI scans of the healthy control subjects revealed a 100 percent accuracy rate for all forty-eight questions asked (three questions asked for each of the sixteen control subjects).[104]

The patient who was selected to participate in the second phase of Monti's study was a twenty-two-year-old male patient who had been diagnosed as being in a vegetative state for over five years prior to his participation in the study, including a month-long specialized assessment by a team of clinicians three and a half years after his traumatic injury. He had responded positively to both the spatial imagery and motor imagery tasks in phase one. He was given six separate fMRI scans in response to six autobiographical questions (for example, "Do you have any brothers?"). In five out of the six scans, the patient's brain lit up in a way that corresponded to either the spatial imagery or motor imagery task, signaling a yes or no response. In all five responses, the patient's answer was accurate. For the sixth (and final) scan, no answer could be ascertained because no brain activity was observed in response. The researchers do not know whether the patient simply chose not to answer the question, fell asleep, or drifted out of consciousness.[105] How many of the other four responders could respond in a similar fashion, if given communication scans, is not known, though I suspect that the researchers are designing such larger-scale studies.

The net result is that, for this one patient, communication appears to have been established, with an 83 percent accuracy rate (five out of six questions). The researchers concluded, "this study showed that in one patient with severe impairment of consciousness, functional MRI established the patient's ability to communicate solely by modulating brain activity, whereas this ability could not be established at the bedside. In the future, this approach could be used to address important clinical questions. For example, patients could be asked if they are feeling any pain, and this information could be useful in determining whether analgesic agents should be administered. With further development, this technique could be used by some patients to express their thoughts, control their environment, and increase their quality of life."[106]

One might think that these breathtaking advances facilitated by functional neuroimaging would be met with open arms, embraced as a beginning of a revolution in thinking about the functional, moral, ethical, and legal status of severely brain-injured patients, particularly those classified as vegetative. Unfortunately, however, such a welcome has not been forthcoming. As Joseph Fins candidly admits, "[M]uch of the work in neuroimaging has been met with concern, skepticism and outright fear by the less than receptive field of neuroethics."[107] Fins elaborates further, asserting, "There is this fear, this prudential quality to neuroethics that frets about this line of scientific inquiry and what it will mean for personhood, social institution, civil liberties and the nature of human nature."[108] The functional neuroimaging revolution, in other words, has rekindled the long-standing debate about what it means to be a person, entitled to the full legal rights of personhood. As Bernard Baertschi recently put it, "[W]e must be wary of putting the cart before the horses: experiments can test for the neural correlates of personhood, but the criterion of personhood must be given first."[109]

If neuroimaging ultimately convinces us that the ability to process and respond to information is still intact in vegetative or minimally conscious patients, would this necessarily imply that consciousness exists? Not so fast, claim the critics. Answering this question depends on the definition of consciousness that one adopts. Even assuming that consciousness is the sine qua non of personhood, one must first specify what one means by the word "consciousness."

Those who criticize the potential of neuroimaging technology advocate a definition of consciousness referred to as "phenomenal" consciousness. Phenomenal consciousness has been described—even by its votaries—as "notoriously difficult, perhaps impossible, to define."[110] This alone should cause some hesitation, at least in the legal community, to tying legal rights to a concept that cannot be clearly defined. Nonetheless, to understand where these critics of neuroimaging are coming from, it is important to disinter their understanding of phenomenal consciousness.

Two forceful advocates for phenomenal consciousness are Guy Kahane and Julian Savulescu of the University of Oxford, who define phenomenal consciousness as the experience of sensations, most notably the capacity to feel, to experience pleasure and pain.[111] They distinguish phenomenal consciousness from sapience, which is defined as a cognitive or motivational state that enables global access to information or memory.[112] Roughly speaking, sapience is the useful tool that grants us access to working knowledge and memory, whereas phenomenality is our ability to experience or feel the information or sensory inputs provided.

With this distinction between sapience and phenomenality drawn, Kahane and Savulescu argue that MCS patients possess phenomenal consciousness but that VS patients do not.[113] In common layperson's terms, they argue that VS patients cannot feel anything, whereas MCS patients can. In response to the functional neuroimaging research of Owen and others, Kahane and Savulescu assert that asking a VS patient to imagine playing tennis or move through her house can yield only evidence of sapience—working knowledge and memory—not phenomenal consciousness (feelings, experience).[114] A VS patient who can engage in such mental imagery tasks on command is more akin to a zombie or artificial intelligence (AI)—able to respond to commands but unable to experience or feel. Because phenomenal consciousness is the only type of consciousness that is morally significant for purposes of ascribing personhood, proponents argue, functional neuroimaging research thus sheds no new light.[115]

But how would the phenomenal conscious votaries respond to Monti's 2010 study suggesting the establishment of communication with one vegetative patient? Recall that Monti concluded that, in the future, fMRI could be used to ask patients whether they were feeling any pain, in order to determine whether additional painkillers were necessary. If such questions could be reliably answered by vegetative or MCS patients, would Kahane and Savulescu concede—at least in the face of an affirmative answer—that such patients possessed phenomenal consciousness? The answer is not entirely clear. What is clear is that asking and obtaining an accurate response from a vegetative or MCS patient to memory-based questions such as "Is your father's name Alexander?" would not yield evidence of phenomenal consciousness to Kahane and Savalescu, since working knowledge and memory, in their view, provide evidence only of sapience, not phenomenal consciousness.

But if fMRI can provide a way to accurately communicate with patients in a rudimentary yes/no fashion to questions such as "Do you feel any pain?" or "Do you feel depressed?" presumably this would provide evidence of phenomenal consciousness. The objections to such communication, I suspect, would not be with the conclusion to be drawn from such answers (that phenomenal consciousness exists), but with the premise upon which the conclusion would be based—namely, that fMRI can provide an accurate means of communication. If future fMRI communication studies fail to show the degree of reliability revealed by the Monti study, a concession about the existence of phenomenal consciousness can be easily avoided. Indeed, one wonders if the accuracy rate obtained by Monti—83 percent (five out of six questions) answered accurately—would be reliable enough for critics. Short of 100 percent reliability, can or should we trust machines to read the minds of the severely neurologically disabled?

Those who advocate for phenomenal consciousness as the dividing line between personhood and nonpersonhood go further than merely discounting the existence of phenomenal consciousness for vegetative patients. Specifically, they assert that because MCS, LIS, and other nonvegetative patients with severe brain injury *have* the capacity to experience pleasure and pain, they are worse off than their vegetative counterparts. As a result, they argue, we should be more willing—not less—to terminate their life support.[116] Presumably, therefore, a future fMRI study that confirms an ability to reliably communicate with vegetative patients would meet the same response. If a vegetative, MCS, or LIS patient can tell us—through fMRI—that she feels pain, depression, or any other negative emotion, would it not be the merciful or humane response to terminate life support?

Indeed, in response to the recent news of Rom Houben, the locked-in patient who was misdiagnosed as PVS for twenty-three years—one commentator, Jacob Appel, advocated euthanasia for totally locked-in patients, analogizing it to being "boiled alive in hot oil daily," and asserting that "the horror of being prisoners in their own bodies might offer a far stronger argument for allowing their suffering to end."[117] Rather than seeing a happy ending in the Rom Houben case—a lifting of Houben's long burden of silence—all Appel could see was a situation that should never have been allowed to happen because Houben's life should have been terminated long ago. It is a classic case of projecting one's subjective preferences onto others, assuming that they would react with the same negativity and horror. As Appel revealed, "I can say with confidence and considerable reflection that I personally would not want to live twenty-three locked-in years, even knowing that 'rebirth' loomed in the future. I regard such a fate as medically-induced torture."[118]

Those who advocate broadly for a right to terminate life support likely will continue to do so in the face of functional neuroimaging evidence of consciousness. They will simply move the relevant ball, shifting their focus from consciousness simpliciter to a narrower concept of consciousness, such as phenomenal consciousness. And to the extent that neuroimaging can establish reliable communication with patients suffering from disorders of consciousness, those who support a right to die will presumably agree that positive answers to questions inquiring about negative emotions—pain, suffering, depression, and so forth—should provide adequate evidence to terminate life support. Indeed, I suspect that if such reliable communication could be established, a positive answer to the question, "Do you wish to terminate life support so that you can die?" would trigger near-universal agreement that life support should indeed be terminated, assuming the patient's positive answer has been verified over a period of time.

Unless and until the reliability of neuroimaging to establish communication has been established—and we are willing to employ it to ask the patient definitive life-or-death questions—it may be threatening to those who advocate the right to die because it could provide objective evidence of consciousness. Such evidence—once it becomes widely publicized—may bolster the public's perception that severely brain-injured patients are alive in a meaningful sense. As two commentators recently confessed, "[G]iven the American political landscape and the law in many states, the slightest hint of conscious activity may make it impossible to discontinue treating a patient, even when most patients would want treatment stopped."[119] This statement reveals that the right-to-die movement feels some threat from the neuroimaging revolution. But the result feared—making it impossible to discontinue life-sustaining treatment even when the patient desires it—is a red herring. If patients want life-sustaining treatment stopped, even when there is neuroimaging evidence of some degree of consciousness, they will continue to be able to do so via advance directives. Patients may need to be more detailed in the instructions they articulate, but it would not be difficult to draft a directive that instructs the discontinuation of life support despite neuroimaging evidence of consciousness. And even in the most demanding states—that is, those that require "clear and convincing evidence" prior to terminating life support—an advance directive that specifically addressed the effect of neuro-imaging evidence should suffice to authorize withdrawal. And if Monti's communication study can be expanded and confirmed, patients who want life-sustaining treatment stopped can simply be asked, just as conscious patients can be asked. In short, the only thing that neuroimaging evidence of consciousness will add is, well, evidence of consciousness.

The comment about the American political landscape reveals more about fears and political predilections than any real contraction of patient autonomy to refuse life-sustaining treatment. It reveals a fear that neuroimaging techniques will cause some to rethink their beliefs about the moral or ethical status of severely brain-damaged patients. If neuroimaging research continues to provide meaningful (even if only implicit) evidence of consciousness, some who presently would pull the plug may begin to hesitate. Functional neuroimaging, in other words, could alter the orthodox presumption about the value of severely brain-injured life. The presumption today is that severely brain-injured life cannot, by definition, be worth living and therefore no one with such a disability would want to be kept alive. Functional neuro-imaging could alter this presumption by providing objective evidence of consciousness and establishing a means of communication. If such a shift in presumptions occurs regarding the value of severely brain-damaged life, it could cause a concomitant political shift toward valuing life in other contexts. A renewed appreciation for valuing brain-damaged life, in other words, could have spillover effects on issues such as physician-assisted suicide, abortion, stem cell research, and other traditionally conservative, pro-life issues. And it may be this fear—a fear about shifting political winds—that underlies some of the surprisingly ardent opposition to neuroimaging technology.

The Treatment Revolution: Drug and Device Therapies

While the neuroimaging revolution has opened up a world of possibilities for diagnosing and communicating with patients who suffer from disorders of consciousness, there has been an equally important revolution in pharmaceuticals and medical devices that promise new avenues for treatment. The most promising results have been achieved with deep brain electrical stimulation, dopaminergic drugs, zolpidem, and branched-chain amino acids (BCAAs).

DEEP BRAIN STIMULATION

Deep brain stimulation (DBS) involves the surgical implantation of tiny electrodes into specific portions of the brain, powered by small external batteries. It is believed that the provision of targeted electrical currents can help stimulate specific neural pathways, which in turn helps modulate certain behaviors. In a very rough analogy, DBS is like jumper cables for the brain. It may accomplish for the brain what a pacemaker accomplishes for the heart.

DBS has been approved by the U.S. Food and Drug Administration for several years as a safe and efficacious treatment for certain tremors as well as for Parkinson's disease.[120] Beginning in 2007, however, evidence began surfacing that suggests DBS may also help improve brain function for severely brain injured patients. Specifically, in 2007, Nicholas Schiff and colleagues published a six-month, double-blind crossover case study involving DBS applied to a thirty-eight-year old traumatic brain injury patient who had been diagnosed as MCS for six years.[121] The researchers (who were blinded as to whether the electrodes were switched on or off) measured the patient's disability score before, during, and after the study, alternating periods during which the electrodes were turned on. The researchers found that the patient's disability improved significantly during periods of electrical stimulation and that this improvement carried over to times when the electrodes were turned off. Several months into the study, the patient began exhibiting the ability to gesture and use an object appropriately—such as brushing his hair—and uttering intelligible words.[122] He also began eating on his own, allowing him to remove his gastronomy tube and gain weight.[123] Schiff noted that the patients' "ability to interact consistently and meaningfully with others was cited by members of his family as the most important change observed. The restoration of communication also allowed the patient to assume a more active (and interactive) role in his treatment."[124] While the patient was still severely disabled, his quality of life had been substantially improved.

DBS is not without its risks or downsides. As with any surgical intervention—particularly in the brain—there are risks of harm and even personality alterations.[125] Moreover, wide variation in the type, location, and extent of brain injury among patients will make it difficult to devise larger clinical trials that can more accurately assess the efficacy of such therapy.[126] But if Schiff's results can be replicated on a larger scale—a big if for now—DBS can potentially alter the standard of care for MCS patients, requiring an assessment as to whether the patient has sufficiently preserved portions of the brain to benefit from such surgical intervention. If a patient showed a potential to benefit from DBS, such intervention would seem appropriate, creating a new paradigm of more aggressive treatment and rehabilitation. It is possible, on the other hand, that improved brain function may cause the patient distress, as the fog of unconsciousness lifts and the reality of one's severe disability is revealed.[127] But this argument can be made for any severely injured, unconscious individual, and it would imply that unconsciousness (unawareness of one's condition) is preferable to consciousness. It would also imply that once unconscious, a severely disabled patient ethically could not be allowed to regain consciousness, effectively mandating status quo maintenance or, more likely, euthanasia or withdrawal of life support.[128] While some ardently believe that a severely disabled or minimally conscious life is not worth living, this is a question about which there is much reasonable disagreement, counseling pluralistic choice and individual autonomy rather than a unitary, one-size-fits-all policy.

DOPAMINERGIC DRUGS

Dopamine is a chemical that facilitates the transmission of nerve impulses in the brain. When dopamine is too low, disorders involving loss of motivation and initiation, reduced memory and attention, loss of pleasure and involuntary movements occur. When dopamine is too high, pleasure seeking, addiction, psychotic, and schizophrenic behavior can result. Dopaminergic drugs increase the amount of dopamine in the brain in various ways, helping some individuals regain consciousness by amplifying or intensifying the transmission of nerve impulses along still-intact neural pathways. Two promising dopaminergic drugs are amantadine and Sinemet.

Amantadine has been approved to combat flu and Parkinson's disease. Beginning in the 1990s, individual case studies began emerging that indicated amantadine could help significantly hasten or enhance recovery of those who suffered severe brain injuries due to either trauma or lack of oxygen (for example, as a result of cardiac arrest), including those in minimally conscious states.[129] Patricia White Bull—one of the PVS miracle stories—was given amantadine by her doctor to treat flu symptoms shortly before her recovery, leading to some speculation that amantadine may have played a role.[130]

Larger studies of amantadine have showed mixed results. For example, a study published in 2005 involved a restrospective review of 123 coma patients with severe traumatic brain injury over a ten-year period, divided into those who were given amantadine twice daily (a total of twenty-eight patients) and those who were not (ninety-five patients). The researchers compared the amantadine patients with the control patients to determine whether a greater percentage of the amantadine patients emerged from their coma. They found that while 46 percent of the amantadine patients emerged from coma versus only 38 percent of control patients, given the small study size and different characteristics of the two groups, this difference was not statistically significant.[131] Another study published in 2005 involved twenty-two traumatic brain injury patients, all of whom were at least six months post-injury, and all of whom were also administered amantadine daily. Six of the patients also underwent PET scanning to determine whether scans would indicate improvements to brain metabolism. The study revealed that on tests of executive function—which includes the ability to plan, provide appropriate responses, and engage in abstract thinking—the patients showed significant improvement. The PET scans of the subset of six patients also showed increased glucose metabolism in the area of the brain associated with executive function.[132]

More rigorous double-blind, placebo-controlled clinical trials—considered the gold standard of scientific research—have also provided mixed results. In such studies, one group of patients is given the drug and another group is given an inactive sugar pill (placebo). The trials are "double blind" because neither the patients nor the researchers know which patients receive the drug. These clinical trials have shown some promise, though they are not uniformly positive. An early, small-scale trial in 1999, for example, studied ten traumatic brain injury patients using a "crossover" method, in which patients received either the drug or placebo during the first phase of the trial, rested for a standard period of time, were then crossed over and received the alternative for the second phase of the trial. The researchers discovered that for the first phase of the trial (which lasted six weeks), both placebo and amantadine patients showed improvement, and over both phases of the trial there were no statistically significant differences in cognitive improvement between the two groups.[133]

A larger double-blind placebo crossover trial was published in 2002, yielding more promising results. The study involved thirty-five traumatic brain injury patients. Group one was given amantadine during the first phase, followed by a placebo in the second phase. Group two was given a placebo in the first phase, followed by amantadine in the second phase. Like the 1999 study, this study revealed that there was significant improvement in both groups during the first six-week phase of the trial. Unlike the 1999 study, however, it revealed that group two—which was given amantadine during the second six-week phase of the trial—continued to experience statistically significant gains during the second phase. Group one—which was given the placebo during the second phase—did not experience any significant gains during this second phase. The study's authors concluded that this difference was "remarkable" because it demonstrated that "patients seemed to improve more rapidly while they were on amantadine" and that amantadine "may have profound economic impacts in shortening the acute and rehabilitation length of stay after [severe traumatic brain injury]."[134]

Another promising dopaminergic drug is Sinemet, which combines the domaninergic drug L-DOPA with carbidopa, a drug that increases the staying power of L-DOPA. As with amantadine, there have been a smattering of published case studies touting miraculous recovery of PVS or other severely brain-injured patients following administration of Sinemet or L-DOPA alone.[135] A larger prospective study of Sinemet was published in 2004 involving eight VS patients who were given Sinemet beginning an average of 104 days post-injury. The study found that seven out of eight patients regained full consciousness with reciprocal interaction within an average of thirty-one days of beginning Sinemet therapy. The other patient improved to a minimally conscious state, able to move a limb on command but nothing further.[136] The authors concluded that the "relatively short time span to recovery of consciousness after onset of [Sinemet] treatment relative to the duration of the VS may indicate that the improvement was most probably related to the medication and not due to natural recovery. Many authors have described recovery in [vegetative state] patients in response to dopaminergic medication and the present study, in this respect, confirms previous observations."[137] While these limited studies of Sinemet are promising, much more research will need to be conducted before any conclusions can be drawn about its use-fulness as a treatment for consciousness disorders.

ZOLPIDEM (AMBIEN)

Another drug that has shown promise for treating disorders of consciousness is zolpidem, marketed under the brand name Ambien. Zolpidem is an insom-nia drug that, unlike most insomnia drugs called benzodiazepines, selectively stimulates a type of neurotransmitter in the brain called GABA. After a brain injury, GABA levels rise significantly, suppressing brain activity and possibly allowing brain tissue to go into a type of hibernation or dormancy until re-covery or regeneration can occur.[138] It is hypothesized that when zolpidem binds to GABA receptors in the brain, the GABA-induced dormancy is switched off, permitting these areas of the brain to regain function.[139]

Early case reports of the use of zolpidem on severely brain-injured pa-tients were nothing short of remarkable. The first published report came from South African researchers in 2000, who relayed the extraordinary recov-ery of a "semi-comatose" young man who showed significant arousal after a single administration of zolpidem. When the drug wore off, the patient re-turned to his previous state. Scanning of the young man's brain after admin-istration of zolpidem showed that large areas of previously inactive areas had become activated by the drug.[140]

More recent case reports reveal similar remarkable stories of recovery. A 2008 published report described the recovery of a thirty-five-year-old man who had severe brain injury following a heart attack. Eight months following his injury, he was given zolpidem, becoming markedly more alert, conversing with providers, tossing around a football, and walking without assistance. His improvement was so dramatic that he was able to be discharged from his rehabilitation facility to his parents' home.[141] Also in 2008, a case was pub-lished involving zolpidem administered to a fifty-year-old mother of three who was in MCS for eighteen months following a heart attack. Within forty-five minutes of receiving zolpidem, the woman was able to read, answer simple questions, perform simple calculations, grasp objects, feed herself, and walk with moderate assistance—all activities she was unable to do prior to zolpidem.[142] The effects of zolpidem wore off after about four hours, at which time the woman lapsed back into a minimally conscious state.[143] The researchers noted that, despite the short half-life of zolpidem, it allowed patients' loved ones to "have their family member back even if only for a few hours a day."[144]

A larger, similarly promising group of case studies was published in 2006. In this group, three PVS patients—two car accident victims and one near-drowning victim, all of whom had been completely nonresponsive and PVS for at least three years—were given zolpidem and monitored for several years. Zolpidem aroused all three. Patient L regained his ability to speak, engage in meaningful conversations, eat food by mouth, perform simple calculations, and make jokes. Patient N regained an ability to state his name and age, respond to noise and visual stimuli, watch television, and react appropriately to what he saw and heard. Patient G (the near-drowning victim) regained an ability to engage in meaningful conversation for short periods of time, answer simple questions, respond to simple commands, noise and visual stimuli, and even catch a baseball.[145] The miraculous effects of zolpidem lasted for approximately four hours, after which time each patient returned to his completely nonresponsive, vegetative state. Repeated daily administration of zolpidem resulted in transient, four-hour arousal each day. These amazing effects were followed and documented for a period of three to six years.[146] The ability of zolpidem to arouse PVS and other severely brain-injured patients in these case studies provoked the South African researchers to apply for a patent, using zolpidem to reverse brain dormancy. The maker of zolpidem has begun a large-scale formal clinical trial to ascertain zolpidem's therapeutic potential for brain-injured individuals.[147]

Of course, not all MCS or PVS patients respond to zolpidem. A recent case in England illustrates the ethical and legal issues that can arise regarding zolpidem, given the limited data regarding its efficacy for treating disorders of consciousness. Specifically, in An NHS Trust v. J.,[148] litigation erupted in the Family Division of the High Court between the family of a fifty-three-year-old woman diagnosed as PVS and the official solicitor, who is required under English law to represent the interests of any PVS patient whose representatives wish to withdraw artificial nutrition and hydration.[149] The family and providers of the woman agreed that she would not want to continue living in a vegetative state, but the solicitor argued that prior to removing her feeding tube, the court should require providers to administer zolpidem to see if it would work. The court agreed with the solicitor and a three-day regimen of zolpidem was provided, to no effect. The family subsequently sought court approval for withdrawal of nutritional support, which was granted, and the patient died shortly thereafter.[150]

Like the English case, other published reports intimate that zolpidem is not a panacea for all disorders of consciousness. For example, in 2008, researchers published a case study of one patient given a single dose of zolpidem who had been diagnosed as MCS for four years. The researchers found no observable improvements in this patient's ability to respond to behavioral tests of awareness.[151] Even less encouraging, in 2009, researchers reported results from preliminary double-blind, placebo-controlled clinical trial of zolpidem given to fifteen patients who were diagnosed as either VS or MCS. The researchers found that only one of the fifteen patients (about 7 percent)— a twenty-eight-year-old man who had been in a vegetative state for over four years—exhibited improvement after zolpidem.[152] Within a half hour of receiving zolpidem, the responsive patient began exhibiting visual tracking and following commands using his arms and legs. On the day he received a placebo, he reverted back to a vegetative state.[153] The researchers hypothesized that there is a subset of individuals with severe brain injury who have the potential to respond to zolpidem and concluded that larger-scale trials are needed to identify the characteristics of those likely to respond.[154] As a result of their preliminary study, the researchers are now conducting such a larger-scale clinical trial, funded by federal money, with the goal of enrolling about one hundred PVS or MCS patients.[155]

BRANCHED-CHAIN AMINO ACIDS

An additional drug therapy that has shown some clinical signs of promise is the use of branched-chain amino acids (BCAAs), of which there are three: leucine, isoleucine, and valine. BCAAs are important in making protein and thus muscle within the body. Brain injury is accompanied by significant reductions of BCAAs, and it is believed that this reduction in BCAA may contribute to a reduction in the efficacy of neural transmissions in the brain, leading to a loss of cognitive function. In addition, BCAAs, particularly leucine, trigger the production of insulin, so increasing BCAAs may positively affect brain insulin levels and hence, cognition. Studies on mice have suggested that dietary supplementation with BCAA can improve brain function in portions of the brain responsible for memory and spatial navigation.[156]

More intriguing than the mice studies, however, are the recent promising studies from Italy involving the use of BCAAs to treat traumatic brain injuries in humans, including MCS and VS patients. Specifically, in 2005, Roberto Aquilani and colleagues published the results of a double-blind, placebo-controlled trial of forty patients with severe traumatic brain injury who were given either a placebo or intravenous BCAAs over a period of fifteen days. The patients' results were compared to a control group of twenty healthy subjects. The researchers compared the disability ratings of the groups before and after the trial, concluding that the patient group receiving BCAA supplementation experienced a statistically significant improvement in disability scores.[157] Given their findings, the researchers recommended that "BCAAs should be given routinely for all rehabilitation patients with TBI [traumatic brain injury] who have reduced plasma BCAA levels."[158]

Aquilani's team published the results of an additional placebo-controlled study in 2008 involving the administration of BCAAs for fifteen days to forty-one patients who were diagnosed as either VS or MCS. The study revealed that the disability rating of the BCAA group improved significantly versus the placebo group. More specifically, within the BCAA group, an astonishing 68 percent of patients (fifteen out of twenty-two) improved to the point that they were no longer classified as vegetative or minimally conscious.[159] Of the nineteen VS and MCS patients assigned to the placebo group, none exited their vegetative or minimally conscious state.[160] The researchers concluded that "short-term parenteral supplementation of BCAAs in rehabilitation patients in a posttraumatic vegetative or minimally conscious state may induce an effective recovery from the vegetative or minimally conscious state in more than two-thirds of treated patients."[161] They admitted that the relatively small sample size of this clinical trial was a limitation, concluding that larger-scale trials were warranted.[162] They also acknowledged that future trials should include a brain scanning component, to allow researchers to ascertain whether the administration of BCAAs causes global or local improvements in brain metabolism.[163]

Although some case reports and initial trials involving BCAA supplementation, zolpidem, and dopaminergic drugs are promising, only time will tell whether the remarkable recovery stories associated with them are isolated outliers or indicators of more widespread hope for the treatment of severe brain injury. It does appear that at least a subset of severely brain-damaged patients, including those in PVS and MCS, may find some relief from one or more of these emerging therapies. As scientists learn more and more about the brain—including its plasticity and dormancy after trauma—the future of drugs or devices to significantly alleviate or even cure disorders of consciousness seems brighter than ever before.

As Good As Dead? Quality of Life

What lessons can be learned from these disorders of consciousness? What salience do they have for legal definitions of death? First, it is important to emphasize that patients suffering from consciousness disorders such as PVS and MCS are not legally dead. Instead, they are severely neurologically disabled; some portion of their brain is functioning, precluding their classification as dead under the whole brain definition. Yet some individuals, including many bioethicists and providers, believe that such patients are "as good as" dead, since their quality of life, given their severe cognitive impairment, is so low. There is a sad but often too accurate saying about the three stages of care provided to severely brain-injured patients: intensive care, followed by no care, followed by don't care. This therapeutic nihilism is echoed in the Appleton Consensus guidelines—representing the collective thought of hundreds of clinicians from around the world—which conclude: "The patient who is reliably diagnosed as being in a PVS has no self-regarding interests. Consequently, unless a previously expressed advance directive requests it, there is no patient-based reason to continue life-sustaining treatment, including artificial hydration and nutrition. It is unkind to allow unrealistic optimism to be sustained and it is unfair to allow the prolonged consumption of societal resources in support of such patients beyond a period of education and adjustment for the family."[164]

As the Appleton Consensus illustrates, the "as good as dead" attitude creates pressure to consider legal avenues to withdraw life-sustaining treatment such as mechanical ventilation or nutritional support.[165] One need look no further than the "vegetative" label itself for evidence of this attitude. The vegetative state has an unmistakably pejorative connotation, implying that VS patients are vegetables—no longer living human beings but material objects, more analogous to carrots than people. Given this particular shibboleth's emotive force, perhaps it is not surprising that a poll of physicians revealed that 94 percent thought PVS patients "would be better off dead" and almost half thought that PVS patients should be declared legally dead.[166]

The attitude is so prevalent, in fact, that recent studies show that the majority of deaths in critical care units are the result of a decision to withhold or withdraw life-sustaining care.[167] Indeed, as James Bernat has recently pointed out, for brain-damaged patients, there is a "self-fulfilling prophecy" in which physicians who believe a patient's chance for recovery is poor will counsel patients or their families to withdraw life-sustaining care. As a result of this counseling, most families understandably give up hope, authorize the withdrawal of care, and the patients will die shortly thereafter.[168]

A physician's belief in his patient's poor prognosis is entitled to some deference, given the physician's medical training and experience. Yet the fallacy of the self-fulfilling prophecy suggests that, in some instances, the patient's chance for recovery is better than the physician's own belief system acknowledges. It is exceedingly difficult for patients' loved ones to know whether providers' assessments are objective or clouded by their own subjective nihilism.

Becker and colleagues, for example, surveyed thirty-one physicians from neurology and neurosurgery departments, soliciting their prognostic evaluation and care recommendations for four real patients who had suffered from major brain hemorrhages. All four patients survived; one experienced severe disability and the inability to care for herself, and the remaining three experienced only moderate disability, requiring some care but able to walk without assistance. The survey revealed that only one physician believed that the patient who survived with severe disability should be withdrawn from life support. Oddly, regarding the other three patients—all of whom achieved a level of recovery rated as moderate disability—a high proportion of surveyed physicians would have recommended withdrawal of life support. For one patient in particular, a third of physicians recommended withdrawal; for the other two patients, a majority of physicians would have recommended withdrawal.[169] The researchers concluded that the survey results "suggested that practitioners tend to be overly pessimistic in prognosticating outcome based upon data available at the time of presentation" and that "individual patients in traditionally 'poor outcome' categories can have a reasonable neurologic outcome when treated aggressively."[170]

Laypersons share their providers' negative attitude toward the vegetative state. It is not uncommon to hear people say they would not want to "live like a vegetable," although they may not understand much about the definition, diagnosis, or prognosis of the vegetative state, nor that their statement could open the door to a court-sanctioned withdrawal of life-sustaining nutrition or other care. Indeed, a recent survey by Laura Siminoff and colleagues confirmed a high degree of confusion among laypersons regarding differences between PVS, other forms of severe brain injury, and brain death. When given a scenario describing a severely brain-damaged patient on mechanical life support, almost 60 percent of respondents thought the patient was dead. When given a scenario describing a PVS patient not on mechanical life support (but receiving nutrition through a gastronomy tube), many fewer respondents—34 percent—thought the patient was dead.[171]

The Siminoff study suggests that ordinary people may be making a judgment that mechanical life support (for example, a ventilator) artificially masks a state that would otherwise result in death. The use of such extraordinary medical technologies may appear to hold a patient prisoner, denying him a natural death. By contrast, a PVS patient whose intact brain stem negates the need for mechanical life support may seem more alive because their ability to breathe on their own necessitates less aggressive medical intervention. With the typical PVS patient (as in the Siminoff hypothetical), there is no extraordinary medical technology holding the patient prisoner, keeping the patient from dying. Admittedly, most PVS patients receive food and water through a feeding tube, yet studies have consistently shown that laypersons have much greater reluctance to withdraw nutrition and hydration as compared to other forms of life-sustaining care—a reluctance that the Siminoff study seems to reconfirm.[172]

Although there is logic in the potential distinction drawn by laypersons between the provision of ordinary and extraordinary medical technology, this distinction differs markedly from the perspective held by most bioethicists and physicians. As discussed in the chapter on brain death, there has been an ardent and consistent push to recognize death of the "higher" brain (for example, PVS or anencephaly) as legal death. In the eyes of higher brain adherents, it is not the mechanically-dependent brain-damaged patient, but the PVS patient, who seems more "dead"—precisely the opposite of the impression held by laypersons in the Siminoff study.

Those who advocate for higher brain death generally do so because they believe that biography is more important than biology. In other words, if the higher brain is the locus of our personality and memories, its permanent functional cessation should be considered the legal death of the person. The continuation of non-higher brain biological functions—the rest of the body—should be disregarded under this theory because biological functions other than those of the higher brain have no connection to our biography, the essence of our personhood.

One obvious result of shifting to a higher brain definition of death would be to declare PVS patients legally dead. Their bodies could be buried, even when the lower brain is still functioning and maintaining the rest of the body without mechanical assistance. Once declared legally dead, PVS patients' oxygen-perfused organs could be harvested. Their assets could be distributed to heirs. Medical resources would no longer have to be "wasted" on the maintenance of their bodies. The overall tone of the higher brain argument is one of "Why bother? Those without a functioning higher brain are just vegetables anyway." It is the quality of life that should matter to the law, the argument goes, not mere biological existence.

This emphasis on quality of life has much innate appeal. After all, who among us would say that they want to live like a vegetable? If one lacks all memory, cognitive capacity, and consciousness of one's surroundings, what could possibly justify the continuation of such a meaningless life, particularly given the high cost of maintaining it and the emotional burden on loved ones? Aside from the constitutionally based autonomy arguments, the logical appeal of higher brain death presupposes a certain faith that such conditions are irreversible and reliably diagnosed.

Yet there are growing doubts within the scientific community regarding orthodox assumptions about the quality of life for such patients. Functional neuroimaging studies, for example, suggest that some patients who cannot behaviorally evince consciousness may in fact possess residual cognitive functioning. This, in turn, implies that they may be able to experience life, in some small, unusual, or little understood way, given them present and future interests that were previously presumed non-existent. As more and more patients regain consciousness or achieve an ability to communicate thanks to technological and medical innovations, it is becoming apparent that the patients themselves consider their quality of life to be much higher than their providers or loved ones realize. Indeed, studies show that quality of life is more closely related to social, not physical, interaction with others.[173]

Perhaps the best example is the patient in a locked-in syndrome, whose quality of life is considered so low that some have asserted a failure to euthanize them is tantamount to medically induced torture. Yet studies of individuals in LIS consistently show that perception of their own quality of life is comparable to healthy control subjects.[174] Indeed, a study published in 2009 by Lulé and colleagues provided data on quality-of-life assessments given to thirty amyotrophic lateral sclerosis (ALS) patients and seventeen LIS patients. The study confirmed the existence of a "disability paradox," in which severely disabled individuals report good quality of life despite their disability. Specifically, the research revealed that, for the ALS patients, the progression of their disease (and concomitant physical disability) did not result in lower quality-of-life scores; instead, quality-of-life scores were actually higher for patients with more severe physical disability.[175] For LIS patients, quality of life was not correlated to the degree of physical impairment.[176] The factors that did positively influence quality of life for these patients were feeling a sense of purpose and control over their own lives,[177] which was aided by strong social support and participation, ability to communicate, and leading productive lives.[178]

The study also showed, perhaps not surprisingly, that the patients' significant others thought that the patients' quality of life was significantly lower than the patients themselves, leading the researchers to speculate that "healthy people may present a defense mechanism having difficulty imagining the feelings and experiences of severely impaired patients."[179] The researchers also revealed preliminary data from a study of providers' perspectives on the quality of life of LIS patients, which showed that two-thirds considered LIS to be worse than either VS or MCS. This data suggested that "[b]iased health-care workers may provide less-aggressive medical treatment or influence the patient's family in ways not appropriate to the situation."[180]

If indeed many people—physicians included—consider LIS to be a worse state than MCS or VS, it is logical to assume that the severe disability bias extends to, and is perhaps amplified with regard to, these patients as well. What seems clear is that the severe disability bias exists, and that it may reflect more about our own subjective discomfort about and unfamiliarity with severe disability than any objective indicators about severely disabled individuals' quality of life. We tend to judge books by their covers.

But if severely disabled individuals themselves report a satisfying quality of life, who are we to disagree with their assessment? More importantly, why would we allow our presumptions against their quality of life to influence their treatment or rehabilitation? Perhaps our biases about their quality of life do not, in fact, influence their treatment or rehabilitation. But if such biases are somehow set aside, why is it so difficult to obtain aggressive treatment for the severely disabled? Perhaps the answer lies in covert distributive justice considerations: why spend so much money on so few? Whether our own biases about quality of life or distributive justice (or both) are to blame, the bottom line is a troubling disregard of patient autonomy and substitution of our own paternalistic preferences and values.

Disorders of consciousness occupy a broad spectrum, from those who are reading this book right now (and hence, fully conscious) to those who are vegetative (and hence, fully unconscious). In between is a twilight zone, occupied by a virtually infinite variety of patients who experience something less than full consciousness, including a growing number who are now recognized as being in a minimally conscious state. In this twilight zone are also those who suffer from progressive dementia disorders (e.g., Alzheimer's), dreamers, those under general anesthesia, recreational drug users, and even those who meditate. None of these less-than-fully-conscious individuals are legally dead, though they are all cognitively impaired, even if only transiently so. Diminished or even absent consciousness, in other words, is a disability—indeed, it can be a can be a pretty severe one—but it is not the functional equivalent of death. Such disabled individuals, in short, are not dead yet.

7

Unbeing Dead Isn't Being Alive

Stepping back and looking at the law *in toto,* there are two distinct political ideologies at play, both of which have managed to capture legal recognition in various ways. On the one hand, there is a "right-to-life" movement, espousing the belief that life begins at conception and urging legal reforms that reflect this belief. On the other hand, there is a "right-to-die" movement, espousing the belief that quality of life, not mere biological life itself, should be the focus of the law. Neither one of these ideologies has dominated, yet their fingerprints are discernible within discrete areas.

The law has agreed on a definition of death yet has been unable to agree on a definition of life. Being not dead, therefore, does not mean being alive for legal purposes. In the eyes of the law, life and death are not antonyms— "unbeing dead," as e.e. cummings said, "isn't being alive." The lack of a legal definition of life should tell us something. It suggests that there may be broader implications perceived with defining life than defining death. If the right-to-life movement secured a uniform law stating that personhood begins at conception, then abortion, discarding frozen embryos, and some contraception could be homicide. A legal definition of death, by contrast, creates only marginal shifts in the timing of the inevitable. Not every embryo will be born, engendering passionate debate about whether the law should allow voluntary termination of pregnancy or punish acts that pretermit a potential birth. But the cold reality is that everyone who is born will eventually die. The question in the context of death, therefore, is not "should" but "when?" Given the ineluctability of death, the stakes seem lower, or at least less politically charged, when the Grim Reaper is standing at the bedside.

While the law has not agreed upon a definition of life, in most cases the living are easy to spot—laughing, interacting, and whistling tunes. But there are many gray areas, between the obviously living and the obviously dead. The common theme among these gray areas is that they are occupied by the biologically, but not biographically, living. Their bodies are biologically alive, but they have never had, or appear to have lost, the ability to laugh, interact, and whistle tunes. The unborn, anencephalic infants, and those in a vegetative state are examples.

Within the gray area occupied by the biographically deficient, the law has refused to draw a distinction between those who have never had a biography versus those who have had a biography but lost it. Thus, both anencephalic infants (who have never had a biography) and PVS patients (who have lost their biography) are considered by the law to be alive. Similarly, for purposes of deciding death, biography (or a lack thereof) is legally irrelevant. An unborn fetus is not dead (though, as we have seen, is not fully a living person either), whereas a person whose whole brain no longer functions is dead. While the former (unborn fetus) has never had a biography, and the latter (brain dead) has lost hers, this distinction does not seem to matter. Neither one has a biography, yet this common characteristic does not result in similar treatment under the law. Indeed, if a lack of biography was what mattered for purposes of defining death, brain death would be declared upon death of the higher brain, not the whole brain.

So if biography is not the sine qua non of either life or death, what is? In the context of defining life, the important initial legal line is drawn between the born and unborn. The ubiquity and importance of the born-unborn distinction is evident throughout law, whether common law, statutes, or the Constitution. In criminal law, for example, we have seen how the "born alive rule" remains an integral part of most homicide prosecutions. Similarly, in tort law, a child can recover for injuries it sustained *in utero,* so long as it is subsequently born. And under property law, while inheritance is allowed for a child *en ventre sa mere* (in the mother's womb) at the time of the testator's death, this necessarily requires that the unborn subsequently be born in order to take under the will.

This is not to say that the unborn are without any legal protection. But they are denied full living status, excluded from legal personhood and consequently not protected as much as you or I. They are in a sort of legal limbo, not legally dead, but not legally "persons" either. Criminal law, for example, is increasingly willing to impose punishment for the intentional destruction of an embryo or fetus through so-called feticide statutes. But feticide statutes generally carry lighter sentences than homicide statutes, implying that the intentional destruction of an unborn life does not have the same value as the life of one who has been born. Likewise, while the frozen embryo cases declare that embryos are entitled to special respect because of their potential for life, they nonetheless conclude that embryos may be discarded if the parents so desire.

Constitutional law, as we have seen, embraces the same born-unborn distinction. In the landmark abortion case Roe v. Wade, for example, the Supreme Court was explicitly asked to declare that the word "person" in the Constitution included the unborn. The Court declined this invitation, concluding that the Constitution's multiple references to persons and people make sense only if understood postnatally, rejecting the idea that abortion constitutes a deprivation of life without due process of law. Constitutional rights, in short, attach only to the born.

The centrality of the born-unborn distinction to both statutory and constitutional law was reinforced in the Supreme Court's partial-birth abortion decision, Gonzales v. Carhart. The Partial Birth Abortion Act (PBAA) formalized the importance of an ethical and legal distinction between the born and unborn. Under the PBAA, a living fetus whose entire head (in the case of head-first presentation) or trunk past the navel (in the case of a breech presentation) is delivered outside the mother's body is sufficiently "born," in the view of Congress, to warrant more vigorous legal protection.[1] While "partial" birth is not "full" birth, it was enough birth to make Congress queasy about a procedure that skirted the line between abortion and infanticide.

The Supreme Court's abortion jurisprudence has drawn an additional legal distinction of significance: between the viable and non-viable unborn. While the unborn are without constitutional rights, the Court has recognized, since *Roe,* that an unborn's life (or potential life) is something that states may claim a compelling interest in protecting after the fetus has passed the point of viability. This does not mean that the Court considers post-viability fetuses to be constitutionally cognizable persons; rather, it merely creates conceptual wiggle room allowing the states to regulate abortions. It effectively declares that post-viability, the states' interest in protecting *potential* life can outweigh the woman's right to choose.

The Supreme Court's recognition of a woman's right to pre-viability abortion has had a direct impact not only on state abortion laws, but also on state criminal and tort laws, allowing such ordinary laws to reflect the states' compelling interest in protecting the *post*-viable unborn. A few state homicide statutes, for example, have been interpreted to apply to the death of a post-viable fetus. And in the majority of states, tort law permits recovery for the "wrongful death" of a post-viable fetus.

Constitutional recognition of a right to pre-viability abortion has also encouraged the creation of private rights of action to compensate individuals whose exercise of those rights has been impeded or frustrated by health care professionals. For example, as we have seen, the torts of wrongful birth and wrongful life could not really exist without constitutional recognition of abortion. And the tort of wrongful conception/pregnancy, while not dependent on the constitutional right to use contraception, has an obvious logical connection to it.

The bottom line is that, when it comes to the law of life, two critical distinctions are made: (1) between the born and unborn; and (2) among the unborn, between the viable and non-viable. A hierarchy of biological life seems to emerge that looks something like this:

> The Born ("persons" with full legal rights)
> The Post-Viablity Unborn (not full legal "persons," but with some substantial legal protections; state has a "compelling" interest in protecting them)
> The Pre-viability Unborn (not full legal "persons," with very few legal protections; may be aborted or discarded)

Unlike life—where there has been no definitional agreement—the law of death has managed to agree on two primary definitions (cardiopulmonary and brain death), but these definitions are harder to apply than one might think. In the context of cardiopulmonary death, for example, there is continuing controversy over the number of minutes that should elapse before declaring death following asystole. Under some donation after cardiac death (DCD) protocols, doctors wait only seventy-five seconds before harvesting organs. Similarly, controversy swirls around doctors' authority to unilaterally impose do not resuscitate (DNR) orders following a patient's cardiac arrest or other life-threatening conditions. These situations, involving a doctor's determination that continuation of care would be "futile," are increasingly common, sanctioned by either specific futility statutes or institutional futility policies. They illustrate how something ostensibly designed to further patient autonomy—DNR orders—has morphed into something employed to deny end-of-life care, even when desperately wanted.

In the context of brain death, there is continuing controversy over diagnostic criteria, error rates, and even how much of the brain must be dead. These uncertainties have engendered ardent debate about whether, as a conceptual matter, it is normatively desirable to continue recognizing brain death as death. Yet the primary factors that led to legal recognition of brain death in the first place—organ transplantation and medical technology that keeps us pink and breathing long after many of us want to go on living—still exist. Legal recognition of advance directives can now give us some degree of control over the timing and manner of our own death, obviating the need for brain death recognition somewhat. But organ transplantation is still heavily dependent on brain death; the vast majority of organs are harvested from individuals declared brain dead.

Without brain death, where would we get organs? Donation after cardiac death, even if expanded significantly, would not come close to providing the same number of organs as brain death. Dispensing with the dead donor rule is another option that some have proposed. But most of us still instinctively flinch at the idea of taking organs from someone who is not considered legally dead. The specter of Monty Python's "live organ transplants" skit—"it's all for the good of the country!"—cuts too close.[2]

Another option for increasing organ availability—and one that has received serious consideration, at least among the medical and bioethics communities—is to liberalize brain death, redefining it as death of the higher brain rather than the whole brain. While higher brain death dispenses with the need to conduct difficult, often ambiguous bedside tests for brain stem function, it poses its own difficulties for definition and diagnosis. How much of the higher brain must be dead? How do we know if the higher brain has irreversibly lost function?

The classic higher brain-dead patient is someone in a vegetative state—individuals such as Karen Ann Quinlan, Nancy Cruzan, or Terri Schiavo. Because such vegetative patients have a functioning brain stem, current law does not classify them as dead. But are they as "good as dead"? In the views of many people, the answer is yes, because vegetative patients have lost their biography, an ability to interact, to remember, and to experience life.

For many years, it was accepted as gospel that vegetative patients are, well, little more than vegetables. But in the early twenty-first century, the medical profession formally recognized that consciousness—believed to be centered in the higher brain—is not an all-or-nothing proposition. Whereas previous medical orthodoxy held that a patient either was or was not capable of consciousness, we now know that consciousness is best understood as a spectrum. Many patients previously classified as vegetative (by definition, incapable of consciousness) are now classified as minimally conscious, capable of fleeting, unpredictable flashes of consciousness, virtually unnoticeable except to the most highly trained eye. Definitively identifying a patient as having an irreversibly dead higher brain, in other words, is much more difficult than imagined even ten years ago.

Higher brain death has also suffered a conceptual setback due to the neuroimaging and pharmaceutical revolutions. Deep brain stimulation, dopaminergic drugs, Ambien, and branched-chain amino acids (BCAAs) have shown some limited promise for awakening some subset of those previously assumed permanently unconscious. Groundbreaking functional magnetic resonance imaging (fMRI) studies involving patients in a persistent vegetative state (PVS) have revealed that some subset of them may be, in fact, aware of their surroundings. They not only seem, physiologically, to hear what others are saying to them, but also to respond appropriately to commands they are given. And in the most recent and remarkable studies of all, they seem to be potentially capable of communicating with us, using fMRI, in response to simple yes/no questions. Because of these pharmaceutical and neuroimaging advances, it is increasingly clear that some patients assumed to be little more than vegetables may be still with us, mentally, and it would be coldly utilitarian—not to mention discriminatory based on disability—to suggest that they should be considered legally dead.

When it comes to constitutional law relating to death, the Supreme Court, in *Cruzan,* assiduously avoided declaring a constitutional liberty to refuse unwanted medical treatment, though it assumed, for purposes of upholding Missouri's "clear and convincing evidence" standard, that such a liberty interest existed. Why the Supreme Court would "assume" the existence of a constitutional right, without actually deciding it, has been the focus of much academic discussion. One possible explanation is that the Court did not want to open the conceptual floodgates to constitutional recognition of a broader "right to die." As Justice Scalia's concurrence in *Cruzan* pointed out, there is a fine (perhaps nonexistent) line between killing yourself by refusing medical treatment versus killing yourself by turning on the car in the garage or taking an overdose of pills. And if there is a right to kill yourself (by whatever means), then it is not an insurmountable logical leap to find a right to obtain a third party's assistance in doing so.

The Supreme Court's decisions in a pair of physician-assisted suicide (PAS) cases, *Glucksberg* and *Quill,* attempted to throw cold water on speculation that an assumed right to refuse unwanted medical treatment ineluctably led to a right to suicide or third party assistance with suicide. Yet Justice O'Connor's separate concurrence in the PAS cases—combined with the other separate concurring opinions—muddied the waters considerably by suggesting that there may be a constitutional right to be free from state-imposed pain at the end of life—that is, a pain free death, or "death with dignity." Moreover, the Court's subsequent decision in Lawrence v. Texas could proffer an alternative analytical framework—unmoored from the *Glucksberg* and *Quill* framework that was focused on history and tradition—that could represent the proverbial camel's nose in the constitutional tent. By rejecting the primacy of historical legal prohibition of suicide and assisted suicide and elevating the importance of modern trends, *Lawrence* potentially frees the Court from a presumption of constitutionality of anti-PAS laws, laying an intellectual foundation on which to recognize a right to assisted suicide in a future case.

For the time being, however, the constitutional status of assisted suicide lies dormant, and the legal action is occurring in the realm of state law. At present, a handful of states—Oregon, Washington, and Montana—legally permit PAS. Outside these states, the legal line is still being drawn between pulling the plug (legally acceptable and required if the patient or patient's family requests) and giving the patient poison to drink (criminal behavior). This thin, fuzzy line—between letting die and killing—was the basis for *Quill* and is still the basis upon which the entirety of law relating to the "right to die" depends. It is a slim and fragile reed.

Constitutionally speaking, there is at least procedural recognition of a "right to life" in the Due Process Clauses, though the Supreme Court has made it clear in its abortion jurisprudence that this right belongs only to the born. Once born, however, you have no constitutional "right to die," because of the historical criminalization of suicide and assisted suicide and because the Court continues to see a meaningful distinction between killing and letting die. In reality, then, there is no real "right" to be born nor a "right" to die. In a very basic sense, your "right" to be born or die is left to nature, the Creator, or whatever cosmic force controls these matters.

The law often reflects political capture by one of two dominant ideological camps, advocating either a right to life or a right to die. The political strength and influence of the right-to-life movement is evidenced in an increasing trend of imposing criminal or civil liability on acts that harm the unborn. It is also evident in Supreme Court acceptance of abortion regulations such as waiting periods and the Partial Birth Abortion Act, and its denial of a right to physician-assisted suicide.

In writing this book, however, I have noticed that, in recent decades, the legal victories of the right-to-life movement are fewer and farther between than those of the right-to-die movement. In short, while the law of life and death is a tide ebbing and flowing between pro-life and right-to-die viewpoints, it is a tide that is moving more in the direction of death than of life. For example, both contraception and abortion have been recognized as constitutional rights. Even the definition of pregnancy has been altered to expand support for contraception and avoid the abortion shibboleth. The law has recognized brain death and shortened the time required to declare cardiopulmonary death—both of which were principally driven by a desire to facilitate organ harvesting. And while organ harvesting undeniably saves the lives of the donor recipients—and therefore could be said to be "pro-life"—it does so by declaring others dead, encouraging or facilitating their death so that others may live. Others may live, in other words, but in order to do so, others must die. The pro-life position that all post-conception life is sacred does not underlie these legal changes.

Similarly, the law has recognized a constitutional right to refuse life-sustaining treatment and the ability of doctors to prescribe lethal medications with a deadly "double effect." Some states, such as Oregon and Washington, have enacted statutes allowing physicians to write prescriptions that will cause the death of their patients. Other states, such as Texas, permit doctors unilaterally to withhold or withdraw life-sustaining care on grounds of futility. These laws have pragmatic utility, but they are far from "pro-life." Instead, they encourage and facilitate death in order to further goals such as more equitable distribution of scarce resources, reducing the expense and heartache associated with prolonged dying, or allowing doctors to exercise their consciences.

The net result of the last several decades of legal changes is an elaborate avoidance of the definition of life and a slow but steady expansion of the definition of death and a concomitant right to die. Whether this legal trend comports with the average American's preferences is an open question. The pro-life versus right-to-die battle pits liberal against conservative, religious against secular, young against old, and rich against poor. Yet many (perhaps most) Americans fall somewhere in the middle of ideological extremes, having deep ambivalence about the definition and meaning of life and death. For these Americans, the law of life and death probably seems disjointed, erratic, unpredictable, and perhaps even threatening.

Indeed, legal reforms viewed as an attempt to encourage death have proved sufficiently threatening to cause popular uproar. The furor over end-of-life counseling during the health care reform debate, for example, evoked the specter of "death panels." While the proposed health reform legislation said nothing about actual death panels—but merely authorized Medicare reimbursement for end-of-life counseling—the popular fear was that counseling could become coercion, encouraging vulnerable seniors to make legal choices to end life sooner rather than later. This concern likely also underlies some of the opposition to greater government involvement in health care generally.

As much as the envelope has been pushed in threatening ways, some advocate pushing it further. For example, there are those who want to change the definition of death to include higher brain death. And when faced with some of the difficulties associated with diagnosing higher brain death, the more radical among the right-to-die movement simply move the pea, proffering a definition of consciousness that is incapable of verification. The most radical of all argue that we should legalize taking organs from those who are not yet dead, such as terminally ill, vegetative, or anencephalic patients.

Many right-to-die reforms are, at their heart, proautonomy. The right to refuse unwanted medical treatment, for example, respects individualism, allowing each person to decide for himself whether he would prefer to forego life-sustaining interventions that do not comport with his own values. DNR orders arguably serve the same autonomy function, at least when they are the result of the patient's (or family's) informed consent. Even abortion arguably furthers autonomy, allowing each woman to make a choice according to the dictates of her own conscience. Those who believe that life begins at conception, implantation, or some other time prior to viability are not forced to undergo abortion. They can choose life. And they can further convince their legislators to withhold taxpayer funding in order to ensure that their tax dollars are not used to facilitate abortion. The truth is that when choice exists (whether constitutionally compelled or statutorily permitted), it accommodates the widest possible array of views—an outcome that is pragmatically desirable for issues about which there is great passion and division.

But there are times when the quest for individual autonomy has been perverted to enhance governmental power to compel a specific outcome rather than respect pluralism. Futility laws, for example, create a strong presumption of death, and those who wish to live are effectively forced to overcome it (if they can). Unilaterally imposed DNR orders can deny patient autonomy, imposing the provider's paternalistic preferences and compelling a quicker death than would otherwise occur. Likewise, advance directives, while theoretically critical to effectuating individual autonomy, are often drafted in a manner that presumes a desire to refuse or withdraw life-sustaining care. The Florida living will statute, for example, provides a template that states, "I willfully and voluntarily make known my desire that my dying not be artificially prolonged under the circumstances set forth below. . . . I direct that life-prolonging procedures be withheld or withdrawn when the application of such procedures would serve only to prolong artificially the process of dying."³ An individual who wanted to continue life-sustaining treatment would not be able to use the sample form provided by the legislature and would presumably need to hire a lawyer to draft such a pro-life document.

Ensuring individual autonomy is laudable, but true autonomy presupposes that the choice is not the result of overt or covert pressure. If the law wishes to effectuate autonomy, these pressures, presumptions, and paternalistic preferences need to be discarded. Unfortunately, expensive medical technology, combined with limited resources, is pushing American law away from individual preferences and autonomy and toward communitarian cost/benefit analysis. The continuation of life can be expensive, particularly toward the end. In an era of dwindling resources, the hard-fought legal autonomy won over the last few decades is beginning to be conceptualized as an autonomy that flows more in the direction of death, not life. The right to die is morphing into an obligation to die.

Consider the legal victories won by the right-to-die movement and the type of autonomy they acknowledge. The law recognizes autonomy to use contraception and abortion. It recognizes autonomy to discard frozen embryos. It recognizes autonomy to refuse unwanted medical treatment, even when life sustaining. It recognizes autonomy to make advance directives, but only if they do not instruct that aggressive end-of-life care should be given. Such pro-life instructions can be ignored, invoking the mantra of futility. And although the law does not recognize a constitutional autonomy to assisted suicide, state laws may give us this right anyway, and increasingly are doing so. Death, it seems, is the destination, and autonomy is the vehicle by which we make this journey.

I began this book by asking you, "Are you alive? What makes you so sure?" Now you know that, in the eyes of the law, your birth and independent existence from your mother place you among an elite group of "persons" entitled to legal protection and constitutional rights. Your status among the living will continue until your death. How your death will be diagnosed is not as simple as you probably once believed, and the law seems increasingly designed to encourage you to die sooner rather than later. This may or may not be a bad thing, depending on your perspective. After all, short of futuristic, successful cryogenics, death—unlike life—is unavoidable. "In the long run," as John Maynard Keynes once said, "we are all dead."

Notes

Introduction

1. *Black's Law Dictionary* 428 (8th ed. 2004).

1. Statutory and Common Law Life

1. *See, e.g.,* Linda McCulloch, Montana Secretary of State, Constitutional Initiative No. 102 (on ballot in 2010), sos.mt.gov/Elections/archives/2010s/2010/initiatives/CI-102.asp (accessed 11/29/09); Ed Vogel, "Personhood Amendment Would Ban Pill RU-486," *Las Vegas Review-Journal,* November 17, 2009, p. 1B; Robin Abcarian, "Roe Foes Push to Redefine 'Person,'" *Chicago Tribune,* October 4, 2009, 2009 WLNR 19555189.

2. *See* Daniel E. Koshland, Jr., "The Seven Pillars of Life," 295 *Science* 2215 (2002). *See also* Lynn Margulis and Dorian Sagan, *What is Life?* (New York: Simon and Schuster, 1995).

3. *See generally* Arthur Caplan and Thomas A. Marino, "The Role of Scientists in the Beginning-of-Life Debate: A 25-Year Retrospective," 50 *Perspectives in Biology and Medicine* 603 (2007).

4. Hugo Lagercrantz and Jean-Pierre Changeux, "The Emergence of Human Consciousness: From Fetal to Neonatal Life," 65 *Pediatric Research* 255 (2009).

5. Amir Halevy and Baruch Brody, "Brain Death: Reconciling Definitions, Criteria, and Tests," 119 *Archives of Internal Medicine* 519 (1993).

6. These facts are borrowed from the California Supreme Court case of Keeler v. Superior Court, 470 P.2d 617 (Cal. 1970).

7. Douglas S. Curran, Note, "Abandonment and Reconciliation: Addressing Political and Common Law Objections to Fetal Homicide Laws," 58 *Duke Law Journal* 1107 (2009).

8. People v. Selwa, 543 N.W.2d 321 (Mich. Ct. App. 1995), *appeal denied,* 557 N.W.2d 307 (Mich. 1996).

9. Ibid., p. 325.

10. Ibid., pp. 325, 326 (emphasis in original).

11. Ibid., p. 328.

12. Ibid., p. 328 n.9.

13. Ibid., p. 331 n.5 (Holbrook, J., dissenting).

14. Ibid., p. 330 (Holbrook, J., dissenting) (citing People v. Guthrie, 293 N.W.2d 775 (Mich. Ct. App. 1980)).

15. Ibid. (Holbrook, J., dissenting) (quoting *Guthrie,* 293 N.W.2d at 775).

16. Ibid., p. 332 (Holbrook, J., dissenting).

17. People v. Guthrie, 293 N.W.2d 775 (Mich. Ct. App. 1980) (quoting LaFave and Scott, *Criminal Law* §67, pp. 530–531).

18. *See, e.g., Selwa,* 543 N.W.2d at 329; People v. Bolar, 440 N.E.2d 639, 644 (Ill. Ct. App. 1982).

19. *Bolar,* 440 N.E.2d at 645. The Court noted that the "fact that the infant expired within moments [of being removed from its mother's womb] is irrelevant." Ibid. The Court also did not appear to be concerned with the fact that the infant did not exhibit any signs of respiration. Ibid.

20. Ibid., p. 644. The current version of the Illinois Anatomical Gift Act can be found at 755 Ill. Comp. Stat. Ann. §50/1–10. In 2007, the Illinois legislature amended its law to allow organ donation after cardiac death. 755 Ill. Comp. Stat. Ann. §50/5–27.

21. *Bolar,* 440 N.E.2d at 644.

22. *Selwa,* 543 N.W.2d at 328 n.9.

23. People v. French, 2003 WL 22872498 (Mich. Ct. App. 2003) (per curiam).

24. Ibid., p. *3.

25. Ibid., p. *5 (Griffin, J., dissenting).

26. Ibid., p. *3.

27. Ibid.; *see also* ibid., p. *6 (Griffin, J., dissenting).

28. Ibid., p. *3.

29. Ibid., p. *6 (Griffin, J., dissenting).

30. Ibid., p. *4 (emphasis in original) (internal citation omitted).

31. *Selwa,* 543 N.W.2d at 328 ("The dissent concludes that the baby's heartbeat as well as the spontaneous respirations were 'artificially induced and mechanically sustained.' However, this is in part inconsistent with Dr. DeWitt's testimony that revealed that the spontaneous respirations were something that the infant did on her own. Furthermore, although the baby required mechanical assistance, that

does not render a finding per se that no circulatory function existed. . . . The necessity of medical intervention to revive or bring one to life does not preclude a finding that a person is born alive. Otherwise, the word 'irreversible' becomes meaningless.") (internal citations omitted).

32. The term "embryo" is generally used to describe the phase of human development up to approximately eight weeks postconception.

33. The term "fetus" is generally used to describe the phase of human development from approximately eight weeks postconception until birth.

34. *See, e.g.,* Hornbuckle v. Plantation Pipe Line Co., 93 S.E.2d 727, 728 (Ga. 1956) ("At what particular moment after conception, or at what particular period of the prenatal existence of the child the injury was inflicted is not controlling, for . . . [i]n . . . general, a child is to be considered as in being, from the time of its conception, where it will be for the benefit of such child to be so considered.") (internal citations omitted).

35. *See* Puhl v. Milwaukee Auto. Ins. Co., 99 N.W.2d 163 (Wis. 1959) *(overruled on other grounds by* In re Estate of Stromsted, 299 N.W.2d 226 (Wis. 1980)).

36. *See, e.g.,* Commonwealth v. Morris, 142 S.W.3d 654, 660 (Ky. 2004) (post-viability fetus is a "human being" under homicide statute); Hughes v. State, 868 P.2d 730, 731 (Oka. Crim. App. 1994) (same); Commonwealth v. Cass, 467 N.E.2d 1324, 1326 (Mass. 1984) (viable fetus is person within meaning of vehicular homicide statute). *Compare* State v. Holcomb, 956 S.W.2d 286, 289–290 (Mo. Ct. App. 1997) (unborn, pre-viable child is person under murder statute); State v. Horne, 319 S.E. 2d 703, 704 (S.C. 1984) (fetus is person for purposes of criminal law).

37. Marka B. Fleming, "Feticide Laws: Contemporary Legal Applications and Constitutional Inquiries," 29 *Pace Law Review* 43, 56–57 n.72 (2008).

38. Lawrence v. State, 240 S.W.3d 912, 915 (Tex. Crim. App. 2007).

39. Ibid., pp. 917–918.

40. Lawrence v. Texas, 539 U.S. 558 (2003).

41. *See, e.g.,* West's Ann. Cal. Penal Code §597. *See also* Sonja A. Soehnel, "What Constitutes Offense of Cruelty to Animals—Modern Cases," 6 *American Law Reports,* 5th ed. 733 (1992).

42. The facts of this case have been gleaned from a 2009 decision of the Indiana Court of Appeals, as well as media reports of the accident. *See* Ramirez v. Wilson, 901 N.E.2d 1 (Ind. Ct. App. 2009); Ruthann Robinson, "Pregnant Lowell Woman Dies in Accident," *NWI Times,* March 22, 2007, www.nwitimes.com (accessed 12/15/09).

43. *Ramirez,* 901 N.E.2d at 3–4.

44. *See* Michael P. Penick, "Wrongful Death of Fetus," 19 *American Jurisprudence Proof of Facts 3d* 107, §1 (2008) (thirty-six states now permit wrongful death actions if the unborn has passed the point of viability at the time of the injury).

45. The pregnant woman who suffers from an injury is of course entitled to her own independent tort recovery.

46. Catherine Palo, "Cause of Action for Wrongful Birth or Wrongful Life," 23 *Cause of Action 2d* 55, §4 (2009).

47. Ibid., §10.

48. Keel v. Banach, 624 So.2d 1022, 1024 (Ala. 1993).

49. Berman v. Allan, 404 A.2d 8, 13 (N.J. 1979).

50. Gleitman v. Cosgrove, 227 A.2d 689, 693 (N.J. 1967).

51. Ibid., p. 691.

52. Ibid., p. 693.

53. *Berman,* 404 A.2d at 11.

54. Ibid., p. 10.

55. Ibid., p. 14 (internal citations omitted; emphasis in original).

56. 42 U.S.C. §1983; Bivens v. Six Unknown Agents, 403 U.S. 388 (1971).

57. Skinner v. Oklahoma, 316 U.S. 535 (1942); Zablocki v. Redhail, 434 U.S. 374 (1978).

58. Common law recognized the torts of alienation of affection and criminal conversation, both of which provide compensation for actions by private individuals that interfere with the harmony of a marriage. These torts, though still existing in a handful of states, do not compensate for acts that prevent marriage from occurring (and hence the constitutional right to marry being exercised), but instead compensate for acts that interfere with an existing marital relationship.

59. Willis v. Wu, 607 S.E.2d 63, 66 (S.C. 2004).

60. Hummel v. Reiss, 608 A.2d 1341, 1343 (N.J. 1992).

61. Ibid., p. 1345.

62. Ibid., pp. 1345, 1347.

63. Barrigan v. Lopez, 68 Cal. Rptr. 3d 73, 78 (Cal. Ct. App. 2007).

64. Ibid., pp. 78–79.

65. Kassama v. Magat, 792 A.2d 1102 (Md. Ct. App. 2002); Molloy v. Meier, 660 N.W.2d 444 (Minn. Ct. App. 2003), *aff'd,* 679 N.W.2d 711 (Minn. 2004).

66. Rich v. Foye, 2007 WL 2702809 (Conn. Super. Ct. 2007); Willlis v. Wu, 607 S.E.2d 63 (S.C. 2004); Coleman v. Dogra, 812 N.E.2d 332 (Ohio Ct. App. 2004), *aff'd,* 844 N.E.2d 1190 (Ohio 2006); Kassama, 792 A.2d at 1102; Anderson v. St. Francis–St. George Hosp., 671 N.E.2d 225 (Ohio 1996).

67. *See, e.g.,* Idaho Code §5-334; Ind. Code §34-12-1-1; Me. Rev. Stat., tit. 24, §2931; Mich. Comp. Laws §600-2971; Minn. Stat. §145.424; Mo. Rev. Stat. §188.130; N.D. Cent. Code §32-03-43; 42 Pa. Cons. Stat. §8305(B); S.D. Codified Laws §21-55-1; Utah Code §78-11-24.

68. These facts are based on Wasden v. Mager, 619 S.E.2d 384 (Ga. 2005).

69. Flax v. McNew, 896 S.W.2d 839 (Tex. Ct. App. 1995).

70. Ibid.; M.A. v. U.S., 951 P.2d 851 (Alaska 1998).

71. Wells v. Ortho Pharm. Corp., 788 F.2d 741(Ga. 1986).

72. Miller v. Johnson, 343 S.E.2d 301, 304–307 (Va. 1986).

73. Dotson v. Bernstein, 207 P.3d 911, 912–913 (Colo. Ct. App. 2009); *see also* R. Donaldson, "Recoverability of Cost of Raising a Normal, Healthy Child Born as a Result of Physician's Negligence or Breach of Contract or Warranty, 89 *American Law Reports, 4th ed.* 632 (1991).

74. *See, e.g.,* Wallis v. Hodson, 26 Eng. Rep. 473 (Ct. of Chancery 1740).

75. 96 *Corpus Juris Secundum,* "Wills" §932 (2009).

76. Uniform Probate Code §2–104(a)(2); 26B *Corpus Juris Secundum,* "Descent and Distribution" §34.

77. Ebbs v. Smith, 394 N.E.2d 1034, 1035–1036 (Ohio Com. Pl. 1979).

78. In re Martin B., 841 N.Y.S.2d 207, 209 (2007).

79. Calif. Probate Code §249.5.

80. La. Rev. Stat. Ann. §9:391.1.

81. *In re Martin B.,* 841 N.Y.S.2d at 211.

82. "Popsicle Idol," *Brisbane News* (Australia), February 23, 2009, p. 5.

83. Gregory M. Fahy et al., "Cryopreservation of Organs by Vitrification: Perspectives and Recent Advances," 48 *Cryobiology* 157, 159 (2004).

84. Ibid., pp. 158–159, 167.

85. Uniform Anatomical Gift Act §6(a)(1) (1987).

86. Ibid., §1(10).

87. Alcor Extension Found., Inc. v. Mitchell, 9 Cal. Rptr. 572, 575 (Cal. Ct. App. 1992).

88. "World Briefing: France: Son Ordered to Bury or Cremate His Frozen Parents," *New York Times,* January 11, 2006, p. A17.

89. *See* "Judge Denies Request for Man's Remains: Brother, Sister Win Legal Battle with Cryonic Foundation," *The Hawk Eye,* July 16, 2009, 2009 WLNR 13586560.

90. Iowa Code Ann. §144C.5(1)(a).

91. Ibid. at §144C.5(1)(f).

92. "Judge Denies Request for Man's Remains," *The Hawk Eye,* July 16, 2009, 2009 WLNR 13586560; Acts 2008 (82 G.A.) ch. 1051, S.F. 473, §22. The cryogenics facility has appealed the trial judge's ruling to the Iowa Supreme Court, seeking the right to disinter Richardson's body and honor his wishes to be neuropreserved. John Mangalonzo, "Cryonics Firm Appeals to High Court," *The Hawk Eye,* August 14, 2009.

93. "Cryonics: A Basic Introduction," Cryonics Institute, www.cryonics.org/prod.html (accessed 12/18/09).

94. 4 Cal. Rptr. 2d 59 (Cal. Ct. App. 1992).

95. Donaldson v. Lungren, 4 Cal. Rptr. 2d 59, 60 (Cal. Ct. App. 1992).

96. Ibid.

97. Ibid., p. 62.

98. Colleen Jenkins, "Frozen Wish Is Met, Sort Of," *St. Petersburg Times*, December 11, 2009, p. 1A.

99. Uniform Anatomical Gift Act, §8(a).

100. Leslie Whetstine et al., "Pro/Con Ethics Debate: When Is Dead Really Dead?" 9 *Critical Care* 538, 540 (2005).

101. *See, e.g.,* California Cryobank, www.cryobank.com (accessed 12/12/09); Midwest Sperm Bank (accessed 12/12/09); www.midwestspermbank.com/catalog.htm; Fairfax Cryobank, www.fairfaxcryobank.com (accessed 12/12/09); The Donor Egg Bank, www.donoreggbankinc.com/profiles.html (accessed 12/12/09).

102. Rob Stein, "Ethicists Decry Embryo Brokerage," *Washington Post,* January 6, 2007, 2007 WLNR 226969.

103. Theresa Erickson, "Abraham Center of Life No Longer in Embryo Business," *Egg Donor and Surrogacy Blog,* www.surrogacyeggdonorblog.com (accessed 12/12/09).

104. D. I. Hoffman et al., "Cryopreserved Embryos in the United States and Their Availability for Research," 79 *Fertility and Sterility* 1063 (2003).

105. Natalie Lester, "Saving Snowflakes: Process Transfers 'Extra' Frozen Embryos to Want-to-Be Moms," *Washington Times,* April 19, 2009, p. M5.

106. Davis v. Davis, 842 S.W.2d 588, 590 (Tenn. 1992).

107. Ibid., p. 595.

108. Ibid.

109. Ibid., p. 596.

110. Ibid., p. 597.

111. Ibid.

112. Ibid., p. 603.

113. Ibid., p. 604.

114. E. Haimes and K. Taylor, "Fresh Embryo Donation for Human Embryonic Stem Cell (hESC) Research: The Experiences and Values of IVF Couples Asked to Be Embryo Donors," 24 *Human Reproduction* 2142 (2009).

115. Denise Grady, "Parents Torn Over Extra Frozen Embryos from Fertility Procedures," *New York Times,* December 4, 2008, p. A26.

116. *See, e.g.,* In re Marriage of Dahl, 194 P.3d 834 (Or. Ct. App. 2008); Roman v. Roman, 193 S.W.3d 40 (Tex. Ct. App. 2006); In re Litowitz, 48 P.3d 261 (Wash. 2002); Kass v. Kass, 696 N.E.2d 174 (N.Y. 1998).

117. In re Marriage of Witten, 672 N.W.2d 768 (Iowa 2003); J.B. v. M.B., 783A.2d 707 (N.J. 2001).

118. *J.B.,* 783 A.2d at 719.

119. *In re Marriage of Witten,* 672 N.W.2d at 783.

120. La. Rev. Stat. §9:126.

121. Ibid., §9:130.

122. Ibid., §§9:126, 9:130.

123. Ibid., §9:127.

124. Ibid., §9:130.

125. Who would have standing to raise such a claim is an interesting legal question, since the frozen embryos themselves cannot bring their own claim. This procedural hurdle may effectively preclude any such claims from being considered, thus allowing for the indefinite storage of frozen embryos.

126. Ibid., §9:131.

2. Constitutional Life

1. U.S. Constitution, amendments V and XIV.

2. *See* John O. Schorge et al., "Contraception and Sterilization," chap. 5, *Williams Gynecology* (New York: McGraw-Hill, 2008); Walter L. Larimore and Joseph B. Stanford, "Postfertilization Effects of Oral Contraceptives and Their Relationship to Informed Consent," 9 *Archives of Family Medicine* 126 (2000).

3. *Black's Law Dictionary* (8th ed. 2004).

4. *Black's Law Dictionary* 1179 (6th ed. 1990).

5. *See MedlinePlus, Merriam-Webster Medical Dictionary,* http://www.nlm.nih.gov/medlineplus/mplusdictionary.html (accessed 11/22/09); Dorland's *Medical Dictionary for Healthcare Consumers,* www.mercksource.com/pp/us/cns/cns_hl_dorlands_split.jsp?pg=/ppdocs/us/common/dorlands/dorland/misc/P_TOC.htm (accessed 11/22/09).

6. American Medical Association, Resolution 443 (A-04) (2004); British Medical Association, "Abortion Time Limits: A Briefing Paper from the BMA" (2005), p. 1.

7. *See, e.g.,* Schorge et al., "Contraception and Sterilization," chap. 5, *Williams Gynecology;* Larimore and Stanford, "Postfertilization Effects of Oral Contraceptives," pp. 127–130; "How Plan B One-Step Works," www.planbonestep.com/plan-b-prescribers/how-plan-b-works.aspx (accessed 12/12/09).

8. Larimore and Stanford, "Postfertilization Effects of Oral Contraceptives," p. 130.

9. *See, e.g.,* Planned Parenthood, "The Abortion Pill (Medical Abortion)," www.plannedparenthood.org/health-topics/abortion/abortion-pill-medication-abortion-4354.htm (accessed 12/23/09).

10. Commonwealth v. Gardner, 15 N.E.2d 222 (Mass. 1938).

11. Ibid., p. 223.

12. Ibid., p. 224.

13. Gardner v. Massachusetts, 305 U.S. 559 (1938).

14. State v. Nelson, 7 Conn. Supp. 262, 1939 WL 931 (Conn. Super. Ct. 1939).

15. Ibid.

16. Ibid.

17. State v. Nelson, 11 A.2d 856, 859 (Conn. 1940).

18. Ibid., p. 861.

19. Tileston v. Ullman, 318 U.S. 44 (1943).

20. Buxton v. Ullman, 156 A.2d 508, 512–514 (Conn. 1959).

21. Poe v. Ullman, 367 U.S. 497 (1961).

22. Ibid., p. 508 (plurality).

23. Ibid., p. 509 (Brennan, J., concurring).

24. Ibid., p. 513 (Douglas, J., dissenting).

25. Ibid., p. 520–521 (Douglas, J., dissenting).

26. Ibid., p. 543 (Harlan, J., dissenting).

27. Ibid., p. 548 (Harlan, J., dissenting).

28. Griswold v. Connecticut, 381 U.S. 479, 480 (1965).

29. Ibid., p. 484.

30. Ibid., pp. 485–486.

31. Ibid., pp. 499–500.

32. Ibid., p. 502 (White, J., concurring).

33. Eisenstadt v. Baird, 405 U.S. 438, 440–441 (1972).

34. Ibid., p. 440.

35. Ibid., p. 443.

36. Ibid., p. 448.

37. Ibid.

38. Ibid., p. 449.

39. Carey v. Population Services Int'l 431 U.S. 678 (1977).

40. Planned Parenthood of Central Mo. v. Danforth, 428 U.S. 52 (1976) (plurality).

41. *Carey*, 431 U.S. at 694.

42. Roe v. Wade, 410 U.S. 113 (1973).

43. Ibid., pp. 120–122.

44. Ibid., p. 153 (emphasis added).

45. Ibid., p. 155.

46. Ibid., p. 156.

47. Ibid., pp. 156–157.

48. Ibid., p. 157.

49. Ibid., p. 140.

50. Ibid., p. 158.

51. Ibid., p. 159.

52. Ibid., pp. 162–163.

53. Ibid., p. 163.

54. Ibid.

55. Ibid., pp. 163–164.

56. Planned Parenthood of Southeastern Pa. v. Casey, 505 U.S. 833 (1992).

57. Ibid., p. 846; *see also* ibid., p. 923 (Blackmun, J., concurring in part and dissenting in part) ("[T]he authors of the joint opinion today join Justice Stevens and me in concluding that the essential holding of Roe v. Wade should be retained and once again reaffirmed.").

58. Ibid., pp. 869–873 (plurality).

59. Ibid., p. 874.

60. Ibid., p. 877.

61. Ibid., pp. 926, 934 (Blackmun, J., concurring in part and dissenting in part).

62. Ibid., p. 944 (Rehnquist, J., concurring in the judgment in part and dissenting in part).

63. Gonzalez v. Carhart, 550 U.S. 124 (2007).

64. Ibid., p. 142 (found at 18 U.S.C. §1531(d)(1)).

65. Ibid., pp. 156–158.

66. Ibid., pp. 134, 137.

67. Ibid., p. 140.

68. Ibid., pp. 135–140.

69. Ibid., p. 142 (found at 18 U.S.C. §1531(b)(1)(A)).

70. Ibid., p. 144.

71. Ibid., p. 146 (quoting *Casey,* 505 U.S. at 877).

72. Ibid., p. 157.

73. Ibid., p. 164.

74. Ibid., pp. 166–167.

75. Ibid., p. 170 (Ginsburg, J., dissenting).

76. John M. Goldenring, "Development of the Fetal Brain," 307 *New England Journal of Medicine* 564 (1982).

77. John M. Goldenring, "The Brain-Life Theory: Towards a Consistent Biological Definition of Humanness," 11 *Journal of Medical Ethics* 198 (1985).

78. Ibid., p. 199.

79. Ibid.

80. Ibid.

81. Ibid.

82. *See* D. Gareth Jones, "Brain Birth and Personal Identity," 15 *Journal of Medical Ethics* 173 (1989) (discussing various approaches to brain life).

83. Goldenring, "Brain-Life Theory," p. 200.

84. Ibid.

85. Steven G. Gabbe et al., "Fetal Cardiovascular System," in *Obstetrics: Normal and Problem Pregnancies,* 5th ed. (Philadelphia: Churchill Livingstone Elsevier, 2007).

86. *See* Elizabeth Price Foley, "The Constitutional Implications of Human Cloning," 42 *Arizona Law Review* 647, 679–687 (2000).

87. There have been constitutional challenges to some of these state bans on embryo or fetal research. *See, e.g.,* Forbes v. Napolitano, 236 F.3d 1009 (9th Cir. 2000) (finding Arizona fetal tissue statute unconstitutional on grounds of vagueness).

88. Pub. L. No. 93-348, 88 Stat. 342, §§202(b), 213.

89. National Commission for the Protection of Human Subjects of Biomedical and Behavioral Research, *Report and Recommendations: Research on the Fetus* 71 (Washington, D.C.: U.S. Department of Health, Education and Welfare, 1975).

90. 40 Fed. Reg. 33526 (1975).

91. 45 C.F.R. §§46.203–46.204.

92. Ibid., §46.204(b).

93. 58 Fed. Reg. 7457 (1993).

94. 42 U.S.C. §289g-1.

95. Pub. L. No. 104–99, §128, 110 Stat. 26, 34 (1996).

96. 65 Fed. Reg. 51976 (2000).

97. "Bush Squeezes Between the Lines on Stem Cells," 293 *Science* 1242 (2001).

98. Ibid.

99. National Conference of State Legislatures, "Embryonic and Fetal Research Laws: Stem Cell Research," www.ncsl.org (accessed 12/15/09).

100. 74 Fed. Reg. 32170 (2009).

101. Sherley v. Sebelius, 704 F. Supp. 2d 63, 70–71 (D.D.C. 2010) (emphasis in original).

102. Order, Sherley v. Sebelius, No. 10-5289 (D.C. Cir. Sept. 9, 2010) (per curiam).

103. *Sherley*, 704 F. Supp. 2d at 71–72 (internal citations omitted).

3. Cardiopulmonary Death

1. György Buzsáki, *Rhythms of the Brain* (New York: Oxford UP, 2006), pp. 16–17.

2. *See* David J. Powner et al., "Medical Diagnosis of Death in Adults: Historical Contributions to Current Controversies," 348 *Lancet* 1219 (1996).

3. George K. Behlmer, "Grave Doubts: Victorian Medicine, Moral Panic, and the Signs of Death," 42 *Journal of British Studies* 206 (2003); President's Commission for the Study of Ethical Problems in Medicine and Biomedical and Behavioral Research, *Defining Death: Medical, Legal and Ethical Issues in the Determination of Death* (Buffalo, N.Y.: W.S. Hein, 1981), p. 13.

4. President's Commission, *Defining Death*, pp. 13–14.

5. Ibid., p. 15.

6. 12A U.L.A. 589, §1.

7. President's Commission, *Defining Death*, p. 59.

8. Robert Steinbrook, "Organ Retrieval Methods Spark Debate," *Los Angeles Times,* July 4, 1992, p. A30.

9. Robert D. Orr et al., "Reanimation: Overcoming Objections and Obstacles to Organ Retrieval from Non-Heart-Beating Cadaver Donors," 23 *Journal of Medical Ethics* 7, 8 (1997).

10. Cara Buckley, "City Plans Ambulance for Organ Collection," *New York Times*, June 1, 2008, p. A35.

11. *See* Calixto Machado, "The First Organ Transplant from a Brain-Dead Donor," 64 *Neurology* 1938, 1938 (2005).

12. Jerry Menikoff, "Different Viewpoints: The Importance of Being Dead: Non-Heart-Beating Organ Donation," 18 *Issues in Law and Medicine* 3, 3–4 (2002).

13. Ibid., pp. 5–6.

14. This is the approach of the Uniform Determination of Death Act. 12A U.L.A. 589, §1.

15. Ibid. ("A determination of death must be made in accordance with accepted medical standards.").

16. *See* "University of Pittsburgh Medical Center Policy and Procedure Manual," 3 *Kennedy Institute of Ethics Journal*, "Appendix," A-6 (1992); Robert M. Veatch, "Donating Hearts After Cardiac Death—Reversing the Irreversible," 359 *New England Journal of Medicine* 672 (2008); Stuart J. Youngner et al., "When is 'Dead'?" 29 *Hastings Center Report* 14, 15 (1999).

17. Australian Organ and Tissue Donation and Transplant Authority, National Health and Medical Research Council, "National Protocol for Donation After Cardiac Death, Draft for Public Consultation" (2009), p. 9; Ethics Committee, American College of Critical Care Medicine, Society of Critical Care Medicine, "Recommendations for Non-Heart-Beating Organ Donation," 29 *Critical Care Medicine* 1826 (2001).

18. Canadian Council for Donation and Transplantation, *Donation After Cardiocirculatory Death: A Canadian Forum: Report and Recommendations* (Vancouver, B.C., Canada: The Canadian Council For Donation and Transplantation, 2005), p. 25; Institute of Medicine, National Academy of Sciences, *Non-Heart-Beating Organ Transplantation: Medical and Ethical Issues in Procurement* (Washington, D.C.: National Academy Press, 1997), pp. 40–41.

19. Buckley, "City Plans Ambulance," p. A35.

20. G. Kootstra et al., "The Non Heart-Beating Donor," 53 *British Medical Bulletin* 844, 848 (1997).

21. *See* Mark M. Boucek et al., "Pediatric Heart Transplantation After Declaration of Cardiocirculatory Death," 359 *New England Journal of Medicine* 709 (2008).

22. Youngner et al., "When is 'Dead'?" p. 16.

23. Tom Tomlinson, "The Irreversibility of Death: A Reply to Cole," 3 *Kennedy Institute of Ethics Journal* 157, 162 (1993).

24. Vacco v. Quill, 521 U.S. 793 (1997).

25. *See* Veatch, "Donating Hearts After Cardiac Death."

26. Youngner et al., "When is 'Dead'?" p. 15.

27. Joanne Lynn, "Are the Patients Who Become Organ Donors Under the Pittsburgh Protocol for 'Non-Heart-Beating Donors' Really Dead?" 3 *Kennedy Institute of Ethics Journal* 167, 170–172, 177 (1993).

28. James L. Bernat, "A Defense of the Whole-Brain Concept of Death," 28 *Hastings Center Report* 20 (1998).

29. Timothy Gower, "Fatal Flaw: Some Doctors Suggest That the Modern Definition of 'Death' is Wrong—And That the Mistake Is Costing Lives," *Boston Globe*, March 9, 2008, p. K1.

30. John Lichfield, "'Dead' Patient Comes Around as Organs Are About to Be Removed," *Independent* (London), June 12, 2008, p. 30; "Dead Man Waking Shocks Doctors," *Toronto Sun*, June 11, 2008, p. 34.

31. Lichfield, "'Dead' Patient Comes Around," p. 30.

32. Y. Y. Chen and S. J. Youngner, "'Allow Natural Death' Is Not an Equivalent to 'Do Not Resuscitate,'" 34 *Journal of Medical Ethics* 887, 887 (2008).

33. Ohio Admin. Code §3701-62-05; Ohio Rev. Code Ann. §2133.25.

34. Sylvia Moreno, "Case Puts Texas Futile Treatment Law Under a Microscope," *Washington Post*, April 11, 2007, p. A3. When Emilio's mother was unable to find another hospital to take Emilio, a Texas trial judge issued a temporary restraining order to prevent Emilio's physicians from terminating his life support. He died—still on life support—before the restraining order had expired. "Texas Works to Defuse Hostility Over Futility Law," *Medical Ethics Advisor*, July 1, 2007.

35. *See generally* James L. Bernat, "Medical Futility: Definition, Determination, and Disputes in Critical Care," 2 *Neurocritical Care* 198 (2005).

36. For an interesting look at the possible variations on approaches to futility, see Richard L. Wiener, "Research Report: A Preliminary Analysis of Medical Futility Decisionmaking: Law and Professional Attitudes," 16 *Behavioral Sciences and the Law* 497 (1998).

37. Ala. Code §22-8A-1; Alaska Stat. §13.52.010; Calif. Prob. Code §4600; Del. Code Ann. tit. 16 §2501; Haw. Rev. Stat. §327E-1; Me. Rev. Stat. Ann. tit. 18-A, §5-801; Miss. Code Ann. §41-41-201; N.M. Stat. §24-7A-1; Tenn. Code Ann. §68-11-1801; Utah Code Ann. §75-22-101; Wyo. Stat. Ann. §35-22-401.

38. Uniform Health Care Decisions Act §7(f) (1993).

39. Ibid., §7(g).

40. *See* N.Y. Pub. Health Law §2966; W.Va. Code §16-30C-6.

41. Texas Health & Safety Code §166.046(a)–(e).

42. Ibid., §166.046(g).

43. Ibid., §166.045(d).

44. Robert L. Fine and Thomas Wm. Mayo, "Resolution of Futility by Due Process:

Early Experience with the Texas Advance Directives Act," 138 *Annals of Internal Medicine* 743, 745, Table 3 (2003).

45. Robert L. Fine, "Tackling Medical Futility in Texas," 357 *New England Journal of Medicine* 1558 (2007).

46. Texas Health & Safety Code §166.046(b)(4)(A).

47. Robert D. Truog, "Tackling Medical Futility in Texas," 357 *New England Journal of Medicine* 1, 2 (2007).

48. President's Commission, *Defining Death*, p. 58.

49. Ibid.

50. Winston Chiong, "Brain Death Without Definitions," 35 *Hastings Center Report* 20, 29 (2005).

51. Tomlinson, "Irreversibility of Death," p. 164.

52. Ibid.

53. Veatch, "Donating Hearts After Cardiac Death," p. 673.

54. Boucek et al., "Pediatric Heart Transplantation," pp. 710–711.

55. Ibid., p. 712.

56. *See* Gina Kolata, "Controversy Erupts Over Organ Removals," *New York Times*, April 13, 1997, p. A28.

57. *Vacco*, 521 U.S. at 802.

58. Alan J. Weisbard, "A Polemic on Principles: Reflections on the Pittsburgh Protocol," 3 *Kennedy Institute of Ethics Journal* 217, 223 (1993).

59. *See* Tracy Weber and Charles Ornstein, "Report Tells of Errors in Organ Case," *Los Angeles Times*, March 2, 2007, p. B1.

60. *See* Charles Ornstein, "Doubts About a Transplant Team," *Los Angeles Times*, August 7, 2007, p. B1.

61. Weber and Ornstein, "Report Tells of Errors," p. B1.

62. Ornstein, "Doubts About a Transplant Team," p. B1.

63. Jessie McKinley, "Surgeon Cleared of Harming Man to Rush Organ Removal," *New York Times*, December 19, 2008, p. A30.

64. Robert D. Truog, "Brain Death—Too Flawed to Endure, Too Ingrained to Abandon," 35 *Journal of Law, Medicine and Ethics* 273, 277 (2007).

65. Norman Fost, "Reconsidering the Dead Donor Rule: Is It Important That Organ Donors Be Dead?" 14 *Kennedy Institute of Ethics Journal* 249, 250, 257 (2004).

66. Robert D. Truog, "Organ Donation Without Brain Death?" 35 *Hastings Center Report* 3, 3 (2005).

67. Laura A. Siminoff et al., "Death and Organ Procurement: Public Beliefs and Attitudes," 3 *Kennedy Institute of Ethics Journal* 217, 225 (2004).

68. Ibid., p. 230, Table 3.

69. Fost, "Reconsidering the Dead Donor Rule," p. 257.

70. Siminoff et al., "Death and Organ Procurement," p. 230, Table 3.

71. In 2008, eighty-eight lethal prescriptions were written in Oregon, but only fifty-four patients took them to end their lives. "2008 Summary of Oregon's Death With Dignity Act," egov.oregon.gov/DHS/ph/pas/docs/year11.pdf (accessed 12/12/09).

72. Fost, "Reconsidering the Dead Donor Rule," p. 253.

73. *Vacco*, 521 U.S. at 801.

4. Brain Death

1. Institute of Medicine, *Non-Heart-Beating Organ Transplantation: Medical and Ethical Issues in Procurement* (Washington, D.C.: National Academy Press, 1997), pp. 23–24.

2. *See* Laura A. Siminoff et al., "Death and Organ Procurement: Public Attitudes and Beliefs," 14 *Kennedy Institute of Ethics Journal* 217, 229 Table 2 (56.7 percent of those surveyed incorrectly believed organs were procured after the respirator was disconnected).

3. P. Wertheimer et al., "Diagnosis of Death of the Nervous System in Comas with Respiratory Arrest Treated by Artificial Respiration," 67 *Presse Médicale* 87 (1959).

4. Earl Walker, *Cerebral Death*, 2d ed. (Dallas, Tex.: Urban and Schwarzenberg, 1981), p. 2.

5. David Lamb, *Death, Brain Death and Ethics* (New York: SUNY Press, 1985), p. 4.

6. "Medical Ethics: Criteria for Heart Transplants," 1 *British Medical Journal* 762, 762 (1968).

7. Ad Hoc Committee of the Harvard Medical School to Examine the Definition of Brain Death, "A Definition of Irreversible Coma," 205 *Journal of the American Medical Association* 337, 337 (1968) (emphasis in original).

8. For example, the Ad Hoc Committee's reference to tendon reflexes is now known to be inappropriate, since tendon reflexes are spinal, not cephalic, reflexes that may continue even after brain death. *See* Walker, *Cerebral Death*, p. 32. In addition, although the pupillary reflex is a cephalic reflex indicative of brain death, what matters most is that the pupils be fixed, with dilation or pupillary size unimportant. Ibid., p. 26.

9. Lamb, *Death, Brain Death and Ethics*, p. 42.

10. *See, e.g.,* H. Tristam Engelhart, Jr., *The Foundation of Bioethics*, 2d ed. (New York: Oxford UP, 1996), p. 247 ("When there is no cerebrum, there is no person. . . . In short, if the cerebrum is dead, the person is dead.").

11. Kansas Stat. Ann. §77-202 (repealed).

12. Ibid.

13. Alexander M. Capron and Leon R. Kass, "A Statutory Definition of the Standards for Determining Human Death," 121 *University of Pennsylvania Law Review* 87, 109–110 (1972).

14. Ibid., p. 107 n.70.

15. Ibid., p. 111.

16. President's Commission for the Study of Ethical Problems in Medicine and Biomedical and Behavioral Research, *Defining Death: Medical, Legal and Ethical Issues in the Determination of Death* (Washington, D.C.: Government Printing Office, 1981), pp. 64–66. Differences in the proposals were small. The ABA proposal defined brain death as "irreversible cessation of total brain function." Ibid., p. 64. The UBDA was a bit more specific, referencing the brain stem explicitly: "[A]n individual who has sustained irreversible cessation of all functioning of the brain, including the brain stem, is dead." Ibid., p. 66; *see also* Uniform Brain Death Act, 12 U.L.A. 63.

17. *See* In re T.A.C.P., 609 So.2d 588 (Fla. 1992) (determining that the Florida brain death statute supplemented, rather than supplanted, the common law cardiopulmonary definition of death).

18. The commission was the President's Commission for the Study of Ethical Problems in Medicine and Biomedical and Behavioral Research. It was created by Congress to study "the ethical and legal implications of the matter of defining death, including the advisability of developing a uniform definition of death." 42 U.S.C. §1802 (1978).

19. 12A U.L.A. 589, §1.

20. Lamb, *Death, Brain Death and Ethics*, p. 84.

21. President's Commission, *Defining Death*, pp. 28–29 (emphasis in original).

22. James L. Bernat, "A Defense of the Whole-Brain Concept of Death," 28 *Hastings Center Report* 14, 18 (1998).

23. Ibid.

24. James L. Bernat, "The Whole-Brain Concept of Death Remains Optimum Public Policy," 34 *Journal of Law, Medicine and Ethics* 35, 39 (2006) ("Clinical functions are those that are measurable at the bedside."). It is clear that Bernat refers to tests of brainstem reflexes when he cites the American Academy of Neurology's Practice Parameters for Determining Brain Death in Adults," which center on the testing of brain stem reflexes. Ibid., p. 40 n.37.

25. Bernat, "Whole-Brain Concept of Death Remains Optimum Public Policy," p. 40.

26. Bernat, "A Defense of the Whole-Brain Concept of Death," p. 21.

27. Bernat, "Whole-Brain Concept of Death Remains Optimum Public Policy," p. 39 n.29.

28. President's Commission, *Defining Death*, p. 75 (emphasis in original).

29. *See, e.g.,* U.S. v. Clintwood Elkhorn Mining Co., 128 S.Ct. 1511, 1518 (2008).

30. Dodd v. U.S., 545 U.S. 353, 359 (2005).

31. President's Commission, *Defining Death*, p. 7 ("It is [] desirable, in the Commission's view, to limit change in the law on death to the minimum necessary for the

problem at hand, i.e., ambiguity about the status of cases of coma with respirator-assistance. Extending the 'definition' of death beyond those lacking *all* brain functions to include, for example, persons who have lost only cognitive functions but are still able to breathe spontaneously would radically change the meaning of death.") (emphasis in original); ibid., p. 41 ("[T]he position taken by the Commission is deliberately conservative."); ibid., p. 59 ("Conservatism seems justified in articulating a rule that will not only be applied within the legal system but will also guide the beliefs and behavior of physicians and the public.").

32. President's Commission, *Defining Death,* p. 76. Brain transplants are not as far-fetched as one might think. Partial brain tissue transplants are already being used to relieve some of the symptoms associated with degenerative brain diseases such as Parkinson's, Huntington's, and Alzheimer's. *See* George Northoff, "Do Brain Tissue Transplants Alter Personal Identity? Inadequacies of Some 'Standard' Arguments," 22 *Journal of Medical Ethics* 174 (1996).

33. Paul A. Byrne et al., "Brain Death—An Opposing Viewpoint," 242 *Journal of the American Medical Association* 1985 (1979).

34. Amir Halevy and Baruch Brody, "Brain Death: Reconciling Definitions, Criteria, and Tests," 119 *Annals of Internal Medicine* 519, 520–521 (1993).

35. Ibid., p. 521; *see also* M. M. Grigg et al., "Electroencephalographic Activity After Brain Death," 44 *Archives of Neurology* 948 (1987); I. Deliyannakis et al., "Brainstem Death with Persistence of Bioelectric Activity of the Cerebral Hemispheres," 6 *Clinical Electroencephalography and Neuroscience* 75 (1975).

36. Robert Veatch has declared that "no one really believes that literally all functions of the entire brain must be irreversibly lost for an individual to be dead." Robert M. Veatch, "The Impending Collapse of the Whole-Brain Definition of Death," 23 *Hastings Center Report* 24 (1993). Tracy Schmidt admits that "[a]t times, physicians are willing to declare 'brain death' when a patient has not fully met the criteria for 'brain death' outlined by the American Academy of Neurology (AAN), but the physicians know from their clinical experience that the individual has no chance of survival." Tracy C. Schmidt, "The Ohio Study in Light of National Data and Clinical Experience," 14 *Kennedy Institute for Ethics Journal* 235, 238 (2004). Schmidt goes on to assert, however, that "OPO [organ procurement organization] policies, along with the hospital's policy and procedures, protect this from occurring." Ibid. Schmidt's confidence that such policies prevent brain death from being declared in such situations is not warranted. Compliance with the AAN's practice guidelines is highly variable within the top fifty U.S. neurologic institutions. *See* David M. Greer et al., "Variability of Brain Death Determination Guidelines in Leading US Neurologic Institutions," 70 *Neurology* 284 (2008). If the top fifty neurologic institutions experience regular noncompliance with AAN guidelines, noncompliance in ordinary institutions is likely even more common.

37. This position has resulted in explicit arguments to discard the dead donor rule and permit the harvesting of organs from those who are not brain dead. *See* Norman Fost, "Reconsidering the Dead Donor Rule: Is It Important That Organ Donors Be Dead?" 14 *Kennedy Institute for Ethics Journal* 249 (2004); Robert D. Truog, "Brain Death—Too Flawed to Endure, Too Engrained to Abandon," 35 *Journal of Law, Medicine and Ethics* 273 (2007).

38. Neurologist Alan Shewmon, for example, has asserted that an integrative concept of death "underlies the mainstream theory of 'brain death.'" D. Alan Shewmon, "'Brainstem Death,' 'Brain Death' and Death: A Critical Re-Evaluation of the Purported Equivalence," 14 *Issues in Law and Medicine* 125, 130 (1998).

39. Lamb, *Death, Brain Death and Ethics,* pp. 5–6; President's Commission, *Defining Death,* p. 17.

40. Shewmon, "'Brainstem Death,'" pp. 135–136; Nereo Zamperetti et al., "Irreversible Apnoeic Coma 35 Years Later," 30 *Intensive Care Medicine* 1715, 1717 (2004).

41. Shewmon, "'Brainstem Death,'" p. 139; Halevy and Brody, "Brain Death," pp. 520–521.

42. *See* Daniel Sperling, "Maternal Brain Death," 30 *American Journal of Law and Medicine* 453 (2004); Peter Singer, *Rethinking Life and Death: The Collapse of Our Traditional Ethics* (New York: St. Martin's Press, 1995), pp. 9–16 (discussing the details of two well-publicized cases of maternal maintenance after brain death); William P. Dillon et al., "Life Support and Maternal Brain Death During Pregnancy," 248 *Journal of the American Medical Association* 1089 (September 3, 1982).

43. Ibid., p. 142.

44. Ibid., p. 128.

45. Ibid.

46. Over 40 percent of all organ donations in the United States are made by living donors. Organ Procurement and Transplant Network (OPTN), "Donors Recovered in the U.S. by Donor Type," optn.org/latestData/rptData.asp (accessed 08/15/09). They donate nonvital organs such as kidneys, lungs, and partial livers.

47. Daniel Wikler and Alan J. Weisbard, "Appropriate Confusion Over 'Brain Death,'" 261 *Journal of the American Medical Association* 2246 (1989); Daniel Wikler, "Brain Death," 2 *Journal of Medical Ethics* 101–102 (1984) (describing whole brain death as "terminally confused" and asserting that "the case for whole-brain death has not been successfully made. . . . The tolerance of logical disorder by the medical community in this matter is quite remarkable.").

48. Truog, "Brain Death—Too Flawed to Endure, Too Ingrained to Abandon," p. 278.

49. Timothy Gower, "Fatal Flaw: Some Doctors Suggest That the Modern Definition of Death Is Wrong—And That the Mistake Is Costing Lives," *Boston Globe,* March 9, 2008, p. K1.

50. Laura A. Siminoff et al., "Death and Organ Procurement: Public Attitudes and Beliefs," 14 *Kennedy Institute for Ethics Journal* 217, 228 (2004).

51. Chiara Scaglioni Tessmer et al., "Do People Accept Brain Death as Death? A Study in Brazil," 17 *Progress in Transplantation* 63, 65 (2007).

52. Charles Amenta, "Defining Death and the Ethics of Organ Donation," *Chicago Tribune,* December 7, 2003, p. C10; C. Pallis, "Return to Elsinore," 16 *Journal of Medical Ethics* 10, 12 (1990) ("The record here is reassuring. Patients fulfilling clinical criteria of brainstem death (and in whom ventilation was continued) have all developed asystole. And none have ever regained consciousness before that. Can we ask for more? I doubt it.").

53. Truog, "Brain Death—Too Flawed to Endure, Too Ingrained to Abandon," p. 275.

54. Charles Ornstein and Tracy Weber, "Close Call in Death Ruling of Potential Organ Donor," *Los Angeles Times,* April 12, 2007, p. A1.

55. *See* Mike Celizic, "Pronounced Dead, Man Recovers," TodayShow.Com, March 24, 2008, today.msnbc.com (accessed 12/28/09); "He Heard MDs Say He's Dead, But He Feels 'Pretty Good Now,'" *Toronto Star,* March 25, 2008, p. A2; Colleen Carroll Campbell, "'Miracle' Stories Can Double as Cautionary Tale," *St. Louis Post-Dispatch,* April 3, 2008, p. C9.

56. An increasing number of states have enacted laws permitting nurses, physician assistants, and even paramedics to pronounce cardiopulmonary death in certain situations. Alaska Stat. Ann. §08.68.395; Ga. Code Ann. §31-7-176.1; Ky. Rev. Stat. §§311A.185, 314.181; Hawaii Rev. Stat. §327C-1; Mich. Comp. Laws Ann. §333.1033(3); Nev. Rev. Stat. Ann. §440.415; Pa. Stat. §450.507; Tex. Health & Safety Code §671.001(d); Va. Code Ann. §54.1.2972(B).

57. The requirement that a licensed physician declare brain death is not universal, as a few states allow nurses to declare brain death in limited situations. *See, e.g.,* Ga. Code Ann. §§31-10-16(a), 31-7-176.1; Nev. Rev. Stat. Ann. §440.415; Va. Code Ann. §54.1.2972(b).

58. *See, e.g.,* Fla. Stat. Ann. §382.009(2) (requiring brain death declaration by the treating physician and a board-certified or board-eligible "neurologist, neurosurgeon, internist, pediatrician, surgeon or anesthesiologist."); N.J. Stat. Ann. §26:6A-4(a) (requiring determination by a "licensed physician professionally qualified by specialty or expertise"); Va. Code Ann. §54.1.2972 (requiring physician licensed in "neurology, neurosurgery or encephalography").

59. Greer et al., "Variability of Brain Death Determination Guidelines," p. 285, Figure 1.

60. Ibid., p. 287.

61. A minority of states specifically require independent confirmation of brain death by another physician in certain situations. Cal. Health & Safety Code §7182; Ala.

Code §22-31-3(a); Fla. Stat. Ann. §382.009(2); Hawaii Rev. Stat. §327C-1(b); Iowa Code Ann. §702.8; Ky. Rev. Stat. §446.400(2); La. Rev. Stat. §9:111(A).

62. Greer et al., "Variability of Brain Death Determination Guidelines," p. 285.

63. Eelco F. M. Wijdicks, "Brain Death Worldwide: Accepted Fact but No Global Consensus in Diagnostic Criteria," 58 *Neurology* 20, 21–23 (2008).

64. 12A U.L.A. 589, §1.

65. N.J. Stat. Ann. §26:6A-4(a). The regulations require a diagnosis of brain death be confirmed (when possible) with an "objective confirmatory test measuring intracranial circulation." N.J. Admin. Code tit. 13, §35-6A.4(b).

66. *See* Eelco F. M. Wijdicks, "The Clinical Criteria of Brain Death Throughout the World: Why Has It Come to This?," 53 *Canadian Journal of Anesthesiology* 540, 540 (2006).

67. American Academy of Neurology, Quality Standards Subcommittee, "Practice Parameters: Determining Brain Death in Adults (1994," *reprinted in* 45 *Neurology* 1012 (1995).

68. Greer et al., "Variability of Brain Death Determination Guidelines," p. 284. Similar problems have been documented in the United Kingdom and Singapore. M. D. D. Bell et al., "Brainstem Death Testing in the UK—Time for Reappraisal?" 92 *British Journal of Anaesthesia* 633 (2004); Ki Jinn Chin et al., "A Survey of Brain Death Certification—An Impetus for Standardisation and Improvement," 36 *Annals Academy of Medicine* (Singapore) 987 (2007).

69. Ad Hoc Committee, "A Definition of Irreversible Coma," p. 337 ("Of great confirmatory value is the flat or isoelectric EEG.").

70. *See* Eelco F. M. Wijdicks, "The Diagnosis of Brain Death" 344 *New England Journal of Medicine* 1215, 1220 (2001) ("Electroencephalography is used in many countries and remains one of the most well-validated confirmatory tests."); Christoph J. G. Lang, "Diagnosis of Brain Death with the Electroencephalogram," 55 *Canadian Journal of Anesthesia* 188, 189 (2008) ("[M]ost countries world-wide consider the EEG as a reliable and valid adjunct in the clinical diagnosis of brain death.").

71. "JAMA Patient Page: Brain Death," 299 *Journal of the American Medical Association* 2232 (2008).

72. Pallis and MacGillivary have asserted that the popularity in the United States of EEG tests to diagnose brain death is a "cultural addiction" without any real scientific basis. C. Pallis and B. MacGillivary, "Brain Death and the EEG," 2 *Lancet* 1085, 1086 (1980).

73. Thomas Rimmelé et al., "Reply," 55 *Canadian Journal of Anesthesia* 189 (2008) ("EEG is no longer recommended as an ancillary test [for brain death], notably because of the numerous false positives and false negatives observed with this assessment."); Lamb, *Death, Brain Death and Ethics*, p. 66 ("The identification of life with electricity is crudely reductionist and is full of false negative and false positive indicators.").

74. Walker, *Cerebral Death*, pp. 66, 72–73.

75. Ibid., pp. 78, 80; Lamb, *Death, Brain Death and Ethics,* p. 67.

76. Fred Plum, "Clinical Standards and Technological Confirmatory Tests in Confirming Brain Death," in Michael Potts et al., eds., *Beyond Brain Death: The Case Against Brain Based Criteria for Human Death* 34, 42–44 (2000); Richard G. Nilges, "Organ Transplantation, Brain Death and the Slippery Slope: A Neurosurgeon's Perspective," in Potts et al., eds., *Beyond Brain Death: The Case Against Brain Based Criteria for Human Death,* pp. 249, 254 (medical research shows 20 percent of otherwise "brain dead" individuals have some recordable electroencephalographic activity; the response of the protransplant medical community has been to classify this activity as "artifactual"); G. R. Park, "Editorial I: Death and Its Diagnosis by Doctors," 92 *British Journal of Anesthesia* 625, 627 (2004) ("Electrical activity may continue after cerebral blood flow has stopped.").

77. N. K. Sethi et al., "EMG Artifact in Brain Death Electroencephalogram, Is It a Cry of 'Medullary Death'?" 110 *Clinical Neurology and Neurosurgery* 729 (2008); Halevy and Brody, "Brain Death: Reconciling Definitions, Criteria, and Tests," p. 521 (documenting case reports and concluding that "[a]lthough this [electrical] functioning does not lead to any clinically apparent interaction with the environment, it clearly satisfies the definition of functioning offered by the President's Commission because it represents organized and directed cellular activity").

78. Sethi et al., "EMG Artifact," p. 729.

79. Walker, *Cerebral Death,* p. 81 ("Comatose patients with intact brainstem functions may have isoelectric EEGs. This condition has been termed cortical or neocortical death."); Lamb, *Death, Brain Death and Ethics,* p. 67 ("The EEG is generated by the cortex of the cerebral hemispheres. . . . An EEG . . . is of no help in the diagnosis of brainstem death.").

80. F. J. Veith et al., "Brain Death I: A Status Report of Legal Considerations," 238 *Journal of the American Medical Association* 1744 (1977); Walker, *Cerebral Death,* p. 37 (interruption of blood flow to brain for five minutes "irreparably damages" it).

81. Xavier Ducrocq, "Consensus Opinion on Diagnosis of Cerebral Circulatory Arrest Using Doppler-Sonography: Task Force Group on Cerebral Death of the Neurosonology Research Group of the World Federation of Neurology," 159 *Journal of Neurological Sciences* 145 (1998); Mel W. Flowers and Bharti R. Patel, "Accuracy of Clinical Evaluation in the Determination of Brain Death," 93 *Southern Medical Journal* 203 (2000).

82. Flowers and Patel, "Accuracy of Clinical Evaluation," p. 203.

83. Ducrocq, "Consensus Opinion," p. 149; Louisa M. Monteiro et al., "Transcranial Doppler Ultrasonography to Confirm Brain Death: A Meta-Analysis," 32 *Intensive Care Medicine* 1937, 1942 (2006) (endorsing use of Doppler as a confirmatory test prior to the more invasive use of angiography, but admitting that "it is only reliable in experienced hands").

84. Flowers and Patel, "Accuracy of Clinical Evaluation," p. 203.

85. Ibid.

86. Ibid.; J-C Combes et al., "Reliability of Computed Tomographic Angiography in the Diagnosis of Brain Death," 39 *Transplantation Proceedings* 16, 19–20 (2007) ("[T]his exam shows, in some cases, a persistent vascularization among patients with BD [brain death] confirmed by conventional angiography. This implies the necessity to repeat the exam to confirm the diagnosis. . . ."); T. A. Ala et al., "A Case Meeting Clinical Brain Death Criteria with Residual Cerebral Perfusion," 27 *American Journal of Neurology* 1805 (2006).

87. American Academy of Neurology, "Practice Parameters," p. 1012.

88. Wijdicks, "Diagnosis of Brain Death," p. 1218. Wijdicks notes that the most common complications, hypotension and cardiac arrhythmia, are often "due to a failure to provide an adequate source of oxygen or to a lack of preoxygenation." Ibid., p. 1216. This failure, in turn, may be due to the fact that the AAN's guidelines state that preoxygenation of the patient is merely optional.

89. Greer et al., "Variability of Brain Death Determination Guidelines," p. 288 (internal citations omitted).

90. Bell et al., "Brainstem Death Testing in the UK," p. 637 ("There are no precise recommendations as to whether the apnoea test should be conducted independently of the other tests as in other jurisdictions, so it is not surprising that individual practice varies. The observation that clinicians are prepared to accept less than recommended thresholds for PaCO2 is worrying particularly in view of observations that in certain patient groups much higher levels may be needed to stimulate respiratory effort and that the UK figure is already lower than in other countries.") (internal citations omitted); Chin et al., "A Survey of Brain Death Certification," p. 991 ("Of the 7 brainstem tests, the caloric [ice water in ear] and apnoea tests seem the most prone to error and variation in practice. . . . Physicans must be aware, not only of the minimum PaCO2 that must be achieved, but also the steps that must be taken to prepare the patient, with the monitoring required and what to do in the event of haemodynamic instability during the conduct of the test. We believe that this is best addressed by providing a detailed written protocol, as well as conducting physician training on the proper conduct of this test.").

91. Wijdicks, "Brain Death Worldwide," p. 21; Wijdicks, "Clinical Criteria of Brain Death Throughout the World," p. 540 (surveying brain death criteria of eighty countries and finding "marked differences in how the apnea test was performed," including the use of a pCO2 target value in only 59 percent of all guidelines).

92. Wijdicks, "Brain Death Worldwide," pp. 22–23, Table.

93. Walker, *Cerebral Death*, pp. 25, Table III-5, 26.

94. Ibid., p. 28.

95. Ibid., pp. 28–29.

96. Ibid., p. 29.

97. Bell et al., "Brainstem Death Testing in the UK." p. 635; Chin et al., "A Survey of Brain Death Certification," p. 991.

98. Walker, *Cerebral Death,* pp. 26–30.

99. M. Y. Wang et al., Brain Death Documentation: Analysis and Issues, 51 *Neurosurgery* 731 (2002).

100. Wijdicks, "Diagnosis of Brain Death," p. 1216.

101. Walker, *Cerebral Death,* p. 31, Table III-9 (In one study, 25 percent of comatose and apneic patients experienced restoration of one or more cephalic reflexes at some point.)

102. Shewmon, "Brainstem Death," p. 143.

103. *See* David Lamb, "Reply to Professor Wikler," 2 *Journal of Medical Ethics* 102 (1984) ("Brain stem death must be seen as the equivalent of decapitation."); Lamb, *Death, Brain Death and Ethics,* p. 39 ("[T]he essential characteristics of life reside in the brain. . . . If brain death is synonymous with physiological decapitation, then brain death is the functional equivalent of systemic death of an individual.").

104. Pallis, "Return to Elsinore," p. 11 ("[A]ll death is, and has always been, brainstem death, and . . . circulatory arrest . . . just happens to be the commonest way in which to bring such death about.") (emphasis in original).

105. Wikler, "Brain Death," p. 101 ("We now have, in effect, a substitute for the brain stem. . . . Temperature regulation, blood pressure, respiration, digestion, even embryological development continue in the brain-stem-dead body if suitably maintained.").

106. Shewmon, "Brainstem Death," p. 136.

107. "Diagnosis of Brain Death: Statement Issued by the Honorary Secretary of the Conference of Medical Royal Colleges and Their Faculties in the United Kingdom on 11 Oct. 1976," 2 *British Medical Journal* 1187 (1976); "Diagnosis of Death: Memorandum Issued by the Honorary Secretary of the Conference of Medical Royal Colleges and Their Faculties in the United Kingdom on 15 Jan. 1979," 1 *British Medical Journal* 332 (1979).

108. Judy Siegel, "Breakthrough Organ Donation Law to Go Into Effect on May 1," *Jerusalem Post,* March 25, 2008, p. 9.

109. "Death and Its Diagnosis by Doctors," 92 *British Journal of Anaesthesia* 625, 625 (2004) ("This Code [Royal Colleges' Code of Practice] is based on clinical criteria, rather than tests such as electroencephalographic activity of the brain, or measurement of cerebral blood flow.").

110. Bell et al., "Brainstem Death Testing in the UK," p. 633.

111. Roland Puccetti, "The Conquest of Death," 59 *Monist* 249, 252 (1976).

112. *See, e.g.,* Jeff McMahan, "An Alternative to Brain Death," 34 *Journal of Law Medicine and Ethics* 44, 47–48 (2006); Ronald E. Cranford and David Randolph Smith,

"Consciousness: The Most Critical Moral (Constitutional) Standard for Human Personhood," 13 *American Journal of Law and Medicine* 233, 233–234 (1987); Michael B. Green and Daniel Wikler, Brain Death and Personal Identity, 9 *Philosophy and Public Affairs* 105, 127–128 (1980).

113. Veatch, "Impending Collapse," p. 20.

114. Ibid., p. 23.

115. Ibid., p. 21.

116. Ibid. Interestingly, others have argued that brain death is antithetical to the dualist mind-body conceptions of Judaism, Christianity, and other major religions. *See* Byrne et al., "Brain Death: An Opposing Viewpoint.

117. Daniel I. Wikler, "Conceptual Issues in the Definition of Death: A Guide for Public Policy," 5 *Theoretical Medicine* 167, 173–174 (1984); McMahan, "An Alternative to Brain Death," p. 47.

118. Veatch, "Impending Collapse," p. 23.

119. Ibid., p. 21.

120. Ibid.

121. Ibid.

122. Ibid.

123. Joyce A. Martin et al., "Births: Final Data for 2005," Centers for Disease Control, 56 *National Vital Statistics Report* 23 (2007).

124. *See* "Frank Admissions End Infant Organ Harvesting," *Los Angeles Times,* August 19, 1988, p. 3; Louis Sahagun, "Harvesting of Baby Organs Not Feasible; Loma Linda Tells Why It Dropped Anencephalic Infants Program," *Los Angeles Times,* August 24, 1988, p. 25; David Ferrell, "Brain Defective Baby; Source of New Heart Ignites Debate," *Los Angeles Times,* November 11, 1987, p. 3.

125. Council on Ethical and Judicial Affairs, American Medical Association, "The Use of Anencephalic Neonates as Organ Donors," 273 *Journal of the American Medical Association* 1614 (1995).

126. Unpublished Meeting Proceedings, American Medical Association Interim Meeting, "The Use of Anencephalic Neonates as Organ Donors—Reconsidered," December 1995.

127. President's Commission, *Defining Death,* p. 40; Lamb, *Death, Brain Death and Ethics,* p. 43 ("Neurologists are not certain whether cessation of higher brain functions entails a total loss of consciousness and awareness. It is extremely difficult to prove that there is a total absence of sentience when the brainstem is still functioning and some systems may still be functioning in deeper parts of the brain.").

128. N.J. Stat. Ann. §26:6A-5.

129. Judy Siegel, "Breakthrough Organ Donation Law," p. 9.

130. Veatch, "Impending Collapse," p. 22.

5. Constitutional Death

1. U.S. Constitution, amendments V and XIV.

2. Gregg v. Georgia, 428 U.S. 153 (1976). *But see* Roper v. Simmons, 543 U.S. 551 (2005) (death penalty for under age eighteen violates Eighth Amendment); Atkins v. Virginia, 536 U.S. 304 (2002) (death penalty for mentally retarded violates Eighth Amendment).

3. *See* Anton J. L. Van Hoof, "Ancient Euthanasia: 'Good Death' and the Doctor in the Graeco-Roman World," 58 *Social Science and Medicine* 975, 980–983 (2004).

4. Tacitus, *The Annals,* Book XV, para. 63–63, in *Complete Works of Tacitus,* ed. Moses Hadas (New York: Modern Library, 1942).

5. William Blackstone, 4 *Commentaries on the Laws of England* 189 (Oxford: Clarendon Press, 1769).

6. Ibid., pp. 189–190.

7. Washington v. Glucksberg, 521 U.S. 702, 712–713 (1997).

8. Hales v. Petit, 75 E.R. 387, 401 (C.B. 1561).

9. Ibid., p. 403.

10. E. P. Evans, *The Criminal Prosecution and Capital Punishment of Animals* (London: William Heinemann, 1907), p. 15.

11. Ibid., p. 167.

12. Exodus 21:23–25.

13. Leviticus 24:18–20.

14. Evans, *Criminal Prosecution and Capital Punishment of Animals,* pp. 186–187.

15. Ibid., p. 190.

16. Norman St. John-Stevas, *Life, Death and the Law: Law and Christian Morals in England and the United States* (Bloomington: Indiana University Press, 1961), p. 233.

17. *Glucksberg,* 521 U.S. at 713.

18. *See, e.g.,* Wackwitz v. Roy, 418 S.E.2d 861 (Va. 1992); State v. Willis, 121 S.E.2d 854 (N.C. 1961).

19. *See* Donaldson v. Lungren, 4 Cal. Rptr. 2d 59, 64 (Cal. Ct. App. 1992); Commonwealth v. Wright, 11 Pa. D. 144, 146 (Pa. Quar. Sess. 1902).

20. State v. Willis, 121 S.E.2d 854, 856 (N.C. 1961).

21. *See generally* John H. Derrick, "Criminal Liability for Death of Another as a Result of Accused's Attempt to Kill Self or Assist Another's Suicide," 40 *American Law Reports, 4th ed.* 402 (1985).

22. Ore. Rev. Stat. §§127.800–127.995; Wash. Rev. Code §§70.245.010–10.245.904.

23. *See generally* John Griffiths et al., *Euthanasia and Law in the Netherlands* (Amsterdam: Amsterdam University Press, 1998); R. Cohen-Almagor, "Belgian Euthanasia Law: A Critical Analysis," 35 *Journal of Medical Ethics* 436 (2009).

24. *See, e.g., Wackwitz*, 418 S.E.2d at 864 (denying recovery); Clift v. Narragansett Television L.P., 688 A.2d 805 (R.I. 1996) (permitting recovery despite continued recognition of suicide as a common law crime); Shamburger v. Grand Casino of Miss., Inc., 84 F. Supp. 2d 794, 798 (S.D. Miss. 1998) (same).

25. *See* Restatement (Second) of Torts §455.

26. Stafford v. Neurological Med., Inc., 811 F.2d 470 (8th Cir. 1987).

27. *See* Scholendorff v. Soc'y of N.Y. Hosp., 105 N.E. 92 (N.Y. 1914); Slater v. Baker and Stapleton, 95 E.R. 860 (K.B. 1767).

28. Washburn v. Klara, 561 S.E.2d 682, 685 (Va. 2002); Howard v. Univ. of Med. and Dentistry of N.J., 800 A.2d 73, 80 (N.J. 2002).

29. Montgomery v. Bazaz-Sehgal, 798 A.2d 742 (Pa. 2002).

30. Union Pac. Ry. Co. v. Botsford, 141 U.S. 250, 251–252 (1891).

31. Sibbach v. Wilson, 312 U.S. 1, 11–16 (1941).

32. Ibid., p. 17 (Frankfurter, J., dissenting).

33. Ibid., p. 18 ("And so I conclude that to make the drastic change that Rule 35 sought to introduce would require explicit legislation.").

34. Cruzan v. Director, Mo. Dep't of Health, 497 U.S. 261 (1990).

35. Ibid., p. 266.

36. Ibid., pp. 268–269.

37. Ibid., p. 269.

38. Ibid., p. 285.

39. Ibid., p. 278 (emphasis added).

40. Ibid., p. 279 (emphasis added).

41. Ibid., pp. 279–280.

42. Ibid., p. 281 ("It cannot be disputed that the Due Process Clause protects an interest in life as well as an interest in refusing life-sustaining medical treatment.").

43. Ibid., p. 287 (O'Connor, J., concurring).

44. Schmerber v. California, 384 U.S. 757 (1966).

45. Ibid., p. 767.

46. Ibid., p. 770.

47. Ibid., pp. 771–772.

48. Winston v. Lee, 470 U.S. 753, 760–766 (1985).

49. Jacobsen v. Massachusetts, 197 U.S. 11 (1905).

50. Ibid., p. 26.

51. Ibid.

52. Ibid., p. 27.

53. Breithaupt v. Abram, 352 U.S. 432, 435 (1957).

54. *Schmerber,* 384 U.S. at 760.

55. Rochin v. California, 342 U.S. 165, 166 (1952).

56. Ibid., p. 172.

57. Ibid., p. 173.

58. Youngberg v. Romeo, 457 U.S. 307, 320 (1982) (internal quotation marks and citations omitted).

59. Washington v. Harper, 494 U.S. 210, 221–222 (1990).

60. Ibid., p. 220.

61. *Rochin*, 342 U.S. at 174.

62. *Cruzan*, 497 U.S. AT 308 (Brennan, J., dissenting); ibid., p. 331 (Stevens, J., dissenting).

63. Ibid., p. 289 (O'Connor, J., concurring).

64. Ibid., p. 290 (O'Connor, J., concurring).

65. *See, e.g.,* Uniform Health Care Decisions Act, §5 (1993).

66. Ibid.

67. In re Guardianship of Schiavo, File No. 90-2908GD-003, Circuit Court for Pinellas County, Probate Division, Feb. 11, 2000, p. 5 (on file with author).

68. Ibid., pp. 5–6, 9.

69. In re Guardianship of Schiavo, 780 So.2d 176, 180 (Fla. Ct. App. 2001).

70. *See, e.g.,* Uniform Health Care Decisions Act, §5(f). The Florida Court of Appeals in the Schiavo case expressly disclaimed any use of the best interests test in her case. *In re Guardianship of Schiavo,* 780 So.2d at 178 n.2.

71. In re Conroy, 486 A.2d 1209, 1231–1232 (N.J. 1985).

72. In re Peter, 529 A.2d 419, 425 (N.J. 1987).

73. *See, e.g.,* Wackwitz v. Roy, 418 S.E.2d 861 (Va. 1992); State v. Willis, 121 S.E.2d 854 (N.C. 1961).

74. *Cruzan*, 497 U.S. at 312–313 (Brennan, J., dissenting) (No third party's situation will be improved and no harm to others will be averted [if Nancy Cruzan remains on life support].").

75. Elizabeth Price Foley, *Liberty for All: Reclaiming Individual Privacy in a New Era of Public Morality* (New Haven, Conn.: Yale UP, 2006), pp. 50–52.

76. *Cruzan*, 497 U.S. at 313 (Brennan, J., dissenting).

77. Ibid., p. 314 (Brennan, J., dissenting).

78. Ibid., p. 343 (Stevens, J., dissenting).

79. Ibid., pp. 344–346 (Stevens, J., dissenting).

80. Ibid., p. 347 (Stevens, J., dissenting) (emphasis in original).

81. Ibid., p. 350 (Stevens, J., dissenting).

82. Ibid., pp. 299–300 (Scalia, J., concurring) (emphasis in original).

83. Ibid., p. 300 (Scalia, J., concurring).

84. Yale Kamisar, "Can *Glucksberg* Survive *Lawrence?* Another Look at the End of Life and Personal Autonomy," 24 *Issues in Law and Medicine* 95, 97 (2008).

85. *Glucksberg,* 521 U.S. at 723.

86. Ibid., p. 711.

87. Ibid., p. 728.

88. Ibid., pp. 728–733.

89. Vacco v. Quill, 521 U.S. 793, 801 (1997).

90. Ibid. (internal quotation marks omitted).

91. Ibid., p. 802.

92. Ibid.

93. Ibid., p. 789 (Ginsburg, J., concurring); ibid. (Breyer, J., concurring).

94. *Glucksberg*, 521 U.S. at 736 (O'Connor, J., concurring).

95. Ibid.

96. Ibid., pp. 736–737.

97. *See, e.g.*, Fla. Stat. Ann. §458.326.

98. *Glucksberg*, 521 U.S. at 745 (Stevens, J., concurring).

99. Kathryn L. Tucker, "The Death with Dignity Movement: Protecting Rights and Expanding Options After *Glucksberg* and *Quill*," 82 *Minnesota Law Review* 923, 928–929 (1998).

100. Oregon Public Health Division, "2008 Summary of Oregon's Death With Dignity Act," Table 1, http://oregon.gov/DHS/ph/pas/index.shtml (accessed 11/02/09).

101. Linda Ganzini et al., "Why Oregon Patients Request Assisted Death: Family Members' Views," 23 *Journal of General Internal Medicine* 154, 155 (2007).

102. Linda Ganzini et al., "Oregonians' Reasons for Requesting Physician Aid in Dying," 169 *Archives of Internal Medicine* 489, 490 (2009).

103. Ibid., p. 491, Table 2.; Ganzini et al., "Why Oregon Patients Request Assisted Death," p. 156, Table 2.

104. Gonzales v. Raich, 545 U.S. 1 (2005).

105. Raich v. Ashcroft, 352 F.3d 1222, 1225 (9th Cir. 2003).

106. International Task Force on Euthanasia and Assisted Suicide, "Zurich Declaration: 'Severe and Enduring Distress' Declared Reason for Assisted Suicide and Euthanasia," www.internationaltaskforce.org/zurich.htm (accessed 1/04/10).

107. *See The American Heritage Dictionary*, 396 (2d College ed. 1985).

108. Leon R. Kass, *Life, Liberty and the Defense of Dignity: The Challenge for Bioethics* (San Francisco: Encounter Books, 2002), pp. 246–247.

109. Lawrence v. Texas, 539 U.S. 558 (2003).

110. Ibid., p. 558.

111. Ibid., p. 578.

112. Ibid., p. 572 (citing County of Sacramento v. Lewis, 523 U.S. 833 (1998) (Kennedy, J., concurring)).

113. Ibid., p. 579.

114. Kamisar, "Can *Glucksberg* Survive *Lawrence?*," pp. 108–119.

115. Sampson v. State, 31 P.3d 88 (Alaska 2001); Krischer v. McIver, 697 So.2d 97 (Fla. 1997).

116. *Lawrence*, 539 U.S. at 599 (Scalia, J., dissenting).

117. Oregon Death With Dignity Act, Ore. Rev. Stat. §§127.800–127.995; Washington Death With Dignity Act, Wash. Rev. Code §§70.245.010–20.245.904.

118. Oregon Public Health Division, "2008 Summary of Oregon's Death With Dignity Act," p. 1.

119. Ibid., Table 1.

120. Ore. Rev. Stat. §127.800(12).

121. Herbert Hendlin and Kathleen Foley, "Physician-Assisted Suicide in Oregon: A Medical Perspective," 106 *Michigan Law Review* 1613, 1616–1617 (2008).

122. Ore. Rev. Stat. §127.825.

123. Ibid., §127.885.

124. Oregon Public Health Division, "2008 Summary of Oregon's Death With Dignity Act," Table 1.

125. Linda Ganzini et al., "Prevalence of Depression and Anxiety in Patients Requesting Physicians' Aid in Dying: Cross Sectional Survey," 337 *British Medical Journal* 1682, 1684 (2008).

126. Ibid., p. 1686.

127. Erin Hoover Barnett, "A Family Struggle: Is Mom Capable of Choosing to Die?" *The Oregonian*, October 17, 1999, p. G1.

128. Ibid.

129. Ibid.

130. Ibid.

131. Ibid.

132. Ibid.

133. Hendlin and Foley, "Physician-Assisted Suicide in Oregon," p. 1625.

134. Oregon Public Health Division, "2008 Summary of Oregon's Death with Dignity Act," Table 1.

135. Baxter v. State, 224 P.3d 1211 (Mont. 2009).

136. Baxter v. State, Decision and Order, p. 13 (Mont. Dist. Ct., Dec. 5, 2009).

137. Ibid., p. 16.

138. Ibid., pp. 16–17.

139. Ibid., p. 17 (internal quotation marks omitted).

140. Ibid., p. 17.

141. Ibid., p. 18.

142. Ibid.

143. Ibid. (emphasis added).

144. Ibid., p. 19.

145. *Glucksberg*, 521 U.S. at 778–779 (Souter, J., concurring).

146. Centers for Disease Control and Prevention, National Center for Injury Preven-

tion and Control, "Suicide: Facts at a Glance" (Summer 2009), p. 1, www.cdc.gov/violenceprevention (accessed 12/31/09).

147. Ibid.

148. *See* "Kevorkian Provided the Gas for Woman's Suicide," *New York Times,* May 17, 1992.

149. Mont. Code Ann. §45-5-102(1).

150. Ibid., §45-2-211(1).

151. Ibid., §45-2-211(2).

152. Baxter v. State, 224 P.3d at 1216.

153. Ibid., p. 1120.

154. Ibid., p,. 1223 (Cotter, J., concurring).

155. Ibid.

156. Verified Complaint, Blick v. Office of the Division of Criminal Justice (Ct. Super. Ct. Sept. 30, 2009), p. 40.

157. Compassion and Choices, "Connecticut Doctors, Compassion and Choices, File Lawsuit to Clarify Ability of Physicians to Provide Aid in Dying to Mentally Competent Terminally Ill Patients," press release, October 7, 2009, p. 1.

6. Not Dead Yet

1. The Multi-Society Task Force on PVS, "Medical Aspects of the Persistent Vegetative State—First of Two Parts," 330 *New England Journal of Medicine* 1499 (1994) (hereinafter *MSTF Part 1*).

2. Ibid., p. 1501.

3. "Vegetative State," *Merck Manual of Diagnosis and Therapy,* 18th ed., ed. Mark H. Beers et al. (Whitehouse Station, N.J.: Merck Research Laboratories, 2006), merck.com/mmpe/sec16/ch212/ch212b.html (accessed 12/02/09) ("Maintaining patients, especially those without advance directives to guide decisions about terminating treatment in a prolonged vegetative state raises ethical and other (e.g., resource utilization) questions."); *MSTF Part 1*, p. 1501 (noting that when a VS becomes permanent, "a physician can tell the patient's family or surrogate with a high degree of medical certainty that there is no further hope of recovery of consciousness or that, if consciousness were recovered, the patient would be left severely disabled.").

4. *MSTF Part 1*, p. 1500.

5. Ibid., p. 1501.

6. Ibid., p. 1502.

7. Nancy L. Childs, et al., "Accuracy of Diagnosis of Persistent Vegetative State," 43 *Neurology* 1465, 1465–1466 (1993).

8. Ibid., p. 1466.

9. Ibid.

10. Keith Andrews et al., "Misdiagnosis of the Vegetative State: Retrospective Study in a Rehabilitation Unit," 313 *British Medical Journal* 13 (1996).

11. Ibid., p. 14.

12. Ibid., p. 15.

13. Ibid.

14. Caroline Schnakers et al., "Diagnostic Accuracy of the Vegetative and Minimally Conscious State: Clinical Consensus Versus Standardized Neurobehavioral Assessment," 9 *BMC Neurology* 35 (2009).

15. Ibid.

16. Ibid.

17. Benedict Carey, "Long Sleep Over, He Helps Reveal Brain's Mysteries," *New York Times,* July 4, 2006, p. A1.

18. "Terry Wallis: The History," www.theterrywallisfund.org/history.html (accessed 12/06/09).

19. Emily Singer, "Why Did Terry Wallis Wake Up After 19 Years in Bed?" *MIT Technology Review,* July 5, 2006.

20. Henning U. Voss et al., "Possible Axonal Regrowth in Late Recovery from the Minimally Conscious State," 116 *Journal of Clinical Investigation* 2005, 2009 (2006).

21. Ibid.

22. *See, e.g.,* British Medical Association, Ethics Department, "Treatment of Patients in Persistent Vegetative State," October 2007, p. 2 ("In the BMA's view, reports of alleged 'recovery' from PVS are likely to indicate an original misdiagnosis.").

23. *See, e.g.,* James L. Bernat, "Ethical Issues in the Treatment of Severe Brain Injury: The Impact of New Technologies," 1157 *Disorders of Consciousness: Annals of the New York Academy of Sciences* 117, 121–122 (2009) (describing Wallis as in a "stable MCS").

24. Eelco F. M. Wijdicks, "Minimally Conscious State vs. Persistent Vegetative State: The Case of Terry (Wallis) vs. the Case of Terri (Schiavo)," 81 *Mayo Clinic Proceedings* 1155, 1156 (2006).

25. Ibid., p. 1157.

26. "Miracle Awakens Mother After 16 Years of Oblivion," *Seattle Post-Intelligencer,* January 5, 2000, p. A4.

27. George Ramos, "Awakening from 16 Years in Near-Coma," *Los Angeles Times,* February 3, 2000.

28. Gina Shaw, "The Puzzle of Donald Herbert: The Latest Brain Injury Case to Make News," 5 *Neurology Today* 20 (2005).

29. Ibid.; Miranda Hitti, "Firefighter's Miracle Recovery Rare in Long-Term Coma Cases," *FoxNews.com,* May 6, 2005, at www.foxnews.com (accessed 12/02/09).

30. Malcolm Ritter, "How Drugs and Doctor's Hope Ended 10-Year Sleep," *Pittsburgh Post-Gazette*, May 16, 2005, p. A1.

31. David Staba, "Illness Claims Firefighter Whose Awakening Made Headlines," *New York Times*, February 22, 2006, p. B1.

32. "Ex-Officer is Alert After Surgery but Not Talking Again," *New York Times*, February 17, 1996, p. A6.

33. Ronald Smothers, "Injured in '88, Officer Awakes in '96," *New York Times*, February 16, 1996, p. A16.

34. Ibid.; "Ex-Officer is Alert After Surgery but Not Talking Again." p. A6.

35. Michelle Williams, "Father's Dramatic Wakeup Thrilled His Boys," *Memphis Commercial Appeal*, February 18, 1996, p. B1.

36. "Policeman Who Briefly Awoke From Coma Dies," *Los Angeles Times*, April 16, 1997, p. A12.

37. Carol DeMare, "'Hopeless' Hospital Patient, 86, Comes Out of Coma," *Albany Times Union*, April 12, 1989, p. A1.

38. Bonnie Steinbock, "Recovery from Persistent Vegetative State?: The Case of Carrie Coons," 19 *Hastings Center Report* 14 (1989).

39. Ibid.

40. Ibid., pp. 4–15.

41. Carole DeMare, "Woman Dies; Spurred Debate on Right-to-Die," *Albany Times Union*, November 26, 1991, p. B1.

42. Dean Barnett, "The 11-Year-Old Massachusetts Girl Who Is Defying the Odds, and the Courts," *Weekly Standard*, January 27, 2006; Patricia Wen, "Stepfather Convicted in Poutre Abuse Case," *Boston Globe*, November 27, 2008, p. A1.

43. Ibid.

44. Ibid.

45. Pam Belluck, "Boston Court Approves Ending Life Support for Girl in Coma," *New York Times*, January 18, 2006, p. A16.

46. "National Briefing New England: Massachusetts: Comatose Girl Shows Responses," *New York Times*, January 19, 2006, p. A20.

47. Patricia Wen, "Girl Gives Dramatic Details in Abuse Case, Says Parents Used Corporal Punishment, *Boston Globe*, April 29, 2008, p. A1; Wen, "Stepfather Convicted in Poutre Abuse Case."

48. Colleen Carroll Campbell, "'Miracle' Stories Can Double as Cautionary Tales," *St. Louis Post-Dispatch*, April 3, 2008, p. C9.

49. "Accident Victim Awakens: Family, Wife Disagreed on Life Support for Him," *Arizona Republic*, June 27, 2007, p. A1.

50. Ibid.

51. Gary Grado, "Crash Survivor's Case Spurs New State Law for Incapacitated People," *(Mesa) Tribune*, July 19, 2009.

52. 2009 Ariz. Legis. Serv. ch. 147 (H. B. 2616) (West).

53. "Man Says Emergence from 'Coma' Like Rebirth," www.msnbc.com (accessed 12/01/09).

54. Steven Laureys et al., "The Locked-in Syndrome: What Is It Like to Be Conscious but Paralyzed and Voiceless?" 150 *Progress in Brain Research* 495, 499 (2005).

55. *MSTF Part 1*, p. 1506.

56. *See, e.g.,* B. Beuthien-Baumann et al., "Persistent Vegetative State: Evaluation of Brain Metabolism and Brain Perfusion with PET and SPECT," 24 *Nuclear Medicine Communications* 643 (2003); C. Tommasino et al., "Regional Cerebral Metabolism of Glucose in Comatose and Vegetative State Patients," 7 *Journal of Neurosurgery and Anesthesiology* 109 (1995).

57. David E. Levy et al., "Differences in Cerebral Blood Flow and Glucose Utilization in Vegetative Versus Locked-in Patients," 22 *Annals of Neurology* 673 (1987).

58. B. Beuthien-Baumann et al., "Functional Imaging of Vegetative State Applying Single Photon Emission Tomography and Positron Emission Tomography," 15 *Neuropsychological Rehabilitation* 276 (2005).

59. B. Wilhelm et al., "Communication in Locked-In Syndrome: Effects of Imagery on Salivary pH," 67 *Neurology* 534 (2006).

60. Christoph Guger et al., "How Many People Are Able to Control a P300-Based Brain-Computer Interface?" 462 *Neuroscience Letters* 94 (2009); Niels Birbaumer, "Breaking the Silence: Brain-Computer Interfaces for Communication and Motor Control," 43 *Psychophysiology* 517 (2006).

61. *MSTF Part 1*, p. 1503.

62. David R. Spiegel, "Treatment of Akinetic Mutism with Intramuscular Olazapine: A Case Series," 20 *Journal of Neuropsychiatry and Clinical Neurosciences* 93 (2008); J. Ure et al., "Akinetic Mutism: A Report of Three Cases," 98 *Acta Neurologica Scandinavica* 439, 439 (1998).

63. Nages Nagaratnam, "Akinetic Mutism Following Stroke," 11 *Journal of Clinical Neuroscience* 25, 28 (2004).

64. J. T. Giacino et al., "The Minimally Conscious State: Definition and Diagnostic Criteria," 58 *Neurology* 349, 350–351 (2002).

65. Ibid., p. 350.

66. Ibid., p. 351. As Laureys and Boly point out, there is no agreement regarding the time interval that is required to differentiate a brief from sustained visual fixation. Moreover, there is controversy within the medical profession as to whether visual fixation is properly considered as a clinical indicator of consciousness. Steven Laureys and Melanie Boly, "What Is It Like to Be Vegetative or Minimally Conscious?" 20 *Current Opinion in Neurology* 609, 610 (2007).

67. Giacino et al., "Minimally Conscious State: Definition and Diagnostic Criteria," p. 351.

68. DeNeen L. Brown, "Sarah Scantlin's 20-year Return to Life," *Washington Post,* July 29, 2005.

69. Ibid.

70. "Colorado Woman in Vegetative State for 6 Years Awakens for 3 Days," Associated Press, March 8, 2007, www.foxnews.com (accessed 6/12/2008).

71. Ibid.

72. Ibid. *See also* "Woman in Coma Says 'I'm Fine,' then Relapses," *Chicago Sun-Times,* March 9, 2007, p. 28.

73. Melanie Boly et al., "Auditory Processing in Severely Brain Injured Patients," 61 *Archives of Neurology* 233, 237 (2004).

74. S. Laureys et al., "Cerebral Processing in the Minimally Conscious State," 63 *Neurology* 916, 916–917 (2004).

75. N. D. Schiff et al., "fMRI Reveals Large-Scale Network Activation in Minimally Conscious Patients," 64 *Neurology* 514, 519 (2005).

76. Adrian M. Owen et al., "Residual Auditory Function in Persistent Vegetative State: A Combined PET and fMRI Study," 15 *Neuropsychological Rehabilitation* 290, 303 (2005).

77. Ibid.

78. W. Staffen et al., "Selective Brain Activity in Response to One's Own Name in the Persistent Vegetative State," 77 *Journal of Neurology, Neurosurgery and Psychiatry* 1383, 1884 (2006).

79. H. B. Di et al., "Cerebral Response to Patient's Own Name in the Vegetative and Minimally Conscious States," 68 *Neurology* 895, 897–898 (2007).

80. Ibid., p. 898.

81. Ibid.

82. Martin R. Coleman et al., "Do Vegetative Patients Retain Aspects of Language Comprehension? Evidence from fMRI," 130 *Brain* 2494, 2496 (2007).

83. Ibid., p. 2502.

84. Ibid., p. 2504.

85. Ibid., p. 2503.

86. Ibid., p. 2500.

87. Ibid., p. 2504.

88. Ibid.

89. M. R. Coleman et al., "Towards the Routine Use of Brain Imaging to Aid the Clinical Diagnosis of Disorders of Consciousness," 132 *Brain* 2451, 2545 (2009).

90. Ibid.

91. Ibid., p. 2548.

92. Ibid., p. 2550.

93. Ibid.

94. Adrian M. Owen et al., "Detecting Awareness in the Vegetative State," 313 *Science* 1402 (2006).

95. Ibid.

96. Ibid.

97. M. Boly et al., "When Thoughts Become Action: An fMRI Paradigm to Study Volitional Brain Activity in Non-Communicative Brain Injured Patients," 36 *NeuroImage* 979, 980 (2007).

98. Ibid., p. 985.

99. *See* Parashkev Nachev and Masud Husain, "Comment on 'Detecting Awareness in Vegetative State,'" 315 *Science* 1221 (2007); Daniel L. Greenberg, "Comment on 'Detecting Awareness in the Vegetative State,'" 315 *Science* 1221 (2007).

100. Boly et al., "When Thoughts Become Action," p. 989.

101. Martin M. Monti et al., "Executive Functions in the Absence of Behavior: Functional Imaging of the Minimally Conscious State," 177 *Progress in Brain Research* 249, 255 (2009).

102. Ibid., pp. 256–257.

103. Martin M. Monti et al., "Willful Modulation of Brain Activity in Disorders of Consciousness," 362 *New England Journal of Medicine* 579, 585 (2010).

104. Ibid., p. 583.

105. Ibid., p. 585.

106. Ibid., p. 588–589.

107. Joseph J. Fins, "Neuroethics and Neuroimaging: Moving Toward Transparency," 8 *American Journal of Bioethics* 46, 49 (2008).

108. Ibid., p. 50.

109. Bernard Baertschi, "The Burden of Self-Consciousness," 8 *American Journal of Bioethics-Neuroscience* 33, 34 (2008).

110. Guy Kahane and Julian Savulescu, "Brain Damage and the Moral Significance of Consciousness," 34 *Journal of Medicine and Philosophy,* 6, 10 (2009).

111. Ibid., pp. 10–12.

112. Ibid., p. 11.

113. Ibid., pp. 16–18.

114. Ibid., p. 16.

115. *See* Dominic Wilkinson et al., "'Neglected Personhood' and Neglected Questions: Remarks on the Moral Significance of Consciousness," 8 *American Journal of Bioethics-Neuroscience* 31 (2008).

116. Ibid., p. 32; Kahane and Savulescu, "Brain Damage and the Moral Significance of Consciousness," pp. 19–20

117. Jacob M. Appel, "The Rom Houben Tragedy and the Case for Active Euthanasia," Nov. 24, 2009, www.huffingtonpost.com (accessed 12/01/09).

118. Ibid.

119. Rob Schwartz and Mirra Schwartz, "The Risks of Reducing Consciousness to Neuroimaging," 8 *American Journal of Bioethics-Neuroscience* 25, 26 (2008).

120. Bridget M. Kuehn, "Scientists Probe Deep Brain Stimulation: Some Promise for Brain Injury, Psychiatric Illness," 298 *Journal of the American Medical Association* 2249 (2007).

121. N. D. Schiff et al., "Behavioural Improvements with Thalamic Stimulation After Severe Traumatic Brain Injury," 448 *Nature* 600 (2007).

122. Ibid., p. 601.

123. Nicholas D. Schiff et al., "Deep Brain Stimulation, Neuroethics, and the Minimally Conscious State," 66 *Archives of Neurology* 697, 700 (2009).

124. Schiff et al., "Behavioural Improvements with Thalamic Stimulation After Severe Traumatic Brain Injury," p. 602.

125. *See, e.g.*, W. Glannon, "Stimulating Brains, Altering Minds," 35 *Journal of Medical Ethics* 289 (2009).

126. Nicholas D. Schiff, "Central Thalamic Deep-Brain Stimulation in the Severely Injured Brain," 1157 *Disorders of Consciousness: Annals of the New York Academy of Sciences* 101, 111 (2009).

127. Walter Glannon, "Neurostimulation and the Minimally Conscious State," 22 *Bioethics* 337, 338 (2008).

128. Schiff et al., "Deep Brain Stimulation, Neuroethics, and the Minimally Conscious State," pp. 700–701.

129. *See, e.g.*, Ross D. Zafonte et al., "Amantadine: A Potential Treatment for the Minimally Conscious State," 12 *Brain Injury* 617 (1998); Teresa S. Wu et al., "Improved Neurological Function After Amantadine Treatment in Two Patients with Brain Injury," 28 *Journal of Emergency Medicine* 289 (2005); C. Schnakers et al., "Measuring the Effect of Amantadine in Chronic Anoxic Minimally Conscious State," 79 *Journal of Neurology, Neurosurgery and Psychiatry* 225 (2008).

130. Heather Clark, "After 16 Years Deep in Sleep, Woman Finds a New World: Family, Doctors Work to Keep Patient Awake," *Charlotte Observer*, December 25, 2000, p. 13A.

131. Shari Hughes et al., "Amantadine to Enhance Readiness for Rehabilitation Following Severe Traumatic Brain Injury," 19 *Brain Injury* 1197, 1202 (2005).

132. M. F. Kraus et al., "Effects on Dopaminergic Agent and NMDA Receptor Antagonist Amantadine on Cognitive Function, Cerebral Glucose Metabolism and D2 Receptor Availability in Chronic Traumatic Brain Injury: A Study Using Positron Emission Tomography (PET)," 19 *Brain Injury* 471 (2005).

133. William N. Schneider et al., "Cognitive and Behavioural Efficacy of Amantadine in Acute Traumatic Brain Injury: An Initial Double-Blind Placebo-Controlled Study," 13 *Brain Injury* 863 (1999).

134. Jay M. Meythaler et al., "Amantadine to Improve Neurorecovery in Traumatic Brain Injury—Associated Diffuse Axonal Injury: A Pilot Double-Blind Randomized Trial," 17 *Journal of Head Trauma Rehabilitation* 300, 308 (2002).

135. W. Matsuda et al., "Levodopa Treatment for Patients in Persistent Vegetative or Minimally Conscious States," 15 *Neuropsychological Rehabilitation* 414 (2005); W. Matsuda et al., "Awakenings from Persistent Vegetative State: Report of Three Cases with Parkinsonism and Brain Stem Lesions on MRI," 74 *Journal of Neurology, Neurosurgery and Psychiatry* 1571 (2003); W. Matsuda et al., "A Case of Primary Brain-Stem Injury Recovered from Persistent Vegetative State After L-dopa Administration," 51 *No To Shinkei* 1071 (1999); A. J. Haig and J. M. Ruess, "Recovery from Vegetative State of Six Months' Duration Associated with Sinemet (Levodopa/Carbidopa)," 71 *Archives of Physical Medicine and Rehabilitation* 1081 (1990).

136. Ben-Zion Krimchansky et al., "Differential Time and Related Appearance of Signs, Indicating Improvement in the State of Consciousness in Vegetative State Traumatic Brain Injury (VS-TBI) Patients After Initiation of Dopamine Treatment," 18 *Brain Injury* 1099, 1101 (2004).

137. Ibid., p. 1104.

138. *See* Ralf Clauss and Wally Nel, "Drug Induced Arousal from the Permanent Vegetative State," 21 *NeuroRehabilitation*, 23, 25–26 (2006).

139. Ibid., p. 26.

140. R. P. Claus et al., "Extraordinary Arousal from Semi-Comatose State on Zolpidem: A Case Report," 90 *South African Medical Journal* 68 (2000).

141. Sara I. Cohen and Thao T. Duong, "Increased Arousal in a Patient with Anoxic Brain Injury After Administration of Zolpidem," 87 *American Journal of Physical and Medical Rehabilitation* 229, 229–230 (2008).

142. Jeffrey L. Shames and Haim Ring, "Transient Reversal of Anoxic Brain Injury–Related Minimally Conscious State After Zolpidem Administration," 89 *Archives of Physical and Medical Rehabilitation* 386, 386–387 (2008).

143. Ibid.

144. Ibid., p. 387.

145. Clauss and Nel, "Drug Induced Arousal from the Permanent Vegetative State," pp. 24–25.

146. Ibid., p. 25.

147. RenGen Therapeutics Plc, "RenGen and the Zolpidem Project," FAQ, www.rengentherapeutics.com/rengenplc/products/zolpidem (accessed 12/11/09).

148. [2006] All E. R. (D.) 73 (Dec.).

149. 1194 WL 1716349 (Sup. Ct.), [1994] 1 F.L.R. 654.

150. Penney Lewis, "Withdrawal of Treatment from a Patient in a Permanent Vegetative State: Judicial Involvement and Innovative 'Treatment,'" 15 *Medical Law Review* 392, 394 (2007).

151. Rajiv Singh et al., "Zolpidem in a Minimally Conscious State," 22 *Brain Injury* 103 (2008).

152. John Whyte and Robin Myers, "Incidence of Clinically Significant Responses to Zolpidem Among Patients with Disorders of Consciousness," 88 *Journal of Physical and Medical Rehabilitation* 410, 413, Table 1 (2009).

153. Ibid., p. 416.

154. Ibid., p. 418.

155. "MRRI Research Study to Investigate How Zolpidem Might Restore Consciousness for Patients in the Vegetative State," *Medical News,* August 31, 2009, www .news-medical.net (accessed 12/09/2009).

156. J. T. Cole et al., "Dietary Branched Chain Amino Acids Ameliorate Injury-Induced Cognitive Impairment," *Proceedings of the National Academy of Sciences,* December 7, 2009.

157. Roberto Aquilani et al., "Branched-Chain Amino Acids Enhance the Cognitive Recovery of Patients with Severe Traumatic Brain Injury," 86 *Archives of Physical and Medical Rehabilitation* 1729, 1731 (2005).

158. Ibid., p. 1733.

159. Roberto Aquilani et al., "Branched-Chain Amino Acids May Improve Recovery from a Vegetative or Minimally Conscious State in Patients with Traumatic Brain Injury: A Pilot Study," 89 *Archives of Physical and Medical Rehabilitation* 1642, 1643 (2008).

160. Ibid.

161. Ibid., p. 1644.

162. Ibid., p. 1645.

163. Ibid.

164. "The Appleton International Conference: Developing Guidelines for Decisions to Forgo Life-Prolonging Medical Treatment, Part II" 18 *Journal of Medical Ethics* 18, supp. 11 (1992).

165. For example, the *Merck Manual of Diagnosis and Therapy* entry for "vegetative state" concludes that "[t]reatment is supportive. Prognosis with persistent deficits is bleak, and withdrawal of care should be discussed with family members." "Vegetative State," *Merck Manual of Diagnosis and Therapy,* 18th ed., ed. Mark H. Beers et al. (Whitehouse Station, N.J.: Merck Research Laboratories, 2006), merck.com/mmpe/sec16/ch212/ch212b.html (accessed 12/02/09).

166. Kirk Payne et al., "Physicians' Attitudes About the Care of Patients in the Persistent Vegetative State: A National Survey," 125 *Annals of Internal Medicine* 104, 105, Table 2 (1996).

167. Steven Laureys and Melanie Boly, "What is it Like to be Vegetative or Minimally Conscious?" 20 *Current Opinion in Neurology* 609, 610 (2007).

168. James Bernat, "Ethical Issues in the Treatment of Severe Brain Injury," 1157 *Annals of the New York Academy of Sciences* 117, 120–121 (2009).

169. K. J. Becker et al., "Withdrawal of Support in Intracerebral Hemorrhage May Lead to Self-Fulfilling Prophecies," 56 *Neurology* 766 (2001).

170. Ibid.

171. Laura A. Siminoff et al., "Death and Organ Procurement: Public Beliefs and Attitudes," 14 *Kennedy Institute of Ethics Journal* 217, 229 (2004).

172. Carol E. Sieger et al., "Refusing Artificial Nutrition and Hydration: Does Statutory Law Send the Wrong Message?" 50 *Journal of the American Geriatrics Society* 544 (2002). This distinction between nutrition and other forms of medical care is also reflected in a recent statement from Pope Benedict XVI, which declares the removal of artificial feeding to be presumptively immoral. Melanie Evans, "Vatican Clarifies Position: Most Patients in Vegetative State Should Still Be Fed," 37 *Modern Healthcare* 4 (2007). The same view has also been expressed by a majority of the Italian National Committee for Bioethics and the Irish Medical Council. Nereo Zamparetti and Nicola Latronico, "Nutrition and Hydration of Patients in Vegetative State: A Statement of the Italian National Committee for Bioethics," 32 *Intensive Care Medicine* 750 (2006).

173. *See, e.g.*, A. Gauthier et al., "A Longitudinal Study on Quality of Life and Depression in ALS Patient-Caregiver Couples," 68 *Neurology* 923, 926 (2007); D. Lulé et al., "Life Can be Worth Living in Locked-in Syndrome," 177 *Progress in Brain Research* 339, 340 (2009).

174. Laureys et al., "The Locked-in Syndrome: What Is It Like to Be Conscious but Paralyzed and Voiceless?" p. 506.

175. Lulé et al., "Life Can be Worth Living in Locked-in Syndrome," p. 341.

176. Ibid.

177. Ibid., p. 344.

178. Ibid., p. 345.

179. Ibid., p. 342.

180. Ibid., p. 347.

7. Unbeing Dead Isn't Being Alive

1. 18 U.S.C. §1531(b)(1)(A).

2. For a video clip of this Monty Python sketch from the the film "Meaning of Life," see http://www.youtube.com/watch?v=8tmLvzubP3I (accessed 5/23/10).

3. Fla. Stat. Ann. §765.303.

Acknowledgments

There is a small army behind every book that manages to find its way into print. There is the author's family, steadfastly offering love, good humor, and an everlasting supply of encouragement. My family has provided this support from day one, never doubting, always excited about the project, despite the fact that it distracted my attention away from them for many days. A million "thank yous" would not be enough to make up for the unflagging enthusiasm of my husband, daughter, mom, sisters and brother-in-law. Beyond my family, there is a cadre of encouraging professional colleagues, who have watched me labor on the project day after day, commiserating with my ups and downs, celebrating my achievements, and facilitating epiphanies that proved invaluable. In this regard I am particularly grateful for Alex Acosta, Tom Baker, Stanley Fish, Michael Lawrence, Matthew Mirow, Joelle Moreno, Janet Reinke and Howard Wasserman.

Importantly, there is the editorial team that brings the raw vision to life, nurturing it from a promising idea into a final project. My editor at Harvard University Press, Elizabeth Knoll, has guided me with enthusiasm, wit, and patience every step of the way. I am eternally grateful for her support. Her team of professional copy editors and assistants—particularly Matthew Hills—has allowed the train to run smoothly and without delay. The anonymous readers who generously shared their time and expertise have shaped the final product for the better.

Last, but certainly not least, there are the students. Those in my constitutional law course and seminars, as well as those in health care law, have shaped my knowledge and continually fueled my curiosity about the law of life and death. My research assistants Rob Brown, Tiernan Cole and Robert Scavone, in addition to cite checking *ad nauseam* and hunting down obscure sources well beyond the bounds of the ordinary law library, have probably learned much more about the vagaries of being alive and dead than they ever wanted to know. But their companionship and aid have proved invaluable.

I have learned something from all of these individuals along the way. As George Bernard Shaw once said (disagreeing with Shakespeare's characterization of life and death in *Macbeth*), "I want to be thoroughly used up when I die, for the harder I work, the more I live. I rejoice in life for its own sake. Life is no brief candle to me. It is a sort of splendid torch which I have got a hold of for the moment, and I want to make it burn as brightly as possible before handing it onto future generations." Thanks to all my family, friends and colleagues who have helped me hand this torch to future generations.

Index